Thomas Reid's Theory of Perception

Thomas Reid's
Theory of Perception

Ryan Nichols

CLARENDON PRESS · OXFORD

OXFORD
UNIVERSITY PRESS

Great Clarendon Street, Oxford OX2 6DP

Oxford University Press is a department of the University of Oxford.
It furthers the University's objective of excellence in research, scholarship,
and education by publishing worldwide in

Oxford New York

Auckland Cape Town Dar es Salaam Hong Kong Karachi
Kuala Lumpur Madrid Melbourne Mexico City Nairobi
New Delhi Shanghai Taipei Toronto

With offices in

Argentina Austria Brazil Chile Czech Republic France Greece
Guatemala Hungary Italy Japan Poland Portugal Singapore
South Korea Switzerland Thailand Turkey Ukraine Vietnam

Oxford is a registered trademark of Oxford University Press
in the UK and in certain other countries

Published in the United States
by Oxford University Press Inc., New York

British Library Cataloguing in Publication Data

Data available

Library of Congress Cataloging in Publication Data

Nichols, Ryan.
  Thomas Reid's theory of perception / Ryan Nichols.
       p. cm.
  Includes bibliographical references and index.
  ISBN-13: 978-0-19-927691-2 (alk. paper)
  ISBN-10: 0-19-927691-9 (alk. paper)
 1. Reid, Thomas, 1710-1796. 2. Perception. I. Title.
  B1538.P38N53 2007
  121′.34092—dc22

                                        2006036374

Typeset by Laserwords Private Limited, Chennai, India
Printed in Great Britain
on acid-free paper by
Biddles Ltd., King's Lynn, Norfolk

ISBN 978-0-19-927691-2

For Gillian McIntosh

Acknowledgments

I have received financial support for research necessary for the completion of this book from several sources. The Ohio State University's Office of International Studies awarded me an International Travel Dissertation Research Grant during which I visited the Special Collections library of the University of Aberdeen in 1998. Graduate Student Travel Prizes from each division of the American Philosophical Association enabled me to present my research on Reid's theory of perception and receive feedback from others. I finalized archival research for this project while on a Kristeller-Popkin Travel Fellowship by visiting special collection libraries at the Universities of Aberdeen, Edinburgh, and Glasgow, as well as the University of Edinburgh's Divinity Library and the city of Glasgow's Mitchell Library. I completed the writing of the book while on leave from teaching for the 2005–6 academic year, which was only possible through generous fellowships from the National Endowment for the Humanities and the Earhart Foundation. I thank all of these funding bodies for their support of my research and their faith in the value of my project.

I also thank several libraries that have allowed me to publish some of Reid's unpublished writings. These include the Special Collections Libraries of the University of Aberdeen, of the University of Edinburgh, and of the New College of the University of Edinburgh.

Some chapters are drawn from or based upon previously published articles. Chapter 4 derives from "Visible Figure and Reid's Theory of Visual Perception," *Hume Studies* 28 (2002): 49–82. The majority of Chapter 6 derives from "Reid's Inheritance from Locke, and How He Overcomes it," *Journal for the History of Philosophy* 41 (2003): 471–92. Chapter 8 derives from "Learning and Conceptual Content in Reid's Theory of Perception," *British Journal for the History of Philosophy* 10 (2002): 49–79. I thank the editors of these journals for their permission to allow me to use these articles in this book.

This project has been shaped and positively influenced by countless comments from a range of individuals. It would be a far inferior book without the help I've received from a variety of sources of support—financial, philosophical, and emotional. I thank participating audiences at the venues at which I presented portions of this book for their invitations to present my work, and for their constructive criticism of it. I also thank those who have corresponded or conversed with me about Reid, or commented on my written work about Reid, including Jonathan Adler, Peter Baumann, Todd Buras, Robert Callergård, James Van Cleve, Terence Cuneo, Rebecca Copenhaver, Phillip Cummins, Philip de Bary, Lorne Falkenstein, Gordon Graham, Giovanni Grandi, Glenn Hartz, George Pappas, Daniel Robinson, Kathleen Schmidt, M. A. Stewart, Paul Tomassi, Kenneth Winkler, Paul Wood, and Gideon Yaffe. The environment at a National Endowment for the Humanities seminar in 2000 on Thomas Reid directed by James Van Cleve was very fruitful for the development of my thinking. Thanks to those participants for many conversations—and to James Van Cleve for his uniquely crafted invitation to me to join the group.

My participation in colloquia sponsored by Liberty Fund about figures and topics in the Scottish Enlightenment has been important both to my efforts to understand the methods and themes of authors of this period and for my attempt to place Reid in his philosophical and cultural context. I thank Liberty Fund for its invitations to partake in these colloquia, and I thank participants at these colloquia for countless fruitful conversations about issues arising in the context of eighteenth-century Scottish thought.

Several of these chapters were originally parts of a dissertation completed under the direction of George Pappas, to whom I offer special thanks. I am exceptionally indebted to Todd, Robert, Terence, George, Gideon, and anonymous referees, who all read chapters or partial drafts of the book manuscript in various stages of development.

My mom and brother, Carol and Dan, have supported me throughout the long gestation of this project. My friends, especially Cathal, Bill, and Emily, have always been willing to lend an ear to discuss the problems of perception—as well as non-philosophical matters of much more importance. I'm thankful to them for their support and friendship. I am most grateful for the inspiration and love of Gill McIntosh.

Contents

Detailed Contents

Tables

Abbreviations

EIP	Thomas Reid, *Essays on the Intellectual Powers of Man*, W. Hamilton and D. Brookes, eds.
IHM	Thomas Reid, *Inquiry into the Human Mind on the Principles of Common Sense*, W. Hamilton and D. Brookes, eds.
EAP	Thomas Reid, *Essays on the Active Powers of Man*
C	Thomas Reid, *The Correspondence of Thomas Reid*, P. Wood, ed.
AC	Thomas Reid, *Thomas Reid on the Animate Creation*, P. Wood, ed.
WGB	George Berkeley, *The Works of George Berkeley, Bishop of Cloyne*, A. Luce and T. Jessop, eds.
T	David Hume, *A Treatise of Human Nature*, L. Selby-Bigge and D. and M. Norton, eds.
NTV	George Berkeley, *New Theory of Vision*. In WGB I.
TVV	George Berkeley, *Theory of Vision Vindicated*. In WGB I.

The recent editions of Hume and Reid prompt a note about the conventions I will use to cite them. Brookes's editions of Reid's *Inquiry* and *Essays on the Intellectual Powers* are new and authoritative. I refer both to page numbers in them and to page numbers in Hamilton's sixth edition of those texts. I also cite the *Inquiry's* chapter and section number (though not all chapters have sections), and the *Intellectual Powers'* essay and chapter number. "EIP 2.9, 133/277b" refers to the second essay, Chapter 9, page 133 of Brookes's edition of the *Intellectual Powers*, and page 277, second column, of Hamilton's edition. The as yet authoritative edition of Reid's *Essays on the Active Powers* remains Hamilton's, though this is soon to change. I also refer to both old and new editions of Hume's *Treatise*, but I employ a different convention to do so. "T 19/1.1.7.5" refers to page 19 of the Selby-Bigge and Nidditch edition. Due to their numbering system, reference to the Norton edition is to book, part, section, and paragraph.

Though we now have a comprehensive volume of Reid's correspondence, Reid's letters have been traditionally published with his other work, as in Hamilton's *Works* and Brookes's *Inquiry*. I refer to Reid's correspondence both by citing its location in C and in his other work, where possible. For example, in Section 3.4 I quote a remark Reid addresses to Hume in a letter, and I cite it as "C 113/IHM 258." Since no column reference (no "a" or "b") is attached to this reference to IHM, this uniquely refers to Brookes's version of the *Inquiry*. (Hamilton was not privy to the Reid–Hume correspondence.)

When citing WGB or CSM, I state the name of the work from which the citation is drawn. Complete references for all these works are in the bibliography.

When citing manuscripts, I refer to the university library holding the document, the shelf-mark, and, where available, the page number and date, as here: Aberdeen MS 2131/4/II/16, 30, 1 Dec. 1768.

Introduction

0.1. Goals

In this book I present an interpretation of Thomas Reid's theory of perception. I also evaluate Reid's arguments for theses he defends in the construction of his theory. This dual aim makes a brief statement of my method useful.

My primary task is to determine the content of Reid's theory of perception. The scope of Reid's theory includes his analyses of: the intentionality of cognition, the senses themselves, sensory experience, the nature of secondary and primary qualities, and the formation of conceptual content in perceptual belief. I devote a full chapter to his response to the Molyneux problem because it ties together several other threads in Reid's theory of perception.

To determine the content of Reid's theory of perception, I must identify what Reid held. Identifying what Reid says does not *ipso facto* inform us of what he held, but it is the first stage in the interpretive process in those cases in which we have antecedent reason to think that the philosopher is freely writing what he writes. Reid—theist, non-skeptic, and clergyman—did not fear violence or worry about being denied a prominent job for writing what he believed.

Reid wrote his most important work, and about 98 percent of his total corpus, in English. He also writes with clarity. English-speaking philosophers have ready access to what he said, and good prospects for understanding what he meant. The English of eighteenth-century Scotland is not our English, but it is familiar in large part because we have inherited the philosophical problems, and most of the accompanying terms, from the Early Modern period. Reid himself has been especially influential in codifying canonical interpretations of Early Modern thinkers through the influence of the "Scottish Common Sense" school of philosophy, which he inadvertently founded. In part this is because many philosophers in fledgling American universities had educational ties to this school of thought.

Reid gave several commencement addresses in spoken Latin and we have extant drafts of these lectures (Reid 1937, and in translation in Reid 1989). They were delivered in 1753, 1756, 1759, and 1762. They are for the most part cogent and philosophical works, and are surprisingly important for clues about the development of Reid's theories. The "Orations," as they are known, foreshadow the two major works I will be discussing, namely the *Inquiry Into the Human Mind on the Principles of Common Sense* (1764/1997) and *Essays on the Intellectual Powers of Man* (1785/1994b).

Achieving our goal of identifying what Reid held is made easier in virtue of our ability to avoid knotty problems facing other interpretive projects in the history of philosophy. With someone such as Leibniz, the interpreter's task is complicated by the fact that Leibniz intended only a small proportion of his written corpus for wide circulation. Leibniz also has a habit of explaining his theories to certain correspondents so as to make his theories amenable to them, without a superseding regard for consistency. By dint of his genius Leibniz corresponded with such a diverse and brilliant group of people that his views are pulled apart under these peculiar pressures. In contrast, at Reid's point in the development of Scottish philosophy, the discipline takes on many of the trappings familiar from contemporary academia. This includes pressures to delay dissemination of one's work until such a time as it can be published formally in a book. Thus Reid's primary scholarly output was in published form and intended for a wide, though scholarly, audience. Only in his correspondence does he risk tailoring the expression of his theories in divergent ways. Even this does not jeopardize our task. Reid's correspondence, though occasionally pregnant with philosophical discussion, does not have the intellectual pedigree of his philosophical forebears, and the group with whom he corresponded was not especially diverse.

Though my primary goal is to determine what Reid held on these matters, I also want to evaluate Reid's theories. This can be accomplished in two ways. I might evaluate Reid's theories on the basis of theories that the majority of philosophers today take to be true. In crude form this degenerates into parody. In more ennobling form this method treats Reid as a philosopher with something of importance to say to today's philosophical community. Alternatively, I might evaluate Reid's theories on the basis of its internal consistency and on his ability to parry objections that were circulating in his milieu. The motivation for this approach is grounded in the belief that Reid was able to deal with these problems on his own terms.

I generally employ the second approach. Like most historians of philosophy, I conceive of the enterprise as philosophical, and not merely exegetical. But the danger attending this aspiration is that such efforts labor under ambiguous goals. Robert Sleigh argues that history of philosophy practiced philosophically sometimes consists in utilizing doctrines associated with or endorsed by a historical figure to create a new theory. But often this "approach is nothing more than an exercise in *a priori* reasoning to no clearly defined end." On the other hand, philosophical history can adopt a different strategy on which one discusses a topic merely "in the company" of historical figures. However, this approach "allows the author a front for probing philosophical problems, presenting arguments, even reaching conclusions, without being held to current standards of rigor" (Sleigh 1990, 3). Sleigh rightly indicts a considerable portion of contemporary work in history of philosophy as failing either to advance our philosophical understanding or to identify what historical figures held.

Nonetheless, simply because a practice's goals are not determinate does not imply that the practice is not valuable or intrinsically valuable. The converse holds too: the mere clarity of the goal of exegetical history does not *ipso facto* bestow upon it any value. I am also uncertain whether Sleigh's distinction between types of history of philosophy is accurate. To make this point stick, I need to define the term "authorial proposition," which refers to a proposition that attributes a proposition with philosophical content to an author. For example, "Reid believed that God's existence could not be proven" is an authorial proposition. If exegetical history takes as its sole goal to determine the truth-values of authorial propositions, then it is not obviously of intrinsic value or of instrumental value to analytic philosophy. Merely knowing what Reid thought about this matter does not assist in determining whether the philosophical claim is true or false.

But this particular characterization of doing the history of philosophy can be improved. Suppose the primary goal of doing history of philosophy is identical to the primary goal of analytic philosophy, which I take to be finding important philosophical truths and avoiding important philosophical falsehoods through analysis of arguments. Suppose this is achieved via the supplementary goal of getting the truth-values of authorial propositions right. If so, we can steer clear of Sleigh's worries about unclear goals while making historical philosophy intrinsically valuable. (See Nichols 2006 for my theory about the purpose and value of doing the history of philosophy.)

Some contemporary work in the history of philosophy meets Sleigh's methodological desiderata through its attention to textual detail, to unpublished material, to social and philosophical context, and by stating philosophical arguments as rigorously as the figure's corpus will bear in the pursuit of philosophical knowledge. I aspire to achieve this result here.

0.2. Reid's Philosophical Development

I will briefly explain Reid's philosophical development and its bearing on his theory of perception, and to do so I draw upon Paul Wood's research. Thomas Reid (b. April 26, 1710, and d. October 7, 1796) was educated at Marischal College, Aberdeen, shortly after the Jacobite uprising of 1715—not the last uprising Reid would witness. This uprising forced the chancellor of the college to flee Scotland, and helped produce a number of rapid changes in the curriculum. After graduating in 1726 he studied for a divinity degree, obtaining it from Marischal in 1731.

Despite his anonymity, Reid's professor George Turnbull is said to have "exercised a greater influence than all other masters and writers put together" on him (McCosh 1875, 91). Turnbull's work is infused with a Newtonian commitment to observation, analysis, and synthesis in both moral and natural philosophy. In the dedication and introduction to his two-volume *Principles of Moral Philosophy* (Turnbull 2005) he makes this explicit. Turnbull also describes the unity of philosophy under a Newtonian method (2005 i, 5–6, 47–66). He uses the new physics in order to prove God's existence in a thesis written in 1726 on the occasion of his supervision over the graduating class that year, which included Reid. This reverence for natural religion was not accompanied by any divisive commitment to sectarianism. In fact Turnbull seems to have left the Presbyterian Church of Scotland to take orders in the Episcopal Church of England later in life (McCosh 1875, 94). But Turnbull did lean toward Berkeleyan idealism. He says that "when we speak of material effects and of space, we only mean, and can indeed only mean, certain sensible perceptions excited in our mind according to a certain order, which are experienced to be absolutely inert and passive, and to have no productive force" (quoted in McCosh 1875, 99). In this respect Turnbull influences Reid not as a model but as a foil.

Under the tutelage of Thomas Blackwell, Reid was privy to a uniquely moderate theological education. Blackwell was the only member of Marischal allowed by the House of Hanover to remain at the college following its purge. Blackwell appeals to reason and to revealed truth in the defense of Christian knowledge and common sense. Reid's rational form of religion and his advocacy of human free will resemble Blackwell's positions, and stands at odds with some of the more radically Calvinist theologies of the day.

In July 1733 Reid secured an appointment as Librarian of Marischal, but the bequest from which Reid was paid (from his ancestor and namesake) was mismanaged. Reid sought to sue the college and the Aberdeen Council in

1736. Taking leave from this post, Reid traveled to England—to London, Oxford, and Cambridge. While at Cambridge he met the Lucasian professor of mathematics, Nicholas Saunderson. Saunderson's abilities to teach geometry and optics despite his blindness left an impression upon Reid that resurfaces in Reid's account of visible figure and in his resolution of the Molyneux problem. (Reid also piqued the Fellows of Trinity College when he deciphered symbols on a sundial, thought to be the work of Newton, which had thwarted previous attempts at decoding (Ramsay 1888, 476).)

Reid's intellectual development in this period after his graduation occurred in the presence of a philosophical club and the faculty of Marischal. Reid was studying Newton's *Principia*, Locke's *Essay*, William King's *De Origine Mali*, Shaftesbury's *Characteristics*, Butler's *Analogy*, and the works of Hutcheson. Reid was also interested in the analysis of force in Newton and Leibniz (Wood 1985a, 3–4).

In 1737 Reid was appointed to the parish of New Machar at King's College, Aberdeen. Reid's election to the post by the college was unanimous but, following on the heels of another dispute, the parishioners rejected him. Reid first preached on May 12, and was physically attacked by those in attendance (Ramsay 1888, 479). Even in a theologically moderate part of Scotland like Aberdeenshire, Reid could not avoid the fervor of religious disagreement and violence, which may have squashed Reid's interest in airing his theological beliefs publicly. Reid would eventually lecture on theology. Yet, discounting the excessively modest references to God's creative work with which Reid peppers his books, he chose not to publish anything of importance in philosophy of religion or theology.

Reid's reading notes from his time at New Machar indicate he studied Berkeley and Hume. Reid's notes on Peter Browne's *The Procedure, Extent and Limits of Human Understanding* (1728) show that at this point he defended Locke's theory of ideas from attack by Berkeley. His study of Hume seems restricted to Hume's arguments about the self. The breadth of Reid's interests while at New Machar is tremendous. In addition to the study of venerable philosophical problems, he researched physics and terrestrial mechanics, eclipses and the transit of Venus, and mathematics and geometry. Evidence suggests that Reid at this time is neither a Berkeleyan nor does he see Humeanism as a skeptical threat.

King's College, at Aberdeen, invited Reid to join the faculty as a regent in October 1751. He initially declined but, after being prevailed upon by his wife and the college, he relented. In this post Reid lectured on mathematics in the first two years, in addition to natural history in the first year, natural philosophy in the second, and a number of topics in the third, including logic, natural law, politics, the arts, and natural religion. This time of philosophical foment occurs in conjunction with the origins of the "Wise Club," an Aberdonian philosophical society. To this group Reid presented the material that would become *An Inquiry into the Human Mind on the Principles of Common Sense*. The Wise Club subjected Hume's philosophical system to rigorous debate. Reid's writings during the time of the Wise Club meetings provide the first evidence of his disaffection with the "Way of Ideas."

Reid uses this term and its synonyms ("Theory of Ideas," "Ideal Theory") to refer to a set of claims about the mind and its relation to the world that were held to be true by the majority of Reid's predecessors. This set of claims became the predominant influence upon Reid's intellectual development and philosophical orientation. For one of the most succinct statements of the Way of Ideas one can turn to a passage from William Porterfield, a psychologist working contemporaneously with Reid. Reid copied the following remarks on a scrap of paper now found in his archived papers:

How body acts upon mind, or mind upon body I know not; but this I am very certain of that nothing can act or be acted upon where it is not, and therefore our mind can never perceive any thing but its own proper modifications, and the various states of the sensorium to which it is present.—So that it is not the external sun and moon which is in the Heavens which our mind perceives, but onely their image or representation impressed upon the sensorium.... From all which it is manifest, that the judgments which our senses induce us to make conceiving the sensible qualities, are exceeding just if considered with respect to the preservation of our bodies, for which they were onely given us; tho' at the same time it is most certain that they are altogether extravagant, and vastly removed from truth.[1]

No action can occur from a distance. We do not directly perceive mind-independent objects, but rather only images. We confuse sensations with objects of perception. We cannot be certain that our perceptual experience informs us of the mind-independent world. Our sensory and cognitive equipment is not reliably aimed at forming true beliefs. In this brief passage Porterfield identifies nearly every aspect of the Way of Ideas that Reid finds odious.

Fully describing the Way of Ideas has proven difficult because Reid's accounts of it are not univocal over time. When discussing abstraction he will select features of the views of his predecessors about abstraction and label it part of the Way of Ideas, whereas when talking about visual perception, another set of claims is identified as part of the Way of Ideas. This patchwork

---

[1] The passage is preceded by Reid's citation, which reads: "Porterfield, Essay concerning the motions of our eyes. Edinburgh Medical Essays, Vol 3, Edinburgh 1752, p. 176 & c." and is found at Aberdeen MS 2131/2/III/02. See EIP 2.14, 176–7/301a.

approach to the history of philosophy has made him into a *piñata* for a group of commentators who accuse him of systematically misrepresenting his predecessors for dialectical purposes (e.g. Yolton 1984). Others rebuff the charge of duplicity but claim that Reid is in danger of being "a *terrible* historian" (Greco 1995, 282). (Unless noted, all emphases in quoted passages are their authors' emphases.) This result is avoided on pains of the odd conclusion that Reid misunderstands his own theories, i.e. that "Reid's assessment of his own work is incorrect" (1995, 279). But this dilemma is a false one, and we needn't choose between preserving Reid's credibility as an historian or as a philosopher. But instead of attempting to identify a set of theses constitutive of the Way of Ideas (a laborious and potentially fruitless task), I will explain the theories of a specific representative of the Way of Ideas wherever appropriate. This enables me to steer clear of some historical controversies. I hope to clarify the meaning of the "Way of Ideas" in the appropriate context, though I will follow Reid's unrestrained use of the term to refer in general to his predecessors' views where such reference is required.

The Wise Club also discussed the work of James Gregory and Alexander Gerard. Gregory's *Comparative View of the State and Faculties of Man, with those of the Animal World* (1764) is another book that emerged from this fruitful environment. Like Reid, Gregory pledges allegiance to a Newtonian method of analysis and synthesis (Gregory 1764, 68). Gregory's book is based upon the premise that human beings are embodied creatures who knowingly interact with a real, mind-independent world. This is why he is comfortable with an approach that compares humans and animals, which would seem inane to philosophers like Descartes, Berkeley, and Kant. Reid shares a key aspect of this vision: unlike the preponderance of work on perception by "empiricists" in Early Modern philosophy, Reid studies the animal parts of the perceptual process with special care.

Gerard and Colin Maclaurin, both professors at Marischal College, influenced Reid's Newtonianism. Gerard provides a succinct statement of what becomes a Reidian position about the study of the mind. Lecturing about psychology, Gerard is recorded to have said that

Psychology is a science of the most extensive utility, for all other sciences are connected with it, & in a manner all our conclusions in it, as well as in Natural Phy. Must be founded on Experiments & observations. ... It is easy to make Experiments upon Body, but more difficult to form experiments concerning the human mind because it is very inconstant.[2]

---

[2] "Ethics or Moral Philosophy," lectures given in 1758–9 at Marischal College. Recorded by Robert Morgan. Two volumes. Special Collections Library of the University of Edinburgh. E.B. 1185 Ger. (1759). Cited in Robinson 1989, 155.

Reid makes this point when he introduces his readers to his attempt to apply Newtonian principles of method to the study of the mind. In addition to this methodological point, Gerard's lectures contain material taught at Marischal on "visible and tangible magnitudes," which provides the seeds for Reid's own development of a theory of visual perception. Below I will cast Reid's theory of visual perception, and his attendant account of visible figure, as a response to Hume because Reid himself presents it in this way. However, evidence indicates that his geometry of visibles presented in the *Inquiry* was constructed in the light of exposure to Gerard's work on this matter. This connection, among many others between Reid's work and that of his local group of colleagues, merits philosophical analysis.

Reid's reputation rose meteorically in the 1760s. He was proposed to succeed Adam Smith in his chair at Glasgow. Through the vicissitudes of the patronage system, Reid took the post in 1764. Faculty disputes seem to have wrangled Reid more there than at King's but Reid's philosophical work continued to flourish. His lectures at Glasgow covered no less diverse a set of subjects than at King's (Wood 1985a, 14). Reid began to employ his method beyond the study of the five senses in the *Inquiry* in order to examine the powers of memory, conception, reasoning, and so forth, in the *Intellectual Powers*. Glasgow's Literary Society took the place of the Aberdonian Wise Club in Reid's life. Between 1765 and 1770 he presented to it much of what would become the *Essays on the Intellectual Powers of Man*, as well as work on Joseph Priestley and materialism (Wood 1985a, 16–17).

Reid's influences help to explain Reid's adoption of his unique method for the analysis of the mind. He did not believe that his colleagues' method arose in a vacuum. He and the others, especially at Aberdeen, were self-consciously implementing the method set forth by Bacon and modified for the better by Newton. The principal lesson he drew from his participation in the intellectual environment of Scotland in the eighteenth century is that Bacon and Newton conducted philosophy in the proper spirit and with the proper aim.

0.3. Overview

I will briefly describe the scope of the book. In Chapter 1 I identify and explain several features of Reid's methodology. Amongst these is his faculty psychology. Reid presupposes that the mind is endowed with a number of powers and faculties, and it is through those powers that Reid explains features of the mental life. Analysis of the power of perception presupposes that there is a unity to our perceptual experience that would be foreign to Berkeley. According to Berkeley, through vision we experience different objects from those we experience through touch; in fact, no two senses take the same objects. Reid rejects this approach in favor of his faculty psychology, which itself is the product of his Newtonian method. The first order of business in this chapter is assessing just what it means to say that Reid adopts a Newtonian method. For Reid, this means that he adopts a hands-on model of inquiry into the mind and the mind's relationship to the body. This commitment marks a vital difference between Reid and his so-called British "Empiricist" predecessors. A brief look at the *Inquiry's* essay on vision reveals that he takes the role of observation more sincerely than most of his predecessors.

Chapter 2 is about the nature of conceptual awareness. Reid characterizes the type of conceptual awareness of interest to his theory of perception as a special subspecies of conception, what he calls *apprehension*. Apprehension is responsible for the presentation of mind-independent objects directly to the mind. Reid describes the conceptual state that apprehension produces as an "immanent act of the mind." This is an intentional state because it necessarily takes objects. Apprehensions thus differ from other mental states, such as moods, which are not intentional.

Hume's philosophical system implies that our states of apprehension do not have determinate intentional objects. Specifically, apprehensions are not directly about mind-independent bodies. Reid goes a step further to interpret Hume as implying that we do not non-inferentially know what are the contents of our thoughts. Reid believes that Hume, whether from neglect or by design, implies that we cannot know what are the objects about which we are thinking. This clears the way to the possibility of knowledge of the contents of our thoughts.

Since the Way of Ideas cannot provide a plausible explanation for our awareness of the contents of our thoughts, Reid is compelled to find an alternative. Reid appeals to the power of "suggestion" and "signification." These terms of art refer to the means by which we come to form intentional apprehensions of mind-independent objects in perception. Sensation experiences catalyze a suggestion relation, which in turn produces perceptual concepts and a perceptual belief. Technically, sensations prompted by our experience of primary qualities *signify* the primary qualities, whereas they *suggest* our conception and belief about the primary qualities. In the *Inquiry* Reid leaves the process of suggestion—by which certain sensations give rise to certain perceptions—mysterious, calling it a "natural kind of magic." But in the *Intellectual Powers* his discussion turns from a focus upon the origin of our concepts to an analysis of cognition in perceptual events. Rather than saying that Reid drops his appeal to suggestion in the *Intellectual Powers*, I say that he modifies and builds upon it in a couple of ways.

Despite its short shelf life, his appeal to suggestion and signification drives his approach to the mind. In Chapter 3 I explain how Reid arrives at his appeal to suggestion by an argument from elimination. Then I explain his application of his theory of suggestion to tactile perception. None of the theories adopted by his predecessors have much hope of success. Reid claims that the Way of Ideas operates upon the assumption that the immediate intentional objects of our thoughts are ideas or other representational intermediaries. The Way of Ideas attempts to reduce contentful mental states to non-contentful features of those states, whereas Reid takes intentional content as irreducible and basic. I give special attention to Reid's *experimentum crucis*, or "crucial test." The crucial test is a thought experiment involving a subject's systematic sensory deprivation. Reid seeks to show that the uses of sensation, custom, and reasoning are singly and jointly insufficient for the formation of our perceptual contents. He takes this as a fine objection to the Way of Ideas, on which sensations and reflection upon sensations are sufficient for providing us with our perceptual contents.

The rest of the book is about more traditional aspects of the perceptual process. In the *Inquiry* Reid examines each sense faculty one by one. He expends little effort on smelling, hearing, and taste, but does treat touch in some detail. Vision, though, occupies about seven times as much textual space as touch. Reid's division of labor is reflected in this book because I single out vision for special analysis in Chapter 4. There I determine the nature of Reid's theory of visual perception, and its implications on a theory of perceptual knowledge. Vision had seemed to Reid's predecessors obviously to be indirect. While he disagrees with this sentiment, his concession to the Way of Ideas is his recognition of a type of visual intermediary, which he calls "visible figure." Reid dares to argue that the presence of visible figure does not thwart his attempt to show that even visual perception can provide us direct access to features of the world. Reid's underdeveloped notion of visible figure requires meticulous analysis. The result is a theory of perception that implies touch and vision afford us differently structured relations to the mind-independent world.

The status of visible figure muddies typical interpretations of Reid's theory as epistemically direct, that is, as claiming that perceptual knowledge arises non-inferentially. But the greatest threat to maintaining a semblance of direct-ness—whether of an epistemic or perceptual form—has to do with the role of sensations. I analyze the relationship between sensations and perceptions in Reid's theory in Chapter 5, and I analyze our consciousness or awareness of sensations in Chapter 6.

I explain in Chapter 5 that Reidian sensations are qualitative feelings and not perceived intermediaries. Indeed, sensations, strictly speaking, are not even necessary for perceptual events. Though this confirms some fears about Reid's theory—that he has in a sense omitted sensations from his theory of perception—I argue that he does this intentionally. I build a case for this conclusion by examining Reid's provocative comments to the effect that our capacity to experience sensations evolved or was created for the purpose of enhancing our survival, and not for the purpose of assisting us in getting information about the mind-independent world.

Reid makes different remarks about the nature of our awareness of sensations in acts of perception. He often says that we rarely attend to our sensations when we perceive primary qualities, and offers several examples to this end. But he also says that we are conscious of, conceive of, and believe in our sensations. This fact creates a problem for our attempt to understand and interpret his theory of perception that parallels the problem just mentioned about our awareness of visible figure in cases of visual perception. In Chapter 6 I attempt to assess the passages used to conclude that a perceiver's awareness of mind-independent primary qualities is indirect due to her need to conceive of her sensations in the process of perception. My assessment of the relevant passages suggests that Reid is not entirely consistent about the nature of our awareness of sensations. Despite this, I argue that the textual evidence better justifies an interpretation of Reid's theory of perception that is comparatively direct.

Reid appeals to suggestion in the *Inquiry* and builds upon that concept in a couple of ways in the *Intellectual Powers*. I discuss the first of these ways in Chapter 7, on perceptual qualities. Frustrated with Locke's metaphysical distinctions between primary and secondary qualities, Reid adopts a cognitive approach. He does not tell us much about qualities per se and instead focuses upon our conception and cognition of qualities. Our notions of primary qualities are built up from the sensations we experience when perceiving an object, whereas our notions of secondary qualities, more remote from the world, are formed via our awareness of our sensations. This implies that our perception of *secondary* qualities must proceed through an intermediating mental state.

The second key way that Reid moves beyond appeal to suggestion lies in his sophisticated analysis of what he calls "original" and "acquired" perception. These are the terms in which he conducts his discussion of the role of cognition in perception, the topic of Chapter 8. These terms refer to stages in the process of constructing full-bodied perceptual contents from rudimentary mental states. With an unfamiliar object we begin the process of perceptual learning by singling it out demonstratively, and eventually arrive at a complex perceptual belief in which we predicate a host of properties of the object. Reid provides analyses of these two stages of perceptual belief formation. But I argue he also makes room for an intermediate stage between these two. Though Reid does not offer a proper theory of perceptual knowledge, what he says about stages of cognition in perception implies that most acquired perceptions depend for their epistemic justification upon inferences somewhere upstream in the process of belief formation.

As a way of tying together threads in Reid's theory of perception, I analyze Reid's treatment of the Molyneux question in Chapter 9. Molyneux's question can be presented in general form as this: "Were a blind person to be given sight, and were a cube and a sphere set in her field of vision, would she be capable of identifying which object is which?" In the *Inquiry* Reid gives both a "no" and a "yes" to Molyneux's question. Though I argue that his answers are consistent, by showing that he is responding to different versions of the question, achieving this result is not the central goal of the chapter. The thrust of Reid's response to Molyneux's issues emphasizes the limitations Reid places upon sensation in the perceptual process. This chapter exhibits the key differences (including methodological differences) between Reid and the Way of Ideas, and confirms several other attributions I make to Reid in the material preceding this chapter.

Reid's aspiration to refute the Way of Ideas arises in almost every chapter in this book. For example, I will argue that Reid holds we can perceive mind-independent objects, not just images, even through vision (Chapter 4). To show this is so, Reid must first show that it is possible that we can conceive of—that is, form intentional mental states about—mind-independent bodies. He does this by arguing that the Way of Ideas fails in its attempts at explaining our apparent ability to do so (Chapter 2). Then he shows that the Way of Ideas, taken to its logical end by Hume, cannot even show that we know what are the intentional contents of our thoughts (Chapter 3). Sensation experiences do not mediate perception (Chapters 5 and 6). Reid's analysis of qualities is aimed at showing that we can conceive of and perceive primary qualities directly (Chapter 7). His discussion of perceptual learning, with his knotty distinctions between forms of perception, is aimed at describing how our senses are not at all "vastly removed from truth" (Chapter 8). Chapter 9 ties together prior themes by analyzing how Reid contests the arguments given by Locke and Berkeley about our cross-modal perceptual abilities. Due to commitments about ideas, Berkeley thought that our senses were not unified; that is, we do not experience the same objects through our senses. Reid rebuts this argument by offering a different analysis of Molyneux's problem, and concludes that our perceptual experience is veridical and unified. Reid thereby fosters the pursuits of natural science in a way impossible for Berkeley, or even Locke.

I conclude the book by drawing together some remarks upon Reid's methodological empiricism, and I attempt to set him apart from these predecessors. By placing thorough limitations upon natural philosophy, he precludes us from understanding or knowing that substance dualism or materialism is true. This feature of his philosophy of mind resembles the views now associated with certain contemporary philosophers of mind who hold that the true nature of consciousness is beyond human comprehension due to the constitutional limitations of our minds. By employing epistemic principles to adjudicate metaphysical disputes, his empiricism resembles the philosophical perspective we have come to associate with some contemporary philosophers of science, who eschew metaphysical posturing in just the way Reid shuns the Way of Ideas' hypotheses.

1

Reid's Method

The importance of Reid's method is best understood in comparison with that of his predecessors. Gregory, Turnbull, Gerard, Maclaurin, and Reid oppose the Cartesian approach to the study of the mind, which takes as its metaphysical point of departure the claim that the mind is an indivisible substance. They equally oppose a Humean approach that departs from a fortified position of skepticism made obligatory by commitment to a radically empiricist thesis about the origins of our concepts. Descartes' brand of metaphysical theorizing never arrives at the world we know, and Hume's empiricism can only reach as far as our impressions.

Reid's Newtonian approach embarks from a place within the physical world and views human beings as embodied squarely in it. Despite the contrast, Hume and Reid both claim Newton's mantle. Since these two have a number of fundamental methodological disagreements, at least one of them must seriously misunderstand Newton if Newton is consistent. So what does Reid mean when he says that he is a Newtonian? This chapter addresses that question by explaining Reid's philosophical method and its goals (see also Callergård 2006). I then explain how Reid applies that method to the problem of perception.

This method sometimes conflicts with Reid's faith commitments. A running problem for Reid is identifying the explanatory limits of the method in such a way as to both forestall materialist hypotheses about the mind and license appeal to supernaturalistic explanations in that and other contexts. This grand problem takes shape in Reid's discussion—or rather, lack of discussion—about his substance dualism. Reid wrote a chapter for the *Intellectual Powers* about substance dualism and the soul but decided not to include it in the published work, which exemplifies ambivalence on Reid's part about ontological questions.

Since Reid's approach to the philosophy of perception is broadly functional, it is not dependent upon any specific account of the ontology of the mind or on God. He begins his philosophy of perception by positing faculties—functional capacities of the mind that, given proper stimulus, produce certain kinds of sensations, beliefs, or judgments. I will explain his faculty psychology and how it obviates the need for him to address troublesome ontological questions in the context of his theory of perception.

1.1. Newtonian Method

The origins of Reid's method lie in the work of Francis Bacon, who, says Reid, was the "only one to teach how this true interpretation of nature is to be acquired by relying on experiments in operation in nature or art" (Reid 1989, 38; see IHM 6.24, 200/200a). Reid's prized student, Dugald Stewart, says that:

the influence of the general views opened in the *New Organon* [by Bacon] may be traced in almost every page of his [Reid's] writings, and indeed, the circumstances by which these are so strongly and characteristically distinguished is that they exhibit the first systematical attempt to exemplify in the study of human nature the same plan of investigation which conducted Newton to the properties of light and to the law of gravitation. (Stewart 1854 i, 259–61)

Reid credits Bacon as a source for several of Newton's insights, dubious though such a claim may be. Reid says, for example, that Bacon provided Newton his model of inductive reasoning (EIP 2.8, 121/271b). According to Reid, their greatest intellectual convergence is this: "Lord Bacon first delineated the only solid foundation on which natural philosophy can be built; and Sir Isaac Newton reduced the principles laid down by Bacon into three or four axioms, which he calls *regulae philosophandi*" (EIP 6.4, 457/436b; see Reid's *A Brief Account of Aristotle's Logic* 6.2 in Reid 2004, 146, or in Hamilton's *Works* ii, 712a–b).[1] Newton's first rule (EIP 2.3, 80/250a; see EIP 1.4, 51/236a–b) and its requirement that natural philosophers appeal to and only to "causes" that are "true and sufficient to explain their phenomena" (Newton 1999, 794) were enormously influential upon Reid's investigation into perception. Reid insists that both the "adequacy" and the "reality" conditions in this rule must be met by theories that attempt to meet Newton's high standards (Marcil-Lacoste 1982, 162).

---

[1] These are Newton's rules: Rule 1. No more causes of natural things should be admitted than are both true and sufficient to explain their phenomena (Newton 1999, 794); Rule 2. Therefore, the causes assigned to natural effects of the same kind must be, so far as possible, the same (795); Rule 3. Those qualities of bodies that cannot be intended and remitted [i.e. qualities that cannot be increased and diminished] and that belong to all bodies on which experiments can be made should be taken as qualities of all bodies universally (795); Rule 4. In experimental philosophy, propositions gathered from phenomena by induction should be considered either exactly or very nearly true notwithstanding any contrary hypotheses, until yet other phenomena make such propositions either more exact or liable to exceptions (796).

Bacon describes several systemic problems in the scientific reasoning of his day in terms of what he calls "idols" as if to suggest that erroneous goals were transmogrified into false gods. The four idols attempt to explain the mistaken ways we interpret nature. Reid indicates that Newton's first rule is inspired by Bacon's discussion of the *idola fori* (Bacon 1994, §59; see EIP 6.8, 527/468ff). By this term Bacon refers to the impediments that language sets for philosophical progress. This point prompts Reid to adopt unfamiliar conventions with respect to the use of the word "cause," conventions that would subsequently lead to some misunderstandings in his readership. "Cause" in its strictest sense does not refer to physical events. Reid holds that the word "cause" only refers to the actions of persons, and not mere matter.

The most tangible positive feature of Bacon's views that Reid adopts for his own is Bacon's repudiation of ancient logic and his affirmation of inductive reasoning. In his discussion of Aristotle's logic, Reid mercilessly criticizes syllogism as an ineffective form of reasoning for any purpose. "No use can be made of it in mathematics" (Reid 2004, 128), and syllogistic logic immeasurably impeded the progress of natural science through the ages (Reid 2004, 145). Bacon's "Novum Organum gave a new turn to the thoughts and labours of the inquisitive, more remarkable, and more useful, than that which the Organum of Aristotle had given before; and may be considered as a second grand æra in the progress of human reason" (Reid 2004, 145–6). Reid adds that induction accounts for the justification of the greatest part of human knowledge.

Reid's familiarity with Bacon and his subsequent appreciation of the intellectual debts Newton owed to Bacon sets Reid apart from other figures who sought to occupy Newton's shadow. Though the concluding General Scholium in the later editions of Newton's *Principia Mathematica* left a profound mark upon Reid, he was unaware of Newton's many vacillations about a famous passage there. Newton says that he has:

not as yet been able to deduce from phenomena the reason for these properties of gravity, and I do not feign hypotheses. For whatever is not deduced from the phenomena must be called a hypothesis; and hypotheses, whether metaphysical or physical, or based on occult qualities, or mechanical, have no place in experimental philosophy. (Newton 1999, 943; for the history of this passage, see Cohen 1962)

Reid repeatedly echoes this methodological commitment. Early in the *Intellectual Powers* he says, "Let us lay down this as a fundamental principle in our inquiries into the structure of the mind and its operations—that no regard is due to the conjectures or hypotheses of philosophers, however ancient, however generally received" (EIP 1.4, 51/236a).

Reid's disdain for the Theory of Ideas leads him away from the authority of tradition and toward reliance upon first-person observation. By Reid's lights a theory of perception is incomplete unless it offers accounts of both the internal, qualitative aspects of perceptual experience, and the relation between perceptual states and bodies in the mind-independent world. Observation accordingly takes two very different forms, one no less legitimate than the other: introspection and investigation of the mind-independent world. The nuanced nature of, say, qualitative mental experience in vision stands alongside the more scientific study of the characteristics of retinal images. From the first kind of observation we learn about colors and the introspectible properties of visual figures, and from the second that the retinal images are produced in pairs and are inverted. Reid's Newtonian commitments structure and unify the way he approaches observations of these different types.

Introspective observation is the primary means of investigation used to learn about the intellectual power of perception. Two intellectual powers aid in this form of observation: consciousness and attentive reflection. Reid says that "the testimony of consciousness can never deceive" (EAP 1.1, 513a), and he does not make that claim about reflection. But the more important difference between consciousness and reflection seems to be this: consciousness is a feature attending all of the operations of our minds all the time (EIP 2.15, 191/308b).[2] This is true though we do not normally reflect upon our mental operations (EIP 1.5, 58/239b). This leads Reid to say:

We may have the former [consciousness] without any degree of the latter [reflection]. The difference between consciousness and reflection, is like the difference between a superficial view of an object which presents itself to the eye while we are engaged about something else, and that attentive examination which we give to an object when we are wholly employed in surveying it. (EIP 1.5, 58–9/239b)

In contrast Reid argues that Locke confounds the two, for Locke says in the *Essay* that "Consciousness is the perception of what passes in a Man's own mind" (Locke 1975, 115/2.1.19). Though reflection is distinct from consciousness for Reid, this does not imply that his analysis of reflection is perspicacious. It is not. In part this is because reflection encompasses other powers; it "is not one power of the mind; it comprehends many," including recollection, attention and judgment (EIP 3.5, 269/347a–b). In any case, reflection is the more useful in developing an empirical science of the intellectual powers (EIP 6.1, 421/420a).

---

[2] Lehrer (1986–7) argues that Reid's discussion of consciousness creates a vicious regress. Mishori (2003) adds to these woes by contending that Reidian consciousness is insufficient to unify our mental states.

By employing reflection upon his observations, introspective and otherwise, Reid is led to a succinct statement of his Newtonian method:

[Scientific] discoveries have always been made by patient observation, by accurate experiments, or by conclusions drawn by strict reasoning from observations and experiments, and such discoveries have always tended to refute, but not to confirm, the theories and hypotheses which ingenious men have invented. (EIP 1.3, 49–50/235a–b; see EIP 2.8, 120–21/271a–b; EIP 5.3, 371/397a; and AC 527a)

Throughout his corpus he upbraids proponents of the Way of Ideas on methodological grounds and attempts to replace its methods with a commitment to observation and induction. I propose to gather together several features of what Reid considers to be the proper scientific method from such passages. Natural philosophers should proceed by:

(1.1) "observing events";
(1.2) conducting "accurate experiments";
(1.3) "reducing [this data] to general rules";
(1.4) then, and only then, drawing conclusions from the above "by strict reasoning."

Reid rightly believes that this method sharply differs from those methods employed by his predecessors.

When Reid refers to the general rules that we form on the basis of our experiments, he refers to laws. The ultimate goal of explanation within natural philosophy is to formulate laws. "To give an account of a phenomenon is simply to demonstrate that such a phenomenon is in accord with some known law of nature" (Reid 1989, 60). He characterizes laws in more detail by saying:

A law is a thing conceived in the mind of a rational being, not a thing that has real existence; and, therefore, like a motive, it can neither act nor be acted upon. … The physical laws of nature are the rules according to which the Deity commonly acts in his natural government of the world; … These laws of nature neither restrain the power of the Author of nature, nor bring him under any obligation to do anything beyond their sphere. (EAP 4.10, 628a–b)

The ultimate goal of explanation is in showing that an event conforms to a known law of nature because explanation can go no further. "Of the laws of nature themselves, however, no explanation can be given except that they are the will of the supreme Founder of all things" (Reid 1989, 60). Reid attempts to arrest the hypothetical speculation of his contemporaries by prescribing this limit.

Reid differs with the Way of Ideas about explanation with regard to the end point of philosophical explanation, and with regard to the means by which we explain a phenomenon. More important than the differences in method is difference regarding the objects over which the method is taken to range. Keith Lehrer accurately identifies this point of contrast between Reid and Hume. The different set of objects of observation from which they form different general rules has greater influence on the outcomes of their arguments than their mutual commitment to empiricism (Lehrer 1998, 15). In an effort to hone the contrast, Lehrer refers to one of Reid's first principles—"that the natural faculties, by which we distinguish truth from error, are not fallacious" (EIP 6.5, 480/441a). Here is another: "That those things do really exist which we distinctly perceive by our senses, and are what we perceive them to be" (EIP 6.5, 476/445b). Together these principles assert that we are entitled to take as foundational the fact that our faculties provide us with reliable experience of the physical world. Reid is definitive: natural philosophy *starts from* our experience of the mind-independent world and should not be constrained to our experiences of our mental states alone. In addition to Reid's stress upon the prominent role that should be accorded to observation, he says that observation is taken to be of the physical world itself. Hume either demurs on both counts, or is unclear about his commitments to these points.

However, though Reid's analysis of the intellectual *powers* of the mind conforms to this Newtonian method, he does not apply it with equanimity in his reflection upon the *substance* of the mind.

Whether intentionally or not, Reid's discussion of the end point of natural philosophy seems tailored to the preservation of his religious commitments. Explanations of natural phenomena stop in laws, which was the great influence of Newton. However, explanations of mental phenomena do not stop in laws that themselves contain mental terms. The philosophies of mind developed by materialists such as Joseph Priestley and David Hartley appeared radical to Reid because Reid is a substance dualist who claims to have proofs for that commitment (see §1.5 below). In response Reid argues that their theories violate Reid's prescriptions about the limits of philosophical reasoning.

Several philosophical and methodological problems arise from this nexus of issues. I mention only two. Reid's appeal to the limits of explanation in natural philosophy seems inconsistent at times because he uses the limits as license for hypothetical speculation of his own. For example, Reid avows that all vegetables have an immaterial being causing in them certain effects that are necessary for the fulfillment of their life processes. Then he writes, "It may be asked to what Order of Beings we must refer those immaterial Agents that act upon inanimate Matter, & those by which Animals and Vegetables are Animated? Are they thinking intelligent Beings or not are they mortal or immortal? What becomes of the Soul of Plants and A<n>imals when they die[?]" Reid pulls up his pen to leave us in darkness: "I am not so much moved by [these] Questions," adding, "To these and such Questions I can answer onely by confessing my Ignorance" (AC 229). Materialists of Reid's day, including Joseph Priestley and David Hartley, would no doubt want to know why Reid believes that the limits of philosophical explanation allow the incredible claim *that* there are angels sustaining plant life, and why they prevent any legitimate inquiry into the *properties* of these beings. Hume aims a harsh barb at Reid when he expresses his wish that "Parsons wou'd confine themselves to their old Occupation of worrying one another; & leave Philosophers to argue with Temper, Moderation & good Manners" (C 19). Though the callous tone is unbecoming, I appreciate Hume's tone of exasperation with Reid on points like this.

Furthermore, Reid's response to materialist theories of the mind is confused. Priestley demanded from Reid an accounting of the *prima facie* conflict between his commitments about the soul and his allegiance to Newtonian observation. Reid repeatedly appeals to the limitations of human knowledge. For example, Reid denies that the desire to know efficient causes can be fulfilled: "supposing natural philosophy brought to its perfection—it does not discover the efficient cause of any one phenomenon in nature. ... Natural philosophers ... have discovered many of her laws ... but they have never discovered the efficient cause of any one phenomenon" (EAP 1.6, 526a). Since a full account of substance dualism must include an explanation of the capacity of the mind to serve as an efficient cause, Reid concludes that the substance of the mind lies beyond the scope of his Newtonian method.

Nicholas Wolterstorff quotes this passage (at EAP 1.6, 526a) and describes this theme in Reid: "What lies at the bottom of Reidian epistemological piety is acknowledging the darkness—or the 'mystery,' as Reid sometimes calls it. ... [I]t becomes evident that darkness is one of the most pervasive themes in his writings" (Wolterstorff 2001, 256; see 259). But Wolterstorff masks a disquieting problem in Reid by praising him for his "piety," "humility and active gratitude," and "trust" (2001, 260–1). Lamentably, what are limits of knowledge in the major works transmogrify in the minor works and manuscripts into what is better described as a veiled appeal to ignorance. I fear that, had Wolterstorff (in his 2001) read and discussed Reid's manuscripts on dualism and materialism (published in 1995 as *Thomas Reid on the Animate Creation*), he would have had to trade his honeyed and ennobling description, however more desirable, for something less pleasant and more true to fact.

A student of Reid's theory of perception should be aware that Reid's substance dualism sits uneasily alongside his general reliance upon observation and induction, but I will not enter this debate here since its complexities would stop us in our tracks. Besides, such a discussion may not contribute to the advancement of philosophical knowledge in the way that a study of Reid's theory of perception will. Thankfully, animadversions on Reid's substance dualism are unnecessary for properly interpreting Reid's theory of perception. Here lies the importance of appreciating Reid's operational analysis of the powers of the mind. Reid marries his Newtonian method with a broadly functional approach to the study of the senses through which, in the *Inquiry*, he considers the physical apparatus, the phenomenology, and the intentional nature of the mental states produced by each sense faculty. At minimum, this method commits Reid to a substantial self (EIP 6.5, 472/443b)—there must be someone doing the observing, and the thoughts of this agent must be unified by some principle. However, ruling upon the ontological status of this self is a different matter entirely.

1.2. Common Sense

The emphasis placed upon common sense in interpretations of Reid, beginning with his colleague and supporter James Beattie and continuing through his contemporary detractors, is frequently greater than Reid's own emphasis upon common sense. Reid's appeal to common sense has been the fulcrum upon which the worst interpretations of his corpus swing, from Kant forward. In the present context, this has led to the dismissal of Reid's theory of perception as naive realism.

Given the historiographical role of "common sense" in misinterpretations, students of Reid's work are faced with the choice of either explaining in detail just what he means by describing his theories as commonsensical, or in stating his theories in ways that minimally play upon his appeal to common sense. I will choose the second route. Thankfully, the role of common sense is much more pronounced in Reid's discussion of the epistemological foundations of knowledge (what Reid canonizes as "First Principles of common sense" in the *Intellectual Powers*) than it is in his theory of perception, enabling us to avoid the thorny aspects of the debate without sacrificing much detail.

Though I will not use the term frequently, I need to disambiguate several of the meanings Reid gives "common sense," which some commentators have said is the most confusing element of Reid's philosophy (e.g. Wolterstorff 2001, 240). Reid uses the term "common sense" as adjective and noun in extremely broad circumstances. Often the term is used in a *general sense* in which he aims to persuade through rhetoric and not through philosophical reasoning, for example, by giving arguments *ad hominem*. (Charitably, one might say that

Reid uses the term in these contexts to promote a philosophical method.) Rhetorical, affected passages that exemplify this meaning of "common sense," like this one, have been largely responsible for Reid's ill repute:

Admired Philosophy! Daughter of light! Parent of wisdom and knowledge! If thou art she, surely thou hast not yet arisen upon the human mind, nor blessed us with more of the rays than are sufficient to shed a darkness visible upon the human faculties, and to disturb that repose and security which happier mortals enjoy, who never approached thine altar, nor felt thine influence! But if, indeed, thou hast not power to dispel those clouds and phantoms which thou hast discovered or created, withdraw this penurious and malignant ray; I despise Philosophy, and renounce its guidance—let my soul dwell with Common Sense. (IHM 1.4, 18/101a)

But this rhetorical appeal to common sense is not as frequent as is its use as an epistemic thesis regarding First Principles (EIP 6.2, 433−4/425b).

Other ways Reid employs the term is to describe a *faculty* of the mind (though not to describe the Aristotelian faculty of the common sense) (EIP 6.4, 423−4/421b); as a *semantic* thesis about what the majority of people mean by a term (EIP 2.5, 98/259a; see EIP 2.8, 125/274a−b); as a *perceptual* claim that we immediately perceive physical, mind-independent objects (IHM 6.20, 170/184a−b); and as a *metaphysical* thesis that there exist the objects we typically believe to exist, which Reid canonizes as a First Principle of common sense (EIP 1.2, 43/232a−b). In that context Reid uses his theory of common sense to refute results that Berkeley draws from his theory of common sense. The perceptual and metaphysical theses arise, among other places, within Reid's enumeration of the First Principles of common sense. Perhaps there is also room to identify a *doxastic* form of common sense since Reid says that beliefs that arise irresistibly within us are common-sense beliefs.

Perhaps the best way to unify these commitments under the aegis of common sense is to describe Reid as using a common-sense method. Some scholars interpret this commitment as Reid's attempt to make the method he inherits from Newton and Bacon his own. For example Marcil-Lacoste says, "Reid's doctrine of common sense is a revolutionary philosophical procedure in which the test of rational arguments will be provided by the experimental discovery of the natural laws of self-evidence and by further experimental discoveries of their implications" (Marcil-Lacoste 1982, 173). Perhaps viewing common sense in this light provides the concept with the range needed to coalesce Reid's disparate uses of the term with his emphasis upon common sense as a final court of appeal in philosophical disputes. Rather than identify it univocally with a faculty, Reid says that "common sense is that degree of judgment which is common to men with whom we can converse and transact business" (EIP 6.2, 424/421b). Specifically, we use common sense when we "judge of things self-evident" (EIP 6.2, 433/425b). As such it is "only another name for one branch or one degree of reason," and he says that this form is not produced by learning (as are the other forms), but rather is "purely the gift of Heaven." This is why, when reasoning through disputes about principles comes to an end, we make appeal to common-sense judgments (EIP 6.2, 426/422b). In this sense of the term, Reid implies that common sense serves a metaphilosophical function.

1.3. Applying the Method to Perception

I have described Reid's method in natural philosophy, but it remains to articulate the way in which he applies this method to the study of perception. One obvious but often overlooked implication is that Reid is not aiming at a "philosophical analysis" of perception, by which I mean that he is not attempting to identify a set of logically necessary and sufficient conditions. Reid develops an empirical explanation of the operation of the senses, their relation to objects in the world, and their place in the mind. For those who expect a set of conditions from Reid, his allegiance to Newtonian methods will seem evasive. He dodges demands to define terms like "perception" and "conception." This tendency works its way into Reid's system as a general principle of some power. In no subject besides the philosophy of mind is there "more frequent occasion to use words that cannot be logically defined." This means that "No man can explain, by a logical definition, what it is to *think*, to *apprehend*, to *believe*, to *will*, to *desire*" (EIP 1.1, 19–20/220b). Reid continues in the early parts of the *Intellectual Powers* to describe what he means by these terms, though he falls short of defining them to his satisfaction.

Instead, he discusses the actual conditions in which human agents succeed in perceiving physical objects, which is why he constructs his account of perception in such a way that it arises out of his introspective and scientific study. Since he does not use a priori reasoning to identify demands upon a theory of perception, he does not satisfy a desire for pre-packaged definitions ready for conceptual consumption.

In virtue of not hypothesizing a priori conditions on an account of perception to which events must conform, Reid stands apart from several historical and contemporary accounts of perception. But we should not thereby infer that Reid merely describes perception. A description of perception would not qualify as a theory because it would not contain philosophical reflection on the process. He builds upon his study of the workings of our faculties in order to identify the laws to which perceptual events conform in what he calls the "proper circumstances" (EIP 2.20, 229/328b). The conceptual and doxastic processes constitutive of a perceptual event can be evaluated in terms of whether they are produced under the earthly conditions that we know are most suitable for veridical human perception.

One mode of developing a theory of perception—Aristotle's in *De Anima* and Reid's—is to isolate the component parts of the perceptual process, explain each of those, then clarify how they operate in concert. Reid describes the physiological systems and events upon which perception supervenes in our world. Our perceptual equipment consists of our sensory organs and those parts of our brains and nervous systems responsible for processing information received from our senses. The physiological component of perception consists in five stages. In a chapter of the *Inquiry* he calls "Of the Process of Nature in Perception," Reid says that the object perceived first must be in contact with an organ of sense, whether immediately (particles from an object entering the nasal cavity) or mediately (rays of light are refracted from the surface of an object to the eye). Next, a physical impression is made upon the organ by the object. The nervous system transmits this impression from the organ to the brain. This impression typically causes a sensation in the mind. Finally, the sensation suggests the perception of the object (IHM 6.21, 174ff/186; see C 213–14).

Though there are physical sub-processes in an account of perception, he denies that a causal theory of perception will be complete. He echoes the remarks about "mystery" above when he asks, "But how are the sensations of the mind produced by impressions upon the body? Of this we are absolutely ignorant, having no means of knowing how the body acts upon the mind, or the mind upon the body.... There is a deep and a dark gulf between them, which our understanding cannot pass" (IHM 6.21, 176/187a). In part this implies that we do not, and perhaps cannot, know what laws govern interaction between the body and mind. In the *Intellectual Powers*, Reid grants that "This train of machinery," this network of physical systems in our bodies, is something "God has made necessary to our perceiving objects" (EIP 2.3, 76/248a). Reid is not claiming that there is any conceptual or metaphysical necessity at work here; rather, in our world, designed by God, this connection obtains. He is careful about this: "though they are conjoined with perception by the will of our Maker, yet it does not appear that they have any necessary connection with it in their own nature" (EIP 2.4, 95/257b; see 2.1, 72/246a). Reid then argues that there is a correspondence between physical states and perceptual states:

As impressions on the organs, nerves, and brain, correspond exactly to the nature and conditions of the objects by which they are made, so our perceptions and sensations correspond to those impressions, and vary in kind, and in degree, as they vary. Without this exact correspondence, the information we receive by our senses would not only be imperfect, as it undoubtedly is, but would be fallacious, which we have no reason to think it is. (EIP 2.2, 76/248b)

Reid believes that a relation of constant conjunction obtains between material impressions and perceptions, but this is not efficient causation. Reid is incredulous that philosophers believe "that the impressions of external objects upon the machine of our bodies can be the real efficient cause of thought and perception" (EIP 2.4, 88/253b; see EIP 2.1, 72/246b). Constant conjunction does not provide good reason to believe that material impressions are efficient causes of perceptions. Furthermore, matter is inactive. Objects that are perceived "do not act at all" (EIP 2.14, 77/301a). But Reid's theory of causation is subject to a tension. He attempts to balance his robust metaphysical commitments about the mind and corollary religious commitments about the soul with his interest in constructing a science of the mind and its operations.

I detect a noticeable shift between Reid's major works in his typically taciturn opinions about the relation between the mind and body. In the *Inquiry* Reid allows that sensations might be caused by physical events in the world and our brain. "Our perception of objects is the result of a train of operations; some of which affect the body only, others affect the mind" (IHM 6.21, 174/186b). Twenty years later he is reluctant to posit a causal connection between the physical and mental. He says that others believe that physical impressions of objects are "the proper efficient causes of the corresponding perception. But no reasoning is more fallacious than this—that, because two things are always conjoined, therefore one must be the cause of the other" (EIP 4.4, 87/253b). Reid's opposition to a causal theory grows with age (Ben Zeev 1986, 102).

His mature discussion of the mind–body relation, as it is manifest in perceptual events, invokes God's action. "It is a law of our nature, established by the will of the Supreme Being, that we perceive no external object but by means of the organs given us for that purpose." He adds, "We perceive, because God has given us the power of perceiving, and not because we have impressions from objects" (EIP 2.4, 95/257a–b). These and similar comments are open to interpretation, but he seems to endorse a theory within the occasionalist family.

In other texts he seems to endorse interactionism. He says, "These different Substances are indeed in our present State so connected that many of the Operations of the mind are performed by means of the Organs of the body. and the good and bad constitution of the body affects the mind" (Reid 2002a,

624). The body causally affects the mind and, he hints, the operations of the mind causally affect our organs. Since Reid uses "cause" in a proprietary way, to refer to agent causes only, he does not use the term "cause" here. Yet Reid's "by means of" relation, which I take to be a real, physical (and not epiphenomenal or purely mental) relation, is enough to prompt his readers to interpret him as offering a kind of interactionism. This text should weigh heavily in determining Reid's mature theory of the mind–body relation because, though he never published it, it occurs in the context of Reid's discussion of the nature of the soul.

But in this same context Reid can be interpreted in a third way, as a skeptic about this connection. "We can give no reason why the picture on the retina should be followed by vision, while a like picture on any other part of the body produces nothing like vision" (EIP 2.4, 95/257b). This comment, following on the heels of his remark about God, has the implication that an appeal to God does not qualify as a "reason," but rather serves the function of delimiting the scope of explanation in natural philosophy (see Tuggy 2000; and Nichols 2007).

Two observations show that these reflections on the mind–body relation are not as confused as they first appear. First, he affirms a form of occasionalism insofar as physical events are *insufficient to cause* mental events, which pushes him toward appealing to God's intervention. He also affirms a form of interactionism insofar as physical events are *a part of the total cause* of mental events. If these statements approximate Reid's views, then they are consistent since this weak form of occasionalism is consistent with this weak form of interactionism.[3]

Second, Reid sanctions some form of skepticism—or at least agnosticism—about the mind–body relation. This is in part because this motley collection of convictions does not induce any knowledge. On one way of viewing the matter, endorsing skepticism about the mind–body relation is consistent either with occasionalism or with interactionism. He may believe that one or the other, or (on weak interpretations) both, are true. But discussion about occasionalism and interactionism is speculation, which falls outside of his Newtonian method. His Newtonian commitments to observability prompt him to desist from claiming to know that one or the other is true.

---

[3] Another option contends that Reid's appeals to God can be stripped of their theological import (De Bary 2002, chapter 10; see Lehrer and Warner 2000). On a strong form of this reading, Reid is interpreted as holding that "nature has fitted out the mental operations of the advanced species in such a way as to permit successful transactions within an often harsh environment … [which] makes Reid's view close to an evolutionary explanation and thus presents some account of the emergence of mental capacities" (Ben Zeev 1990, 42). This is motivated by an interest in rebutting the charge (in Norton 1976a) that the justification of Reid's first principles of contingent truth depends upon God's existence and benevolence.

Despite his agnosticism about the causes of specific mental events, Reid persists with his theory of perception and focuses upon those mental components of the process that can be understood. The mental aspects of perception unify what we receive from our senses, nervous systems, and brains. Reid takes for granted that his readers know that "perception" and its cognates are equivocal in this way, and that his readers will be able to determine from the context which aspect of the faculty it is—mental or physical—to which he refers. Reid typically intends to denote the mental components of the process with the term, as here:

[W]e shall find in [perception] these three things: First, Some conception or notion of the object perceived; Secondly, a strong and irresistible conviction and belief of its present existence; and, Thirdly, That this conviction and belief are immediate, and not the effect of reasoning. (EIP 2.5, 96/258a)

Aaron Ben Zeev has an insightful way of characterizing this point. He says, "these cognitive features are expressive of the perception itself, and are not an additional, separate process" (1986, 105). Reid's remark, which he repeats elsewhere (see EIP 2.20, 226/326b; and IHM 6.20, 168/183a), is not intended to state necessary and sufficient conditions.[4]

Implicit in the foregoing are further conditions, including that there must be a causal process by which the object produces the conception and belief in

---

[4] A failure to employ univocal definitions of the term is responsible for substantial confusion in the secondary literature, often found in studies that compare contemporary theories of perception to Reid's. Suppose we use Frank Jackson's definition of "mediate perception" and apply it to Reid's theory of perception, as J. Todd Buras has done. In Buras's words: "x is a mediate object of (visual) perception for S at t iff S perceives x at t, and there is a y such that x ≠ y and S perceives x by virtue of perceiving y" (2005, 462). Buras offers necessary and sufficient conditions of an indirect or "mediate" theory of perception with Jackson's definition because he believes Jackson's description of the logical structure of mediated perception "fairly represents the content of the terms in the early modern debate," including Reid. Buras argues that Reid's theory of perception is a mediated theory, and, specifically, that perceptual events are "referentially" mediated by our sensations (2005, 464).

Two problems arise. Though Jackson's discussion can be used by interpreters to clarify Reid's theory, Jackson's characterization does not represent the goings-on in Early Modern debates about perception (which is not to imply it was intended by Jackson for this job). Specifically, Reid does not take as his aim the construction of a logical analysis of "perception" or "indirect perception," though he does believe that some features distinguish perception from other mental operations. Second, Buras follows Jackson by characterizing "mediate" or "indirect" perception as having the following necessary condition: my perception of object x must be, "by virtue of perceiving y," the intermediary. As applied to Reid, the intermediary is a sensation. Jackson is especially clear about the relation between the agent and the intermediary. In order for my perception of x to be indirect and mediate, I must not merely *be aware of* or apprehend or *experience* a sensation. I must *perceive* the sensation. In other words, one event of perception must occur within another if a perception of an external object is to be indirect, according to Buras. But, as we have witnessed above, Reid defines perception to be an operation of the mind that takes mind-independent bodies and primary qualities as its intentional objects. Given these two points, it appears to be an analytic truth that Reidian perception is not mediated on the definition used by Buras.

us (IHM 6.21 and EIP 2.2), and that "Perception is applied only to external objects, not to those that are in the mind itself" (EIP 1.1, 23/222a; see EIP 1.1, 26/224a). A few unusual implications about his use of "perception" follow from these points. First, Reid sometimes allows that "perception" can occur in cases of hallucination (EIP 2.28, 214/320b; see Van Cleve 2004b, 129). Second, he does not attempt to include any sensory experience within the scope of the perceptual event in this characterization. This is odd since we take a certain type of qualitative sensory experience to be what distinguishes perception from other forms of mental activity, like belief.

A further complicating factor in discussing perception in Reid is the fact that he often uses "perception" in accord with his formal definition on which it refers to the conception and belief of a mind-independent body. More frequently Reid uses "perception" and its cognates as multi-purpose terms referring to features of the process by which we are aware of mind-independent bodies, without invoking his formal definition. This has created substantial confusion in the literature on Reid. To avoid this problem in this book, when I invoke Reid's formal definition of the term, I will use "perception$_{C\&B}$," and in other cases I will simply use the term "perception." Though not pretty on the page, this use of terminology is helpful in maintaining clarity of thought.

1.4. Faculty Psychology

Reid writes much more about our faculty of perception than about any other faculty. In order to put his theory of perception in proper view I must situate it amidst the other intellectual powers and identify the reasons for his faculty psychology.

I have already identified one motive, which is that Reid is interested in gaining knowledge about the function of the active mind at the expense of studying its substance. Reid also adopts a faculty psychology in response to the Way of Ideas. He traces a methodological flaw in the philosophies of mind of many of his predecessors to their complex descriptions of powers of the mind:

[T]here are many activities relating to the human mind of which we will try only in vain to render an account. How the mind thinks, in what way it is conscious of its thoughts and operations, completely escapes us. By no hypothesis shall we be able to explain or to give an account of these faculties.

This is because these faculties cannot be explained in terms of simpler laws: "Surely these faculties are, in truth, primary and simple, not composed of,

nor to be reduced to, other faculties but implanted in our minds by God."
He adds, "For in the mind, no less than in the material worlds, there are first
principles of which no explanation can be given" (Reid 1989, 60). We will see
this commitment at work in his discussion of intentionality and his criticisms
of Hume in that context.

Reid recommends starting with a robust set of faculties. In contrast, he
believes the Way of Ideas begins with only one: the ability to perceive ideas,
which Richard Routley memorably labels "@-ception". This follows from an
intuition that we should individuate faculties on the basis of their objects since
the only immediate objects of awareness are ideas, according to the Way of
Ideas. The principles of the Way of Ideas:

have not only led philosophers to split objects into two, where others can find but
one, but likewise have led them to reduce the three operations now mentioned to one,
making memory and conception, as well as perception, to be the perception of ideas.
But nothing appears more evident to the vulgar, than that what is only remembered,
or only conceived, is not perceived. (EIP 4.2, 314/369b)

Locke suggests that we can adopt many different propositional attitudes
to ideas, but ideas will be the intentional objects of all the intellectual
powers. Reid's approach affects a considerable shift in thinking (Mishori 2003,
142–4). Not only is the propositional attitude one adopts in imagination,
for example, distinct from the attitude adopted in a perception, but also
the objects themselves are of a different kind. Perceptual states take mind-
independent qualities and bodies as their immediate intentional objects, while
the imagination takes hypothetical states of affairs as its.

The claim that the mind has distinct faculties is not a matter of dispute
in seventeenth- and eighteenth-century philosophy. What is debated is the
explanatory efficacy of appeals to the distinct faculties. Reid would eventually
be faced with vitriolic criticism from Priestley for having profligately multiplied
the faculties. According to the Way of Ideas, all the intellectual faculties take
ideas as their immediate intentional objects. As a result they cannot be
individuated by appeal to their intentional objects. This point hides in the
shadows of a warning Hume issues at *Treatise* 1.3.7. An error "inculcated
in the schools," he says, "consists in the vulgar division of the acts of the
understanding, into *conception, judgment* and *reasoning*." Such a distinction errs
because these three forms of cognition "all resolve themselves into the first,
and are nothing but particular ways of conceiving our objects" (T 1.3.7, 96n).
Hume has no reason not to add perception to this list. This is in part because
we can "consider" a "single object," we can dwell on several objects, and we
can think about objects in a certain order. These acts of cognition depend upon

the mind producing mental states that are either about other mental states, or about mind-independent objects and their qualities. Reid's faculty psychology proceeds upon an opposite conviction insofar as he believes these processes mark different faculties. This conviction is borne of Reid's observations of the way his mind works in the world.

In the *Inquiry* Reid says that "nature seems both to have planted and reared" a subset of our powers. These are the powers we have "with the brutes." The set includes the intellectual powers of perception (sight, smell, hearing, touch, taste) and memory, and active powers such as lust, rest, and a form of anger. This set of powers has the best claim to being innate, in the sense that a human being has the disposition to develop those powers without further experience. The remaining powers, however, encompass abilities that are unique to human beings and are the products of "human culture" (IHM 1.2, 13/98b). These powers cannot be developed without the agent's having further experience within a society. This set includes intellectual powers such as judgment, reflection, and abstraction, and active powers of friendship, public spirit, and gratitude. One way to understand this distinction is by considering its implication that human beings left feral would acquire the powers of the brutes, but not the powers of human culture. Typically innate powers are solitary, while others depend upon social interaction.

Here in the *Inquiry* Reid glides over differences between powers and faculties, but in the *Intellectual Powers* he suggests that the term "faculty" is "most properly applied to those powers of the mind which are original and natural, and which make a part of the constitution of the mind." Faculties contrast with those powers that are not faculties because the "non-faculty" powers are those "acquired by use, exercise, or study, which are not called faculties, but *habits*" (IHM 1.1, 21/221b). This distinction is not co-extensive with the solitary/social distinction above. The implication is that the set of intellectual powers is divided exhaustively between faculties and habits. Having said this, Reid does not fully abide by this distinction.

In addition to *faculties* and *powers*, there are *operations*. The term "operations" refers to "every mode of thinking of which we are conscious." Thus operations subsume a broad category in Reid's architecture of the mind. The term is significant because it conveys Reid's conviction that the mind is active. Body is "extended, divisible, moveable, inert" and "a dead, inactive thing, which moves only as it is moved, and acts only by being acted upon." But the mind "is from its very nature, a living and active being. Everything we know of it implies life and active energy" (EIP 1.1, 20/221a). Operations are instances of the usage of faculties and powers. Acts of remembering my sixteenth birthday or events of perceiving a maple tree are operations.

For present purposes the most important category in the taxonomy is that of *power*. By describing a set of powers distinct from the intellectual powers as "active," Reid is not to be taken to imply that the intellectual powers are not active in their own right. The particular division is to some extent a matter of convenience (Brooks 1976, 73). The active powers are divided into three primary categories: mechanical, animal, and rational, which in turn contain subcategories. The mechanical powers are composed of instincts and habits, and animal powers include appetites, desires and affections. The rational powers are too few in number to merit further subcategories, though there are some powers that Reid seems to leave unclassified, e.g. those of imitation and attention.

The group of intellectual powers is smaller in number and presented more straightforwardly because it is not further divided into subcategories. The principal powers are abstraction, conception (or simple apprehension), consciousness, judgment, memory, perception, reasoning, reflection, and the sense of good taste. (For comprehensive tables of these divisions, see Brooks 1976, 74–6.) But this is artificially clear, and a host of ambiguities in classification remain. For example, Reid seems to categorize imagination in two ways and seems to use it as a synonym for two powers. Also, Reid is aware that powers can operate in tandem, making it difficult to identify an individual operation as belonging to one power and not another.

Thankfully, despite these difficulties, few will look askance on Reid's faculty psychology since in many ways his approach has been adopted in the philosophy of psychology. Reid's philosophy of mind has partially set the table for subsequent psychology. One of the standard histories of the development of psychology as a science proclaims, "Insofar as Reid systematized the psychological tradition of his time he undoubtedly shaped the tradition in such a way as to make it potentially suitable to become a component of psychology as a science" (Kantor 1969, 157). This contrasts sharply with earlier assessments of Reid from within psychology (e.g. Brett 1921).

Though we have motivated Reid's method and his execution of the method in the form of his faculty psychology, the intended explanatory force of setting mental events in the context of this system of faculties and operations is not obvious. Reid's Newtonianism compels him first to observe introspectively the activities of his mind, which leads him to the classificatory scheme he has. Sufficient observation allows Reid to reason inductively about the faculty used to produce states of a similar type, and draw conclusions about the conditions under which the faculty operates properly. For example, Reid describes the way in which we use the faculty of reflection to formulate new concepts from old and apply the new concepts in perceptual belief formation.

But his schema is also intended to be psychologically descriptive of the mind and is not proposed merely as a heuristic. The faculties are fundamental to explanation, and are to serve as terms in general laws of thought. Reid believes that memory, say, is a fundamental feature of our cognitive experience (EIP 3.2, 255/340b), and can be used to explain why certain beliefs are known through its codification as a First Principle (EIP 6.5, 474/444b). Apparently this trend continues: "The modern psychologist is either a 'faculty psychologist' or he confines himself to pointing" (Robinson 1989, 50).

It is tempting to appeal to Newton's use of laws in an explanation of Reid's appeal to faculties, in part because Reid himself does this. But the status of faculties as fundamental to Reid's enterprise in developing a natural philosophy of the mind is difficult to ascertain in part because Reid's adoption of Newton's methodology is subject to considerable interpretation (see Callergård 2006, chapter 2). For Newton, it remains possible that gravity is not a fundamental law, but instead can be explained in terms of more general laws, which offers a point of contrast. In addition, Newton's opposition to mechanical accounts of gravity was not based upon any a priori commitments, in contrast to some of Reid's claims about the fundamental status of the faculties. Newton simply could not find mechanisms that would fulfill the strictures of his first rule of philosophizing and thereby successfully explain the regularities that he explains by appeal to gravity.

This contrast between Reid and Newton about the limits of explanation in natural philosophy enhances our understanding of Reid's philosophy of mind and his vociferous objections to materialism. The ensuing problems Reid inherits mirror those present today in the dualist camps dedicated to constraining materialist explanations of the mind. In contrast to Newton's opposition to explaining gravity in terms of other, simpler mechanisms, Reid's opposition to materialist explanations of the mind and its faculties stems from hypotheses of his own, founded upon religious commitments. Reid does not succeed in his attempt to unify natural philosophy under Newton's rules because of the differences between the standards of explanation he employs about physics from those he employs about the mind (Nichols 2007; Tapper 2003). Reid pays allegiance to Newton's emphasis on observation, but he rebuffs explanations of mental or spiritual phenomena in terms of material mechanisms without a fair hearing. Reid's dilemma involves taking his commitment to empirical observation in scientific explanation as far as possible, but holding on to his religious commitments while doing so. Reid's solution was to refrain from publishing writings that used his religious commitments to constrain scientific explanation, including, for example, his views about the immaterial "Soul of Plants."

1.5. Belief

Reid refers to several faculties in the course of accounting for perceptual events because several faculties are involved in perception. A seemingly simple act of coming to believe that you see your brother on the sidewalk involves, to some extent or other, intentional awareness, visual perception, memory, belief, and judgment. Aspects of perceptual learning creep into the process at points, too. In Reid's typical definition of "perception" he explicitly makes mention of intentional awareness (under various names, including "conception" and "apprehension"), perception, and belief. Though I discuss conception in detail further below, I will briefly address the relation between belief and perception.

Belief is regarded as unaccountable and basic, like other faculties. The term, like the names for other faculties, refers to the faculty itself and to the operations of the faculty. Reid holds that belief is a physically necessary condition on human perception: we can't form perceptions in this world without belief. (I doubt Reid intends it to be conceptually necessary, but I won't enter into that issue here.) I take it that this is what he means when he defines perception as incorporating a belief component, and by calling belief an "essential ingredient" here:

[T]here are many operations of the mind in which, when we analyse them as far as we are able, we find belief to be an essential ingredient. A man cannot be conscious of his own thoughts without believing that he thinks. He cannot perceive an object of sense, without believing that it exists. He cannot distinctly remember a past event, without believing that it did exist. Belief therefore is an ingredient in consciousness, in perception, and in remembrance.

Not only in most of our intellectual operations, but in many of the active principles of the human mind, belief enters as an ingredient ... In every action that is done for an end, there must be a belief of its tendency to that end. (EIP 2.20, 228/327b)

He makes several other provocative statements in this compact passage, including: "Belief is always expressed in language by a proposition, wherein something is affirmed or denied"; "there can be no belief without conception" (EIP 2.20, 228/327b); and "belief in general is the main spring in the life of the man" (EIP 2.20, 228/328a). In the *Inquiry* Reid says that belief is typically the product of either instinct or habit (IHM 6.20, 170/184a–b). But explaining what these comments mean, and showing that his theory of belief can be consistent—let alone plausible—is a challenge that would require considerable space. Revealing a few tensions within Reid's account will circumvent future misunderstanding.

The first unique feature of Reid's theory of belief is that belief is psychologically irresistible: "My belief is carried along by perception, as irresistibly as my body by the earth" (IHM 6.20, 169/184a). When confronted with a mirage that I perceive to be a shallow body of water, it is not incumbent upon me, or psychologically necessary for me, to believe *that there exists a shallow body of water before me* or *that there exists an optical illusion created by external conditions to which I am now subject.* Suppose the first time I experience an optical illusion I do not know it. I would continue to form a belief, not about the existence of what I perceive, but about the existence of what I think I perceive. It seems that the letter of Reid's law is mistaken. However, he can respond by arguing that he uses "perception" as a success term. This would imply that, when I experience my first optical illusion, I do not, strictly speaking, "perceive" any body of water.

Second, belief is a matter of degree. If we understand what this means, we can be more charitable to his claim that belief accompanies all kinds of mental state. Reid says, "belief admits of all degrees, from the slightest suspicion to the fullest assurance" (EIP 2.20, 228/327b). This commitment is strange given Reid's critique of Hume on belief since it exploits Hume's sliding scale of the vividness of ideas. If belief is a matter of degree, but it requires the assent to a proposition, then where is belief's quantitative aspect?

Third, belief is a ubiquitous feature of our mental lives. Reid implies in the inset passage that belief is an ingredient of consciousness, memory, and perception. This further emphasizes how different Reid's theory is from contemporary accounts. If every conscious operation I conduct is accompanied by belief, and if all belief is "always expressed in language by a proposition," then Reid has over-intellectualized the mind in a radical way at odds with a common-sense philosophy. Taken at face value, this would imply that liminal forms of sensory awareness, like one's awareness of colors in peripheral regions of the visual field, are items about which propositional beliefs are formed. The principal problem with offering a literal interpretation like this lies in the failure of the resulting view to come to terms with our psychological reality: we simply do not form beliefs with propositional content for each conscious experience we have. This problem has not stopped some commentators from offering this interpretation (see Chapter 8).

In order to accommodate these claims in a consistent theory of belief, I construe Reid's use of the term in a way different from contemporary uses. I draw a distinction on Reid's behalf between wide and narrow uses of "belief." Used narrowly, belief refers to a conscious mental state in which an agent affirms a proposition. Used widely, the term refers to conscious or non-conscious mental states, which need not constitute the affirmation of a proposition. In order to accommodate the texts, beliefs in this wide sense resemble states of conception more than narrow beliefs. In order to differentiate these beliefs from states of mere simple apprehension, Reid must hold that these wide beliefs positively dispose an agent toward the proposition of which the belief is composed. Reid's claims about belief, when the term is used widely, appear obviously false upon a contemporary account of belief as a state that is a conscious affirmation of a proposition. This distinction I offer serves as a heuristic that provides some background to Reid's claims about belief, and affords us of the means to be charitable to him at these junctures.

This does not settle the matter. I revisit the vicissitudes of Reid's theory of belief, and its connections with consciousness and conception, in Chapter 7 in the context of the nature of our awareness of our sensations. If for every conscious state of awareness I assent to a proposition about it, then I must form beliefs about all my sensations. But if sensations suggest perceptual beliefs about mind-independent bodies, then it appears that there are two beliefs in perceptual events: one about my sensation, another about the object. If this is the way that perception works, then Reid's theory is burdened by commitments to a rich, unconscious mental life.

1.6. Substance Dualism

In the brief discussion of the way in which Reid half-heartedly attempts to marry weak forms of interactionism and occasionalism, I remarked that he seems to employ multiple notions of causation. Reid claims that the faculties have causal powers and that physical events result in certain mental events. But he argues that this is explanatorily incomplete and requires elucidation in terms of agent causation. There are agent causes and there are physical causes.

He concurs with what he takes to be Hume's claim that causation amounts to nothing more than constant conjunction, but he restricts this form of causation to the material world. This is consistent with the position that matter is wholly passive. In contrast, agents bring into the world substantive acts of causation. Agent causation "differs *toto genere*. For a physical cause is not an agent. It does not act, but is acted upon, and is as passive as its effect." He adds, in the same 1789 letter to James Gregory, "that every physical cause must be the work of some agent or efficient cause" (C 206–7).

The agent's causal powers arise due to their inherence in a substance, the everlasting self (Reid 2002a, 620ff). Echoing a conclusion of Descartes' in the Second Meditation, Reid describes the mind as that "which thinks, remembers, reasons, wills." This much we can know from introspection but, in contrast to Descartes, Reid immediately tells us what we cannot: "The essence both of body and of mind is unknown to us" (EIP 1.1, 20/220b). But this does not prevent us from attributing the operation of our powers to the "mind or soul" of human beings.

Reid gives his commitment to substance dualism the imprimatur of common sense when he enumerates his First Principles of contingent truths. In the first two principles Reid commits himself to the inexplicability of consciousness and to a substantial self. The genesis of these commitments lay in his common-sense method, which he uses to argue against the Way of Ideas' tendency to spiritualize the body and materialize the mind (IHM 7, 209/205b).

There is little more to say about the metaphysics of Reid's substance dualism, at least as drawn from his published work. Reid says he believes "the mind to be immaterial" and that he has "very strong proofs" for this belief (EIP 2.4, 89/254a). But he doesn't describe the implications of this commitment upon his body of thought, or offer any detailed analysis of these proofs in his published material. Reid's move at the outset of the *Inquiry* epitomizes his approach: though it is an inquiry into the human mind, he turns immediately to a discussion of the operations of the mind (IHM 1.2) and avoids wrestling with ontological issues. This is consistent with his methodological emphasis upon observation. Yet the trend disguises the importance of substance dualism to Reid's philosophy of mind, and the potentially greater importance of the knowledge of substance dualism to Reid's philosophical method.

The most direct statement he makes about his dualism occurs in a manuscript entitled "Three lectures on the nature and duration of the soul," which is reprinted in Brookes's edition of the *Intellectual Powers*. Reid explains that because of the superiority of the powers of the soul over the powers of the body, we have a "Strong Presumption that they must be beings of a quite different Nature" (Reid 2002a, 617; see 625–6ff). He professes an indivisibility argument for the immateriality of the soul (617 and 624). Throughout these manuscripts Reid refers to the soul as an "Immaterial Substance." He defends the survival of the soul after death with a kind of moral argument (620ff.).

Reid believes that "of all Questions in Philosophy this concerning the future Existence of the Soul is the most important" (Reid 2002a, 627). Why then did he omit this manuscript from inclusion in the *Intellectual Powers*? One reason for Reid's decision not to publish them arises from his epistemological appraisal of his belief that the soul is immaterial and immortal. He reduces his readers' expectations up front by confessing that "It is perhaps Impossible for us to say with Certainty that the mind may not exist in a Point" (618). At the conclusion of his discussion, Reid amplifies this conclusion:

I shall onely farther add that [as as] {though} this Question concerning a future State of Existence is of the highest Importance to Mankind yet it must be acknowledged that [all] the Arguments that Philosophy suggests upon this head are not of such Strength but that they may leave some doubt even in the Minds of wise and thinking Men.

The Arguments I have advanced are I think abundantly sufficient to prove that we have no reason to conclude that the soul shall perish with the body. ... But as there are very different degrees of probability which fall below that degree of Evidence which we call certainty, so I think it must be acknowledged that all the Evidence we have of a future State from Reason or Philosophy amounts to Probability only and not to certainty. ... These things must depend upon the Will and Pleasure of the Almighty: Nor can we without arrogance pretend to know these things without a Revelation from Heaven. {Such a Revelation God has been pleased to give us}. (Reid 2002a, 629–30)

Reid discusses the *epistemology* of his dualism and the afterlife in greater detail than dualism itself. By studying the way Reid claims to know dualism is true, we can understand what he believes are the limits of a philosophy of the mind. This is important for two reasons.

First, one of his central disagreements with the Way of Ideas is about methodology. By clarifying the principles of Reid's method and differentiating them from those of the Way of Ideas, we better understand Reid's place in the Early Modern canon. Second, we will repeatedly witness Reid's use of epistemic principles in the defense of theses in his philosophy of mind. He privileges metaphysical positions that enable him to preserve common-sense epistemological commitments shared by the majority. His discussion of the epistemology of dualism is no different.

Reid appears unaware of the tension between his defense of our knowledge of dualism—and his accompanying attack on our ability to know materialist theses—and his empirical, observational method. Reid's dualism compels him to place the mind outside the realm of science, whereas his empirical method places the mind inside the realm of science—where "science" refers to the domain of empirical knowledge.

Reid attempts to set himself apart from the Way of Ideas because he believes he doesn't posit hypotheses in the way that they do. He's right about this. His is not an armchair philosopher of mind. The thousands of words in *Inquiry*, chapter 6, about Reid's observations on the physiology of squinting should be enough to quiet doubters. Reid is an empiricist in ways the other "British Empiricists" are not.

Yet Reid's epistemological analysis of his commitment to substance dualism and his opposition to active matter threaten to place the ontology of the mind outside the realm of science. He fights enthusiastically against the onset of materialism by arguing that materialism does not respect the proper limits of human knowledge. Reid eventually employs Newtonian methodological principles in the service of substance dualism. Doing this and placing the mind outside science affords Reid some protection for his substance dualism. Reid employs this tact in his unpublished responses to Priestley's 1774 *An Examination of Dr. Reid's Inquiry in to the Human Mind, on the Principles of Common Sense*; ... (see Tapper 2003).

One fringe benefit to this tension in Reid's treatment of the mind is that it allows us to follow his lead and study his theory of perception without extensive analysis of ontological issues.

1.7. Sensing and the Senses

The sense faculties differ, according to Reid, in two significant ways: with respect to the type of sensation to which they give rise and the type of quality of which they inform us. Reid classifies smelling, tasting and hearing together as "very simple and uniform, each of them exhibiting only one kind of sensation and thereby indicating only one quality of bodies" (IHM 5.2, 54/119a). These three senses provide us with three distinct types of sensations. While they are each used to perceive secondary qualities, we perceive different secondary qualities through them. Reid begins with smell and taste because he thinks that hearing presents a wider and more complex range of sensations for our experience. We hear "four or five hundred variations of tone." There is a "prodigious" variety of individuatable sounds that differ in tone, volume, pitch, and media through which the sound waves travel. We can also experience pressure exerted upon the ear by sound (IHM 4.1, 49/116b–117a). Though this raises questions about the relation between hearing and tactile sensations of pressure, Reid does not pursue the matter.

Touch and sight possess more structural sophistication than the other three senses. The sense of touch affords us experience of both secondary and primary qualities. Sensing primary qualities provides us knowledge of the mind-independent world. Vision too affords us knowledge of secondary *and primary qualities*, which creates a friendly rivalry between vision and touch for the fairest sense.

Several reasons favor believing touch is more important to Reid for a theory of perception. Reid holds that we do not see distance from the eye (as opposed to relative distance between visible objects), but we perceive distance through touch. The sense of touch is also of considerably more aid to Reid in his attempt to refute the Way of Ideas. Lastly, provided the agent has the proper training, "there is very little of the knowledge acquired by sight, that may not be communicated to a man born blind" (IHM 6.2, 78/133). Upon close examination, vision even seems to be a hindrance to Reid in his refutation of the Way of Ideas. This is because, in his effort to explain aspects of the phenomenology of vision, Reid is compelled to introduce what seems to be a perceived intermediary, visible figure. Of all the senses, it is Reid's analysis of vision that most closely resembles the representationalist theories Reid associates with the Way of Ideas.

Despite these observations, immediately preceding the above quotation Reid describes vision as of a "superior nature" to touch (IHM 6.2, 78/133b). Reid evinces admiration for the designedness of the eye and the way in which its contemplation draws the mind naturally to its creator. He also observes that through sight we rapidly gain immeasurable amounts of information, which are not only difficult to access by touch, but in many cases are impossible to access.

In setting out his research as he does, he implicitly explains the means by which he distinguishes the senses. He does not, however, offer any extended theory about this division or about why there are only five. The fact that Reid considers only five could be seen as problematic. This is not because he employs "perception" in analogical senses, as he does, in order to say that we can "perceive" beauty, design, and moral facts. The problem for Reid's enumeration of the senses has to do with other forms of sensory awareness such as kinesthetic and proprioceptive awareness. What reason does Reid have for leaving them out of his classification?

Consider proprioceptive sensations through muscular motion and tension, and the way that they inform us of the location and movement of our limbs. A case can be made for denominating this ability as a sixth sense. The uniqueness of such sensory experiences meets one of Reid's criteria for individuating a sense faculty. Reid is aware of this type of sensory experience, though his comments are inchoate. He describes a "sensation, which accompanies the flexure of joints, and the swelling of muscles" (IHM 4.7, 66/126a). Reid frequently employs the term "the five external senses," a phrase which invokes a tacit distinction between the external five senses and the internal, proprioceptive muscle sense (IHM 2.1, 25/104b). Perhaps Reid can allow that proprioception does qualify as an internal sense faculty. Thomas Brown later criticized him for failing to make clear how this proprioceptive muscle sense relates to sensation experience, and for failing to identify the sorts of concepts one can acquire from this sense (Brown 1828 i, 504–5). Nonetheless, Reid's comments about our muscle sense show that he was aware that such a sense provides us a unique means of sensory experience and information about the world.

1.8. Summary

Reid studies the mind and the faculty of perception through the joint use of introspective observation upon his use of his own senses, and empirical investigation on his and others' use of different senses in different circumstances. His goal is to formulate general laws about the operation of perception and about its relation to objects in the world. This contrasts with the goal of stating necessary and sufficient conditions for the concept of "perception." Perception is the faculty through which we form beliefs about the physical world by means of our senses. For the purpose of developing his theory of perception, Reid simply presupposes that there is a physical world. The substance of the mind is inconsequential to the heart of Reid's examination of perception. This is because his faculty psychology and his aim to account for the operation of perception do not depend upon the mind being either material or spiritual. He presupposes that there are five senses, even though he recognizes a form of proprioception.

2

Intentional Awareness

I have offered an explanation of the framework of Reid's method and his faculty psychology and explained Reid's depiction of the function of perception. He says that perception is the faculty through which we form conceptions and beliefs about physical bodies in our environment through the use of our sense organs. Perception incorporates a conceptual component. In this chapter I examine what it means for us to conceive and apprehend. In the following chapter I explain the way that conception is incorporated into perceptual events.

Reid's theory of conception, like his theory of perception, is developed in the shadows of the Way of Ideas. He holds that the Way of Ideas engenders skepticism about the external world by positing perceived intermediaries between our mental states and bodies. But the Way of Ideas spawns a more insidious type of skepticism, even if it is lesser known. It fosters skepticism about our knowledge of the contents of our conceptions. In the previous chapter I noted Reid's concern that the Way of Ideas attempted to "reduce" the plethora of faculties to a single one—the simple apprehension of ideas. David Hume goes one step further by explaining our awareness of ideas in terms of relationships between sensory impressions. Reid interprets Hume to mean that the immediate intentional contents of our ideas are not external bodies or imaginary beasts, but instead are sensory impressions. Sensory impressions are the things out of which ideas are "derived," as Hume puts it. This introduces a troublesome additional step in the process of cognition. Impressions bear relations of association that together explain the intentional contents of our ideas. Impressions are like syntax for a language and relations amongst them are like grammatical rules. Reid believes that the presence of these hidden rules, coupled with the fact that people are unaware that they are conceiving of ideas in virtue of their impressions, poses a problem for Hume. It inhibits our ability to know non-inferentially what are the intentional contents of our ideas.

Reid avoids Hume's implication by presupposing intentionality as a primitive, irreducible feature of thought. We are able to take physical, mind-independent objects as the direct intentional objects of our apprehensions without apprehending any representational intermediary. I can conceive of the chest of drawers and the immediate object of my thought is the chest itself, not an intermediary that represents the chest. He thereby defends the directness of conceptual apprehension, which is conceptually prior to subsequent defenses of the directness of perception.

2.1. "Simple Apprehension" and Intentional Content

Conceptual apprehension can take many different items as objects. I can conceive of F, conceive of F being x, or conceive *that F is x*. F might be a physical or spiritual or fictional thing. Conception can also take many different forms. I can entertain a thought about a chest of drawers, I can imagine it being green, or I can form the belief *that the chest is painted in an unsuitably dark green*. One feature is common to these examples of conception. My various thoughts are about things. They are also about certain things and not others. I imagine mythical creatures worshiping together, I form a judgment about the Pythagorean theorem, and I perceive the chest of drawers. This ubiquitous feature of conceptions, this capacity of conceptions to be about things, is their intentionality.

Reid develops his positive account of intentionality first by appeal to a distinction that maps a division between *de re* and *de dicto* forms of belief:

[T]he words conceive, imagine, apprehend, have two meanings, and are used to express two operations of the mind, which ought never to be confounded. Sometimes they express simple apprehension, which implies no judgment at all; sometimes they express judgment or opinion. ... When they are used to express simple apprehension, they are followed by a noun in the *accusative* case, which signifies the object conceived; but, when they are used to express opinion or judgment, they are commonly followed by a verb, in the *infinitive mood*. ... When the words are used in the last sense, the thing conceived must be a proposition, because judgment cannot be expressed but by a proposition. When they are used in the first sense, the thing conceived may be no proposition, but a simple term only-as a pyramid, an obelisk. (EIP 1.1, 25/223b)

Beliefs can be described and attributed in two ways. Consider the ambiguous statement *Ortcutt believes someone is a spy*. This can be given a *de dicto* or *de re* reading. A *de dicto* attribution parses this statement as *Ortcutt believes that there is someone who is a spy*. This restricts the scope of the existential quantifier by placing it within the belief. The existential quantifier in *de re* beliefs has wider scope because speakers uttering *de re* beliefs individuate an object in thought and posit some relation between that object and the predicate. A *de re* attribution renders the statement as *some person is an X and Ortcutt believes X is a spy.* One might characterize the distinction as being that *de dicto* attributions relate the speaker to a proposition, while *de re* attributions relate the speaker to an object (Quine 1956).

When Reid uses terms including "notion of," "concept of," and "belief about" in the context of his theory of perception, and when he speaks of "simple apprehension," he attributes *de re* beliefs to perceivers. He even builds a doxastic component into his definitions of "perception," as witnessed. However, a number of reasons give me pause in applying these terms to the terms *de re* and *de dicto* in the exegesis of Reid. First, he doesn't use those terms himself. Second, in addition to being anachronistic, historical squabbles about these terms make their use to describe Reid's theory problematic. These terms are typically used to clarify language in the context of belief attribution. Third, Reid insists that he can have conceptions that take non-existent items as intentional contents. This implies that intentional objects do not need to be "things" in space-time. In this sense, the term *de re* is misleading. Lastly, speaking of perception as incorporating *de re* conceptual states underdescribes the intentional content of these mental states. *De re* states can take mind-independent or mind-dependent, physical or non-physical objects as intentional objects. When we form a belief through our joint use of the intellectual power of perception, we individuate a mind-independent object in our environment and predicate of it some property. In this limited sense, existence is a "property" since Reid holds that we implicitly attribute mind-independent existence to the intentional objects of all perceptual states. This is constitutive of what it means to perceive something (IHM 6.12, 124/158b). For the same reason, I cannot use Russell's term "knowledge by acquaintance" to describe this feature of Reidian perception, for according to Russell we are immediately acquainted only with sense-data.

I propose to use the term "intentional" to refer to the object-oriented content of mental states, "intentional awareness" to refer to the nature of the agent's apprehension, and "intentional object" to refer to the thing that the mental state is about. Some states of mind are not intentional. This group includes moods such as feeling groovy and other emotional states such as being depressed.

Basically, for Reid the intentional object of perceptual states is always a physical quality. I will augment this thesis in later discussions about whether secondary qualities, illusions, and sensations can in principle be the objects of perception. On Reid's comparatively direct theory of perception, the intentional object of my perception of a chair will be the chair and/or one or more of its primary qualities. On an indirect theory of perception, the intentional content of a perception of a chair will be a mind-dependent representation of the chair, like an idea.

Beliefs with intentional content are not identical to concepts with intentional content. Concepts with intentional content are necessary for beliefs with intentional content but the converse is not true. Our focus is upon conception because it is the more fundamental form of intentional awareness:

[A]lthough conception may be without any degree of belief, even the weakest belief cannot be without conception. He that believes, must have some conception of what he believes … [C]onception enters as an ingredient in every operation of the mind. Our senses cannot give us the belief of any object, without giving some conception of it at the same time. [T]hough there is no operation of the mind without conception, yet it may be found naked, detached from all others, and then it is called simple apprehension, or the bare conception of a thing. (EIP 4.1, 296/360b−361a)

Having a conception is often taken in the intentional sense of the term when "conception" and "apprehension" are used by Reid, as when he says: "a certain sensation of touch both suggests to the mind the conception of hardness, and creates the belief of it" (IHM 5.3, 58/121a; see Wolterstorff 2001, 7–8).

If conception is "an ingredient in every operation of the mind," then does it follow that all mental operations are intentional? If conception implies intentionality, this result is ineluctable and, along with Brentano, Reid would affirm by implication that intentionality is the mark of the mental. However, Reid's use of "conception" varies considerably. One form of conception is present in my beliefs and a different form is present in my experience of depression. Reid does not suggest that the experience of moods requires intentionality. Furthermore, he recognizes that we typically experience sensations without thought about them. A few minutes ago you were experiencing the feeling of the hardness of this book in your hands, but that sensation did not prompt you to experience any conscious intentional mental state directed at that sensory experience. Thus when Reid says that conception is an ingredient in all mental states, the evidence suggests that this does not mean that all mental states—conscious ones and unconscious ones, sensations and moods, perceptions and beliefs—are intentional. His use of conception is considerably wider in scope than that. Determining how wide it is presents problems since Reid takes the faculty of conception as a primitive in his system and, as such, it is inexplicable.

States of conceiving and believing are intentional states in virtue of the fact that these propositional attitudes are composite forms of simple apprehension:

Conceiving, imagining, apprehending, understanding, having a notion of a thing, are common words, used to express that operation of the understanding, which the logicians call simple apprehension. ... Logicians define simple apprehension to be the bare conception of a thing, without any judgment or belief about it. (EIP 4.2, 295/360a)

This definition of "conception" refers to a rudimentary intentional awareness—awareness of things. This use of the term does not refer to the application of discursive concepts (Wolterstorff 2001, 11; Alston 1989, 43). The interpretation of Reid's comments about "simple apprehension" and "conception" that I have presented applies to his theory of perception in the following sense. Reid stresses that all perception is conceptual, and that conception is an "ingredient" in perception. What he means by this can now be explained as the thesis that all perceptions contain intentional content.

The Way of Ideas has its own means of explaining intentionality, as well as different standards for explanation. Reid encounters a difficulty in communicating his opinions to his audience, which is only familiar with the Way of Ideas' paradigm. "But here, again," says Reid, "the ideal system comes in our way." This is because the Way of Ideas has reversed the proper order of explanation in the process of perception. It "teaches us that the first operation of the mind about its ideas, is simple apprehension—that is, the bare conception of a thing without any belief about it" (IHM 2.4, 29/106b). Reid is voicing an explanatory point. The Way of Ideas proceeds from simple apprehensions that are about ideas to "comparing" the "agreements or disagreements" between our ideas. By comparing our apprehensions of ideas, we then form perceptual beliefs and perceptual judgments. But Reid claims that there is something amiss about this elucidation of the process. "[A]pprehension, accompanied with belief and knowledge, must go before simple apprehension, at least in the matters we are now speaking of"; or, in other words, "simple apprehension is performed by resolving and analysing a natural and original judgment" (IHM 2.4, 29/106b–7a). The Way of Ideas misconstrues the order of explanation. Hume overtly attempts to account for beliefs, memories, and perceptions in virtue of impressions and ideas, and in turn accounts for impressions and ideas in terms of the principles of association. Reid offers an analogy to explain this point. When we perceive an apple, we perceive the apple as a whole. Though it is true that the apple is "compounded of simple principles and elements," our perception of the apple as a unified object precedes our analysis of the apple's parts and precedes an analysis of the components of our sensory experience. For example, we typically see the apple as an apple, and only later individuate in thought the hue of the apple's skin. Likewise, our intentional awareness of objects occurs naturally within perception. We perceive objects and blithely presuppose that our perceptions are about the objects we think they are about.

Reid speculates that a false understanding of the origins of our beliefs, memories, and perceptions generates this mistake. Now Reid is making a genetic point about the etiology of our coordinated mental states, i.e. mental states that combine the use of simple apprehension with the use of another faculty. We perceive external objects before we are able to conceive them:

> Conception of Objects is not the first Act of the Mind about them. External Objects are perceived by our Senses before they are simply conceived. If a Man had never seen colours he could never have conceived them and the same may be said of all the Simple objects of Sense. As to things in the Mind its Operations Affections and Passions we can onely conceive them after having been conscious of them. ... Hence it appears that Conception accompanied with belief or Judgment does in most cases preceed simple Conception. And instead of saying that our Judgments are formed by compounding & putting together simple Conceptions, it is much nearer the Truth to affirm that our Simple conceptions are formed by analyzing those natural and original Judgments which we have from our external Senses or from Consciousness & other judging powers. ... (Aberdeen MS 2131/8/ii/02; compare EIP 4.3)

Reid seeks an account of how we come to have certain simple apprehensions, namely those that we form independently of other faculties. He proposes an account of states in which, for example, I simply apprehend or entertain a thought about the chest of drawers in terms of perceiving or remembering the chest. Reid holds that in our experience conception operates in coordination with other faculties prior to operating independently of other faculties.

Two points follow from Reid's criticism that the Way of Ideas has inverted the order of explanation. First, the Way of Ideas presupposes that simple apprehension is a basic faculty. Reid concurs with this point. But this is the only basic faculty allowed by the Way of Ideas. By "basic" I mean that it is the only faculty in terms of which explanations of operations of other faculties are to be offered. So the explanatory method adopted by the Way of Ideas implicitly repudiates Reid's faculty psychology. Reid is more ecumenical because he holds that a large number of faculties are to be taken as basic in this sense, including memory, belief, judgment, and perception. This implies that Reid does not take it upon himself to account for the faculty of perception in terms of more general laws or principles. Those who adhere to the Way of Ideas, "Ideal Theorists," do seek to explain perception (and belief, memory, and judgment) in terms of the simple apprehension of ideas.[1]

---

[1] The "basic" and "non-basic" language may call to mind discussions about "Classical Foundation-alism" to which Reid makes first-rate contributions. The present discussion is closely related to Reid's objection that the only empirical beliefs allowed to be foundationally justified by the Way of Ideas are self-evident beliefs about the contents of first-person states of consciousness. In contrast, Reid's discussion of the first principles of contingent truths in *Intellectual Powers* 6.4–5 yields much wider

Second, the Way of Ideas presupposes that the only objects of simple apprehension are ideas. Ideas are mind-dependent, typically imagistic mental objects. A worrisome implication of this second point is that the Way of Ideas engenders skepticism about the external world.

2.2. Present Context

I call Reid's argument that the intentional content of our mental states is fundamental and cannot be reduced his "Blind Book" argument due to a thought experiment he employs in stating it. In his thought experiment Reid imagines an illiterate savage who cannot understand the way letters and words communicate the meanings of English words and sentences. This is intended as an analogy to express the fact that, if the Way of Ideas is true, we cannot understand that the syntax of impressions bears a relationship to the meanings of ideas. If Hume is correct, says Reid, we have as much chance of knowing the contents of our thoughts as does a blind book in reading itself. Reid's statement of this argument is somewhat obscure and is in a condensed form. The most efficient means to introduce Reid's argument is through a discussion of this problem as it appears in the contemporary philosophy of mind.

I am able to think about a wide range of objects and to represent them in my mind—Shanghai's skyline, Abraham Lincoln, centaurs, the next Prince of Wales, Petra, and blueberries and the taste of them. When thinking about any of these things, I can determine what I am thinking about by introspection. But how does a thought of Petra come to take Petra as its intentional content? One common theory is that the thought comes to be about Petra in virtue of an internal representation or idea of the word "Petra." Such internal representations are symbols in the way that the word "Petra" is a symbol. The representative capacity of the word "Petra" is fixed by relations it bears to speakers of the language. The intrinsic character of the syntax does not determine the representative capacity of the word. Considered as black shapes on a white surface, or as a sequence of sound waves audible to the human ear, "Petra" is mere syntax.

---

foundations for empirical knowledge than those offered by his predecessors. However, the present discussion is not concerned with stopping an *epistemic* regress. Instead, my use of the term "basic" in this context refers to Reid's attempt to stop an *explanatory* regress. Just as Reid holds that demand for further justification of the beliefs produced by memory, perception, reasoning, etc. is misguided, so the demand for further explanation of the origins of the faculties of memory, perception, reasoning, etc. is also misguided. These faculties are explanatorily basic, and cannot be accounted for in terms of a yet more basic faculty such as simple apprehension.

Explaining mental representation in terms of an underlying structure of internal representations in a language of thought, or "mentalese," is a contemporary variation on the Way of Ideas. The intentional content of thoughts is explained in terms of syntactic structures. The "defining thesis of the linguistic or symbolic conception of thought," says Laurence BonJour, is that the:

representative capacity or content [of thoughts] is not somehow fixed by their intrinsic character, but is instead imposed upon them from the outside by relations of some sort in which they are involved. Just as the word "telephone" could, given its intrinsic character, have represented anything else or nothing at all instead of representing the class of objects that it actually does represent, so is it also allegedly the case with the corresponding thought-symbol. (BonJour 1991, 332-3)

On the "linguistic" theory, the relations that my thoughts about Petra bear to other symbols in my thought-symbol vocabulary fix the intentional content of my thoughts about Petra. Creators of this theory are ambitious insofar as they attempt to explain the intentional content reductively. The capacity of thoughts to represent is not simply asserted, or taken as a primitive in the philosophy of mind. The explanation accounts for mental representation in terms of features of the mind that are themselves devoid of any representational content, and accounts for the intentional in terms of the non-intentional.

It is a fact that in the vast majority of cases I know the intentional contents of my thoughts. Barring complications surrounding Twin Earth cases, which require special treatment, I know that I am thinking about Petra and not Abraham Lincoln. I know that the city of Petra is located in present-day Jordan, and that millennia ago it was a thriving Nabataean center of trade. BonJour asks whether this theory can "explain how mentalese symbols come to have a particular meaning or interpretation or content in a way that makes that meaning or interpretation or content accessible to the person who allegedly thinks by means of them?" (BonJour 1991, 334). He answers negatively and fashions a widely applicable argument against this type of theory:

According to the linguistic conception, all that is present in my mind (or brain) when I think contentful thoughts is symbols of the appropriate sorts; these symbols are meaningful or contentful by virtue of relations of some sort in which they stand, but this meaning or content is represented in the mind only by the symbols themselves, not by any further content-bearing element or feature. But ... merely having access to a symbol or set of symbols does not by itself yield any access to their representative content. ... Thus, merely having such thought-symbols present in my mind (or brain) by itself gives me no understanding of their content. (BonJour 1991, 336)

Of course, appealing to a further set of symbols, members of which also only derive their intentional content by relations to other members, will gain no traction on this problem. BonJour concludes that "the acceptance of the linguistic conception seems to lead inexorably to the conclusion that I have no access to the content of my thought, no internal grasp or understanding at all of what I am thinking" (BonJour 1991, 336). Since this is absurd, we have an argument against the theory.

What can replace the linguistic theory of thought? BonJour suggests that thoughts must have at least some of their content "by virtue of their intrinsic, non-relational character" (BonJour 1991, 346). This is necessary in order to know—non-inferentially and introspectively—what we are thinking about. This might be construed in terms of the "intrinsic character of the thought to specify precisely that particular property to the exclusion of anything else, the property in question must itself be somehow metaphysically involved in that character. The point is that no surrogate or stand-in of any sort will do, since any account of the relation between such a surrogate and the property itself will raise all the same difficulties" (348). At least some thoughts must have the intentional objects they do intrinsically.

Any explanation of this position will involve a robust metaphysics in order to support this special relationship between thought and content. BonJour invokes Aquinas' theory of perceptual forms to clarify what it means to say that a thought has an "intrinsic character." Reid not only voices the critical argument that BonJour offers, but Reid also makes a veiled appeal to the medievals for assistance in sorting out the metaphysics of the resulting theory. The version of the linguistic theory of cognition in Reid's milieu comes courtesy of David Hume.

2.3. Reid's Interpretation of Hume

Reid believes that Hume endorses an account of thought that seeks to explain intentional content in terms of states without intentional content. But Hume's discussion of impressions and ideas is fraught with exegetical challenges. Many commentators (e.g. Price 1940) loosely interpret that discussion as addressed to issues of meaning in order to skirt some interpretive problems. Reid lacked the mechanics to carry out this reading, but he knew better than to claim that his own interpretation was the best possible understanding of Hume. He expresses his frustration at his inability to discern a univocal, consistent distinction between impressions and ideas—the foundation of Hume's theory—in Hume's work:

[W]hy has not the author told us whether he gives the name of *impression* to the object seen, or to that act of my mind by which I see it? When I see the full moon, the full moon is one thing, my perceiving it is another thing. Which of these two things does he call an *impression*? We are left to guess this; nor does all that this author writes about impressions clear this point. Everything he says tends to darken it, and to lead us to think that the full moon which I see, and my seeing it, are not two things, but one and the same thing. (EIP 1.1, 33/227b)[2]

Two points follow. First, Reid is implicitly criticizing the method that Hume has used to arrive at his division of the objects of thought into impressions of ideas. This division is not itself the product of the use of the experimental method. He explicitly raises this point in his logic lectures, where he says, "Hume would argue that if it be neither an idea nor an impression, it cannot be. But it will equally follow from these premises that these divisions are imperfect. Upon this account, till they are able to demonstrate the perfection of them, we ought never to look upon them as conclusive, nor exclude any one thing from being because our notions of it don't tally with the beds made for them" (Edinburgh MS Reid 1763 Dk. 3.2, Lecture 15).

The second observation is that interpreting Hume has been difficult—then and now. Reid is not suggesting that the *Treatise* is a *Choose Your Own Adventure* novel, but it remains true that expert commentary on the nature and relation of Humean impressions and ideas continues to lack significant consensus. This serves as a testament to the difficulties in which Reid finds himself—and as ample reason to be charitable to him.[3] Some commentators erect creative bridges between what they see as a deep division between

---

[2] Reid says: "It would have been unnecessary to explain so obvious a distinction, if some systems had not confounded it. Mr Hume's system, in particular, confounds all distinction between the operations of the mind and their objects. When he speaks of the ideas of memory, the ideas of imagination, and the ideas of sense, it is often impossible, from the tenor of his discourse, to know whether, by those ideas, he means the operations of the mind, or the objects about which they are employed. And, indeed, according to his system, there is no distinction between the one and the other" (EIP 1.1, 26/224a; see EIP 2.12, 164/294a).

[3] Historically, other Hume commentators have found similar difficulties interpreting the intentionality of Humean ideas. These include Jonathan Bennett (1971, 225), Francis Zabeeh (1960, 68–9), and John Laird, who says Hume's "doctrine was that impressions were *non-representative*, and *atomic*" (1967, 29–30). Marjorie Grene says that Humean ideas are sometimes described as non-representational, but adds that "ideas are also presented as *of* their corresponding impressions, which are their objects. ... In contrast to ideas, impressions, or rather, impressions of sensation, which are the chief starting point in Book I ... arise, we know not how (or as moral philosophers know not how), and cannot be 'about' anything else" (1994, 166).

Many commentators also argue that Humean ideas clearly do not bear intentional content, including John Passmore (1980, 90), Constance Maund (1937), and numerous Hume scholars working today. Norman Kemp Smith provides the classic expression of this interpretation by saying: "Hume has also spoken of ideas as 'representing' the correspondent impressions; and some of his critics have taken this as showing that he at times regards them as ideas *of* their impressions, i.e. *meaning* them, *referring to* them. ... [But] there is no evidence that Hume ever thought of so regarding them" (1941, 205n).

But what Kemp Smith has in mind when discussing meaning and reference is unclear. In this context Laird responds on Reid's behalf: "Mr. Kemp Smith's statement, strictly interpreted, asserts that

incompatible sets of claims that Hume makes about ideas and impressions.[4] Others (such as Stephen Everson[5] and Barry Stroud[6]) echo Reid's point and recognize that Hume's corpus warrants incompatible interpretations of his use of "impressions" and "ideas."

As a result of these challenges Reid frequently resorts to metaphor to assess Hume's commitments. Reid says that Hume's "ideas are as free and independent as the birds of the air, or as Epicurus's atoms when they pursued their journey in the vast inane. But why should we seek to compare them with anything, since there is nothing in nature but themselves? They make the whole furniture of the universe" (IHM 2.6, 34/109a–b). Later he says Hume's "self-existent and independent ideas look pitifully naked and destitute." While "Descartes, Malebranche, and Locke" "treated them handsomely" and "made them representatives of things, which gave them some dignity and character," by Hume ideas and impressions are "turned out of house and home, and set

a representation does *not* mean or refer to what it represents. I find this hard to believe. ... What is the prodigious difference between 'meaning and reference' on the one hand, and 'representation and application' on the other?" (Laird 1943, 175). Laird continues: "In ordinary English usage the 'of' in 'idea of'—Hume's habitual term—is referential. I can see no reason for supposing that, for him, 'to conceive or form an idea of' means anything different from 'thinking of', and I can see very little point in his insistence that an idea not derived from an impression had *no* meaning ... unless he meant that the 'derivation' implied some sort of reference to 'matter of fact' of the impression order" (143, 176).

⁴ According to Donald Livingstone, Hume does endorse the Way of Ideas, but this can be obscured because there is a secret, "radically different and distinctively Humean" use of "the term 'perception' " that is to be found "virtually buried some 200 pages later in what are notoriously the most difficult sections" of the *Treatise* (Livingstone 1984, 10). Lennon holds that Hume operates with two logically independent analyses of impressions and ideas simultaneously—phenomenalist and realist accounts, which Hume fails to keep distinct (Lennon 1979). This resembles an earlier suggestion of Robert McCrae. McRae goes so far as to suggest that the best way to describe Hume on cognition and meaning is that Hume endorses two completely distinct theories. He motivates the interpretation as follows: "There are two distinct ways in which Hume describes the relation between an idea and its corresponding impression. First, an idea is the representation of an original impression—'the ideas I form are exact representations of the impressions I felt' [T 1.1.1.3/3]. Secondly, an idea is caused by an original impression—'our impressions are the causes of our ideas' [T 1.1.1.8/5]. Corresponding to these two kinds of relation, there are ... two theories of meaning in Hume. According to the first the meaning of a term consists of an idea *qua* representing something. According to the second the meaning of a term consists of the cause of the idea. Consistently with this we find that Hume in his writings works with two types of definitions, one analytical and the other causal" (McRae 1969, 489).

⁵ The distinction between ideas and impressions "as formulated by Hume in terms of 'force and liveliness' has proved recalcitrant to analysis and elucidation—and has as a result seemed to many to be both false and carelessly executed" (Everson 1988, 401). "Officially ... Hume is allowed to claim no more than that impressions of sensation arise 'in the soul originally, from unknown causes'. This solipsistic constraint, however, is not one that Hume observes with constant diligence. Throughout his discussion of the theory of ideas he lapses into talk of the senses—talk to which he is not entitled without apology" (1988, 412).

⁶ "The obviousness of the fact that there is a difference between perceiving and thinking does not make Hume's account of that difference obvious. In fact, it is not even clear what his account comes to. If it is taken fairly literally it does not seem to be very plausible" (Stroud 1977, 28).

adrift in the world, without friend or connection, without a rag to cover their nakedness" (IHM 2.6, 35/109b). I expect that this last comment is directed at a point in the *Enquiry* where Hume says:

All events seem entirely loose and separate. One event follows another; but we never can observe any tie between them. They seem *conjoined*, but never *connected*. And as we can have no idea of any thing which never appeared to our outward sense or inward sentiment, the necessary conclusion *seems* to be that we have no idea of connexion or power at all, and that these words are absolutely without any meaning, when employed either in philosophical reasonings or common life. (*Enquiry* 7.2.6, 74)

Hume stands out as the only proponent of the Way of Ideas to have allowed such an untoward implication, which is why Reid describes a sharp contrast between Hume and his predecessors.[7]

While this comment is from Hume's *Enquiry*, Reid finds the elements for his Blind Book argument in *Treatise*, Book I. For any purported idea, we either identify the Humean impression from which it arose, or do not. If we fail, then the idea is meaningless, contrary to first appearance. Herein lies what Reid calls Hume's "articles of inquisition": every idea must either be derived from a corresponding impression, or be composed of simple ideas which themselves are derived from corresponding impressions. "Derived" means *copied from* and "corresponding" means *resembling*.

The difference between impressions and ideas is not merely qualitative in nature. Hume describes the class of impressions as being constituted by "sensations, passions and emotions," and says ideas are "the faint images of these in thinking and reasoning" (T 1.1.1.1, 1). My belief *that Petra was an ancient*

---

[7] Reid is reduced to metaphor because he is perplexed not only by Hume's distinction between impressions and ideas, but by the ontological status of impressions. Reid attempts to remain neutral about this. Impressions might be physical or phenomenal mental states. Perhaps some impressions are physical and others mental. "Mr Hume," Reid says, "gives the name of impressions to all our perceptions, to all our sensations, and even to the objects which we perceive" (EIP 2.4, 88/254a). Reid avoids taking a stand because he did not feel it necessary to do so for his dialectical goals. Reid merely needs to specify the conceptual role that impressions play in Hume's philosophy of mind. Irrespective of their ontological status, Hume still holds "that our impressions arise from unknown causes, and that the impressions are the causes of their corresponding ideas. By this he means no more but that they always go before the ideas; for this is all that is necessary to constitute the relation of cause and effect" (EIP 2.12, 165/294b).

Hume describes certain impressions of touch and sight as extended, physical and as bearing parts (T 1.4.5.9/235), which makes Reid's neutrality important. Reid expresses his uncertainty about the ontological makeup of impressions when saying, "The common theory of ideas—that is, of images in the brain or in the mind, of all the objects of thought—has been very generally applied" (EIP 3.7, 279–80/353a). His arguments do not depend upon a phenomenalist reading of impressions. But Reid doesn't let the matter rest there. In the passage about the Way of Ideas from which this comment is drawn Reid explicitly addresses an objection to analyses of mental states that reduce them directly to physical impressions on brains (EIP 3.7, 281/354a).

Nabatean city is a propositional attitude and my visual impression of the rose-colored facades is not. Despite occasional texts in the *Treatise* to the contrary, these are different kinds of state. Impressions do not take anything mind-independent as their intentional objects. Reid thinks of Humean impressions in the way that he thinks of what he calls "sensations." Either way, impressions do not enable us to think about mind-independent objects.

The contents of ideas arise, or "proceed either mediately or immediately," entirely from our impressions (T 1.1.1.11, 7). Hume says, "Now since all ideas are deriv'd from impressions, and are nothing but copies and representations of them, whatever is true of the one must be acknowledg'd concerning the other" (T 1.1.7.5, 19); that "every idea is deriv'd from some impression, which is exactly similar to it" (T 1.2.3.2, 33; see T 2.1.11.8, 319); and "impressions can give rise to no ideas, but to such as resemble them" (T 1.2.5.23, 63; see T 1.1.1.5, 3, T 1.2.6.3, 66). It is obvious and "requires no farther examination" to believe that complex ideas such as beliefs, possessors of intentional content, are formed from simple ideas, themselves copies of simple impressions of sensation. "We shall here content ourselves with establishing one general proposition, *That all our simple ideas in their first appearance are deriv'd from simple impressions, which are correspondent to them, and which they exactly represent*" (T 1.1.1.7, 4).

Charity to Hume can obscure the fact that there are two distinct relations he posits between ideas and impressions here. First, complex and simple ideas, i.e. all ideas, are produced and derived from impressions, with the caveat that complex ideas are produced and derived from impressions by way of being produced and derived from concatenations of simple ideas. Second, all ideas represent only other impressions and ideas. In this context the two-place "represents" relation means that ideas only take other impressions and ideas as their intentional contents. Still another idiom through which to express this crucial observation is to say that ideas are only about other impressions and ideas. Where one complex idea takes another as its intentional object, Hume assures us that, eventually, the trail will end in a complex idea taking an impression as its intentional content. Reid finds this second (intentional) relationship between ideas and impressions of considerable importance for evaluating Hume's philosophy of mind. I will focus on it at the expense of examining what Hume says about the first (causal) relationship.

Hume makes explicit a further feature of this thesis about the intentionality of ideas when he addresses the scope of those items that can possibly be the intentional objects of ideas. Ideas cannot represent mind-independent objects like tables and chairs directly, if they can represent those things at all. This follows from the division of labor between ideas and impressions, and the role they are given in an explanation of cognition. "We may observe," says

Hume, "that 'tis universally allow'd by philosophers, and is besides pretty obvious of itself, that nothing is ever really present with the mind but its perceptions or impressions and ideas" (T 1.2.6.7, 67; see Abstract 648–9). To say nothing is "present with the mind" means nothing is represented by the mind that is not an idea or an impression; in other words, nothing is the intentional content of an idea but other ideas and impressions. Here Hume claims that ideas *only* represent impressions and ideas. He supports this thesis with a perceptual relativity argument, which he concludes by saying that "The most vulgar philosophy informs us, that no external object can make itself known to the mind immediately, without the interposition of an image or perception" (T 1.4.5.15, 239; see 1.4.5.19, 241). Hume uses the terms "image" and "perception" synonymously. "Perception" is defined early in the *Treatise* as referring to impressions and ideas. Therefore, whatever representational capacity images possess, it too must be reduced to simple impressions. (Chapter 4 analyzes Reid's objections to Hume's perceptual relativity argument.)

From the interpretation on offer, and in order to make sense of Reid's argument, I infer that Reid holds that Hume endorses the following principle:

(2.1) Ideas only take other impressions and ideas as their intentional contents.

On the basis of Hume's texts, including those adduced above, we can also infer that Reid is justified in attributing (2.1) to Hume. Taking "copy" for "represent" or "be about," Reid understands what I have captured in (2.1) as the claim "that every object of thought must be an impression or an idea—that is, a faint copy of some preceding impression" (IHM 2.6, 33/108b).

The next relevant piece of Hume's theory has to do with the nature of impressions. Hume says that the assertion that "our senses offer not their impressions as the images of something distinct, or independent, and external, is evident; because they convey to us nothing but a single perception, and never give us the least intimation of any thing beyond" (T 1.4.2.4, 189). Later in the *Treatise* he says that our impressions, that is:

our passions, volitions, and actions, are not susceptible of any such agreement or disagreement; being original facts and realities, compleat in themselves, and implying no reference to other passions, volitions, and actions. Tis impossible, therefore, they can be pronounced either true or false, and be either contrary or conformable to reason. (T 3.1.1.9, 458)

Impressions do not have representational content. This way of putting the point is intended to allow that someone can use impressions to represent something else, but that this is a purely extrinsic feature of impressions. For example, a red light hanging above asphalt may represent the wrath of a local god. What the red light represents is contingent upon its relations to other local laws, social norms, rituals, and so on, and is not intrinsically determined by the nature of red lights. Hume requires this of impressions because they are that in virtue of which the representational content of ideas is to be explained. From this I identify another key principle in Hume's discussion about impressions and ideas, namely:

(2.2) Impressions do not have intentional content.

Others see good grounds for attributing this point to Reid. One commentator suggests that Humean "Impressions are, in effect, sensations in Reid's sense—mental phenomena which are not intrinsically representational" (Hopkins 2005, 349).

Stopping with (2.1) and (2.2) would leave obscure the features of impressions in virtue of which the ideas they produce have intentional content. As Hume's comments quoted thus far imply, ideas are related to the impressions they are about because of the associative relations amongst those impressions. Hume posits relations of contiguity in time and place, along with resemblance and mind-dependent causation, in order to account for the origins of all of the contents of our simple and complex ideas. Without recapitulating this familiar theory, I propose that we bring forward a third Humean principle about impressions and ideas, and that is:

(2.3) The intentional content of ideas is reducible to (or derivable from) associative relations amongst impressions.

Before turning to Reid's *reductio* of Hume's theory, I raise and respond to one criticism of this section. Someone will surely object (i) that the view attributed to Hume is unjustified given the texts quoted and cited, and (ii) that Reid's interpretation of Hume, as explained here, also suffers from a lack of textual support. So the section fails to establish Reid's interpretation of Hume or Hume's own theory.

I have attempted to disarm these charges in several ways. Studying Hume and the surrounding literature has convinced me that the interpretation of Hume I offer as Reid's is warranted, even if other conflicting interpretations are as well. So to make the first point stick, it is not enough to say that there may be other equally justified interpretations of Hume. Frankly, I'm not even arguing that there is no *better* justified reading of Hume. My limited dialectical goal has been to show Reid's interpretation follows from a reasonable use of the texts in their context in the eighteenth century. A number of problems plague the second criticism. Reid is not in the business of reconstructing the theories of his predecessors. Reid's history of philosophy is pastiche, and not precise. In addition, I have mentioned Reid's frequent comments that he is unable clearly to understand Hume's characterization of impressions, ideas, and their relations. Furthermore, the context of Reid's argument against Hume's theory of thought mostly occurs in texts that Reid himself did not publish or prepare for publication. Indeed, they were commencement addresses—in Latin—given to graduating classes. For these reasons, my expectations in understanding Reid's interpretation of Hume are limited. I hope to have provided the best semblance of order to Reid's self-avowedly diffuse comments on Hume's theses about ideas and impressions.

2.4. The Blind Book Argument

The previous section, with the interpretive risks it takes, pays substantial dividends because it provides background to a fascinating argument that Reid levels against Hume, though, as is customary, Reid does not mention him by name in this context.

Reid credits Hume himself with planting and nurturing the seeds of this *reductio* argument. By stating this, Reid's intent is to point to Hume's genius and not to give offense. A glimmer of Reid's meaning lies in Hume's own use of his analysis of ideas, impressions, and their relationships to deconstruct certain of our concepts, which Reid interprets antagonistically. The concepts that Hume deconstructs include concepts of cause and effect (T 1.3.14.1, 155), time (T 1.2.5.26, 64), substance (T 1.4.5.3, 232), matter (T 1.2.6.7–9, 67), and the self (T 1.4.6, 251). Hume's chief instrument in this operation is stated here in general form: "Now since nothing is ever present to the mind but perceptions, and since all ideas are derived from something antecedently present to the mind, it follows that 'tis impossible for us so much as to conceive or form an idea of anything specifically different from ideas and impressions" (T 1.2.6.8, 67). Since matter is in space-time, it follows that the "idea" of matter is actually devoid of meaning. As Hume says about the idea of the enduring self, "there is no such idea" (T 1.4.6.2, 251), and so on.

Reid restates Hume's position as a threat:

The articles of inquisition are few indeed but very dreadful in their consequences; Is the prisoner an impression or an idea? If an idea, from what impression copied? And if it appears that the prisoner is neither an impression, nor an idea copied from some impression, immediately, without being allowed to offer anything in arrest of judgment, he is sentenced to pass out of existence and to be, in all time to come, an empty unmeaning sound or the ghost of a departed entity. Before this dreadful tribunal, cause and effect, time and place, matter and spirit, have been tried and cast. (IHM 6.8, 98/144 a–b)

If the idea is not copied from a corresponding impression, or from some further idea, which is in turn copied from an impression, then it "is sentenced to pass out of existence." In sum, Reid says that Hume "adopts the theory of ideas in its full extent; and, in consequence, shews that there is neither matter nor mind in the universe; nothing but impressions and ideas" (EIP 2.12, 162/293a). Reid alleges that these "articles of inquisition" have maximum force and maximum scope, to employ Kenneth Winkler's helpful distinction. Winkler says the scope of the theory of ideas is "universal, and its force unforgiving: it seems to say that any alleged thought or conception lacking an appropriate pedigree is unintelligible or meaningless" (Winkler 1991, 552). All purported mental states are brought to trial (maximum scope), and when found guilty the verdict is that the state is unqualifiedly meaningless (maximum force).

According to this interpretation of Hume, my thought of Petra is of Petra in virtue of there being appropriate associative relationships between this idea and a set of sensory impressions. Sensory impressions—in this case pictorial snapshots of color experienced while looking at Petra's buildings—are themselves meaningless and without intentional content. How is it, then, that they produce or explain, or can produce or can explain, the intentional content of my thought about Petra?

If Hume's explanation of the process by which our thoughts acquire their intentional contents is correct, then we would know neither what are the intentional contents of those states nor even that those states have intentional contents. Hume's theory would imply that "we can have no idea of anything but our sensations, and the operations of mind we are conscious of" (EIP 2.12, 164/294b; see EIP 2.14, 180/303a). Reid's use of the term "sensations" to refer to qualitative mental states corresponds roughly to Hume's use of the term "impressions." By "operations" Reid refers to uses of faculties of the mind. So he allows that, if Hume is right, we can know we are employing the faculty of reason and not the faculty of perception, for instance. This point arises from the *Intellectual Powers*. But the central texts pointing to this underdeveloped and (with the exception of Haldane 1989, 1993) unknown epistemic argument occur in Reid's commencement addresses delivered at King's College, Aberdeen.

There Reid begins:

For by what divination could I be taught that these images painted in my *camera obscura* are representations? How am I to be taught that the forms present and imprinted on my mind represent things that are external or that have passed out of existence? (Reid 1989, 62)[8]

In this pair of rhetorical questions Reid distinguishes two problems for an explanation of cognition in terms of ideas. First, how can one know *that* those ideas purporting to have intentional content have it? Second, if that question can be answered, how does one know *what* an idea with intentional content is in fact about?

Reid amplifies this twofold problem while commenting on Hume's belief that ideas are representational. Reid asks us to:

suppose that ideas represent things like symbols; in this way, words and writing are known to express everything. Let the intellect, therefore, be instructed by ideas, not in the manner of a *camera obscura* with painted images but like a written or printed book, teaching us many things that are external, that have passed away, and that will come to be. This view does not solve the problem; for who will interpret this book for us? If you show a book to a savage who has never heard of the use of letters, he will not know the letters are symbols, much less what they signify. If you address someone in a foreign language, perhaps your words are symbols as far as you are concerned, but they mean nothing to him. Symbols without interpretation have no value. (Reid 1989, 62)[9]

Before we can state the implicit argument, these passages require comment. First, the term "camera obscura" refers to an antiquated apparatus by which a stream of light enters a dark room or (for portable units) a dark box through a small aperture. The entering light is focused through the hole and projects the images of objects on the outside of the room on to the opposite wall upside-down. The model of the mind suggested by the Way of Ideas structurally resembles the workings of a camera obscura. But in this passage Reid offers to change the simile to explain Hume's theory of cognition. He does this because he does not want his argument to depend upon an imagistic version of the Way of Ideas. Reid was wise to make this point since Hume sometimes

---

[8] Reid wrote these commencement orations in unsophisticated Latin, and they are published as Reid 1937. A good English translation was published as Reid 1989, from which I have drawn in quoting Reid. However, I have made several minor modifications to this translation in cases in which the translation omits a point of importance. I will not bother to note each divergence because I include Reid's Latin for each quotation from the orations, as here: "Qua enim Divinatione edocear, formas has in camera mea obscura depictas esse representamina; Quomodo edocear formas præsentes & menti impressas res preteritas aut externas adumbrare" (Reid 1937, 34–5).

[9] "Ponamus postremo Ideas res representare, tanquam Signa; sic verba et Scripturam omnia exprimere notum est. Sit ergo Intellectus Ideis instructus, non tanquam camera obscura cum imaginibus depictis, set tanquam liber scriptus vel impressus, multa externa, præterita, et futura nos edocens. Neque hoc Nodum solvit, quis enim hunc Librurm nobis interpretabitur. Si homini barbaro qui nunquam de litteris audivit, librum ostenderis, litteras signa esse nescit, multo magis quid significent. Si quem lingua ignota alloquare, verba tua tibi fortasse signa sunt illi vero nihil significant. Signa, sine interpretatione nihil valent" (Reid 1937, 35).

describes impressions as images and sometimes does not. Even if they are not, and instead are syntax of another kind, Reid insists that the problem remains.

Reid employs a family of terms that includes "meaning," "symbol," "know," "represent," "signify," and "interpret." He does not explicitly define these terms; he presumes that he uses them in their customary ways. Reid seeks to understand how Hume accounts for intentional content. Thus when Reid rhetorically asks about what uninterpreted symbols might "mean" to the agent, he is implicitly voicing his skepticism about the agent's ability to know what those symbols represent by reflecting on the content of the symbols.

If these theses are true, then:

> (2.4) If agents know the contents of their intentional mental states, they must successfully interpret their impressions.

Reid holds that (2.4) follows from an implicit definition of "know" coupled with (2.1)–(2.3). When Reid says, "Symbols without interpretation have no value," he gives us a reason for (2.4). Syntactic states like impressions require an interpretation in order to make that out of which they are built meaningful.

Reid's use of the book and savage example supports (2.4) and highlights what he believes knowledge is not. In order to know the contents of my thoughts it is not necessary that I am able to manipulate symbols. If these symbols are not intrinsically representational, then I will not know what they signify unless I have a lexicon enabling me to translate them. Suppose a "mental language" refers to any unified set of syntactic symbols used in cognition. Since the mental language is not accessible to me through consciousness or introspection, I cannot know what the words in the language mean. In fact, strictly speaking, I will not even know that those "words" or "sentences" bear any content at all. That is, I will not know I am even using a language. This is the way to read the argument, despite the fact that in his metaphor he refers to letters in the book as symbols and as signifying things, as opposed to referring to words.

Naturally Reid assents to the antecedent of (2.4), which he takes to be obvious:

> (2.5) Agents know what are the intentional contents of their ideas. (premise)

For purposes of the *reductio* we can read "ideas" as referring to any thought with intentional content.

Though it is obvious that Reid endorses (2.5), special support for it comes from another quarter. Reid's analysis of our ability to know what we are thinking about when we are thinking about non-existent objects confirms the premise in a manner that dramatically exhibits Reid's understanding of our access to the contents of our thoughts. Reid adopts a theory of fictional objects on the basis of which we can think about and predicate of them in common-sense ways, despite the fact that they in no way exist or subsist. We do not need to interpret or reflect upon the contents of our thoughts in order to do this. He arrives at that position by reasoning from the Way of Ideas' implications about our cognition of fictional objects. As with Hume's theory, Reid accuses the Way of Ideas in general of impugning our ability to think of things like centaurs. He defines the territory he wishes to defend here: "I conceive a centaur. This conception is an operation of the mind, of which I am conscious, and to which I can attend. The sole object of it is a centaur, an animal which, I believe, never existed. I see no contradiction in this" (EIP 4.2, 321/373a). He adds, "conception is often employed about objects that neither do, nor did, nor will exist" (EIP 4.1, 311/368a; see EIP 2.11, 160/292a). Then he goes so far as to say that he knows "no truth more evident to the common sense and to the experience of mankind" (EIP 4.1, 311/368a–b; see Nichols 2002a).

Reid believes that he can conceive of fictional objects directly and without any intermediating ideas or representations, curious though it may sound. This conceptual claim is conjoined to an epistemic claim when he addresses the alternative view presented by the Way of Ideas. One of the twin pillars of the Way of Ideas is the false assumption that "in all the operations of understanding, there must be an object of thought, which really exists while we think of it; or, as some philosophers have expressed it, that which is not cannot be intelligible" (EIP 4.1, 312/368b). This is because all cognition is done in the currency of ideas, and ideas exist whenever someone is thinking. "The [proponent of the Way of Ideas] says, I cannot conceive a centaur without having an idea of it in my mind. ... Perhaps he will say, that the idea is an image of the animal, and is the immediate object of my conception, and that the animal is the mediate or remote object." To this Reid first responds by arguing that, upon introspective inspection of the content of his thought, there appears to be only one object of conception, not two. Second, the object of conception:

is not the image of an animal—it is an animal. I know what it is to conceive an image of an animal, and what it is to conceive an animal; and I can distinguish the one of these from the other without any danger or mistake. The thing I conceive is a body of a certain figure and colour, having life and spontaneous motion. The philosopher says, that the idea is an image of the animal; but that it has neither body, nor colour, nor life, nor spontaneous motion. This I am not able to comprehend. (EIP 4.2, 321–2/373a–b)

Reid claims to have knowledge of the contents of his own mind such that, when he entertains thoughts about fictional objects, he knows he is thinking directly about a non-existent centaur. To use his terms, it is our "attentive reflection" alone that gives us "clear and certain" knowledge of the contents of our thoughts. Even in difficult cases of thoughts about things like centaurs and unicorns, their intentional contents are so transparent in a moment's reflection that we can identify them "without any danger or mistake."

From the foregoing premises of Hume, a controversial proposition follows:

(2.6) Agents successfully interpret the impressions out of which their ideas are composed. (from (2.4) and (2.5))

Reid disputes (2.6). We do not and need not interpret our impressions in order to know the contents of our thoughts. These form two distinct criticisms, but Reid's savage-and-book example has a way of blending them together. I propose to distinguish them.

First, when we identify the representational contents of a thought, we do so merely through an awareness of the thought. That is:

(2.7) It is not the case that agents interpret their impressions.

Agents do not interpret impressions because impressions are uninterpretable syntax. Suppose, after you stub your toe, your friend inquires of you what that pain represents, means, or is about. Taking those terms at face value would imply that your friend has made a category mistake by considering something which is not meaningful, and has no intentional content, as being meaningful and having intentional content.

We can reapply Reid's analogy with language to convey the present point. Meaningless markings—scribbles—that do not have intentional content cannot be interpreted. The act of interpretation requires an agent to identify one item as standing for another. By nature of Hume's account of the mind, impressions are not about and do not represent anything. If Hume is correct, then we are like savages who, though staring at books, do not know that the symbols they contain are anything but scribbles. According to Reid's thought experiment, a savage presented with a book written in the English language and a book written in a sequence of meaningless markings could not determine that one was rich in semantic content while the other was not. On the grounds of (2.7), Reid infers that he has reduced Hume's position to absurdity by showing that it implies a contradiction.

The second of Reid's two points is that:

(2.8) It is not the case that, were impressions interpretable, agents would be able successfully to interpret their impressions.

Suppose someone informs the illiterate savage that the pages at which he is staring contains symbols that have meanings and that represent other items.

At this point the savage knows that he is being presented with a book with meaningful sentences, and not with a book of meaningless markings. However, without a proper lexicon the agent is still unable to interpret the meanings of the words and sentences in the book. In a similar way, if Hume is correct, I am unable to know the intentional contents of my thoughts.

Furthermore, suppose the members of a set of mental states S_2 (impressions) used to interpret the members of a set S_1 (ideas) will *ex hypothesi* be composed of non-contentful states, and will require an interpretation. The same is true of the members of any set S_3 used to interpret members of S_2, and so on *ad infinitum*. This consideration rides under the surface of Reid's discussion. Unless intentional relations are at some point taken as basic, one will not be able to ground knowledge of the intentional contents of our thoughts. Suppose I were to give the savage a second book, which correlated one set of symbols with another. If he does not know the meanings of the second set of symbols, he will be no closer to knowing the meanings of the first.

(2.7) and (2.8) follow from the preceding premises, but they show that (2.6)—the claim that agents successfully interpret the impressions out of which their ideas are composed—is false. In turn (2.6) is entailed by the conjunction of Hume's commitments about ideas and impressions (captured in (2.1)–(2.3)) and a statement that agents know what the contents of their thoughts are, i.e. (2.5). Reid affirms that we have a great deal of self-knowledge of the contents of our thoughts, so he will not give up (2.5).

For the completion of his *reductio* he must identify which feature of Hume's account of impressions and ideas he wishes to give up. Just what proposition Reid rejects on the basis of the contradiction he has derived from Hume is underdetermined. He does not make this explicit in the commencement speeches. There too he draws his conclusion in metaphor—"this hypothesis of ideas does not loose the knot but twists together several others that are most difficult" (Reid 1989, 62).[10] Since Reid is intent on banishing Hume's associationist account of intentionality in its entirety, Reid does not formally conclude his argument by pinpointing whether it is the nature of ideas, the nature of impressions, or the relationship between those two kinds of mental state that generates the problem. Presumably this is in part because these features are not independent of one another. Giving up any one of them would necessitate a sharp revision to the other two.

Reid's argument is another way (in addition to the arguments of *Intellectual Powers*, Essay VI) of reducing the Way of Ideas to absurdity. The two enduring

---

[10] "Revera hæc Idearum Hypothesis nodum nullum solvit complures eosque difficillimos nectet" (Reid 1937, 35).

differences between the argument presented here and the arguments of the *Intellectual Powers* are that this argument is impressively prescient, and this argument strikes at the heart of the Way of Ideas. In contrast, many of the arguments in the *Intellectual Powers* take the form of familiar *reductios* to skepticism. Reid's Blind Book argument is predicated upon the same intuition about meaning as is the Chinese Room Argument, and his assertion and defense of (2.5) parallels and foreshadows the critical point presented by Searle in that argument.[11] Others will see similarities with Wittgenstein's musings on the interpretation of rules.[12] But perhaps BonJour's argument is the clearest contemporary statement of this objection to the Way of Ideas.

2.5. Unaccountable Intentionality and the Poverty of Humean Replies

If acts of conception do not take as their intentional objects what we think they take as their intentional objects, skepticism ensues. Therefore, conception must be direct. But arriving at that conclusion by *reductio* does not serve to explain how it is that our minds have the power of uniquely picking out and individuating objects, let alone how we have the power of conceiving of non-existent objects. Reid flirts with medieval resolutions to the problem.

Reid says that the medievals believe that conception "is an act of the mind, a kind of thought. ... Conceiving, as well as projecting or resolving, are what the schoolmen called *immanent* acts of the mind, which produce nothing beyond themselves" (EIP 4.1, 300/363a). Each thought is imbued with its content and

---

[11] In the Chinese Room a monolingual English speaker is "locked in a room, and given a large batch of Chinese writing" and "a second batch of Chinese script" and "a set of rules for correlating the second batch with the first batch." The rules "correlate one set of formal symbols with another set of formal symbols," and in this context the term "formal symbols" refers to what to the subject is nothing but syntax. The subject "can identify the symbols entirely by their shapes." A third set of Chinese symbols and English instructions enable the subject "to correlate elements of this third batch with elements of the first two batches" and state that the subject is "to give back certain sorts of Chinese symbols with certain sorts of shapes in response" (1980, 417–18). So one set of formal symbols S_1 is input into the room, and another set of formal symbols, S_n, is output by the agent. The agent uses a second set of symbols S_2 to "correlate" those in S_1 with the outputs in S_n. But merely adding more formal symbols in the form of another set S_3, which are used to "correlate" symbols in S_2 with symbols in S_n, gets the agent no closer to meanings of any of the symbols.

[12] In the *Investigations* Wittgenstein has a number of examples that resonate with Reid's. For example, walking in the woods I happen on a sign nailed to a tree. On the sign is an arrow pointing left. I cannot know that I am correctly interpreting the rule since no interpretation I submit is capable of determining its meaning. Furthermore, if all the other symbols in my conceptual repertoire were, like this one, uninterpretable (by me), then I would not know that this in fact was a symbol at all (Wittgenstein 1953, §197–9/80).

structure by an intentional essence, which is either an attribute of the mind of God or an independently existing metaphysical entity. In Aquinas' terms froghood takes two forms: *esse intentionale* and *esse naturale* (*De Potentia*, q2, a1). My thought of a frog is of a frog in virtue of the fact that it is participating in the *esse intentionale* of froghood, whereas a frog is a frog in virtue of the frog's *esse naturale*. The object of thought is immanent; its form mysteriously causes us to conceive of it in the way we do.[13] Thoughts are intrinsically about what they are about, which obviates the need for representative intermediaries. Reid is sympathetic to this point. If faced with a choice between an appeal to formal causation and positing ideas, he holds that only formal causation would be sufficient to explain the phenomena:

[I]s it not necessary, I ask, for this intermediate object [an idea] to be joined also to the object perceived? Without doubt, this is necessary, for in no other way can the mind affect the object, or the object the mind. ... This point appears to have been fully grasped by Aristotle who for this reason taught that ideas or forms were sent forth from the object. (Reid 1989, 66)[14]

Reid is faintly describing the regress argument submerged in a premise of his Blind Book argument. A thought of a frog either directly or indirectly represents a frog. Suppose I explain that my thought about the frog indirectly represents the frog because it represents an intermediating mental state—a visual or tactile impression of the frog, say—that in turn represents the frog. What is true of my thought is no less true of this intermediating state: it either directly or indirectly represents the frog. If it indirectly represents the frog, then we must continue our search for what it is in virtue of which that state represents the frog. If it directly represents the frog, then we need to know two things: how it does; and why the intermediating state can be directly about the frog while my original thought of the frog cannot. Remarks like this have led some commentators to interpret Reid as advocating a theory on which a thought has the intentional content it does in virtue of a formal cause (see Haldane 1993, 2000, and especially 1989, 300–1).

---

[13] Brentano makes a similar point and he echoes the scholastics using the same terminology of "immanence" that Reid uses: "Every mental phenomenon is characterized by what the scholastics of the Middle Ages referred to as the intentional (and also mental) inexistence of the object, and what we, although with not quite unambiguous expressions, would call relation to a content, direction upon an object ... or immanent objectivity" (Brentano 1973, 88). But, contrary to Brentano's thesis, not all forms of mental activity are intentional in this way for Reid. Exceptions include sensations and moods. Reid neither universally generalizes the claim that mental states are intentional, nor claims that the intentional objects are mere phenomena. But, with Brentano, Reid does take intentionality as primitive and irreducible.

[14] "nonne quæso oportet medium hocce objecto etiam conjungi? Sine dubio: aliter neque mens, objectum, neque objectum, mentem afficere potest. ... Aristoteli hoc probe perspectum fuisse videtur, qui idcirco Ideas seu Species ab objecto emissas esse voluit" (Reid 1937, 38).

How can the Ideal Theorist escape this predicament? Recall Hume's comments that ideas are "loose and separate" and "conjoined, but never connected." Hume recognizes that his theory implies that "these words are absolutely without any meaning, when employed either in philosophical reasonings or common life." But he doesn't stop there. He manages to find "one source [of meaning] which we have not yet examined." He says, "We suppose that there is some connexion between them" (*Enquiry* 7.2.2, 75). His suggestion seems to be that an act of *supposing* they have meaning plays a role in *giving* the terms that refer to ideas and impressions meaning. This is prima facie odd. Consider also that "supposing" refers to a relation that is still constrained by the Way of Ideas. What we suppose seems to be expressed in a second set of ideas, whose members take members of the first set as intentional objects. Winkler remarks, Hume's "interest in acts of supposing or relative ideas is no sign that we have moved into territory where the theory of ideas does not hold sway; in the *Enquiry*, relative conceptions and acts of supposing are well within its scope" (1991, 556). The Ideal Theorist cannot escape the predicament.[15] This is cause to think that Reid must have something like Aquinas' appeal to *esse intentionale* and *esse naturale* in the back of his mind as a solution.

[15] Here's one argument Hume might use to account for content without falsifying the plausible assumption that we have first-person access to the contents of our own thoughts, and without positing an internal interpreter of representational states. Following Hume, let's use "perceptions" to refer to impressions and ideas. Hume might distinguish between (a) the relations holding between two perceptions, and (b) the relations holding between perceptions of those perceptions, i.e. between first-order and second-order perceptions. This distinction is motivated by Hume's description of the nature of identity attributions. Specifically, when attributing identity to oneself, one appeals to the adroitness one observes in the mind's movement from one perception to the next. This invokes a third-person perspective from which one views perceptions. The subject seems identical through time because, from the observer's point of view, the transitions from perception to perception are swift. Likewise one may reflect on this scenario by employing third-order perceptions. In this case one would stand over two subjects, as it were. How would Hume know that the observer and the subject are identical? So long as the transition from a first-order perception to a second-order perception was itself straightforward, then the agent at the third remove would think the other two are identical, or so it might be alleged.

There are several problems to which this attempt succumbs. This would only work were Hume to hold that we are only necessarily conscious of perceptions at the first-order level. But he says that we are conscious of all perceptions. Hume says, for example, that: "The only existences, of which we are certain, are perceptions, which being immediately present to us by consciousness, command our strongest assent, and are the first foundation of all our conclusions." He continues: "as no beings are ever present to the mind but perceptions; it follows that we may observe a conjunction or a relation of cause and effect between different perceptions, but can never observe it between perceptions and objects" (T 2.1.1.47/212; see 1.4.2.13–14/193). Second, this view seems to leave the advocate of the representational theory of the mind with a self precisely divided between various strata of observers and subjects. (This itself might be strangely inconsistent with Hume's bundle theory.) Thus, were this proposal to succeed, it would only show that Hume can evade the problem of an inner interpreter of representations, which does not absolve the representational theory of mind from the need to preserve first-person knowledge of one's mental states.

However, Reid explicitly repudiates the appeal to forms as it occurs in Aristotle's theory of cognition. Aristotle "thought, That there can be no sensation, no imagination, nor intellection, without forms, phantasms, or species in the mind; and that things sensible are perceived by sensible species and things intelligible by intelligible species" (IHM 7, 207/204b; see EIP 1.1, 30/225b–26a). While this theory, especially in the hands of Aquinas, can seem to imply a direct theory of thought, appearances are deceiving. Both Aquinas and Aristotle introduce intermediaries, like sensible species. Though their accounts have advantages over Hume's, Reid doesn't believe they are coherent:

> The whole doctrine of the Peripatetics and schoolmen concerning forms, substantial and accidental, and concerning the transmission of sensible species from objects of sense to the mind, if it be at all intelligible, is so far above my comprehension that I should perhaps do it injustice, by entering into it more minutely. (EIP 2.8, 106/268a; see EIP 5.6, 389–90/405b)

Reid's Newtonian method implies that the doctrine is highly implausible since it appears to be an hypothesis of the first rank. Also, the Peripatetics and schoolmen presuppose that "in every kind of thought there must be some object that really exists; in every operation of the mind, something to work on" (EIP 2.20, 320/372b). Reid identifies this claim with the Ideal Theory and rejects it, in part through his argument about our awareness of fictional objects (at EIP 2.8, 128/274b; and EIP 4.2, 312/368b). The assertion that a non-existent half-horse, half-man emits or produces forms that enter Reid's mind is indecipherable.

The appeal to substantial forms holds allure for Reid chiefly because it offers a more commonsensical alternative than the Way of Ideas. Keep in mind that Reid is a philosopher for whom a robust metaphysics is almost always to be preferred over skepticism. But invoking substantial forms in order to explain intentional thought is unsatisfactory on Newton's methods, and generates more problems than it solves. Reid responds to the problem by revoking the demand upon him that he have a metaphysical theory that accounts for intentional thought. He repudiates the need for such a theory, and claims that intentionality is an inexplicable, unaccountable feature of cognition.

This contrasts with Hume. Hume argues that, if no one is able to trace the origins of a purported intentional content back to a set of simple impressions, then that idea is devoid of intentional content. I remarked on Hume's wide-ranging use of these "articles of inquisition" and Reid adds to the list in a now published manuscript, "Of Power." Hume argued that the conception of power is not the product of sense or consciousness, and, says Reid, Hume "rashly concluded that there is no such conception in the human mind" (Reid 2001, 3). "Supposing we were unable to give any account how we first got the conception of power, this would be no good reason for denying that we have it. One might as well prove that he had no eyes in his head for this reason[:] that neither he nor any other person could tell how they came there" (Reid 2001, 5). Reid's response to the challenge to explain the fact that our thoughts have intentional contents is to admit it cannot be explained in terms that are devoid of reference to intentionality.

Instead Reid presumes that the intentionality of perceptual states is irreducible and must be taken as a basic datum in one's philosophy of mind. He sets out his case by foreshadowing Brentano:

Most of the operations of the mind, from their very nature, must have objects to which they are directed, and about which they are employed. ... To perceive, without having any object of perception, is impossible. The mind that perceives, the object perceived, and the *operation* of perceiving that object, are distinct things, and are distinguished in the structure of all languages. (EIP 1.1, 26/224a)

Those mental states that have intentionality have it necessarily. Those states, perceptual states amongst them, "*must* have objects *to which* they are directed, and *about which* they are employed" (my emphasis). Unlike Brentano, Reid only claims that "most" operations of the mind have intentionality.

Reid implicitly denies that the intentional objects of perceptual beliefs are sensations. My perception of the oak takes the oak as its direct intentional object. It is not about the oak in virtue of being about my sensory impression of the oak. The intentional objects of perceptions are physical objects. To be precise, "The objects of perception are the various qualities of bodies" (EIP 2.17, 200/313b; see EIP 2.19, 218/322b).

I said that, for Reid, a thought's intentional object is related by necessity to the thought. In other words, my thought about the chest of drawers could not be the thought that it is unless its intentional object is the chest of drawers, which amounts to a form of semantic externalism. But Reid rightly tells a different story about the relation between a thought's content and its causes in sensory experience. There is no privileged logical connection between sensations and intentional contents, let alone between a token sensation and a token intentional content (EIP 2.20, 227/327a). No sensation is intrinsically related to any intentional content. The result is that none of the empirical relationships to which Hume points can establish that a certain perceptual state takes the object that it does. Hence, Hume's goal of individuating the meaning of an idea in virtue of identifying the sensations, or in Hume's terms, the impressions, from which it is caused and which it resembles, fails.

The associative relations between an agent's ideas and impressions cannot make it the case that, for any particular idea and any particular impression, the idea is about the impression. Restating Hume's theory, Reid puts this point rhetorically as follows:

There are ideas present in the mind, representations of things that are external or have passed away; the mind, conscious of these ideas, perceives things that are external and have passed away with the ideas playing a middle role. Now, granted that there are ideas of things in the mind of which the mind is conscious, by what skill or by what indications, I ask, can the mind either know or even portend that these ideas are representations of other things? (Reid 1989, 61)[16]

Reid still makes the point in epistemic terms, but an implication of his assertion that the mind cannot know these facts is that intentionality must be taken as a primitive, unaccountable feature of mind. Anything can resemble anything else, can be temporally contiguous with anything else, and can seem to cause anything else. As Hume puts it: "To consider the matter a priori, anything may produce anything" (T 1.4.5, 247), which is why Reid credits Hume for assistance in his refutation of Hume (C 31). The upshot is that Hume's account of intentional content, or more loosely "mental representation," is not able to meet minimal standards of coherence. Keith Lehrer accurately identifies Reid's objection:

[Hume's] impressions and ideas are not states which are about objects and, moreover, concatenation of them will not be a state which is about an object either. ... Hume had assumed that our thought of such things [horses and people] must be constructed out of impressions or ideas. But he failed to confront the problem of immanence or intentionality. ... The fundamental problem for Hume's empiricism is the problem of accommodating the intentionality of thought. ... Hume cannot account even for our conception of impressions. (Lehrer 1998, 16, 17)

Intentionality cannot be reduced to non-intentional states on pains of failing to account for rudimentary, commonsensical features of thought.[17]

---

[16] "Ideæ sunt, in mente presentes, rerum externarum & præteritarum representamina, mens harum Idearum conscia, mediantibus ijs res externas et præteritas percipit. Dato jam quod sint Ideæ rerum in mente, quarum mens est conscia: Qua arte quæso aut quibus Indicijs, scire vel etiam augurare potest mens, has Ideas esse aliarum rerum Representamina" (Reid 1937, 34).

[17] Reid's objection to Hume's theory of thinking directly informs his theory of perception. He diagnoses his predecessors' theories of perception as invoking a contiguity principle on which "there must be some immediate intercourse between the mind and its object so that one may act upon the other," which is thought to imply that "as the external objects of sense are too remote to act upon the mind immediately, there must be some image or shadow of them that is present to the mind, and is the immediate object of perception" (EIP 4.2, 312/369b). Suppose that there are intermediaries in perception in terms of which the having of our intentional contents is explained, much as Humean

Hume and Humeans have sought to avoid this charge in several ways. Some Hume scholars concur with Reid's interpretation here, but deny the force of the rhetorical question. One scholar argues that mere causation is itself sufficient for intentionality: "The intentional relation is taken to be a causal relation ... [The] intentional cum causal relation is always from cause to effect: the cause means or is about the effect, that is, the cause functions as the cognitive content and the effect as the intentional object" (Flage 1991, 53, 54). Though perhaps a justified interpretation of Hume, this seems incredible if taken as a philosophical thesis. Another defender of Hume says that we bark up the wrong tree when we want to know any more than what Hume tells us when describing associative relations (Waxman 1994, 51; see T 1.3.5.1–2, 84). Reid's multi-purpose response is that Hume's tripartite appeal to association, that is, his "enumeration of the relations of things which are apt to lead us from one object to another, is very inaccurate ... [and] far too scanty in reality" (EIP 4.4, 348/386b).

Another group of Hume scholars are refreshingly forthright about the difficulties plaguing Hume on cognition. Jonathan Bennett pulls no punches. He rejects several of Hume's key theses about ideas and impressions and, motivated by charity, reintroduces a consistent set of principles about meaning (Bennett 2001 ii, 202–20). Don Ross introduces precisely Reid's problem (though not as Reid's problem). "From the causal and mechanical perspective," he says, "this tale of reverberating impacts [of impressions in the mind] is, for Hume, the whole story of mind. It provides us, however, with no account of the *content* of thought, since the notion of content appeals to *semantic*, and not merely mechanical, *structure*" (Ross 1991, 346). Ross concurs that Hume's theory of cognition, as stated by Hume himself, seems to fail for Reid's reasons, but he does not concede Hume's defeat: "We do not need, as Hume insists, *metaphysical foundations* for resemblance; but we do need more *details* about it" (1991, 349). For Reid, as for BonJour and a small minority today, this response reveals that the full force of the argument has not been understood.

A final strategy is employed by another group of Hume's defenders, which argues that Hume has a "special" use of the term "meaning." Even though a mental state is meaningless, it can nonetheless "refer to something real" (Wright 1983, 125). Members of this group resist interpreting Hume's use of the Way of Ideas as having maximum scope and force. Instead they suggest that "We can successfully refer and genuinely talk about something ... even

---

impressions are used to explain ideas. Reid says: "we know as little how perception may be produced by this image as by the most distant object" (EIP 2.14, 178/302a). Reid applies Newton's first rule of philosophy—that explanations must be true and sufficient to explain the phenomena—in rejecting the Way of Ideas' use of images in an account of perception.

though there is a sense in which we don't know what we are talking about, or what we are saying" (Strawson 1989, 122–3). This sequacious commentary unintentionally reflects the poverty of Hume's stated theory. Reid holds precisely their interpretation of Hume, namely that we don't know what we're talking about. But his hopes for self-knowledge are more ambitious than the ones held by these commentators.

Proponents of arguments that mirror Reid's Blind Book argument are typically led to his corollary conclusion that intentionality is an unaccountable feature of mind. By "unaccountable" Reid means that the phenomenon cannot be derived from a law of nature (see Section 1.1). This is why Reid holds that the capacity to have intentional thoughts is "primary and simple, not composed of, nor to be reduced to, other faculties" (Reid 1989, 60). Searle can be read as capturing the conclusion of Reid's objection to Hume. He doesn't put the point in terms of Reid's faculty psychology, but he does say that "intentional notions are inherently normative. They set standards of truth, rationality, consistency, etc., and there is no way that these standards can be intrinsic to a system consisting entirely of brute, blind, non-intentional causal relations" (Searle 1993, 51). Intentionality is a primitive.

It is difficult to refrain from inquiring into *how* our conceptions are intentional. Consistent with his discussion about the limits of philosophical explanation within the framework of his Newtonian method, Reid warns his readers against insisting upon such a point. To ask further questions about intentionality, where that is interpreted as a request for an explanation in terms of yet simpler mechanisms and faculties, implicitly presupposes that we have not reached the limits of philosophical explanation. According to Reid, we have reached those limits.

We must be wary of Reid's claim that philosophical reasoning is at an end, and that the search for an explanation is at an end. He applies this tact elsewhere in his corpus in discreditable ways directed at silencing his opponents, as here when writing about Hume on God and design:

No man can ever conclude from experience that even the least effect that appears to have the least bit of design in it can be without a designing cause. It appears very odd that one who considers the structure of the human body should think such a glorious fabric produced by chance. We need not reason with the man, who can allow himself to entertain such a thought and therefore he should be left to himself. (Edinburgh MS Reid 1763 Dk. 3.2, Lecture 59).

Reid's claims that explanation stops at the point he wants it to, and that his interlocutors can go no further, are in danger of embarrassing misuse. But as for intentionality, Reid is not suggesting, because we have reached such a limit, that no one can ever explain how our thoughts are intentional. He makes no claim that such an explanation is in principle impossible; on the contrary, he hopes for the promise of such answers at some future point. But, given the available explanations in his time—principally Hume's account of intentionality in virtue of the principles of association, and Aristotle's and Aquinas' account in virtue of forms and phantasms—Reid prefers silence.

2.6. Summary

This chapter represents an analysis of Reid's discussion of the intentionality or aboutness of our mental states. This is the feature of perception that accounts for the fact that our perceptions are directed at objects. Reid argues that unless this feature of the mind is taken as a primitive into one's philosophy of mind, then a radical form of skepticism—skepticism about the contents of one's thoughts—will result. On pains of absurdity, Reid holds that the intentionality of thoughts is a basic and unaccountable feature of them.

Reid's explanation of why intentionality *simpliciter* is basic in his theory of perception is conceptually prior to Reid's explanation of how our perceptions come to have intentional content. The profundity of the error in Hume's use of impressions, ideas, and the principles of association compels us to begin our discussion of Reid's theory of perception here. Now that we know that our minds are capable of intentional thought, and that this is irreducible, we turn to the matter of showing how our minds are capable of intentional thought through our perceptual faculty. How do our perceptual experiences take as their intentional objects things like mind-independent, physical bodies and their qualities?

3

Perceptual Awareness through Touch

The Blind Book argument, and the argument presented in this chapter, run in parallel because they reveal failures of the Way of Ideas to ground a plausible philosophy of mind. The Blind Book argument concludes that the Way of Ideas sacrifices what Reid takes as a non-negotiable feature of our mental life: my non-inferential knowledge of the intentional contents of at least some of my thoughts. This runs parallel to the argument I will present in this chapter, which Reid also states through a thought experiment. Reid mounts an argument on the basis of the poverty of our sensory stimulus to show that, no matter what sensations I experience, they will not be sufficient to explain what Reid takes to be a non-negotiable feature of our mental life: the fact that I am able to have perceptions and perceptual beliefs about mind-independent primary qualities.

The similarities in the two arguments' motivations give way to differences in their structures and conclusions. The thought experiment I will now present and explain reveals a chasm between the mind-independent world and our ability to have determinate thoughts about it. Reid grants for the sake of argument that the principles of the Way of Ideas theoretically allow that we can have perceptions whose intentional objects are primary qualities by putting the conclusions of the Blind Book argument in abeyance. He then contends that the Way of Ideas nonetheless lacks the resources needed to explain how my perception of an object is about the object. So the two arguments are structurally dissimilar. The Sensory Deprivation argument of this chapter is best construed as an abductive argument against several of the Way of Ideas' proposals to explain our intentional awareness of primary qualities through perception. The Blind Book argument is best construed as a deductive argument that proceeds by way of reducing Hume's principles about ideas and impressions to absurdity.

Whereas intentionality is taken as a primitive in Reid's philosophy of mind, Reid has more to say about the process by which we form intentional perceptual beliefs about mind-independent bodies. The Sensory Deprivation argument clears the ground for Reid's alternative explanation of this process. A reductive explanation of our primary quality concepts in terms of ideas and impressions is anathema to Reid. But he agrees with Locke that it is absurd to hold that those ideas are innate in us from birth. His alternative is to posit what he calls *natural signs*. Reid principally uses his doctrine of natural signs to express his theory of perception, but he also applies it in other areas of his corpus, for example to explain the effects of music on the mind (Reid 2004, 287). Through his discussion of natural signs Reid offers a partial explanation of the manner in which sensations "suggest" perceptions of objects. This is partial because, as Reid is quick to admit, it is incomplete. He describes his own view as requiring inevitable appeal to something mysterious. However, though this may leave us short, his triumph lies in showing that no reductive explanation of our ability to have intentional perceptual states from the Way of Ideas is plausible.

This appeal to natural signs serves as a crude alternative to the accounts given by George Berkeley and by Etienne Bonnot, Abbé de Condillac, of concept formation through sensory experience. Both these individuals hold that we form our concepts of primary qualities merely through our sensory experience. At the end of this chapter I develop several objections that these two philosophers may wish to pose to Reid, and I explain what Reid may say in response.

3.1. Reid's Argument from Elimination

Failure to study Reid's rejection of the views of his predecessors has led to misunderstanding, and then ridicule, of Reid's own proposals to explain the intentional content of perceptions.[1] This is understandable because Reid's theory about our acquisition of concepts of primary qualities appears obscure to those unaware of its origins. In order to motivate and better understand Reid's appeal to innate features of our constitution, I will identify the ways in which Reid's position is constructed in response to the theories

---

[1] Peter Winch, for example, observes that Reid's suggestion terminology is awkward, misleading, and prima facie inconsistent with Reid's maxim that "Common words, therefore, ought to be used in their common acceptation" (EIP 1.1, 18/219b). Winch voices more substantive criticisms by saying that the presence of suggestion relations renders Reid's account of perception indirect (Winch 1953, 330). He adds that Reid's account of perceptual knowledge precludes non-inferentially justified belief (1953, 332). But, amidst his eager arguments and interesting points, he makes no effort to understand why Reid would be offering the account he offers, and thus misunderstands Reid's use of suggestion and natural signs.

of intentional perceptual content offered by his predecessors. At the risk of anachronistic prose, I use the term "intentional perceptual content" or "intentional perception" to refer to an intentional mental state that occurs in virtue of one's use of one's perceptual faculty. My perceptual awareness of an apple on my desk has an intentional perceptual content. My belief that Medusa is the mother of Pegasus lacks perceptual content since I do not use my senses to form that belief, but it does have intentional content, according to Reid.

My perception of the apple before me has the intentional content that it does in virtue of the way that normal human beings have been created. Reid says that the battery of sensations I experience when perceiving an apple—tactile, visual, and gustatory—signify the apple by being natural signs of the apple. The cognitive constitution of human beings is built in such a way that certain sensations bring to mind perceptual states that take certain objects as their intentional contents. He recognizes that this appeal to the innate semiotic capacities of our minds is not a *theory* of the intentionality of perception—far from it. But he implicitly attempts to justify this conclusion through arguing by elimination that other attempts to account for the intentional perceptual contents are false.

First he says, "We have no way of coming at this conception and belief [about hardness], but by means of a certain sensation of touch, to which hardness hath not the least similitude" (IHM 5.3, 57/121a) and then adds, "it is a fact that such sensations are invariably connected with the conception and belief of external existences" (IHM 5.3, 61/122b). So Reid affirms:

(3.1) There is a contingent, counterfactual dependence of our intentional perceptions upon our sensations.

Hardness, which Reid defines as the firm cohesion of the parts of a body, is a primary quality of mind-independent objects. Reid affirms the following critical theses about the attempts to explain the acquisition of intentional concepts of primary qualities:

(3.2) Intentional perceptions of mind-independent qualities and bodies are not innate ideas in us since birth.
(3.3) Sensation experiences conjoined with human reasoning are insufficient for producing intentional perceptions of mind-independent qualities and bodies.
(3.4) Sensation experiences conjoined with relationships of resemblance are insufficient for producing intentional perceptions of mind-independent qualities and bodies.
(3.5) Sensation experiences conjoined with custom and habit are insufficient for producing intentional perceptions of mind-independent qualities and bodies.

If (3.1) is true and the prospective explanations canvassed in (3.2)–(3.5) fail, then any successful explanation of our simple apprehension of mind-independent qualities and bodies must involve more than associative relations, reasoning, or habits. Reid believes that:

> (3.6) Sensation experiences conjoined with human reasoning and/or relationships of resemblance and/or custom and habit are insufficient for producing intentional perceptions of mind-independent qualities and bodies.

Reid does not believe that appeals to reasoning, resemblance, and habit collectively have explanatory power, a belief not obviously justified on the basis of (3.2)–(3.5). He says, "by all rules of just reasoning, we must conclude, that this connection is the effect of our constitution, and ought to be considered as an original principle of human nature, till we find some more general principle into which it may be resolved" (IHM 5.3, 61/122b). Reid seeks to appeal to explanatory principles that do not entail innate ideas and that are not the product of experience. Only then will he account for the fact that we can conceive of primary qualities. In other words:

> (3.13) The only remaining explanation sufficient to account for intentional perceptions must appeal to natural signs from our constitution.

Descartes, Locke, and Berkeley are roughly represented in Reid's use of (3.3), (3.4), and (3.5).

3.2. Overestimating the Explanatory Power of Experience

We can see in several of these theses reliance upon experience, which Reid will argue is overestimated. In a reaction to Cartesian philosophy, many natural philosophers and scientists in the British Isles adopted explanatory models that not only minimized but did away with any appeal to principles of our human constitution. To Reid, this was going too far. I want to set the context for Reid's Sensory Deprivation argument by examining one way in which his predecessors did take this trend too far—and why Reid believes this fails.

Some physiologists embraced a Berkeleyan model of explanation in order to account not only for mental phenomena, but also for features of visual experience. This is a theme in the work of Robert Smith and William Porterfield, which was influential in Reid's time and which Reid knew directly. They both share a broadly Berkeleyan optimism about the power of experience and habit to provide us concepts, and also to explain motor processes in visual perception.

When I look across the room, I see one chest with two eyes. Smith claims that seeing things singly, and hearing things singly, is a matter of learning and habit. As applied to vision, the habit in question is the association of a location on the retina with the mind-independent location of the object (1738 i, 137–48; see Falkenstein 2004, 108–9). Later Porterfield would espouse a similar view, which gained widespread acceptance at the time. Porterfield argues for the conclusion that "The true cause of this uniformity in the motions of our eyes to me seems wholly to depend on custom and habit: for it is not to be doubted but these motions are voluntary, and depending upon our mind, which, being a wise agent, wills them to move uniformly" (Porterfield 1759, 114–15). This proposal omits recognition that non-cognitive dispositional states producing perceptual beliefs require stimuli in order to bring them about.

Parallel eye movement is a motor phenomenon, not a perceptual phenomenon. The accounts of eye movement in Berkeley, Smith, and Porterfield are subject to empirical disconfirmation in two ways (Daniels 1989, 36). First, the fact that motions of each eye are allegedly under our voluntary control implies that adults should be able to move each eye at will. Since adults cannot do this, Reid concludes that the joint movement of our eyes is not merely a matter of custom or habit (IHM 6.10, 113/152b). Second, if the joint movement of the eyes is the product of a habit acquired through experience then there will be a period in infancy in which the eyes do not move jointly and in parallel. But Reid's earnest observations disconfirm this implication (IHM 6.10, 113/152b).

The associationism and concomitant appeal to the role of custom in these accounts cannot cope with the data. In order to explain parallel eye movement, and the dependence of visual perception upon it, we must appeal to our constitution (IHM 6.13, 132/163b). The visual system has been created in such a way as to operate under a principle that requires sensory stimulation on corresponding points of the retinas in order to prompt the perception of objects. We are innately disposed to move our eyes in parallel because the will of God has arranged it, says Reid. He allows that we can gain knowledge about the physical apparatus of the eye and brain, and their joint activity. But Reid's reference to God and to the endowment of our constitution signal that any attempt to reduce these phenomena to aspects of experience is misguided.

When Reid says that "there is something in the constitution, some natural instinct, which directs us to move both eyes always the same way" (IHM 6.13, 132/163b), his appeal to natural instincts is of a piece with his appeal to natural signs. At the time of Reid's writing and in the milieu of trends in natural philosophy that we see in Smith and Porterfield, his interest in arguing for limits to the role of experience in explanations of not only motor phenomena, but also mental phenomena, appears wise and sensible. This is so even if his means to advance such arguments is unusual.

3.3. The Sensory Deprivation Argument

His principal effort to establish this conclusion involves an elaborate thought experiment.[2] Reid adopts the scientific terminology of Robert Hooke and calls it his *experimentum crucis*, his "crucial test." Reid seeks to learn "whether from sensation alone we can collect any notion of extension, figure, motion, and space." His thought experiment involves an adult blind subject who, despite being able to reason and remember, has no concepts about extension whatsoever. In addition to losing his sight, he has "lost all the experience, and habits, and notions he had got by touch; [he lacks] the least conception of the existence, figure, dimensions, or extension, either of his own body, or of any other; but to have all his knowledge of external things to acquire anew, by means of sensation, and the power of reason, which we suppose to remain entire" (IHM 5.6, 65/125b). The implication is that the subject is not only devoid of any prior sensory experience, but he lacks a "body image," a sense for the relative spatial location of one's appendages (Ganson 1999, 51).

To appreciate Reid's argumentative strategy, recall Hume's challenge to anyone so bold as to deny that sensory impressions and accompanying associative principles are sufficient for the formation of any idea:

[E]very simple idea has a simple impression, which resembles it, and every simple impression a correspondent idea. Every one may satisfy himself in this point by running over as many as he pleases. But if any one should deny this universal resemblance, I know no way of convincing him, but by desiring him to shew a simple impression that has not a correspondent idea, or a simple idea that has not a correspondent impression.

---

[2] In addition to his major argument, Reid has a minor one. Reid targets the claim that each concept has a corollary sensation. He writes: "when I grasp a ball in my hand, I perceive it at once hard, figured, and extended. The feeling is very simple, and hath not the least resemblance to any quality of body. Yet it suggests to us three primary qualities perfectly distinct from one another, as well as from the sensation which indicates them" (IHM 5.5, 63/123b). According to his predecessors' theories, we are capable of distinguishing a sensation for each perceptual concept we acquire through sensory experience. But we lack a multitude of sensations that would be necessary for Berkeley's views about concept formation (see Daniels 1976, 38). This argument shows that a single sensation can give rise to a plurality of intentional concepts, which implies that the sensation–concept relation is not isomorphic.

If he does not answer this challenge, as it is certain he cannot, we may, from his silence and our own observation, establish our conclusion. (T 1.1.1.5, 3–4)

Reid argues that our ideas of figure, motion, and extension do not have any correspondent impression from which they are derived. He argues that Hume's conclusion is formed:

rashly and unphilosophically. For it is a conclusion that admits of no proof but by induction; and it is upon this ground that he himself founds it. The induction cannot be perfect till every simple idea that can enter into the human mind be examined, and be shewn to be copied from a resembling impression of sense or of consciousness. No man can pretend to have made this examination. (EAP 1.4, 520a)

Either the argument is inductive, as it is advertised, or deductive. If deductive, then it is invalid. If inductive, Hume's claim to be "certain" that there are no exceptions to this principle is inconsistent with the argument's form (see IHM 5.7, 69–70/127–8, IHM 75–6/132a–b, and Somerville 1995, 146). In addition to raising this criticism about the structure of Hume's argument, Reid also seeks to meet him on his own ground by finding a counterexample to Hume's generalization.

As the laboratory technician conducting this crucial test, Reid imagines administering a series of tactile sensations to the prone subject by poking and rubbing objects against the subject's skin. The sensations are administered in sequence. After each one the reader is invited to inquire whether the subject is capable of forming perceptual beliefs with intentional content about primary qualities. In keeping with the earlier discussion, I take "notions of external existences, of space, motion, and extension, and all the primary qualities of body" to refer to intentional perceptions (see AC 180–1).

First the subject is pricked with a pin:

Common sense may lead him to think that this pain has a cause; but whether this cause is body or spirit, extended or unextended, figured or not figured, he cannot possibly, from any principles he is supposed to have, form the least conjecture. Having formerly no notion of body or of extension, the prick of a pin can give him none. (IHM 5.6, 65/125b)

Reid is adapting an example from Berkeley for his own purposes (see Berkeley 1948 ii, 179). Having experienced the single pinprick, the subject is not able to apprehend any primary quality. The momentary sensation is minimally tactile and includes some element of pain. This constitutes the first stage of his reasoning:

(3.7) Were the subject's sole sensory experience (a) a single momentary tactile sensation of pressure (b) experienced via a stimulus at a single location, then the subject would not acquire any intentional perceptions of extension or figure.

Sensations are not extended, according to Reid, so they are not spatially located in parts of the body or in the brain, even though their stimuli are spatially located by way of the body and nervous system (Falkenstein 2000). We cannot say that the subject experiences the sensation as "covering a large area of his body" or as "being at a single spatial location of his body." Such locutions may be taken to imply that he possesses some form of intentional awareness of his body in the first place. Likewise, when Reid remarks that an object is dragged across the body, *ex hypothesi* the subject does not experience it as moving through space.

In the next stage of the experiment a blunt object is pushed against the subject's body "with a force gradually increased until it bruises him." In this case the sensations extend through time. This makes no difference in the subject's conceptual abilities, though. The subject has nothing more than "another sensation or train of sensations," which allows him to "conclude as little as from the former" (IHM 5.6, 66/126a). The subject experiences a pressure sensation, which is eventually accompanied by a pain sensation:

(3.8) Were a tactile sensation added to the subject's sensory experience that is (b) experienced via a stimulus at a single location, (c) extends through time, and (d) increases in force over time, then the subject still would not acquire any intentional perceptions of primary qualities.

In the third stage an object is applied to the subject's body so that it "touches a larger or a lesser part of his body." Reid presumably refers to an experience of a sensation of pressure stimulated over a wide part of the surface of his body, e.g. imagine a pillow is laid upon his chest. As opposed to a pinprick, it may be thought that if enough of the body's surface is covered, the subject can acquire a notion of "surface area." Reid asks, "Can this give him any notion of its extension or dimensions?" and answers, "To me it seems impossible that it should":

When my two hands touch the extremities of a body; if I know them to be a foot asunder, I easily collect that the body is a foot long; and if I know them to be five feet asunder, that it is five feet long; but if I know not what the distance of my hands is, I cannot know the length of the object they grasp; and if I have no previous notion of hands at all, or of distance between them, I can never get that notion by their being touched. (IHM 5.6, 66/126a)

The use of the expression "distance between" seems to hover between concepts of distance and concepts of spatial extension, making Reid's example ambiguous. But this should not worry us. One way of understanding the concept of extension is in terms of the volume of space occupied by the surfaces of the object, which can be described as the distance between its surfaces. So Reid argues that our apprehension of the notion of spatial extension cannot arise merely from tactile sensations and reflection upon them. The subject cannot form an intentional perception of the pillow that it is extended:

> (3.9) Were a tactile sensation added to the subject's sensory experience (e) that is stimulated by covering a large surface area of skin, then the subject still would not acquire any intentional perceptions of extension, dimensions, or distance between.

At the fourth stage Reid imagines that "a body is drawn along [S's] hands or face, while they are at rest." Though this produces a new sensation in the subject, Reid "cannot conceive" how this would provide him with any notion of "space or motion." The reason is that neither sensory feelings produced by an object dragged along the skin, "nor any combination of feelings, can ever resemble space or motion" (IHM 5.6, 66/126a). In other words:

> (3.10) Were a tactile sensation added to the subject's sensory experience that (c) extends through time and (f) is stimulated by an object in motion, then the subject still would not acquire any intentional perceptions of space or motion.

Reid's claim that the falsity of (3.10) cannot be conceived, along with other aspects of the tone of this passage, seems (and only seems) to suggest that he seeks to justify (3.10) a priori. I suspect, though, that Reid was only speaking rhetorically.

Next the subject moves his limbs, thereby experiencing a new type of sensation, a muscle sensation. Altering the position of his arm from one place to another might be thought to prompt the formation of the notion of movement or motion. By doing so the subject experiences a new sensation, which accompanies the "flexure of joints, and the swelling of muscles." Reid remains insistent that this would not lead to any new conceptual apprehension. He says, "how this sensation can convey into his mind the idea of space and motion, is still altogether mysterious and unintelligible" (IHM 5.6, 66/126a). (Thomas Brown would later agree with Reid's criticisms of Berkeley but disagree with Reid's repudiation of the role of the muscle sense in concept acquisition (Brown 1828 i, 504–5).) The heart muscle pumps blood but in those instances in which we experience a sensation of the beating of our heart, it gives "no conception of space or motion." This leads to the fifth step:

(3.11) Were a sensation added to the subject's sensory experience, one that (g) accompanies the subject's muscle movements, the subject still would not acquire intentional perceptions of space or motion.

With this Reid is ready to draw some conclusions. He begins by emphasizing the contrast between his theory and his predecessors':

It appears as evident that this connection between our sensations and the conception and belief of external existences cannot be produced by habit, experience, education, or any principle of human nature that hath been admitted by philosophers. At the same time, it is a fact that such sensations are invariably connected with the conception and belief of external existences. Hence, by all rules of just reasoning, we must conclude, that this connection is the effect of our constitution, and ought to be considered as an original principle of human nature, till we find some more general principle into which it may be resolved. (IHM 5.3, 61/122b)

[P]hilosophers have imposed upon themselves and upon us, in pretending to deduce from sensation the first origin of our notions of external existences, of space, motion, and extension, and all the primary qualities of body. ... [The primary qualities] have no resemblance to any sensation, or to any operation of our minds; and, therefore, they cannot be ideas either of sensation or of reflection. The very conception of them is irreconcilable to the principles of all our philosophic systems of the understanding. The belief of them is no less so. (IHM 5.6, 67/126b)

He implies that it is inconceivable that a tactile sensation resembles a primary quality (IHM 5.3, 59/121a). His penultimate conclusion is:

(3.12) The subject's sensory experience and/or reasoning and/or resemblance and/or custom does not enable the subject to acquire any intentional perception of any primary quality.

Once established, (3.12) yields:

(3.13) The only remaining explanation sufficient to account for intentional perception must appeal to natural signs from our original constitution.

This argument appears to be directed at Berkeley rather than Descartes. But Reid emphasizes his opposition to Cartesian, intellectualist explanations of perceptual awareness when he adds: "They [sensations] are natural signs, and the mind immediately passes to the thing signified, without making the least reflection upon the sign, or observing that there was any such thing" (IHM 5.5, 63/124a; IHM 5.3, 61/121a). Reid takes aim at Locke too—specifically, at Locke's definition of knowledge (at *Essay* 4.1.2)—when he remarks that suggestion relations necessitate "no comparing of ideas, no perception of agreements or disagreements" (IHM 2.7, 38/111a). None of these proposals does justice to the organic and fluid acquisition of our concepts of mind-independent qualities.

In order to clarify Reid's conclusion, several modifications of the reasoning are needed. The first adjustment concerns the notions of qualities that Reid says the subject cannot acquire. At the first stage, for example, Reid describes the subject as unable to acquire intentional perceptions of extension and figure. At the second stage he does not mention any determinate notions. In the fourth he cites the subject's inability to form notions of space and motion. As he iterates each step of his reasoning, Reid refrains from generalizing over all notions of primary qualities, but this is not to be taken as implying that, for example, the subject at the fourth stage might acquire a notion of figure and extension despite his inability to form notions of space and motion. For Reid the acquisition of the concepts of motion and hardness *presuppose* the possession of the concept of extension (Grandi 2003, 23−7).

Next, Reid mentions a number of distinct features of tactile experiences, which I have identified with letters (a) through (g). The list of features represents only a fraction of the possible characteristics of tactile sensations. For example, Reid does not mention the felt temperature of objects that his subject experiences with his tactile sensations. A critic could appeal to this feature to argue that the thought experiment is incomplete. For this reason I emphasize the wide scope of the conclusion present in Reid's statements of it. Reid holds that no combinations of any tactile sensations, or any sensations at all, will yield notions of primary qualities for S.

Lastly, the status of the Sensory Deprivation argument is itself uncertain. I have spoken of stages of reasoning rather than premises of an argument because Reid does not characterize this thought experiment as an argument. However, it seems to be intended to establish a philosophical thesis; at least, it is not intended to establish an empirical result. One way to interpret this "argument" and the crucial test thought experiment is as an attempt to establish a modal claim, namely that, necessarily, explanations of concept acquisition restricted to experience, sensations, and learning are insufficient to account for the intentional content of perceptions. Since thought experiments typically deal with the possible, this reading is tempting. A weaker alternative would be to aim merely at showing that such explanations are insufficient for concept acquisition. Others have made similar points about Reid's argument and his similarly anti-sensation analysis of the Molyneux problem. The lesson is that "neither the semantics nor what it is to possess the concept [of a primary quality] makes any mention of sensation. Acquisition is only slightly more complex. ... Sensation's role in acquisition is at most a well-entrenched contingency" (Hopkins 2005, 350). This predominately negative reading seems to be an interpretation that is consistent with the texts and that leaves some of the teeth in the reasoning. On this weak reading, we are then faced with identifying what type of reasoning is implicit in it. The texts and their context indicate that Reid is mounting an argument to the best explanation on behalf of his conclusion, and not a deductive or inductive argument.

3.4. The Nature of Sensations

Plainly distinguishing between the qualitative character of sensations and the intentional character of perceptions is clearly important to Reid because he uses sensations to explain how we acquire concepts through perception. The Way of Ideas conflates sensation and perception. "[T]he purposes of common life do not make it necessary to distinguish them, and the received opinions of philosophers tend rather to confound them," nonetheless, distinguishing between sensations and perceptions is essential for "any just conception of the operations of our senses" (6.20, IHM 167/182b). Reid describes sensations in a way that renders them qualitative experiences functioning as signs of qualities.

A number of texts support the thought that Reidian sensations are purely qualitative states. The first is drawn from Reid's discussion of Berkeley's influence. Unlike ideas, Reid says that sensations do not intrinsically represent properties of mind-independent objects (IHM 2.2, 26/105a). Berkeley claims at *Principles* 1.8 that ideas cannot take agents or material objects as intentional objects. They cannot be "pictures or representations" of "those supposed originals or external objects" (WGB ii, 44). Reid reapplies Berkeley's *esse is percipi* thesis to argue that Reidian sensations do not and cannot take mind-independent objects as their intentional objects. A sensation, he says, "has no similitude to anything else, so as to admit of a comparison" (IHM 2.2, 26/105a). Berkeley's description of ideas of sense, reinterpreted as proxy for sensations, "appears to me to be perfectly agreeable," adding that the "very essence of [a sensation] consists in its being felt" (EIP 2.11, 156/289b). In his correspondence with Hume, Reid is more explicit: "I can attend to what I feel, and the sensation is nothing else, nor has any other qualities than what I feel it to have. Its *esse* is *sentiri*, and nothing can be in it that is not felt" (IHM 258; see C 113). According to these passages, the phenomenal, purely qualitative experience is all and only what is involved in a sensation state.

Second, in Reid's description of the nature of pain he says that pains are the feeling of them:

The form of expression, *I feel pain*, might seem to imply that the feeling is something distinct from the pain felt; yet, in reality, there is no distinction. As *thinking a thought* is an expression which could signify no more than *thinking*, so *feeling a pain* signifies no more than *being pained*. What we have said of pain is applicable to every other mere sensation. ... [T]he sensation by itself ... appears to be something which can have no existence but in a sentient mind, no distinction from the act of the mind by which it is felt. (IHM 6.20, 168/183a)

This sentiment is consistent across the major works. In the *Intellectual Powers* Reid says, "In sensation, there is no object distinct from that act of the mind by which it is felt" (EIP 2.16, 194/310a).

Third, Reid addresses this issue by distinguishing two meanings to the word "feeling." The first refers to a mode of perceiving through touch. The second "is the same thing as *sensation*, which we have just now explained; and, in this sense, it has no object; the feeling and the thing felt are one and the same thing" (EIP 1.1, 38/229b–230a). Advocates of adverbial theories that understand sensations to be ways of sensing take this to imply that sensations are not intentional states of mind. In another passage Reid distinguishes between two aspects of the experience of hunger in a way that adds support to an interpretation on which sensations are non-intentional states:

The appetite of hunger includes an uneasy sensation, and a desire of food. Sensation and desire are different acts of the mind. The last, from its nature, must have an object; the first has no object. These two ingredients may always be separated in thought; perhaps they sometimes are, in reality; but hunger includes both (EIP 2.16, 196/311a).

Here too Reid says that the sensation accompanying a perception "has no object."

Next, Reid says, "the name sensation should, in philosophical writings, be appropriated to signify this simple act of the mind, without including any thing more in its signification, or being applied to other purposes" (EIP 1.1, 37/229b; see EIP 2.16, 199/312b; and IHM 2.2, 26–27/105a). If a mental operation were simple, this would seem to imply that it has no internal structure. This offers support for the view that sensations are incapable of having the type of act/object structure that intentional states require. But Reid also says that "there is still in these sensations something of a composition" (IHM 3, 47–48/116a).

The prevailing view in the literature on this issue states that Reid offers an "adverbial" theory of sensations. This is supported by the texts used thus far, and by appeal to Reid's opposition to the Way of Ideas. Contemporary advocates of the adverbial theory of sensation have given Reid's theory renewed voice. They are interested in avoiding varied problems (perceptual, metaphysical, and ontological) associated with the reification of sensation states. One might wonder to what degree Reid's analysis of sensations is similar to adverbial analyses given by Chisholm, Ducasse, and others. Chisholm himself says that the inspiration for his development of an adverbial theory of sensation lies in Reid's work (1957, ch. 8). A number of statements of this view resemble Reid's in content and presentation, including this one: "although it is undeniable that pains exist and people have them, it is also clear that this describes a condition of one entity, the person, rather than a relation between two entities, the person and a pain. For pains to exist *is* for people to have them" (Nagel 1965, 342). An adverbial theory of sensation typically attempts to explain phenomenological aspects of perceptual experience while not reifying intermediating objects of perception like ideas. Also adverbial sensations do not possess any intrinsic representative properties. These commitments are not presented as necessary conditions upon an adverbial theory—one might have an adverbial theory and claim that sensations are all we know (perhaps Condillac), or have an adverbial theory and claim that there are intermediating ideas (perhaps Descartes).

But while the similarity between Reid's theory and typical contemporary adverbial theories is not cosmetic, there remain important differences that make the assertion that Reid is an adverbialist ill advised. Reid's approach serves epistemic purposes, which marks a difference of philosophical strategy. Theories like Reid's have been resurrected to assist in the construction of a more parsimonious account of the mind than is otherwise available. Reid is not motivated by intuitions about parsimony and reduction, or even by an interest in blocking a representative realist theory of perception per se. He wants to be true to the phenomenology of sensation experience and offer a theory of sensation that comports with observations of the perceptual process in members of our species.

Others are correct to say, about this similarity between Chisholm's theory and Reid's, that Reid's "theory" of sensation fostered a contrast with the view that we passively receive ideas, but that it lacks the systematic structure needed in order to justify the claim that Reid offers an adverbial theory (Madden 1986, 272). Reid wants to insure that at least some perceptual knowledge is non-inferential. If we are aware of mind-independent bodies only by virtue of being aware of our sensations, which represent them, then we will be hard-pressed to prove that we have non-inferential knowledge of the external world. Despite affinities between Reid's discussion and adverbial theories, Reid does not employ his proposal for the same sorts of problem-solving purposes as his contemporary followers. (Of course, the fact that Reid tailors his theory for different ends does not imply that his theory thereby evades criticisms addressed to adverbial theories (see Jackson 1977, ch. 3).)[3]

---

[3] One critic, J. Todd Buras, argues that the adverbial theory of sensations leads to a vicious regress. The "adverbial interpretation must insist, as intimated earlier, that sensations are accompanied by other

3.5. Natural Signs and Suggestion

Reid puts this account of sensations into the service of his theory of natural signs. In the right circumstances, a grimace or a pressure sensation or even a material impression on the retina can be a natural sign that prompts one to form a perceptual concept. Seeing a grimace may prompt the formation of belief that the subject who is grimacing is in physical pain. A pressure sensation may prompt a perception of the hardness of the table upon which one's hands rest. A retinal impression can signify the visible figure of an object of perception. Thus there are a number of different categories of "natural sign." In each category, a different type of input will yield a different type of output, though all outputs are cognitive.

Reid is explicit that his two terms of art, "suggestion" and "natural sign," are interdefinable. He says that the "connection which Nature hath established betwixt our sensations and the conception and belief of external objects" is describable in two ways. In the first, "a certain sensation of touch both suggests to the mind the conception of hardness, and creates the belief of it: or, in other words, that this sensation is a natural sign of hardness" (IHM 5.3, 58/121a–b). Officially, sensations signify qualities and suggest conceptions and beliefs about qualities. Reid's relation between sensation and object has been called a "cognitive semiotic connection" (Jacquette 2003, 281). Many sensations are signs. What they do is suggest. What they suggest are intentional perceptions of primary qualities. What makes the process natural, according to Reid, is that it occurs without aid of reasoning or resemblance.

Reid knowingly borrows these terms of art from Berkeley, but he has his own reason for keeping them in his lexicon:

modes of thought which take sensations as their objects. Since Reid acknowledges no unconscious modes of thought, the accompanying modes of thought are themselves objects of thought" (Buras 2005, 232). From here, he develops a regress argument: "They therefore either take themselves as objects or they are the objects of yet another mode of thought. Suppose they take themselves as objects. This commits Reid to an invidious distinction. There are no grounds to deny that sensations are reflexive, if we grant that other modes of thought are. Suppose the thoughts by which we take sensations as objects are themselves objects of yet another mode of thought. In this case, a regress looms: the thought by which we take sensations as objects is the object of another mode of thought, and so on ad infinitum. Since all modes of thought are conscious for Reid, the regress is vicious. The result would be an actual infinity of conscious thoughts accompanying every sensation—which is absurd" (2005, 232).

The adverbialist denies the exclusive disjunction with which Buras leads. It is false of an adverbial theory that either sensations take themselves as objects or they are objects of other mental states. Sensations can perform their work as natural and artificial signs without being objects of other states of mind. Sensations are like epiphenomenal qualities in that they have no causal powers as such, even though they have significatory powers to draw the mind on to qualities. Epiphenomenal qualities avoid Buras's disjunction. Implying a vicious regress is not one of the adverbial theories problems. Reid's theory of consciousness does face a regress problem (see Lehrer 1986–7), but this does not bear on his theory of sensations.

Because the mind passes immediately from the sensation to that conception and belief of the object which we have in perception, in the same manner as it passes from signs to the things signified by them, we have therefore called our sensations *signs of external objects*; finding no word more to express the function which nature hath assigned to them in perception, and the relation which they bear to their corresponding objects. (IHM 6.21, 177/188a; see IHM 6.24, 190/195a)

This is akin to the way we do not notice the sounds of a language we speak, but rather move directly to the meanings of the spoken words (IHM 6.2, 81–2/135a). The sounds of spoken language are mere signs, not objects of thought themselves.

For a sign to signify something a "real connection" between the two must be present. This connection can be the product of nature or a product of the "will and appointment of men." If of the will of men, the sign is artificial, which provides the contrast class for natural signs. Reid says, "words, whether expressed by articulate sounds or by writing, are artificial signs of our thoughts and purposes" (IHM 2.21, 177/188a). Familiar cultural signs, such as the red light, which signals us to stop our cars, are artificial signs.[4]

Reid in no less than three places draws distinctions between types of natural sign. I select his second taxonomy of signs and use that to explain the relationship between sensations and intentional content. For the sake of completeness, see Table 1 for all three of Reid's sets of distinctions.

In the second taxonomy, at IHM 59–60/121b–22a, Reid articulates a tripartite distinction of natural signs, which I will call "experiential signs," "instinctual signs," and "constitutional signs." (Reid does not give each type a proper name.) The types are distinguished on the basis of the means by which we know (or do not know) of the connection between sign and thing signified.

Experiential signs suggest the perception of physical states of affairs wherein the connection between the sign and state of affairs is established only by experience and empirical research—as in "mechanics, astronomy, and optics" (IHM 5.3, 59/121b). Our observations of the skies eventually suggest to us facts about the orbits of the planets around the sun, but not without research and reasoning on our parts. The sound of a fire engine is a sensation that suggests the presence of a fire engine, but only in virtue of past experiences of that sound conjoined with the presence of fire engines. The majority of the sensation experiences that are signs can be denominated as experiential signs.

---

[4] Reid claims that the suggestion of perceptual beliefs in vision is "immediate" (IHM 6.8, 101/146b; see Falkenstein and Grandi 2003, 125–6). Reid says that visible figure is "suggested immediately by the material impression upon the organ" (IHM 5.8, 74/131b). This indicates that there are two forms of suggestion by sign, immediate and mediate. He says little explicitly about this.

Table 1. Three sets of distinctions between types of natural sign[5]

Types of Sign	Inquiry 2.7	Inquiry 5.3	Inquiry 6.21
	38/111a–b	59–60/121b	177–8/188a
Instinctual		Origin: "discovered to us by a natural principle" Signifies: seeing angry face prompts fright in infant	
Constitutional	Origin: "natural and original" Signifies: all sensations suggest one's persistence through time; tactile sensations suggest extension and solidity	Origin: discovered "as it were, by a natural kind of magic" Signifies: all sensations suggest one's persistence through time; tactile sensations suggest extension and solidity	Origin: "original principle of our constitution" Signifies: tactile sensations suggest extension and solidity
Habitual	Origin: "experience and habit" Signifies: aural sensation suggests coach passing		Origin: by "custom" Signifies: visual sensations with proper experience signify distance
Experiential		Origin: "discovered by experience" Signifies: beliefs about chemistry and mechanics	Origin: by "reasoning" Signifies: "all that reason discovers of the course of nature"; no examples; chemistry and mechanics?

Reid adds that all of our acquired perceptions can be found in the category of experiential signs (see Chapter 8). Specifically, visual perception in accord

---

[5] Reid has no compelling reason to offer three distinct sets of signs, and he has many reasons not to do so. We might censure Reid, but we can also make a developmental point. The troublesome category of signs by custom, incipient in the *Inquiry*, takes form in the *Intellectual Powers*. Reid devotes extended

with experiential signs "by custom" explains our ability to get information about the distance of objects, even though distance is not a direct object of visual perception (IHM 2.21, 177/188a).

Instinctual signs are the second type of sign in his second taxonomy. They suggest mental states "wherein the connection between the sign and thing signified, is not only established by nature, but discovered to us by a natural principle, without reasoning or experience" (IHM 5.3, 60/122a). Elsewhere Reid seems to describe this category of sign when saying that some signs signify things and prompt beliefs "previous to experience" (IHM 6.24, 190/195a). This form of suggestion captures the instinctual way that certain sensations inform me of my body's reaction to features of the world. An acrid smell signals that I should not ingest that which is emanating the smell. This sensation produces this effect independent of any experience or learning on my part. Had I never experienced such a smell before, the smell would nonetheless produce this effect. This category of sign is capable of explaining a number of behaviors. "An infant may be put into a fright by an angry countenance, and soothed again by smiles and blandishments. A child that has a good musical ear, may be put to sleep or to dance, may be made merry or sorrowful, by the modulation of musical sounds" (IHM 5.3, 60/122a). Our innate language of gestures and facial features—which adults use as well—compose the bulk of this group of instinctual signs.

Constitutional signs are the third type of sign in Reid's second taxonomy. These signs suggest mental states wherein the connection between the sign and intentional content is unknown. Constitutional signs are building blocks for all perceptual beliefs, and are the signs upon which experiential signs are built. In this group are numbered signs "which, though we never before had any notion or conception of the thing signified, do suggest it, or conjure it up, as it were, by a natural kind of magic, and at once give us a conception and create a belief of it" (IHM 5.3, 60/122a). (Placed into the present context, this remark calls to mind Hilary Putnam's dismissal of "magical theories of reference" (Putnam 1981, 3).) Concepts of primary qualities are formed in virtue of tactile sensations functioning as constitutional signs. For example, we obtain a concept of hardness in virtue of "an original principle of our nature, annexed to that sensation which we have when we feel a hard body" (IHM 5.3, 60/122b). Later he adds, "Nature, by means of the sensations of touch, informs us of the hardness and softness of bodies; of their extension,

---

attention to the distinction between original and acquired perception there. Under the aegis of this distinction Reid explains the roles of custom and learning in the formation of complex perceptual beliefs and the accretion of levels of cognition in perception (see Chapter 8).

figure, and motion; and of that space in which they move and are placed"
(IHM 2.21, 178/188a). In the proper circumstances the sensation cues or calls
to mind the quality of hardness, though the workings of the process are not
transparent to reason. It remains unknown and mysterious, as he remarks here
of the notion of space: "It seems then by a kind of inspiration or original
perception we know that there is space of which our bodies occupy a part"
(Aberdeen MS 2131/8/II/21, 5). Constitutional signs are the crucial category
for our purposes, since Reid believes they do the work missing from the
accounts of his predecessors. Constitutional signs provide the contrast between
the sign theories of Berkeley and Reid. Berkeley does not differentiate what
we have called habitual and experiential types of sign from constitutional signs.
Constitutional signs are in a class of their own, and cannot be wholly explained
by appeal to custom and habit.

If we restrict our attention to the second and most prominent set of
distinctions between natural signs, several pressing questions remain. One
regards the ambiguous relationships between types of sign. Reid does not
explain how the first and third forms of sign interrelate. Constitutional signs
prompt us to form perceptions with intentional content about primary qualities
of bodies. By means of experiential signs certain sensations allow us to form
beliefs about specific objects that we individuate and re-identify because we
have had prior experience of them. I perceptually apprehend a horse-drawn
coach in virtue of my hearing the sound of its wheels on a gravel road. So, in the
perceptual process, constitutional signs appear to be prior chronologically and
conceptually to instances of experiential signs. In order to apprehend through
perception that the object I hear is a coach, I must have prior sensory experience
of the coach itself, which Reid recognizes. But on pains of circularity this
prior sensory experience of the coach must at some point involve sensations
that do not fall within the realm of experiential signs. Since sensations are not
intentional, there must have been sensations that I experienced without prior
knowledge that they signified things such as coaches and horses.

Our apprehension of the coach qua coach is not given to us immediately
through the instinctual or constitutional forms of sign; this is why it belongs
in the experiential category. Since we learn through experiences what coaches
are, and with what sensations they are associated, our experiences of the coach
and its parts can be resolved into those sensations that suggest the primary
qualities of the coach. Helpful though it would have been, Reid does not
analyze in detail the train of operations that give rise to our initial concept
of a coach. Even so, our concept of a coach, and of any similarly complex
thing, depends upon our prior concepts of the primary qualities. In other
words, I would not possess the intentional awareness of a coach had I not

acquired and applied concepts of extension, motion, position, and shape. Not wanting to invoke ideas, Reid refrains from using a distinction between simple and complex ideas to address the means by which we acquire sophisticated concepts and use them in perception. But if I am correct, Reid intends the class of experiential signs to piggyback upon the more fundamental classes of instinctual and constitutional signs.

3.6. Sensations and Intentional Perceptual Awareness

Reid does not attempt to explain in any more detail how sensations generate intentional content in perceptions. This is part of the point of introducing the schema in the first place. One valuable lesson he has learned from past failures is that any appeal to further mechanisms or principles will either fail or lapse into hypothetical speculation. This is why he opposes the theses stated in Section 3.1—they attempt reductively to explain how our sensory experience gives rise to intentional content in perceptions. This leaves us with the vexing task of understanding how constitutional signs serve to represent intentional perceptions of primary qualities.

One way that sensations can signify qualities is in virtue of the intentional content of the sensations themselves. If sensations have intentional objects, or in other words, if sensations are intrinsically intentional, and those objects are mind-independent qualities, then we have an explanation of how it is they signify. Consider the hardness I experience as I touch a tabletop. This experience suggests to me that the surface of the table is hard, and *ipso facto* extended. My sensation may be thought to represent the table's hardness because of the intrinsic character of that experience. One theory of this form is found in what Locke says about primary qualities. Our ideas of sensation can represent extension and motion in the way that a photographic image resembles the landscape of which it is a picture.

One commentator says Reid holds that "some of our mental contents—sensations—point beyond themselves and beyond the purely mental to objects. Thus sensations must carry within them external referentiality, which points towards the objects and qualities of objects which make up our experience." This is thought to be what Reid means when he says "sensations function as signs" (Rollin 1978, 265). This account treats sensations as intentional states in much the same way that memories, beliefs, and perceptions are intentional. The content of the thought *the cat is on the mat* is about a cat being on a mat because of the speaker's meaning in uttering that statement. The interpretation of sensations under discussion holds that their representational power derives from the fact that they "carry within them external referenti-ality." Sensations *intrinsically* possess intentional properties through which we individuate and refer to mind-independent qualities.

A theory describing the representational capacity of sensations as "intrinsic" contrasts with a theory on which the representational capacity of sensations arises in virtue of arbitrary relationships between sensations and the things they represent. On the latter theory, which I am advocating as an interpretation of Reid, sensations *extrinsically* represent primary qualities. Reid repudiates theories on which sensations intrinsically represent. Such an interpretation is odd because it attempts to account for the intentionality of perception, which cannot be done, in terms of something, sensation, that Reid does not believe is intentional.

In addition to the textual evidence cited above for a non-intentional interpretation of the content of sensations, there are a few further considerations we can make against the claim that sensations are intrinsically representational. Sensations signal qualities of objects only when properly coupled with an original principle of suggestion, so their representational capacity derives from the union of their qualitative content, the perceptual context, and the principle of suggestion that links the sensory experience with the object. Reid says that specific sensations suggest the qualities they do only because God has ordained it and not for any reasoning having to do with the intrinsic character of sensations (EIP 2.16, 198/312a). Like Berkeley, Reid also uses pain as a paradigm of sensations, denies sensations have an act/object structure, claims that the essence of a sensation lies in its being felt, and holds that every sensation occurs in a mind. But this agreement must not be taken to extend to Berkeley's further claim that sensations are intentional objects of perceptual states (Cummins 1975, 61–3). The *qualitative content*, but not the *representational capacity*, of sensations is intrinsic to them.

Second, recall the contrast between what Reid calls "natural" and "artificial" signs. If the sign and thing signified is the product of human art and contrivance, the sign is artificial. Hearing the word "frog" suggests in our minds a thought of the amphibians we know by that name, but the word "has no similitude to the substance signified by it; nor is it in its own nature more fit to signify this than any other substance" (IHM 5.3, 58/121b). The representational relationships governing our use of the word "frog," our apprehension of its meaning, and the sensations that cue our perceptions of frogs are all arbitrary and the product of human activity. In a similar way, sensations of pressure suggest concepts of hardness and thereby represent hardness. Sensations only represent primary qualities insofar as they represent extrinsically.

Yet this does not imply that sensations of pressure are not natural signs (and are artificial signs). Reid draws the distinction between natural and artificial signs by appeal to their relationship to human experience, and not in terms of the arbitrary relationship between the intrinsic content of a sensation and the thing it signifies. The representational relationship between a sensation of pressure and the primary quality of hardness is extrinsic in several senses. The qualitative content of the sensation experience does not take the token quality of hardness as its intentional object. Furthermore, the relation between the sensation as natural sign and the thing signified is contingent. The conventions that have given way to our constitutional signs, whether the effects of God or nature, are in our cognitive psychology as original principles. By the vicissitudes of our constitution, its divine endowment and the history of our species, we are disposed to form certain intentional perceptions in response to certain sensations. In this sense all sensations that function as constitutional signs do so extrinsically and not by their intrinsic features.[6]

Before leaving the issue, I wish to draw a distinction of considerable importance between whether sensations *take or have* intentional objects, and whether sensations *are* intentional objects of other mental states. These issues are logically independent. One may hold that sensations take objects but are not objects, or that they do not take objects but are objects. I will deal with the question of whether sensations are objects of intentional mental states (the more prevalent issue) in Chapter 7, when we examine the role of sensation in the larger perceptual process. Here we have—and have only—determined that the representational power of those sensations that function as natural signs lies in the role they play, and not in any intrinsic property. They are thus extrinsically representational.[7]

---

[6] Others have now adopted a similar apparatus to make the same point in reference to Reid. Van Cleve distinguishes between "autonomous" and "dependent" forms of representation. Dependent representations are only representations in virtue of the fact that they activate autonomous sources of information. Furthermore, the two are only contingently linked. Autonomous states are intrinsically representational, and require no interpretation on the part of an agent (Van Cleve 2004a, 409–10; see Copenhaver 2004). Conceptual and perceptual forms of acquaintance are autonomous in this respect. Sensations are dependent because they represent only in virtue of the fact that our minds or brains are wired to form concepts in response to sensations.

[7] Hume objects to Reid's argument on the grounds that Reid's crucial test presupposes that there are innate ideas. Hume levels this objection to Reid after being given parts of Reid's *Inquiry* via their mutual friend Hugh Blair. Replying to Reid through Blair, Hume writes: "If I comprehend the Author's Doctrine, which, I own, I can hitherto do but imperfectly, it leads us back to innate Ideas" (Wood 1986, 416). Since there are no innate ideas, Reid must be mistaken. John Wright (1987 and 1991) has explained and defended Hume's objection to Reid. But Reid does not endorse a theory of innate ideas. Instead, he posits innate, original capacities. When coupled with the propensity of certain sensations naturally to suggest certain primary quality concepts, Reid needn't affirm that the mind stores innate ideas.

3.7. Berkeley's Objection: Straw Man

Though that problem is assuaged, Reid's crucial test is plagued by other difficulties. One may object to Reid's unwillingness to consider transcendental features of our experience of the world. Specifically, Reid presupposes that it is metaphysically possible that the subject has the experiences described in the Sensory Deprivation argument without having any "body image." Perhaps he is wrong to do so.[8] At the least, Reid does not consider the pressure sensations of the agent's body as he rests on the table, sensations which are stimulated along a length and width. But rather than focusing upon these problems I turn to a bigger threat.

Reid's predecessors, Berkeley in particular, would reply that the theories of concept acquisition with which Reid has saddled them are pale imitations of their actual theories. Berkeley will claim that sensations give rise to concepts only when they are properly combined in thought. His approach lies in his groundbreaking operational analysis of perceptual apprehension. On this theory one's perceptual awareness of a primary quality is equivalent to an awareness of those sensations one would have, were one to experience the quality. For example, Berkeley says that distance concepts are composed of a series of imagined sensations. "Looking at an object I perceive a certain visible figure and colour, with some degree of faintness and other circumstances, which from what I have formerly observed, determine me to think that if I advance forward so many paces or miles, I shall be affected with such and such ideas of touch" (NTV §45 WGB i, 188). Berkeley expends more effort analyzing concepts such as distance than he does concepts of specific shapes, but he would claim that a nexus of closely related tactile sensations constitutes one's concepts of shapes. Keith DeRose comments:

Berkeley does not think of our concepts of solidity and tangible figure (for example, the concept of a sphere) as being images of single tactile sensations, but rather to be a knowledge that certain types of tangible ideas tend to go together, particularly in conjunction with certain actions. … Of course it is absurd to think that the sword is like a tactile sensation, but now it can be held that to think about the sword or any of

---

[8] Reid's third-person description of the subject's experience invokes the concept of the subject's body, but Reid precludes the subject from invoking a concept of his own body as he experiences sensory stimulation. A subject need not have a discursive concept of "body" or "my body" in order to experience the sensations Reid administers. An adult who has no language skills would be capable of experiencing the battery of sensations. However, it isn't obvious that it is physically possible that the subject can experience those tactile sensations without any body image. One might build an argument against Reid from intuitions about the categories and the unity of apperception. Reid must claim that this is physically possible since otherwise he begs the question. Setting aside Reid's anaemic pleas about what he finds himself unable to conceive, he hasn't addressed such an objection.

its qualities is to know what sensations one would have if there were a sword present and if certain actions were taken. (DeRose 1989, 341).

On this counterfactual account, a concept of a primary quality is formed on the basis of a range of tactile sensations. The tactile sensations to which Berkeley entitles himself are diverse, including kinesthetic, skin, and muscle sensations. Were the subject of Reid's crucial test permitted to experience a range of tactile sensations at once, then, the suggestion goes, he would be able to form ideas of what he would experience were he to have similar sensations. DeRose concludes that Reid has not given Berkeley his due.[9]

Some responses are open to Reid. First, Berkeley's discussion of the phenomenology of sensation experience is insufficiently detailed to tell us *when it is* that an agent moves from having no concept of body to having a concept of body. Without a response to this issue, Berkeley's theory is incomplete.

But a Berkeleyan might reply with a similar point of his own. Even if Berkeley cannot identify the moment at which an agent acquires a primary quality concept from sensations, Reid has not given the agent an opportunity to reach that point. The subject in Reid's rapid-fire crucial test is not portrayed as exemplifying the patience that a human being may need to acquire concepts. While Reid does allow the subject the use of "the power of reason" (IHM 5.6, 65/125b), Reid takes no pains to describe the role that reflection might play in the process. Instead Reid inadvertently trivializes the role of reflection by feeding the subject one sensation at a time, thereby leaving him very little to reflect upon. An agent like the subject who is deprived of his sensations would need a panoply of sensation experience, and the time to bring coherence to it, if he is to have any hope of achieving an intentional perceptual awareness of primary qualities. This may require the agent to move his body, to understand how certain sensations follow upon others, and how his body is capable of creating sensations. Reid has arguably begged the question against Berkeley on this count.

Wolterstorff offers a different Reidian response to Berkeley. What is left undeveloped in the foregoing analysis of the dialectic is Berkeley's core commitment to a non-realist (either phenomenalist or idealist) analysis of objects. DeRose says that the apprehension of hardness amounts to an apprehension of the sensations one thinks would be had if one were to push against the object

---

[9] We should not be misled by Berkeley's appeal to visual sensations in the passage above. Visual sensations can play a role in my acquisition of concepts of primary qualities despite the fact that they are not necessary for that process. Berkeley's own account of natural signs assists in explaining how. When experience has associated the look of a sword with previous tactile sensations, the visual sensation alone can prompt me to model the types of sensation I would have were I to feel the sword. With sufficient experience, by sight alone I can come to know that the thing I see has primary qualities such as hardness and extension, that is, by sight I know that it would feel thus and so when I touch it.

(DeRose 1989, 341). Wolterstorff wants to know what "is the force of thinking of the sensations we would have if *it* were in front of us? What is that *it*?" (Wolterstorff 2001, 90). The force of the rhetorical question lies in challenging Berkeley to explain his counterfactual analysis of sensations without committing himself to a realist analysis of objects. The analysand is either a primary quality of a material body or not. If it is, then Berkeley's counterfactual analysis would imply that the subject cannot directly apprehend its primary qualities for any attempt at apprehending its primary qualities would only yield a set of counterfactual statements regarding the subject's sensation experience.

The second lemma better represents Berkeley. If the analysand is not a primary quality of a material body, then we must admit that Berkeley's account is aiming at something very different from Reid's account. On this reading I am uncertain what DeRose's counterfactual analysis of concepts of primary qualities amounts to. The concept *hardness* refers to or picks out those sensations I would experience, were I to feel a hard body. But now the concept of hardness occurs in its own analysis. The same is true of the example about the sword.

We must press this point: how do I come to know the counterfactual conditions about sensations that characterize my concept of hardness without presupposing that I already have a concept of hardness? To see the force of this point, imagine Berkeley as the subject of Reid's thought experiment and upon his table. At some point, after experiencing several tactile sensations of pressure, Berkeley suddenly utters that he now has concepts of extension, hardness, solidity, and motion. He says that solidity is that series of sensations he would have, were he to experience a solid body. Reid would conclude that this subject had not understood the purpose of the thought experiment. Primary qualities are by definition mind-independent and are not the sorts of things that do not exist if I do not sense them. In contrast to Berkeley, Reid simply *assumes* that there are mind-independent primary qualities of which we form intentional perceptions, and then seeks a scientifically acceptable account of our notions of them.

3.8. Condillac's Objection: From Straw Man to Statue

Condillac's memorable thought experiment[10] in the *Treatise on Sensations* provides a detailed reconstruction of what it would be like to acquire an

---

[10] In this section I draw upon Condillac's discussion in the *Treatise on Sensations*, not from the earlier *Essay on the Origin of Human Knowledge*. In the *Essay*, sensations and perceptions refer to the same

intentional concept of a primary quality. The thought experiment is quite similar to Reid's crucial test but with the opposite aim. Condillac intends to support a radical sensationalist theory of the acquisition of intentional content without any assistance from innate ideas or abilities. A brief comparison of their two thought experiments will illuminate Reid's crucial test, and a problem with it.[11]

Imagine an adult human being who has had no sensations, no innate concepts, no innate abilities, and no prior sensory experiences. The subject can reason and can remember events once she experiences them. Condillac describes her as being like a statue. We may follow him in the use of the term, even though it is metaphorical; this subject is fully outfitted with natural human capacities, but is devoid of all experience. The subject is given use of her senses one at a time, beginning with smell (because it is the simplest). A rose is placed below her nose and she experiences an olfactory sensation. Sensations are qualitative and non-intentional states of mind for Condillac—at least by

type of mental state, though they have different sources. As he defines these terms, perception is "the impression produced in the presence of objects; *sensation*, the same impression regarded as coming from the senses" (Condillac 1987, 489/1.3.16). Early in the book he says that "the idea of perception can only come from reflection on what we experience while some sensation is affecting us" (Condillac 1987, 443/1.2.1.1). He argues that sensations are representative. As a result he claims that "perceptions of light, color, solidity, and other sensations are more than sufficient to yield all the ideas we commonly have of objects" (1987, 436/1.1.2.9). But this is coupled with the announcement, in the first sentence of the book, that "all we ever perceive is our own thought" (1987, 433/1.1.1.1). In short, this makes our perceptions about modifications of our own mind. An "idea," though, is "the knowledge we get from [the impression] as an image" (*Essay* 1.3.16). Condillac believes that the representational capacity of visual sensations produces ideas in a subject merely by the subject being aware of her visual sensations. This transition from sensation to idea resembles Hume's discussion of the transition from impression to idea. Condillac says: "I look in front of me, up, down, to the right, and to the left. I see a light diffused in all directions and several colors that are certainly not concentrated in a point. I need nothing else. There, independently of any judgment and without the help of the other senses, I find the idea of extension in all its dimensions" (1987, 517/1.6.12).

Condillac has explained the origin of the intentional content in perceptions, but at a high price. Since sensations are representative, but do not represent mind-independent primary qualities, the color sensations to which he averts are not representative of external objects. They are experienced as being extended and directional, but their intentional content is not constituted by features of mind-independent bodies. Falkenstein pinpoints the problem as being that "these spatially disposed colours are not in us as physical impressions. Instead, they are paradoxically taken to be impressions on an unextended mind." Falkenstein adds: "Since the subject of perception is immaterial, it follows that the 'impression' that constitutes perception (recall the definition of perception as an impression arising in the subject in the presence of objects) cannot be a physical impression made by objects on the sense organs. It must be some other sort of modification of the soul, and the presence of external objects must serve merely as its occasional cause" (Falkenstein 2005, 414). As a result Condillac's claim in the *Essay* that visual sensations "trace out extension" is confused.

[11] It is a tantalizing prospect to suppose that Reid read Condillac's *Treatise*, which, published in 1754, predates Reid's *Inquiry* by a decade. To my knowledge there is no direct evidence that he did—no mention of Condillac in the corpus, no reading notes, etc. However, the choice of examples and the approach of his thought experiment provide some reason to think Reid did read Condillac.

the writing of the *Treatise*. Condillac takes pain sensations as paradigmatic and adopts a view on which sensations are not representational: "If I actually experience pain, I would not say that I have the idea of pain; I would say that I sense it" (1982, 1.3.14/167). So, when having an olfactory sensation of a rose, the subject does not form any awareness of the rose as external to her. Since the subject has no innate abilities, she is unable to conceive of mind-independent qualities of the world if only given a sense of smell.

Condillac suggests (without using personal pronouns to describe the "statue") that "to itself, it will be the smell itself of this flower.... In short, smells are for it only its own modifications or states" (1982, 1.2.2−3/175). Some smells generate pleasant sensations, others unpleasant sensations. This accounts for the origins of pain and pleasure. She experiences pleasure when confronted with a pleasant smell, for example, but she cannot yet have desires. Condillac emphasizes the role of pain and pleasure since they will prompt the subject to remember the olfactory sensations, and, eventually, to have the desire to re-experience or avoid the sensation.

The statue becomes capable of making comparisons between smells by demonstratively re-identifying them with the aid of her memory. Condillac stresses the utility of surprise. The statue will be shocked out of complacency when a smell constantly in its experience is replaced by an unknown smell. "The more abrupt the transition from some of them to others, the greater its surprise and also the more striking the contrast between the pleasures and pains accompanying the changes." This prompts the statue to compare them more carefully, which leads Condillac to remark that "pleasure and pain are always the prime movers of its faculties" (1982, 1.2.18/180). Unpleasant smells prompt the statue to compare them with pleasant smells, and to wish to return to pleasant smells. This gives rise to what she presents to herself as her needs (1982, 1.2.25/182). The experience of needs creates the capacity for imagination. She wants to experience a smell that she is not now experiencing. In contrast to Condillac's inference that "pleasure and pain" are "prime movers" in the development of the subject's ability to acquire new perceptual contents, Reid does not mention the ways pain and pleasure sensations would structure a subject's reflection upon his or her sensations.

But how does Condillac believe that the statue will develop intentional perceptions of primary qualities? Condillac says that even upon having (and only having) the faculties of smell, hearing, and vision, she would be unable to develop intentional perceptions of primary qualities like extension, shape, and space. By setting the bar so high Condillac's approach resonates with Reid's. Condillac not only advocates a form of radical empiricism opposed to Reid's appeal to natural signs, but he does so in a way that abides by some of Reid's conditions. Specifically, Condillac and Reid agree that an (allegedly Humean) isomorphism, on which one sensory impression gives rise to one idea, is false.

First, let's consider which tactile sensations are incapable of producing intentional contents about mind-independent objects. Suppose the statue to have no sense other than touch. If so, the temperature of the air and her sensations of her internal organs are important in this process. Yet, even if the air is warmed or the heart caused to pump faster, or even if she is struck in the same location repeatedly, she will gain no notion of extension. If someone moves her arm, she will not acquire the concept of movement or motion (1982, 2.2/226–7). Whereas it does not occur to Reid to give his subject a diversity of simultaneous sensations, Condillac gives the statue "at the same time warmth on one arm, cold on another, a pain in the head, a tickling in the feet, a discomfiture in the bowels, etc." (1982, 2.3.1/228). However, Condillac says that even this will not produce any apprehension of three-dimensional extension.

The reason lies in an obscure necessary condition for acquiring intentional perceptual content: "because an [extended] object is a continuum formed by the contiguity of other extended objects, the sensation that represents it must be a continuum formed by the contiguity of other extended sensations" (1982, 2.4.2/230). Despite what is said in the last part of this sentence, Condillac recognizes that sensations "belong only to the mind" and do not "extend" beyond it. After all, if sensations are themselves extended, then having sensations *ipso facto* generates an awareness of extension. What are we to make of this condition?[12]

Condillac seems to hold that tactile sensations must be experienced as being spread across space, even though they themselves are not spatial. I am uncertain how precisely to state this condition in such a way as to make Condillac's proposal consistent.

Condillac believes that the statue can fulfill this requirement by touching her own body in certain ways described at *Treatise* 2.5. For Condillac "impenetrability" is not a sensation but a property of bodies, while "solidity" is the sensation associated with impenetrability. He says:

Since the essence of this sensation of solidity is to represent at one and the same moment two things that exclude each other, the mind will not perceive solidity as one of those states in which it finds only itself; it will perceive it necessarily as a state in which it finds two things that are mutually exclusive and as a result it will perceive it in these two things. (1982 2.5.3/233)

---

[12] Some such condition is necessary, but it is not sufficient for Condillac. The subject must also "analyze, that is to say, it needs to observe its 'I' successively in all the parts where it appears to be found" (*Treatise* 2.4.3/231).

Eventually "naturally, mechanically, by instinct and without being aware of it," the hand will move upon some part of the statue's body. This will produce two sensations of solidity, which places the hand and the chest "necessarily outside of each other." We can add, on his behalf, that the statue would concomitantly experience an additional muscle sensation in the arm that moves the hand.

If any set of sensation experiences is capable of giving rise to perceptions about extension and figure, then a set of these sensation experiences has the best opportunity of doing so. This is due to the qualitative richness and apparently spatial phenomenal qualities experienced simultaneously. Condillac implies that this simultaneous union of three distinct tactile sensations cannot be experienced by a reflective, properly functioning adult without her developing an object-oriented perceptual awareness of extension. Of course, three is the minimum number of sensations specified by this thought experiment. To understand Condillac's meaning, try wrapping the fingers on your right hand around your left forearm. This elicits a host of sensations, some of which are felt as though they are spatially located in the forearm, fingers, thumb, and palm. Do this low enough on your forearm so that your middle finger extends just far enough to come all the way round to your thumb. Corresponding to the location of those sensations in phenomenal space are corollary sensations felt as if they were in your forearm, preventing your fingers from coming to rest upon your palm. You also sense the warmth of your arm in your palm, and you can experience muscle sensations. Constrict your fingers and simultaneously flex your forearm to experience a pair of distinct muscle sensations that appear to be in a contiguous phenomenal space.

In this way I form a notion of the impenetrability of a region of space occupied by a part of my own body. This is not quite a notion of mind-independent extension. Perhaps this region of a statue's own body through which his fingers cannot move would be perceived as being a region of phenomenal space. The primary quality of mind-independent extension is not clearly separated in thought from a Berkeleyan concept of extension as being a set of counterfactuals about my sensation experience.

But consider Condillac's transition between first feeling the nexus of sensations in that case, and then experiencing another set of sensations associated with one's fingers wrapping around something such as a teacup. In this case I experience a similar set of sensations as being located in my fingers, but I lack a corollary set of sensations as being located in my forearm. The pressure sensations in my fingers signal that there is a region through which they cannot move, and which is also not occupied by other sensations. That is, there is a mind-independent region of space that abuts my fingers; this space does not "feel back," as it were. When the hand touches something that is *not* the statue's own body, the statue receives no response even though it experiences a sensation of solidity through its hand.

Barring appeals to innate abilities and ideas, and to a "natural kind of magic," this is a subtle and plausible account. I leave it as an open question whether Condillac is correct that this robust sequence of sensation experiences can prompt a perceptual content that takes the extension of a mind-independent body as its intentional object. The present point, critical of Reid, is that he does not even consider this type of confluence of simultaneous sensations in his crucial test. The rich phenomenology of Condillac's discussion up to this point alone—we have not recounted the ways the other senses assist the statue's use of touch to learn more about mind-independent qualities—shows that Reid's Sensory Deprivation argument lacks comparative imagination and sophistication. Since Reid withholds this robust sensory experience from his subject, and thus does not reflect on the implications of this sensory experience upon acquiring intentional contents of primary qualities, he attacks a straw man.[13]

3.9. Reid's Reply to Condillac: A New Manuscript

The contrasting features of their thought experiments lead to implicit criticisms of Reid by Condillac. But, surprisingly, Reid has answered several of these points in an early, unpublished manuscript version of his Sensory Deprivation argument. The date of the manuscript remains uncertain, though Giovanni Grandi convincingly argues that it belongs to a period from between 1758 and the first half of 1759 (Grandi 2003, 35–7). Whatever the precise date of composition, Reid wrote these notes several years prior to the publication of the *Inquiry*.

---

[13] One further point of contrast is this. For Condillac, developing the capacity to experience mental states with intentional content is a gradual process. But Reid was worried that, on his view, we would get all our intentional concepts at once. After all, he offers no developmental account of our acquisition of the ability to have perceptions with intentional content. Reid says: "I do not mean to affirm, that the sensations of touch do, from the very first, suggest the same notions of body and its qualities which they do when we are grown up. Perhaps nature is frugal in this, as in her other operations. The passion of love, with all of its concomitant sentiments and desires, is naturally suggested by the perception of beauty in the other sex; yet the perception does not suggest the tender passion till a certain period in life. ... Perhaps a child in the womb, or for some short period of its existence, is merely a sentient being; the faculties by which it perceives an external world, by which it reflects on its own thoughts, and existence, and relation to other things, as well as its reasoning and moral faculties, unfold themselves by degrees" (IHM 5.8, 72/130b). Tactile sensations do not suggest concepts "till a certain period of life," in which respect they are more like the feeling of love than they are like the joint motion of the eyes. This is helpful, if obvious. But Reid shows no more subtlety with regard to the temporal features of sensations in this context.

In this manuscript, Aberdeen MS 2131/8/II/21, Reid exhibits a begrudging admiration for an argument like Condillac's, and addresses Condillac's conclusion about the means by which we learn of extension. Reid says:

> If it should be said that we perceive the extension of a body by its touching any two remote parts of our body the question occurs how we came to learn the distance of these two parts of our body the head & feet for instance. Suppose then I say that I learn the distance of my head & feet, by moving my hand from one to the other. The velocity of this motion & the time give me a perception of the distance between them. And I acknowledge I can find no better account of the matter. But if this is the true account it follows First that the perception of time or duration must be previous to that of extension & consequently that without memory it were impossible to have acquired any idea of extension. (Aberdeen MS 2131/8/II/21, 1)

Reid is discussing an intuition similar to the intuition driving Condillac's thought experiment. Suppose the subject touches her right foot with her right index finger. Then she touches her head with her right index finger. Reid implies that in order to come to an awareness of extension through this experience, she must first perceive or at least be aware of the duration between the moment she touched her foot and the moment she touched her head. Presumably he says this on the grounds that this is necessary for the two experiences to be uniquely individuated by the subject. Reid has a point, but I find it difficult to pinpoint the way in which the subject must necessarily be aware of duration in order to individuate these two tactile sensations.

Either the subject is or is not able to be aware of unique sensory experiences without having a concept of duration. If the subject can individuate sensory experiences without a concept of duration, then it appears that Reid's criticism is misguided. The thought experiment does not presuppose one notion of a primary quality and explain the others in virtue of it. If the subject cannot individuate sensory experiences without a concept of duration, then the thought experiment does not get off the ground. If Reid believes that it is necessarily true that the subject has perceptions of intervals of time in order to be aware of the subject's own experience of two distinct sensations, then Reid should have given a proof for that claim instead of stating the thought experiment.

One way to express this problem with Reid's necessary condition is by observing the role of memory in the subject's experience. The subject is pricked with a pin, and at a later moment, experiences the pressure exerted by a blunt object against his skin. At a third and later moment, he remembers the first sensation, and at a fourth moment he recollects the second sensation. These two distinct memories are sufficient to individuate the first sensation from the second one. The subject needn't have a further mental state through which he is aware of the duration between the two sensory experiences. One can remember X, then remember Y, without needing to remember the time between X and Y. One can also remember something without remembering the time at which one originally had the experience. (Given Reid's analysis of memory, he should agree. See EIP Essay 3.) So it seems an awareness of duration between one tactile sensation and another, as construed as time between, is not necessary for the agent to individuate the two tactile experiences. In other words, Condillac's thought experiment does not beg the question in the way Reid seems to think it must in the manuscript. It follows that this particular objection to the effect that the subject's awareness of two distinct tactile experiences could not give rise to an intentional perceptual awareness of extension fails.

Reid next implies that the subject must have the capacity of memory in order to use this pair of tactile sensations to develop intentional awareness of extension. He is correct that the subject must have some kind of rudimentary ability to recollect the immediately preceding sensation. But how this functions as a criticism is unclear. On the ground rules set by Condillac, the subject is simply given the ability to remember. In the *Inquiry*, Reid does not prohibit the subject from having memory. This inchoate objection to a position similar to Condillac's is unsuccessful.

So far I have applied the comments in Reid's manuscript to Condillac's thought experiment in order to determine whether Reid has the resources to respond to it. On one important count Reid's sophisticated manuscript treatment of the Sensory Deprivation argument falls short of addressing Condillac's proposal. Namely, Condillac's thought experiment does not involve *two successive* tactile sensations, but *three simultaneous* tactile sensations. Not even in the manuscript does Reid consider that the body felt might itself be a part of one's own body. Thus, even if Reid's criticisms were on target, they would not show that Condillac's thought experiment is misguided.

The heart of Reid's manuscript discussion is this:

Suppose a blind man by some strange distemper to have lost all the experience and habits he had got by feeling all notion of extension, figure & motion {even of the figure & dimensions of his own body} but to retain his reasoning & reflecting powers. If he felt a post before him this would not at first hinder his running his head against it. Several unlucky knocks might make him attend to those feelings that went before them and by degrees raise the fear of one when he had those sensuous feelings. When he moved his hand or foot ~~this motion was attended by &~~ he would be conscious of a certain effort {of mind} and a feeling consequent it. This feeling he might {call} motion but it is certainly extremely different from our notion of motion for it would include no notion of space or change of place. He moves his hand variously further & further in the in the [sic.] air These he may conceive as various modifications of what he has called motion in his hand but as that motion includes not extension so neither can its modifications. By one of these modifications he runs his hand against his nose. Some accidents of this kind would teach him the way to his nose and that it was something related unto him. That by a gentle motion of his hand towards it he might feel it & by a more violent motion he might hurt himself. In like manner he may find out other parts of his body & learn ~~the way~~ to conduct his hand to them.

Suppose then that by a long course of observation and reflection he hath learned to give names to the several parts of his face his nose forehead brows eyes mouth lips chin & cheeks &c and that he can at pleasure move his hand to any of them say that he can move one hand to one and another to another part at once. Let us no[w] consider what idea he can from all this Collect of his Face. It seems to be a vastly complex one Made up of an Effort of his hand variously modified as it passes over the severall parts of his face the feelings of the Swelling of the Muscles and Pleasures of the Joints in his hands and fingers the feelings of his face that correspond with these. When I endeavour to put all these together they Seem not to have the least Resemblance to my Idea of a Face. Whether It Resembles the Idea a Blind Man hath of a Face I cannot tell. But it seems to be so far from being got at once by feeling the Face that it must necessarily in the most active and attentive Mind be the work of years the effect of an infinite number {of sucessive} feelings & various modifications of these feelings joyned together they seem to me not to convey the least Idea of Space. Shew me once how by any or all of these feelings we get an idea of length and the difficulty is over. But I confess I am utterly at a loss to conceive how that Idea is got by a blind Man. (Aberdeen MS 2131/8/II/21, 2–3)

This remarkable passage diverges from the *Inquiry's* version of the thought experiment in a number of important ways.

First, certain tactile sensations at the earliest stages of the process are accompanied by feelings of pain and pleasure, and also by emotions such as fear; Reid neglects to discuss these features in the *Inquiry*. Next, in the manuscript the agent is active and moves his own body, his head, as well as his hand and foot; in the *Inquiry* the agent is passive. Third, in the manuscript, Reid concedes that the agent has an intentional concept that he would associate with motion, even if it is inchoate and indeterminate; Reid denies this in the *Inquiry*. These three points are all small steps toward proving to his readers that Reid understands the phenomenological experiences that lead Condillac to the conclusion that our sensory experience alone is sufficient to bring us to intentional awareness of primary qualities.

This still falls short of Condillac's insight, but Reid inches closer to it with two other differences in the manuscript. Through the movement of his arm, by his own locomotion, he comes to touch his hand against his nose. The agent nearly simultaneously experiences at least three distinct sensations—a tactile sensation in his nose at the point of impact, a tactile sensation in his fingers at the point of impact, and a muscle sensation phenomenally located in his arm. I say "at least" since Reid recognizes in the text that the agent may also experience pain. Here Reid describes a sensation experience immensely richer than anything he canvasses in the *Inquiry*. Condillac believes an experience like this would yield an intentional awareness of extension in a reflective subject.

I say "in a reflective subject" because Condillac imagines that the subject acquires a keen familiarity with the subject's qualitative experience over the course of a long period of patient attention and deliberation. Reid too senses the importance of this point in the manuscript. Reid introduces a temporal component to the agent's experience by commenting that his concept of his face may be the "work of years" of attentive reflection upon sequences of tactile sensations. In the *Inquiry* Reid denies that the agent can acquire any primary quality concept under these conditions.

Given the rich phenomenology predicated of the subject in the manuscript's thought experiment, why does Reid still believe that he will not acquire an intentional awareness of any primary qualities? To be clear, Reid does not deny that the subject could under ideal circumstances acquire such an intentional awareness. In the *Inquiry* Reid denies that the subject can acquire an intentional perceptual content about any primary quality (figure, extension, motion, duration, etc.). In the manuscript version he allows that the subject may form an eviscerated idea of motion, which can be read as a concession to Condillac's argument. More importantly, Reid turns his attention to considering "what idea he can from all this Collect of his Face." A notion of one's face is, as Reid admits, "a vastly complex one." Surely his interlocutors would prefer that Reid discuss instead the subject's effort at arriving at the much simpler notion of extension. Reid is at risk of attacking a straw man when he hypothesizes that the subject's sensation experiences collectively do not "have the least Resemblance to my Idea of a Face." Why must someone like Condillac claim that the subject's sensation must *resemble* the intentional contents to which they give rise? Surely Condillac has plausible reasons to deny that. Reid says that the subject's notion of his face does not seem to be "got at once by feeling the Face that it must necessarily in the most active and attentive Mind be the work of years the effect of an infinite number {of sucessive} feelings & various modifications of these feelings." Again, why must someone like Condillac believe that the subject would acquire an intentional perceptual awareness of her face at once? Condillac in fact does deny that such an awareness would come at once.

The manuscript discussion brings into greater relief the central problem present in the published version of the crucial test. Reid does not seem to appreciate those sorts of examples that most obviously favor Condillac's claim that sensations and reflection upon them can give rise to a subject's intentional perceptual awareness of extension. These examples include wrapping one's fingers around one's forearm and gripping a teacup.

Consider the subject's experience (a) through (g), and add to that the supplementary experiences Reid imagines the subject to enjoy in the manuscript version of the thought experiment. No matter what sensations Reid adds to the subject's experience, the subject remains unable to become intentionally aware of primary qualities. Reid could be making a universally generalized claim such as:

> (3.14) For any set of sensations experienced by the subject, the subject will be unable to become intentionally aware of any primary quality; or
>
> (3.15) If the subject has a set of sensation experiences that have heretofore not enabled the subject to become intentionally aware of any primary quality, then the subject probably will not be able to become intentionally aware of any primary quality by adding one more sensation to the set.

How (3.14) could be justified abductively, that is, through an argument to the best explanation, eludes me. But through this thought experiment he is incapable of offering a deductive argument. So (3.14) does not explain Reid's central intuition about the implications of sensory deprivation, and (3.15) is quite similar to (3.14) but for the use of "probably" in the consequent. It seems that Reid is tacitly employing an intuition about the additivity of sensations like the one captured in (3.15). But how does he justify it without begging the question?

Both these proposals rest on a belief that, no matter the size or diversity of the set of tactile sensations, adding one more will never enable the agent to form a perceptual belief that takes as its intentional content a primary quality. Ironically, we can present Reid with the same methodological concern with which he addresses Hume above. The small list of tactile sensations experienced by the subject is insufficient inductive evidence to draw a universally generalized conclusion. Clearly, it is not a priori known that one more tactile sensation will not elicit the intentional awareness of a primary quality when it is added to any set of sensation experiences. But if the matter is to be decided empirically, then Reid's thought experiment is ineffectual. What we need instead are actual experiments in cognitive psychology. The most charitable interpretation of Reid's argument takes it as an abductive argument. This absolves him of a fallacy, but it leaves woolly just how he is to reach his universally generalized conclusion. Reid does attack a straw man in the Sensory Deprivation argument, and, given his discussion in the manuscripts, it appears he was aware that the case he presents on behalf of his interlocutor later in the *Inquiry* is less promising than it could be.

Why then does Reid choose to shield his readership from the fuller discussion of his thought experiment contained in his manuscripts? One answer is that Reid believes that the additional phenomenology imputed to the agent in the manuscript version is irrelevant to his acquisition of an intentional awareness of primary qualities. This is not especially plausible. The additional experiences with which Reid endows his subject in the manuscript do seem relevant and would have given Reid's published argument more credibility. Besides, Reid says that "the ideal system must stand or fall" upon the crucial test (IHM 5.7, 70/128a). Surely, under those circumstances, he would wish to give his interlocutor's explanation the best run for its money by including a full panoply of sensations within the agent's experience.

Other mundane answers are: perhaps Reid did not see the importance of some of his comments in the manuscript version; perhaps he saw their importance but did not want to revise the *Inquiry* to accommodate them; perhaps in the course of writing the *Inquiry*, Reid overlooked the pages on which these earlier comments were written. In support of this suggestion, the document on which these paragraphs are found contains a number of comments on disparate topics, and they bear evidence of being written at very different times. We will probably never know.

3.10. Summary

Reid continually reminds us that natural signs are only placeholders for a conceptual *sine qua non*. The gap between our sensations, which Reid recognizes are produced in part by way of nerve impulses, and our concepts about mind-independent qualities, exemplifies the cavernous, "deep and a dark" fissure between mind and body (IHM 6.21, 176/187a). But this needn't thwart further investigation into his philosophy of mind. An epistemologist takes justification to be what converts true belief into knowledge even though she has only hints about this, and no account of justification. She doesn't hesitate to continue to use the concept in her work. In this way Reid (in the *Inquiry*) takes the notion of a natural sign to be what bridges the gap between sensations and concepts, even though he has no "theory" of natural signs. Those writing on suggestion line up to recognize this point—or at least the obscurity of Reid's account—and move on.[14] So will we.

[14] Robinson 1976, 48; Gallie 1989a, 225; Gallie 1997, 332; N. K. Smith 1941, 41; Daniels 1976, 35; Winch 1953, passim; DeRose 1989, 347; and Yolton 1984, 214.

I suggest we think of Reid's case against the Way of Ideas' inchoate theory of cognition as having two major stages motivated by distinct concerns. The first is the Sensory Deprivation argument, which we can construe as an argument that the poverty of the sensory stimulus prevents us from acquiring intentional contents of mind-independent qualities. This argument is based upon Reid's crucial test thought experiment. Even if the Sensory Deprivation argument does not achieve its intended result, we can say that it was successful at foisting the burden of proof upon those who deny Reid's conclusion.

Equally important for Reid (despite the way he lays down the gauntlet with the crucial test) is the second stage of his argument. Reid has argued that the accounts of Descartes, Locke, and Berkeley fail to explain our acquisition of primary quality concepts. Reid plugs the gap with an appeal to natural signs. But why not instead adopt a form of skepticism about concepts? Reid takes Hume to adopt a skeptical position about the very nature of intentional thought. The facile way to interpret Reid's response to Hume is to retread Reid's comments to the effect that it is an implication of common-sense epistemic principles that we know thought is intentional. Yet this customary reply overlooks some of Reid's most fascinating and original arguments against the Way of Ideas. By explaining and stating Reid's anti-skeptical arguments against Hume, we show why Reid entitles himself to the belief that there is intentional content to perception.

We now turn to Reid's analysis of visible figure, which exemplifies the same anti-sensation mentality. Visible figure is the only primary quality perceived by sight, and in this case, perception of visible figure can occur without the experience of any sensation corresponding to it. In a sense, then, the analysis of hardness allows Reid to assess the Way of Ideas' analysis of touch, and the analysis of visible figure allows Reid to assess its analysis of vision (Hopkins 2005, 350).

4

Visual Perception

Through the power of suggestion our sense of touch puts us in unmediated contact with features of the mind-independent world. This means that we do not need recourse to intellectual powers other than perception in order to be aware of mind-independent qualities. In other words, we need neither rely upon reasoning to form our concept of extension, contrary to Descartes, nor upon custom and habit to form such concepts, contrary to Berkeley. This also means that we do not need to perceive or be aware of intermediating objects like ideas in order to perceive mind-independent qualities, contrary to (Reid's interpretation of) Hume. Reid's arguments for the directness of conceptual and perceptual apprehension put us on a path toward a theory of perception that affords us an intimate relation with the mind-independent world.

But the relation between the world and our perceptual powers is too sophisticated to allow for an orderly theory. The richness and variety of vision requires a nuanced analysis that will complicate Reid's theory. Reid takes his task to be to account for the actual workings of our intellectual powers. The groundbreaking sophistication of his theory of vision comes at the expense of a trim and tidy direct realism, a price Reid is happy to pay.

The complicating factor in Reid's theory of vision is the presence of what he calls "visible figure" and "visible magnitude." Reid heaps scorn on the Ideal Theory for reifying intermediaries in the form of ideas and impressions in both cognition and perception. But visible figure seems to be a perceptual intermediary. Despite appearances, Reid does maintain our intimate connection with the mind-independent world through vision, but this connection is subtle and recondite.

A portion of the difficulty in analyzing Reid's theory of vision lies in his reticence to speculate about the nature of visible figure, which leaves his interpreter with a task that is constructive and not merely explanatory. I set out several constraints that Reid implicitly places on visible figure, both textual and philosophical, and then I describe a tripartite distinction between types of visible figure. This facilitates an interpretation on which visible figure is a relational property. In the second half of this chapter I will examine the perceptual status of visible figure.

4.1. An Inconsistency in Reid

We can make a prima facie case for the inconsistency of Reid's theory of perception with his rejection of the Ideal Theory, in order to motivate our discussion. Most scholars believe Reid adopts a theory on which the immediate object of perception is a physical body because he wishes to avoid problems generated by the veil of perception in the Ideal Theory. As early as the dedication of the *Inquiry* Reid says that the Way of Ideas "leans with its whole weight upon a hypothesis ... [t]hat nothing is perceived but what is in the mind which perceives it" (IHM 4/96a). Reid attributes to the Way of Ideas thesis:

(4.1) No immediate objects of perception are mind-independent.

Let's leave (4.1) at this level of generality for now and show how Reid's rejection of the Ideal Theory conflicts with his theory of visual perception.

Reid's attempt to banish perceptual intermediaries in his analysis of vision is complicated by his recognition of visible figures as the immediate objects of our visual systems. With sight, "we perceive originally the visible figure and colour of bodies only" and not, for instance, their extension (IHM 6.20, 171/185a). It seems that visible figures are perceptual intermediaries since it seems the objects of acts of visual perception are visible figures. Reid might be taken to affirm that:

(4.2) The immediate objects of visual perception are only visible figures and colors.

Reid's repudiation of the Ideal Theory in (4.1) and the nature of his account of visual perception in (4.2) seem to be in conflict. Specifically, they are inconsistent with the following phenomenal description of what we see:

(4.3) The visible appearances of things to the eye, such as the shapes and colors we see, are not mind-independent objects.

On behalf of (4.3), consider the content of the visual experience when looking at a clock high on the wall in the morning light. Examined under normal conditions, the clock's metric measurements show it is perfectly circular. A spectography test places the reflectance properties of its surface in the midst of the wavelength normal perceivers would describe as a platinum white. Yet the phenomenology of the experience exhibits an elliptical shape in a sallow yellow hue, which fails to describe the mind-independent clock. Barring the adoption of naive realism, which says that the clock really is elliptical and sallow, a minimal appreciation for the phenomenology of visual experience suggests (4.3) is true.

If Reid is taken to endorse a direct theory of perception for all our sense modalities, then Reid cannot deny (4.1) and affirm both (4.2) and (4.3). In addition to differing with received wisdom about Reid, such a hybrid theory—on which touch is direct and vision indirect—is counterintuitive, and may be philosophically problematic.

Reid did not fully appreciate this conflict, though he notices that vision presents unique difficulties for his comprehensive theory of perception. He analyzes the nature of the representational relations between visible figures, which he occasionally calls "perspectival appearances," and what he calls "real" and "tangible" figures, i.e. the tactile surface properties of physical objects. He uses the result of this analysis, his "geometry of visibles," to show that the faculty of visual perception can give us reliable information about three-dimensional objects.[1] The implications of Reid's geometry of visibles and his implementation of the notion of visible figure have not been examined in the context of Reid's theory of perception, remaining a curiosity in the history of geometry. Reid himself does not know what to make of this: "To what category of beings does visible figure then belong? I can only, in answer, give some tokens, by which those who are better acquainted with the categories, may chance to find its place" (IHM 6.8, 98/144b).

What is visible figure? Only if an answer to this question enables Reid to differentiate visible figures from ideas will he evade the puzzle I've articulated. However, it is not enough that Reid succeeds in describing something that is sufficiently different from impressions and ideas to avoid the puzzle, but which fails to exist or fails to explain the requisite visual phenomena. We must also have some independent reasons for thinking that the thing (or property or entity) to which "visible figure" refers actually exists.

Before we redress this criticism, we must fix some terms. For our purposes "visible figure" and "apparent figure" will be synonymous. Reid also, but rarely, uses the term "perspective appearance" to refer to visible figure (IHM 6.2, 81/135a). The terms "visible magnitude" and "apparent magnitude" are also synonymous. Norman Daniels observes that in this world visible and apparent figure and visible and apparent magnitude are synonymous due to contingent facts about our environments and ourselves (Daniels 1989, 15–16). Reid believes it is possible that other creatures apprehend real figure through

---

[1] This relationship has been explored in Daniels 1989; Weldon 1982; Angell 1974; Yaffe 2002; Hagar 2002; and Van Cleve 2002.

seeing, hence the need for the distinction (IHM 6.9, 108–112/150–52). Also, Robert Hopkins suggests that visible place and visible extension "are simply components of visible figure: place being the direction in which a given point lies; extension being a matter of the angular distance between the directions of two points forming the extremes of a line of contiguous points" (2005, 346). Likewise "real figure" and "tangible figure," and "real magnitude" and "tangible magnitude," are treated in the same way. (Variations amongst these four pairs of terms are present at IHM 6.1, 79/133a–b, IHM 6.3, 82–84/135–136, IHM 6.7, 95–99/142–144, EIP 2.14, 178/302a–b, and EIP 2.20, 223/325a.) The real or tangible magnitude and the real or tangible figure of an object are intrinsic properties. The apparent or visible magnitude and the apparent or visible figure are not intrinsic properties of an object.

We may understand "magnitude" to refer to the volume of an object (in two or three dimensions), which is enclosed by shape, and "figure" to refer to the set of surfaces that enclose its volume. Magnitude is a property of the size or largeness of objects—whether objects of vision or of touch. Tangible magnitude is measured on the metric scale, while visible magnitude is measured in terms of the volume of two-dimensional space an object occupies in one's visual field relative both to the three-dimensional object causing it, and to the other two-dimensional objects in one's visual field. Visible magnitude is composed of the visible surface area of the object and the distance of the object to the eye. Tangible figure is determined by the shape of an object construed as its set of surfaces and edges in length, width, and breadth.

A final terminological comment is that magnitude and figure do not ordinarily co-vary. A scale model of a fighter jet might share the shape with an actual jet, but it differs in size. Likewise, the fighter jet might occupy the same volume of space as my flat, but the two differ in shape. This obvious difference between the two does not prevent Reid from typically using "visible figure" in such a way as to refer not merely to the bounded, two-dimensional color expanse but also to the volume (in length and width) that the figure occupies. For example, Reid says that every "visible figure will bear the same ratio to the whole of visible space, as the part of the spherical surface which represents it, bears to the whole spherical surface" (IHM 6.9, 104–5/148a). In this passage Reid predicates of visible figure a relative volume of two-dimensional space, thereby using "visible figure" to refer not only to the shape of the object but also to its size. This ambiguity is not insidious, but must be remembered amidst the bevy of related terms.

4.2. "Perception" and Constraints on Visible Figure

These are the constraints that Reid places upon visible figure and its status in the perceptual process. Visible figure must:

(a) be capable of being represented by figures cast upon the inner surface of a sphere;
(b) be interderivable with tangible figure;
(c) be mind-independent;
(d) regularly suggest our perceptions of bodies;
(e) have "no distance from the eye, no convexity";
(f) be something of which we can be perceptually aware;
(g) be regularly suggested by material impressions on the retina.

Some of these traits, e.g. (a) and (b), assist in fixing the functional role of visible figure in Reid's geometry of visibles; others, such as (d) and (f), describe the relation of visible figure to perceivers; and constraints like (c) and (e) begin to characterize its ontological status. These constraints each assist in plotting a course through Reid's account.

What little Reid says directly about visible figure occurs in his geometry of visibles, where he proposes a thought experiment. Imagine an eye placed at the center point of a sphere, able to rotate 360° in any plane containing the center. The most salient feature of this experiment is that this eye, "perceiving only the position of objects with regard to itself, and not their distance, will see those points in the same visible place which have the same position with regard to the eye, how different soever their distances from it may be" (IHM 6.9, 103/147b). The sorts of experiences that structure our association of visible figures with the distance, depth, and three-dimensionality of tangible figures do not habituate this eye. Reid explains the nature of the visible figures seen by this hypothetical eye: "[E]very visible figure will be represented by that part of the surface of the sphere on which it might be projected, the eye being in the centre. And every such visible figure will bear the same ratio to the whole of visible space, as the part of the spherical surface which represents it, bears to the whole spherical surface" (IHM 6.9, 104−5/148a). This marks our first constraint: visible figures (a) must be capable of being represented by figures cast upon the inner surface of a sphere.

Contrary to Berkeley, Reid claims that with knowledge of the tangible figure and of the position of one's eyes relative to the object one can deduce the visible figure.[2] Reid says, "the visible figure of a body may, by mathematical reasoning, be inferred from its real figure, distance, and position, with regard to the eye" (EIP 2.14, 181/303b–304a). Given facts about the dimensions of a real figure and information about its angle and distance from an eye, we can derive the dimensions of its visible figure by appeal to standard three-dimensional planar geometry, i.e. we needn't yet appeal to his geometry of visibles. But visible figure must have geometrically describable properties in order to permit the interderivability central to Reid's discussion. I will refer to this constraint as (b) interderivability, specifically the interderivability of visible figure from real figure coupled with facts about the distance of the real figure from the eye. Interderivability between visible figure and real figure provides evidence that an object whose visible figure we see and an object whose surfaces we touch are in fact unified (IHM 6.8, 98–99/144b).

Reid believes the derivation can work in the other direction as well but he only mentions this briefly. He says, "It was shewn ... that the visible figure of a body may, by mathematical reasoning, be inferred from its real figure, distance, and position, with regard to the eye: in like manner, we may, by mathematical reasoning, from the visible figure, together with the distance of the several parts of it from the eye, infer the real figure and position" (IHM 6.23, 188/193b). He often uses the terms "tangible figure" and "real figure" to refer to the three-dimensional properties of external objects. But in contexts like this one it must refer to the facing surfaces of physical objects. Likewise, properties of the visible figure as one sees it will only correspond to the properties of the facing surface of a body. This interderivability does not allow one to know the full shape of the reverse sides of objects.

This constraint suggests that real figure and visible figure are distinct, but this falls short of identifying their ontological relationship. For this we can turn to Reid's response to Berkeley. He says:

When I use the names of tangible and visible space, I do not mean to adopt Bishop Berkeley's opinion, so far as to think that they are really different things, and altogether unlike. I take them to be different conceptions of the same thing; the one very partial, and the other more complete; but both distinct and just, as far as they reach. (EIP 2.19, 222/325a)

---

[2] Berkeley argues for a contrary position in the *New Theory of Vision* §149–59 (WGB i, 232–5). He claims that geometrical objects are not visual but tangible, and that visible figure functions merely to suggest tangible shape and size. According to Reid, Berkeley's description of this relation is too weak and falls short of explaining the interderivability between visible and tangible figure. Atherton (1990) identifies Berkeley's central purpose in the *New Theory* as "making a case against those who think what we see represents bodies existing in external space" (14). Reid expressly attempts to counter Berkeley's position with his geometry of visibles.

Reid is not asserting that the real and visible figure are merely "different conceptions" or different ideas. Our conceptions of a visible figure and real figure are indeed different conceptions, but the figures themselves are not mental entities. Reid argues that visible figure is external and independent of minds by noting what would follow if it weren't: "[I]f visible objects were not external, but existed only in the mind, they could have no figure, or position, or extension" (IHM 6.11, 119/155b). He leaves us in no doubt by saying: "the visible figure of bodies is a real and external object to the eye, as their tangible figure is to the touch" (IHM 6.8, 101/146b). If visible figure is nothing other than a physical object conceived of in a certain way, then visible figure is (c) mind-independent.

Furthermore, when I see a visible figure, my mind is drawn to a conception and belief of an external object or quality (IHM 6.2, 81/135a–b). "Visible figure, therefore, being intended by nature to be a sign, we pass on immediately to the things signified" (IHM 6.8, 102/147a). Experience has taught us that we are warranted in correlating visible figures with real figures "every hour and almost every minute of our lives" (EIP 2.14, 182/304a). Hence, visible figure (d) suggests perceptions of physical objects.

Reid adds that (e): "The visible figure hath no distance from the eye, no convexity, nor hath it three dimensions; even its length and breadth are incapable of being measured by inches, feet, or other linear measures" (IHM 6.23, 188/193b). Visible figures lack a number of spatial properties that are associated with normal mind-independent objects, but he stops short of saying they have no spatial properties. This is indeterminate between two options: visible figure has none of these spatial dimensions, or it has these spatial dimensions but it is identical with the eye or some part of it. But given the other constraints upon an account, especially the next two, visible figure is not an eye or part of one.

Reid adds a developmental point in this context when saying: "But when I have learned to perceive the distance of every part of this [globe] from the eye, this perception gives it convexity, and a spherical figure; and adds a third dimension to that which had but two before" (IHM 6.23, 188/193b). "It" refers not to the visible figure but to the globe as it is perceived. Before perceptual learning has occurred, the visible figures are not signs of real figures for the agent. Once perceptual learning has occurred, seeing visible figures enables the perception of distance. Reid says, "the distance of the several parts of an object, joined with its visible figure, becomes a sign of its real figure." This reconfirms (d).

Passages quoted thus far should make clear the fact that visible figure is something of which we can be aware. Reid refers to "the perception of visible figure" (IHM 6.21, 176/187b). In fact, he says: "we perceive originally the visible figure and colour of bodies only" (IHM 6.20, 171/185a). Thus (f)—that it is something of which we can be perceptually aware—is a constraint on an account.

In Reid's discussion of the physical process of perception he mentions the curious role of visible figure. "It may farther be asked," he says, "whether there be any sensation proper to visible figure, by which it is suggested in vision? Or by what means it is presented to the mind?" (IHM 6.8, 99/144b). Elsewhere he discusses a related point, saying that "there are certain means and instruments, which, by the appointment of nature, must intervene between the object and our perception of it" (IHM 6.21, 174/186a). The nervous system transmits a physical impression from the organ to the brain. For most senses the impression then causes a sensation in the mind, which in turn suggests an intentional perceptual content. But he adds, "The perceptions we have, might have been immediately connected with the impressions upon our organs, without any intervention of sensations." This cautionary modal claim is common in Reid and resonates with lessons from his crucial test. But in the next sentence he makes a factual claim about what we actually perceive. "This last seems really to be the case in one instance—to wit, in our perception of the visible figure of bodies" (IHM 6.21, 176/187b). Visible figure is "immediately connected with the impressions upon our organs" because the material, retinal impression directly causes the visual perception of objects. In this way vision is unique because retinal impressions, not sensations, prompt our awareness of visible figure (IHM 6.8, 102/147a). So our awareness of visible figure is (g) suggested by retinal impressions, not sensations.[3]

---

[3] This constraint has courted controversy. Gideon Yaffe (2003a) argues instead that color sensations suggest our awareness of visible figure. He adopts this line for several reasons: out of charity for Reid, who he sees as unable to respond to a problem about visual focusing; because of alleged problems with the theory that material impressions can suggest awareness of visible figure; and due to a key text at IHM 6.8, 99/145a. The most compelling motivation lies in Yaffe's appreciation for Reid's philosophical method. He explains: "I argue, from underestimating the importance to Reid of a neo-Aristotelian, teleological conception of the human mind: Reid is at pains to discover the 'intensions of nature' in the construction of the mind; he wants to sort the things our minds are able to do into those things that we are designed to do for their own sake, and those we are designed to do solely for the sake of achieving something else" (103). Yaffe glosses this assertion as the claim that "we are given none of our features in vain." However, this more potent form of teleology is stated without supporting texts (108). This penultimate stage in his argument leads to the conclusion that "conception of and belief in the existence of visible figure is suggested by a sensation that follows the encounter with visible figure" (104).

Several facts work against Yaffe's interpretation. Falkenstein and Grandi offer a convincing reply both to Yaffe's case for his own interpretation, and to his criticisms of the interpretation that material impressions suggest awareness of visible figure. (Yaffe replies to them as well; see 2003b.) They argue against Yaffe's claim (2003, 110ff.) that Reid's intent in developing his geometry of visible space was to

Understanding constraints (a)–(g) will diffuse the patulous problem described above. These constraints imply that visible figures are different from ideas. For example (c) states that visible figures are mind-independent, and (b) implies that visible figures bear a much closer relationship to physical bodies than do ideas. In fact, visible figure is mind-independent in the ways needed to render it a primary quality, not a secondary quality. Reid's coarse description of visible figure is reason to think that visible figures are relevantly dissimilar from ideas, but this is only the first of two steps he must take in order to avoid inconsistency. Now we must look to find something—frankly, anything—that can bear the weight of these constraints.

found a new science, by showing that Reid's concern was to oppose those geometers who mistakenly took themselves to be studying the figures that we actually see. Since Reid did not take himself to ground a science of the visibles, they argue that Yaffe is mistaken to lean upon the teleological considerations that he does (Falkenstein and Grandi 2003, 124–5).

The fact that Yaffe's argument is motivated by teleological considerations provides a stumbling block to its success. Reid recognizes that it is possible to have a color sensation that does not suggest the perception of visible figure. Yaffe says that the "mere fact that this is possible shows that our power to have color sensations was not given to us with the intention that we perceive visible figure" (2003a, 109). But the sufficient condition Yaffe establishes for identifying a purpose for something is implausible. In this case X does not have purpose Y (for Z or Z's) so long as God could have brought about a world in which X's do not cause or bring about Y's. In other words, it seems as though if it is a feature's purpose to cause something, then it must necessarily cause that thing in our world. Why must God only act purposefully in ways that are necessary? Besides, what form of necessity or "perfect possibility" is at work here? Furthermore, Yaffe distinguishes not only God's purposes but God's primary and secondary purposes in endowing us with sub-faculties of perception. This occurs at significant distance from Reid's texts.

Yaffe also claims that, according to Reid, we are given none of our features in vain (2002, 108). But Reid is no Leibniz, and attributing a limited form of the Principle of Sufficient Reason does not bode well. Also, Yaffe has provided no texts to suggest that Reid endorses a maxim like this. Were Reid to endorse it, this would not imply that, of a given feature, we will be able to identify its purpose. At the conclusion of the article Yaffe adduces four passages in *Intellectual Powers* 2.14 in which he believes that Reid appeals to Nature's intentions in structuring perception as it has. Only one has directly to do with the relation between sensation and perception (and it does not address the role of visible figure). As important, these passages refer to Nature's intentions only to imply that knowledge of what they are is beyond us, e.g. "Who knows but their [mind and body] connection might have been arbitrary, and owing to the will of our Maker?" (IHM 6.21, 176/187b; Yaffe 2003a, 113).

Lastly, an ambiguity permeates the argument. When Yaffe asks what "visible figure is suggested by" (2002, 106), he might intend a couple of different hypotheses: what is a geometrical visible figure suggested by, what is a conception and belief of visible figure suggested by, or what is a seen visible figure suggested by? Yaffe alters the claim when he says that "we are endowed with vision in part because nature intends that we see visible figure" (2002, 108–9). This represents two changes: the purpose is not identified as the purpose of perceiving visible figure but of vision per se, and the appeal is not to perception$_{C\&B}$ of visible figure but to the seeing of it. Yaffe does gloss "perception" as "conception of and belief in the existence of visible figure," but Reid says that it is rare that we perceive visible figure in this way (IHM 6.2, 81/134b–135a). Reid says that only painters, when painting, regularly conceive of and perceive visible figure. Since we do not normally do so, basing his argument upon the premise that we must identify the purpose of our conception and belief of visible figure seems unable to achieve the intended result.

4.3. Taxonomy of Visible Figures

There is no rigorous account of the metaphysical and perceptual status of visible figure, though a number of possibilities have been mentioned. Given certain texts (e.g. IHM 6.7, 95/143a), one might argue that visible figures are retinal impressions. Second, perhaps visible figures resemble the physical impressions of touch *and sight* described by Hume (T 1.4.4.9, 235). Third, perhaps visible figures are rather mental impressions of some kind. Anthony Pitson (1989) says that Reid's use of "appearance" refers to the color an object seems to have. He favorably quotes Reid's comment that "It is impossible to know whether a scarlet colour has the same appearance to me which it hath to another man" (IHM 6.2, 80/134a). Here the notion of appearance is used "by Reid to refer to a feature of the perceiver's state of mind" (Pitson 1989, 84). Closely related, fourth, one might construe visible figures as forms of conception or as mental events in some sense. Phillip Cummins pursues an explanation in this neighborhood. He argues that in cases of visual perception, according to Reid, "our conceptions vary, such that first a coin is perceived as round and, subsequently, is perceived as elliptical. Conceptions, not actual objects, determine the objects intended in perception and the objects of conception need not exist" (Cummins 1974, 332). This interpretation has some textual support (EIP 4.1, 301/363a−b). Finally, as a last resort one might argue that visible figures are non-existent objects. According to Lorne Falkenstein, Reid is, or rather, "would appear to be," he says, "forced to admit that our beliefs in visible figures are beliefs in something that does not actually exist in the external world, though they serve as signs for the things that do so exist" (Falkenstein 2000, 318).

I will not burden the present discussion by re-evaluating these proposals in depth (see Nichols 2002c). Suffice it to say that each of these proposals possesses debilitating difficulties because each fails to exemplify at least two of our constraints. Retinal impressions cannot be objects of awareness (EIP 2.4, 95/257a−b) but visible figures can be. Besides, retinal impressions cannot suggest themselves. Physical Humean impressions seem to inherit the same troubles. The proposal that visible figures are mental appearances or images pushes us back into the difficulty of differentiating Reid's theory of visual perception from the Way of Ideas. It is often a similar Berkeleyan view (NTV §41−45/WGB i, 186−188; see Cummins 1987, 168) that serves as Reid's main target. Besides, sensory experiences cannot bear informational content of the sort required to meet the interderivability constraint. Cummins's proposal that visible figures are some form of conception points us in the right direction, but taken on its own merits it cannot account for the objectivity or externality of visible figures, or the interderivability constraint. Problems too numerous to mention render the notion that visible figures might be non-existent or subsistent objects implausible.

One of two lessons I draw from the problems attending our understanding of visible figure is that it plays multiple roles in Reid's theory of perception. The second is that the alternative accounts of visible figure do not explain the implications of Reid's geometry of visibles on visible figure. When Reid uses the term "visible figure" in that context, he is using it in a very different way from other contexts. As a result I distinguish between three ways to analyze—or three types of—visible figure: geometrical, seen, and perceived figure.

Imagine a vase suspended in the middle of an otherwise empty room. In the geometrical sense of the term, the vase possesses a visible figure for each set of coordinates in the room from which it can be viewed. As we've seen, Reid chooses to represent visible space using a model in which the eye is a point in the middle of a sphere and visible figures are represented as patches on the inside surface of a sphere.[4] From this proceeds Reid's geometry of visibles.

The geometry of visibles supersedes any of the achievements of Locke, Berkeley, and Hume in technical brilliance. For our purposes it is the results that are important, not the proof itself. Reid argues that theorems about figures projected on to the inner surfaces of spheres are proof-theoretically equivalent to theorems about visible figures and lines. This is more intuitive than might appear, and Yaffe has reconfirmed this result (Yaffe 2002).[5] The upshot of Reid's proof is that the figure that the vase would project to any set of coordinates could be deduced with information about the vase's dimensions and its distance from those coordinates. This sense of visible figure I call *geometrical figure*.

Any physical, mind-independent object will thus possess an infinite number of geometrical figures. Geometrical figure need not be identified with any particular projection of points on any particular sphere. In fact, Reid's geometry

---

[4] There may be some confusion about the claim that, because visible figures are patches on a sphere, they can represent three-dimensional objects. If such figures are two-dimensional, one might argue, their representational abilities are inadequate to the task. Reid says that visible figures are two-dimensional (e.g. at EIP 3.5, 273/349b), but they are unlike surfaces in plane geometry. In short, geometrical visible figures occupy three-space. Even so, the argument on which only three-dimensional (and not richly two-dimensional) objects can represent other three-dimensional objects (in the sense of visual representation relevant here) is unsuccessful.

[5] To understand the need for this proof, consider that some visible phenomena cannot be captured in a planar geometry. Lie on your back in the center of a square room with a flat ceiling. Look up at the four corners of the room. The angles you'll see are obtuse, i.e. the square contains angles that add to more than 360°. Reid's geometry of visibles explains this phenomenon. While this visible square cannot be drawn on a plane it can be drawn on a sphere.

of visibles is not wedded to a spherical model. We might say that the geometrical figures of an object are the collections of points modeled from all hypothetical lines of sight toward the object, where said collections of points mathematically represent the dimensions of the object's real figure.

Reid's remark about the ability of the blind to ascertain features of visible figure improves our understanding of geometrical figure. He says:

I require no more knowledge in a blind man, in order to his being able to determine the visible figure of bodies, than that he can project the outline of a given body, upon the surface of a hollow sphere, whose centre is in the eye. This projection is the visible figure he wants: for it is the same figure with that which is projected upon the *tunica retina* in vision. (IHM 6.7, 95/143a)

In geometrical form, visible figure is mathematizable. The visible figure and the retinal impression share all relevant *geometrical* (not perceptual or sensory) properties with the material impression. Hopkins describes a kind of objectivity of visible figure by saying that, "despite its relativity to a point, visible figure is a genuine property of the environment. For it is a matter of geometry in which directions from a given location the various parts of an object lie" (2005, 346). "Same" in the above quotation refers to the sameness of these properties only.

Notice that an object's geometrical figures are not necessarily unique. A tilted circle may possess the same geometrical visible figure as an ellipse when their sets of properties are modeled from the right coordinates. This is because the geometrical figures of these objects are determined by the direction in which their surface points lie from the eye (see Van Cleve 2002, 379 ff). The same will hold for some geometrical figures of three-dimensional objects. The geometrical figure of a cube from a certain set of coordinates may be identical to the geometrical figure of another polyhedron, like a square prism or a pyramid. This we know through common experience—a frontal view of a cube with edges having a length of one foot will not provide me enough information to determine whether this seen figure represents a cube. For all I know I may be looking at the bottom of a pyramid. Of course from long distances the square and the cube will at best appear as points in my visual field. Under standard conditions—in which the distances are not too great to prevent me from seeing the shape of the object, lighting is adequate, etc.—the visible figures projected by pairs of objects are *coincident*. But some pairs of three-dimensional objects do not have any coincident figures. Cubes and spheres have no coincident figures under standard conditions. Amongst two-dimensional figures seen in a frontal view, squares and circles don't either.

(This will take on added importance below since Molyneux's famous questions range over figures without any coincident visible figures.)

The second type of visible figure is produced when a single geometrical figure is instantiated in the world and represented to the eyes, or to be precise, to an eye. (Reid's geometry of visibles is designed for monocular vision.) I propose to call this *seen figure*. Seen figure only refers to the representation of physical objects to the eyes. In this sense of the word "see" I do not see; my eyes do. Reid's geometry of visibles allows us to deduce the dimensions of a seen figure from data about surface dimensions of a physical object and its distance from the hypothetical eye. This is possible because a seen figure inherits the relevant geometrical features of geometrical figure. Seen figure too will mathematically represent real figure, *ceteris paribus*.

The third and final type of visible figure is *perceived*$_{C\&B}$ *figure*. Perceived$_{C\&B}$ figures are seen figures of which we conceive and believe. When I typically perceive a vase I form a conception and belief of the vase itself, and not of its visible figure. Yet, as those who have attempted to sketch or paint would attest, in some circumstances one does perceive$_{C\&B}$ the visible figures of objects.

Geometrical figure aids in shoring up claims of immediate perceptual knowledge from vision. This is due to the help of his geometry of visibles and the proof-theoretic equivalence between statements about visible figures and statements about patterned shapes on spherical surfaces. In addition Reid's geometry of visibles is fascinating because it is non-Euclidean. But discussing geometrical figure at length is orthogonal to the present purpose of analyzing Reid's theory of perception. Since we so rarely conceive of and believe in visible figure, perceived$_{C\&B}$ figure is also unimportant for present purposes. Seen figure, on the other hand, is an essential component of all visual perception and it deserves further scrutiny. Its status is as unclear as it is important. I wish to understand seen visible figure better by analyzing it in terms of some of the key constraints enumerated above.

4.4. Seen Visible Figure

Geometrical figure is a relational property holding between a set of coordinates and the facing surfaces of a figure. When a geometrical figure is instantiated in the world, the product, a seen figure, inherits the geometrical properties of its predecessor. Some believe that the ontological status of relations differs from the ontological status of relational properties. The rationale for the ontological difference between relations and relational properties is that the class of dyadic relations includes items such as *is smaller than*, whereas the class of relational properties includes properties referred to by predicates like *a is smaller than b*, or F(a,b). While I do not dispute the fact that these two terms differ, the second is merely an instantiation of the first. I see no harm in allowing that an instantiation of a relation like *is smaller than* is a relational property in the present context. The important point is that seen figure is a relational property.

One early obstacle to the textual consistency of this suggestion hinges upon Reid's beliefs about relations. If he evinces no support for realism about relational properties, or if he denies realism about relational properties, then my proposal has an important strike against it. In other words, it is important that Reid hold that relations exist and are not reducible.

In fact, Reid is best interpreted as a realist about relational properties. First, one might think that with an ontology like Reid's, even if he does not explicitly describe relations as irreducible, we are warranted in assuming that they are. But we needn't rest our response to this question upon such a plea. For, while Reid developed no theory of relations, he does claim that relational properties can be immediately perceived. Reid describes two ways we arrive at concepts of relational properties, the first of which is by perceptually comparing relata: "By this comparison, we perceive the relation, either immediately, or by a process of reasoning. That my foot is longer than my finger, I perceive immediately; and that three is the half of six. This immediate perception is immediate and intuitive judgment" (EIP 6.1, 422/420b). Despite the propositional form Reid gives to these examples—perception$_{C\&B}$—this passage requires that we see relational properties like the comparative length of my index finger and thumb. If something is an object of visual perception for an agent who is in the proper circumstances and whose intellectual powers are healthy, then the object is real enough for our purposes. This is because the ontological status of seen figure as a relational property proves to be no obstacle to its being perceived.

This in turn raises a further problem about the mind-independence of seen figure. One might wonder how something seen couldn't but be dependent on a mind. About this, first, seen figures are independent of immaterial minds because they are relational properties between *eyes* and objects. Reid says that because "the eye" perceives "only the position of objects with regard to itself, and not their distance, [it] will see those points in the same visible place which have the same position with regard to the eye" (IHM 6.9, 103/147b). Visible figures of this kind are relations, and are relations between eyes and objects. Second, seen figures are also mind-independent in the sense that they are independent of any particular visual system. The seen figure projected from a vase to the coordinates my eyes currently inhabit is the same seen figure that would be projected from the vase to another's eyes, were hers to occupy the same coordinates. This secures the objectivity of seen figure across perceivers, and is an important step to show that Reid's visible figures are not simply a species of idea or sense-data.

Constraint (c) on the account of visible figure requires it be objective and mind-independent. Though seen figure conforms to those requirements, it is not clear that it is actually seen. That an eye takes or can take visible figures as objects is more often assumed than argued for in Reid. In part this is because he does not want to violate established linguistic practice according to which we "see" bodies. Nonetheless, when he needs to be clear on the matter he is. For example, Reid remarks that, "when I look at a globe which stands before me, by the original powers of sight I perceive only something of a circular form, variously coloured" (IHM 6.23, 188/193b), and, "we perceive originally the visible figure and colour of bodies only, and their visible place," and not, for instance, their extension (IHM 6.20, 171/185a). Visible figure is the only type of object represented to our eyes. As the phenomenon of perceptual relativity makes clear, Reid is right about this. But his terms are ambiguous. We've seen that he often uses "perceive" to refer to perception$_{C\&B}$, but here he is not using it in that way, for we do not form conceptions and beliefs of visible figure. He says as much himself: "the visible appearance of objects is hardly ever regarded by us. It is not at all made an object of thought or reflection, but serves only as a sign to introduce to the mind something else" (IHM 6.2, 81/134b−135a).

Another constraint (b) requires visible figures to possess geometrical properties that enable its use in derivations of real figure. We should insure that our interpretation makes good on this point. Just as a single geometrical figure is a relational property between a specific collection of points and a geometrical object, seen figure is a relational property between an eye and a physical object. Relational properties can and do possess geometrical features. A golf ball might possess the property of occupying 1/48th the volume of a basketball. My delete key possesses the property of being 15 inches north and 30 inches west of my cup of coffee. The geometrical properties of seen visible figures will be substantially more complicated than these traits. Given the current position of my eyes, the seen figure of my computer monitor will not be a simple rectangle because in my visual field it is as though it were projected on to the surface of a sphere.

Reid most clearly describes seen figure as meeting constraint (a), being capable of being represented by figures cast on the inner surface of a sphere, and constraint (b), interderivability with tangible figure, when he says that "A projection of the sphere or a perspective view of a palace is a representative in the very same sense as visible figure is," adding that "wherever they have their lodging in the categories, they will be found to dwell next door to them"

(IHM 6.8, 99/144b). He intends that the "perspective view," i.e. the seen figure, possesses the same representational properties as does the geometrical figure.

Reid emphasizes that the representational properties of visible figures have been widely misunderstood. Geometers have mistakenly taken themselves to describe the visibles with Euclidean theorems and diagrams. But Reid warns:

> When the geometrician draws a diagram with the most perfect accuracy; when he keeps his eye fixed upon it, while he goes through a long process of reasoning, and demonstrates the relations of the several parts of his figure; he does not consider, that the visible figure presented to his eye, is only the representative of a tangible figure, upon which all his attention is fixed; he does not consider that these two figures have really different properties; and that what he demonstrates to be true of the one, is not true of the other. (Reid 1997, 102−3)

This correction emphasizes that visible figure represents but is not identical to the corresponding tangible figure.

4.5. Color and Seen Figure

The upshot of this discussion of seen figure is that it seems to meet the constraints Reid places upon what he calls "visible figure." But some questions about the relation between color and seen figure are as yet unanswered. It is important to say something about the matter now if we are to avoid reducing seen figure to color experiences. The only qualitative mental states present in the experience of visible figure are color sensations. Says Reid, "When I see an object, the appearance which the colour of it makes, may be called the sensation, which suggests to me some external thing as its cause; ... At the same time, I am not conscious of anything that can be called *sensation*, but the sensation of colour. The position of the coloured thing is no sensation" (IHM 6.8, 99/145a). Reid claims that the only sensation to accompany our visual perceptions is the sensation of color. We have no sensation of the magnitude or figure (i.e. size or shape) of objects of visual perception. His treatment of color contrasts with his treatment of visual shape and magnitude due to differences between our awareness of color, and our awareness of magnitude and shape. So to determine whether and how seen figure is associated with sensations, we need to determine whether seen figure is colored.

Evidence suggests that seen figure is not necessarily colored. But Reid's views about the nature of color and the semantics of color terms are perplexing (see Falkenstein 2000 and Pitson 2001). Colors for Reid are only unknown causes of known sensory effects. Reid uses "color" and other secondary quality terms to refer to the unknown base properties that cause effects in our sensory systems, effects which most other philosophers label with the same terms, e.g. "red." Technically physical objects are colored and our color sensations are not colored, hence the importance of maintaining a distinction between colors and color sensations.

With that explanation in hand we can turn to a thought experiment in which Reid disassociates color from figure:

> Let us suppose, therefore, since it plainly appears to be possible, that our eyes had been so framed, as to suggest to us the position of the object, without suggesting colour, or any other quality: What is the consequence of this supposition? It is evidently this, that the person endued with such an eye, would perceive the visible figure of bodies, without having any sensation or impression made upon his mind. (IHM 6.8, 101/146a–b)

Since seen figures can exist apart from experiences of color, visible figure is not necessarily conjoined with or reducible to experiences of color.

We might turn this around to ask whether the sensation of color necessarily depends on seeing visible figure. Reid imagines another type of perceptual difficulty with which he denies this direction of dependence. Suppose:

> the eye were so constituted that the rays coming from any one point of the object were not, as they are in our eyes, collected in one point of the retina, but diffused over the whole: it is evident that such an eye as we have supposed would shew the colour of a body as our eyes do, but that it would neither shew figure nor position. (IHM 6.8, 99/145a)

This person senses color, but her visual system cannot detect figure. We can in principle sense color without seeing visible figure, so color sensations do not reduce to seen figures.

None of the foregoing serves to deny that seen figure and the experience of color are closely related in the actual world. They are constantly conjoined in our normal experience. In a bevy of passages Reid associates the present-ation of color to the mind with the position of the object relative to the perceiver:

> [T]he position of the coloured thing is by the laws of my constitution presented to the mind along with the colour. (IHM 6.8, 99/145a)

> Visible figure is never presented to the eye but in conjunction with colour: and, although there be no connection between them from the natures of things, yet, having

so invariably kept company together, we are hardly able to disjoin them even in our imagination. (IHM 6.7, 97/143b)[6]

Colour by our Constant Experience is so associated with Visible Figure & even with Tangible Figure that we are apt to think they cannot exist Separate. That Visible Figure can be without colour I think evident by supposing the whole field of Vision of one uniform Colour excepting one Triangle perfectly black or without Colour. We should have as distinct an Idea of the Triangular Space as if it was coloured. (Aberdeen MS 2131/6/III/5; in Reid 1997, 324–5)

The way our bodies now experience color is coincident with experience of seen figure, provided our systems are functioning properly.

However, in the last inset passage Reid insists that it is physically possible that they are experienced separately. In this case Reid alleges that we can see figure without color. Arguably, the triangular space hypothesized to be in the midst of one's visual field is not truly colorless. Besides, in this case the agent would still be aware of a contrast between what has and what does not have color. However, to argue that it is a priori true that any object in the visual field is colored would perhaps beg the question against Reid. I conclude that Reid believes that awareness of figure and color are in principle separable.

In addition to the manuscript text above, Reid elsewhere claims that it is not merely possible that awareness of color and awareness of figure are separated, but that this occurs in the actual world. Reid says: "Nor is the supposition we have made altogether imaginary: for it is nearly the case of most people who have cataracts, … they perceive the colour, but nothing of the figure or magnitude of objects" (IHM 6.8, 99–100/145b). Since sensations of color can be experienced without a concomitant perception of visible figure or magnitude, Reid infers that it is not sensations of color that suggest the perception of visible figure. He repeats this point shortly thereafter by addressing himself to the preceding discussion: "In answer therefore to the question proposed, there seems to be no sensation that is appropriated to visible figure. … It seems to be suggested immediately by the material impression upon the organ … " (IHM 6.8, 101/146a).

Adducing these texts shows that, for Reid, visible figure and awareness of it are not identical to and cannot be reduced to color and awareness of color. Yet a point of philosophical significance about the underlying relation

---

[6] Compare Berkeley's comments at NTV §43 (WGB i, 186–7). Though color and figure are, *ceteris paribus*, constantly conjoined in our experience, this doesn't imply that the same color experiences attend all seen visible figures. Since Reid was attuned to phenomena like color-blindness and cataracts he would allow, wisely, that subjects might not experience the *same* color even though their eyes will detect the same visible figure.

between figure and color is yet to be made. One of Reid's arguments for color sensations focuses on our ability to identify mind-independent color qualities over a range of lighting conditions and environments. An awareness of color constancy describes the ability of an agent to attribute changes in the appearance of colors to mind-independent features of either the object seen or the light through which the object is seen. The color sensation is independent of the object's color. It is an effect of the object's color on our minds. Awareness of size or magnitude constancy can be described as the agent's capacity to attribute changes in magnitude to either the real or the apparent magnitude. Likewise, awareness of figure or shape constancy results from the agent's capacity to attribute changes in figure to the real or apparent figure. One philosophically important difference between our awareness of color and our awareness of visible size or shape is that our awareness of size (and shape) constancy can be described without recourse to a private mental state, since visible shape and size—visible figure—is mind-independent and publicly observable (see Ganson 2002, 236–7). This serves to pull apart our awareness of visible figure and our awareness of color sensations, which in turn has interesting implications for the Molyneux problem (see Chapter 9 and Hopkins 2005, 348). Seen figures are objective and mind-independent in ways that color sensations are not.

Given a theory of properties upon which he can maintain the account of visible figure he has, the analysis developed thus far is sufficient to extricate Reid from the inconsistent set of three propositions stated above. This is the second step in that process. For seen figures are mind-independent properties, unlike ideas. In this way (4.3) is falsified and Reid's rejection of the Ideal Theory is not inconsistent with his theory of visual perception. As we will see next, it seems that Reid has good non-ad hoc reasons for positing seen figure in order to account for the phenomenon of perceptual relativity.

4.6. Awareness of Seen Figure

At the beginning of the chapter I emphasized the metaphysical ambiguity of visible figure by quoting Reid's jocular admission that he does not know where in the categories to put it (IHM 6.8, 98/144b). The primary burden of the first part of this chapter was to distinguish amongst different types of visible figures, and identify the metaphysical status of that type of figure, seen figure, of most importance for his theory of perception. But the metaphysical ambiguity of the thing is accompanied by a vexing uncertainty about its epistemic status. Furthermore, the problems that surround the nature of our awareness of visible figure in visual perception mirror like problems about the nature of our awareness of sensations in other forms of perception, discussed in Chapter 6.

Reid does not clearly explain our perceptual relationship to visible figure. He tells us that we do not regularly perceive$_{C\&B}$ seen figure (IHM 6.2, 81/134b–135a). But we have read texts that express the position that we are somehow aware of seen figure. Reid says that visible figure is the object of perception, but his frequent qualifications imply that this form of awareness does not take the form of the *perceiving*$_{C\&B}$ relation. He says it is not the mind but "the eye" that perceives visible figure (IHM 6.8, 103/147b), and that visible figure is "presented to the eye" (IHM 6.7, 97/143b). It is seen, as opposed to perceived (IHM 6.23, 188/193b). It is considered a sign for real figure (IHM 6.8, 102/147a). It is an object of "original" perception (IHM 6.20, 171/185a). Picking up this distinction in the *Intellectual Powers* we read that, by sight, "we perceive visible objects to have extension in two dimensions, to have visible figure and magnitude, and a certain angular distance from one another" (EIP 2.21, 236/331b).

If we interpret "perceive" in such passages as "perceive$_{C\&B}$" then Reid contradicts himself. In the interest of charity we shouldn't do this. Thankfully, there is plenty of textual evidence that he has something else in mind. In these and other passages about "original" perception Reid does not invoke any sort of *conceive that* or *perceive that* locution, as we might expect him to do were he using the formal notion of perceiving$_{C\&B}$. The most charitable course is to suppose that Reid implicitly invokes his non-propositional, *de re* form of intentional apprehension when using the term "perception" in these and other cases (e.g. at EIP 2.17, 200–1/313b and EIP 2.19, 217/322a). Reid confirms that this interpretation is the right one in those passages that describe the eye as what perceives. With this non-literal use of "perceive" Reid wants to capture the fact that seeing is not merely a physical relation, meanwhile stopping short of implying that we conceive of and believe in visible figures.

While those who have reconstructed Reid's geometry of visibles have not explicitly addressed the nature of our awareness of seen figure, they seem to have taken it for granted that there is some type of intentional mental state involved in the apprehension of seen visible figure (e.g. Weldon 1982, 364 and 365). I propose to use the term *visually aware* to refer to a state of intentional apprehension within states of visual perception. This form of conceptual acquaintance with the mind-independent relational properties of objects is the type of mental state undergirding his theory of perception generally. The intentional conception Reid invokes in the context of his theory of perception is the same form of direct apprehension that Reid adopts when criticizing his predecessors' theory of thinking. According to our earlier discussion, Reid claims that we possess mental states whose intentional content is directly about features of the mind-independent world. When Reid defines perception to include a conceptual component, it is this type of intentional apprehension that he has in mind.

By drawing from Reid's distinctions amongst faculties and powers of the mind, we can provide the above response with additional plausibility. Reid notes that attention, consciousness, and conception are different mental states (EIP 1.1, 24–5/222b–223a). We are broadly aware of a number of things in a semi-conscious manner. He says that we are "conscious of many things to which we give little or no *attention*. We can hardly attend to several things at the same time" (EIP 1.2, 42/231b). As applied to vision, we are routinely aware or conscious of objects in our field of vision, even though we do not give them our attention or form *de re* thoughts about them. In the discussion of the Blind Book argument, Reid notes that when we read a text, the letters and words on its pages are objects of awareness but are not objects of full attention or *de re* conceptions. In standard conditions, our awareness of visible figures and words is merely a sign for something else, something that we often do attend to and conceive.

Of course, Reid gives visible figure special status by using the verb "perceive" to describe what we do to it, whereas he does not say that we "perceive" words on a page when reading. So the appeal to Reid's gradations of awareness as represented in his faculty psychology does not fully explain the nature of our awareness of visible figure. Yet it does provide a plausible framework in which to find a Reidian response to the problem.

At this point someone may argue that even if Reid's theory of visual perception is not inconsistent with his rejection of the Way of Ideas—and thus in some sense succeeds in being direct—it follows neither that Reid's theory of visual perception is direct in any philosophically important sense of the term, nor that it will be compatible with an account of non-inferential perceptual knowledge. Thankfully, Reid employs his account of visible figure in responding to a perceptual relativity argument, and my aim in the remainder of this chapter will be to apply Reid's theory of visual perception and attendant notion of visible figure to this argument. This will put us in a position to appreciate the ways in which, on its own terms, Reid's theory of visual perception is and is not direct, and is and is not compatible with accounts of non-inferential perceptual knowledge.

4.7. Hume's Perceptual Relativity Argument

Since Reid addresses the perceptual relativity argument about vision fashioned by Hume, we will reconstruct this argument. Hume says that, contrary to the "universal and primary opinion of all men," philosophy teaches us that:

> nothing can ever be present to the mind but an image or perception, and that the senses are only the inlets through which these images are conveyed, without being able to produce any immediate intercourse between the mind and the object. The table, which we see, seems to diminish, as we remove farther from it: but the real table, which exists independent of us, suffers no alteration: it was, therefore, nothing but its image, which was present to the mind. These are the obvious dictates of reason. (*Enquiry* 12.9, 152; see T 1.4.1.12, 187)

In this circumscribed argument Hume purports to show that the object of sight from perspective P is not identical with the object of sight from perspective Q, even though common sense dictates that an agent sees the same object from both perspectives. Reid does not reformulate the argument in exacting detail, but his discussion leads me to believe he construes it in the following way:

> (4.4) The shape and dimensions of the immediate object of awareness vary relative to the position of my eyes with respect to the object.

After all, the immediate object of my awareness when looking at a table from 100 yards away has different dimensions from the immediate object of my awareness when the table is 4 feet away.

> (4.5) The mind-independent table *ex hypothesi* does not possess shape and dimensions that vary relative to the position of my eyes.
> (4.6) So, the mind-independent table is not an immediate object of awareness.
> (4.7) So, at most we immediately perceive ideas or images.

In the inset passage, Hume does not address the epistemological implications of the argument, but we will add a further conclusion on his behalf since Reid believes the epistemic consequences are of crucial importance, namely:

> (4.8) So, we do not have non-inferential knowledge of mind-independent objects.[7]

---

[7] Reid focuses on Hume's argument, but at NTV §44–§49 (WGB i, 187–9) Berkeley presents a similar argument but his conclusion differs from Hume's. At *Principles* §15 Berkeley says that: "it must be confessed this method of arguing doth not so much prove that there is no extension or colour in an outward object, as that we do not know by sense which is the true extension or colour of the object" (WGB ii, 47). I thank Kenneth Winkler for this observation

Hume uses the terms "present to the mind" and "see" to describe modes of awareness in this argument. Using these terms equivocally may generate confusion, particularly from Reid's point of view. Reid distinguishes between higher-order modes of perceptual awareness—involving conception and belief—from the lower-level states of simple apprehension involving demonstrative acquaintance. I have formulated (4.7) as Reid took the argument; (4.7) exemplifies a contrast with standard theories of Reidian direct perception.

George Pappas, for example, renders the perceptual component of what he dubs "Reidian direct realism" as follows: "Typically we immediately perceive objects and their qualities, i.e., we perceive them without perceiving intermediaries" (Pappas 1989, 156). The term "immediately" here and in other work on this issue (e.g. Alston 1989) has a specific meaning that is unearthed by contrasting Reid's theory with an indirect one. Pappas says: "Indirect perception of external physical objects requires not merely that there be perceived intermediaries, but also that the perception of the physical object should be dependent upon the perception of the intermediary" (1989, 159). This constitutes necessary and jointly sufficient conditions for *indirect* perception. These conditions are: (i) in order to perceive the external physical object O, the subject must perceive an intermediary R, "where R ≠ O, and where R is not a part of O nor is O of R," and (ii) the subject's perception of O must be dependent upon the subject's perception of R (1989, 156–7). Hume's argument through (4.7) reputedly shows that the perception of mind-independent physical bodies must be indirect. Ideas and images clearly are not parts of objects.

4.8. Hybrid Theories of Perception

An assumption underlies (4.4) through (4.6) that I think the advocate of a direct theory of perception is wise to reject. Hume assumes that the competing views he considers are purchased wholesale. In other words, if the table is not the immediate object of sight then it is not immediately sensed in any way whatsoever. Reid's theory implies otherwise. Even if my visual awareness of the table is mediated by an idea of the table, it does not follow that I cannot directly sense the table *with my hands*. Simply because the object of sight is not the mind-independent table, it does not follow that the table cannot be an immediate object of some other sense. This should not come as a surprise since Reid explicitly remarks about the many differences between the senses. Though in all senses the object is conceived to be "independent of our perception," many differences remain amongst them. For example, he says, "in one, the distance, figure, and situation of the object, are all presented to the mind; in another, the figure and situation, but not the distance; and in others, neither figure, situation, nor distance" (IHM 6.12, 124/158b).

Reid insists that the process of vision is structured differently from the process of our other sense modalities. Suppose we clarify Pappas's perceptual thesis. Where "perceptually aware," a companion term to "visually aware," refers to intentional states experienced in vision *and other senses*, Pappas's thesis might read:

> (4.9) Typically we are immediately perceptually aware of objects and their qualities, i.e. we are perceptually aware of objects without being perceptually aware of intermediating objects.

The scope of (4.9) is ambiguous. We have two options:

> (4.10) Through every sense modality we are typically perceptually aware of mind-independent objects and their qualities directly; or
> (4.11) Through at least one sense modality we are typically perceptually aware of mind-independent objects and their qualities directly.

But to hold a substantive direct theory of perception Reid need only affirm (4.11). Reid claims we are typically perceptually aware of mind-independent qualities directly through touch. As we have seen, he says that through perception we are immediately aware of mind-independent bodies and qualities. This resonates with results from his Sensory Deprivation argument, in which he minimizes the role of sensations in the process through which we gain intentional awareness of physical bodies. Now enters Hume, who takes himself to have shown:

> (4.12) Through no sense modality do we typically perceive mind-independent bodies and their qualities directly.

However, Reid believes Hume does not argue for (4.12) but only for the negation of (4.10). This leaves it open for Reid to affirm (4.11).

But does Reid concede the falsity of (4.10)? The answer depends upon what we have to say about vision, since amongst the other senses it is the best candidate for an indirect analysis. I will argue in what follows that, due to the relational nature of seen figure, Reid's theory implies that we are directly aware of mind-independent qualities of objects through vision. Thus Reid's theory implies (4.10).

When setting out the prima facie case against Reid at the outset of the chapter I suggested that philosophers might look askance at hybrid theories.

I now want to dispel the worry that a theory on which the structure of one sense modality differs from the structure of the others is for that reason implausible. Despite the way in which such an insight complicates one's theory of perception, drawing this distinction is the only way to make theoretical room for phenomenological facts about our senses. These facts are not lost on other philosophers who favor introspective analysis. One such philosopher argues that the sense of vision possesses some important structural differences from the sense of touch:

> What must be emphasized about touch is that it involves the use of no mediating field of sensation. There is in touch no analogue of the visual field of visual sensations which mediates the perception of the environment…. The role of bodily sensation in tactile perception is wholly disanalogous to the representational role of visual sensation in visual perception…. [I]n tactile perception no intervening third sensuous entity gets between one and the object. (O'Shaughnessy 1989, 38, 45, 49)

What O'Shaughnessy dubs "visual sensation," Reid calls "visible figure" and "visible magnitude." Finer points of comparison aside, complicating the theory of perception in this way renders one's theory more plausible, not less, since only by doing so can one account for the ways in which the phenomenology of touch and sight differ.

So, even if Hume's argument were entirely successful, one could still endorse (4.11) and lay claim to a significant form of direct perception.

4.9. Touch, Vision, and "Immediate Object"

Reid attempts to refute Hume's argument at several stages, first with the distinction between visible and tangible figure occurring at IHM 6.2, 81–2/135a–b. When I see a table at 10 yards and then at a 100, its "visible appearance, in its length, breadth, and all its linear proportions, is ten times less in the last case than it is in the first." Reid has much to say about the placeholder "immediate object of awareness" in (4.4)—"table" in Hume's statement of the argument. It can either refer to the seen figure of the table or to the table itself. The first premise is true if we take "immediate object of awareness" to refer to the seen figure of the table.

Reid invokes his distinction between visible/apparent figure/magnitude from real/tangible figure/magnitude. "The real magnitude of a line is measured by some known measure of length—as inches, feet or miles" (EIP 2.14, 180–1/303b). In contrast, seen figure is a property dependent upon the position of the eyes of the perceiver relative to the external object:

The real magnitude of a line is measured by some known measure of length—as inches, feet, or miles: the real magnitude of a surface or solid, by known measures of surface or capacity ... is measured by the angle which an object subtends at the eye. Supposing two right lines drawn from the eye to the extremities of the object making an angle, of which the object is the subtense, the apparent magnitude is measured by this angle. (EIP 2.14, 181/303b)

The real figure of the table is measured by different means, sensed by a different faculty, and is extended in three dimensions.

With this distinction and the notion of seen figure it presupposes, Reid charges Hume with equivocation. "This ingenious author has imposed upon himself by confounding real magnitude with apparent magnitude" because, in Hume's syllogism, "apparent magnitude is the middle term in the first premise; real magnitude in the second" (EIP 2.14, 182/304b). Assuming there are mind-independent objects, this point seems sufficiently obvious so as not to merit further discussion. Indeed, to this extent Reid *concurs* with Hume: our eyes do not immediately see the real magnitude of objects. But, Reid adds, we shouldn't expect them to. "This [real] magnitude is an object of touch only and not of sight; nor could we even have had any conception of it, without the sense of touch" (EIP 2.14, 181/303b). Neither a body's "real magnitude, nor its distance from the eye, are properly objects of sight, any more than the form of a drum or the size of a bell, are properly objects of hearing" (EIP 2.14, 182/304a). Seen figures are the only objects of our visual systems. Once we have separated the wheat from chaff, Hume has only shown that vision is suited to perceive things in a way that touch is not. This is not equivalent to (4.6), so Reid grants both (4.4) and (4.5) then denies (4.6).

It doesn't follow from this point about equivocation in (4.4) and (4.5) that the way in which I am visually aware of things is direct. This, in addition to my comment about hybrid theories, may give the false impression that Reid holds that we directly (or immediately) perceive the objects of touch, but that we do not directly perceive the objects of vision. No doubt there are some definitions of "immediate" and "direct" that would render Reid's theory of perception indirect. Of course some definitions of these terms would have it that none of the sense modalities are immediate on Reid's analysis. Many anachronistic applications of these terms to Reid's theory threaten to make the process of showing that Reid endorses a direct theory of perception trite and effortless. This occurs when we begin with philosophically privileged accounts of perceptual directness, and apply the analysis without a clear vision of what it is intended to illuminate. We need to identify what Reid thinks is philosophically important about directness in the context of visual perception in order to make headway.

Reid imposes the constraints upon visible figure that he does primarily in order to show that visible figure is radically unlike the Way of Ideas' impressions and ideas. Suppose the foregoing analysis of visual perception is correct, and suppose that through visual perception I am immediately aware of seen figure and not tangible figure. Reid resolutely argues that it does not follow from this point that we are visually aware of ideas or images or sense-data of objects, as in (4.7). Seen figure is not merely a representational intermediary. It is a relational property between objects and eyes of perceivers. This gives visible figure its mind-independence, public observability, and objectivity. Ideas, images, and sense-data lack these philosophically important traits. Seen figure is constituted by real (not ideal, not mental) relational properties. The philosophical importance of these characteristics is obvious: only because ideas lack them can Hume move from (4.6), the claim that the mind-independent table is not an immediate object of awareness, to (4.7), the claim that at most we immediately perceive ideas or images of mind-independent objects. In other words, since seen visible figure has these features, Hume is not entitled to infer (4.7), even if (4.6) were true. Reid rightly thinks that securing these traits for the immediate objects of perception is the chief task of a direct theory of visual perception, for only with them does visual awareness bring us into contact with the world.[8]

Reid takes his response to what I've identified as premise (4.6) a big step further by arguing that the law-like variation in the seen figure of an external object is best explained by an appeal to the objective, mind-independent relation a given seen figure bears to its correspondent real figure. In other words, he thinks that the specific way the immediate objects of visual awareness vary, far from disconfirming his theory, lends it considerable support:

[T]he real table may be placed successively at a thousand different distances, and, in every distance, in a thousand different positions; and it can be determined demonstratively,

---

[8] One lesson to take from Reid's analysis of this part of Hume's argument is that we must be especially careful when using terms like "immediate object" and "direct" since they are prone to ambiguity. The way philosophers have defined accounts of direct perception—including definitions attributed to Reid—has forced Reid's actual view out of consideration in much the same way that Hume's argument does. Return to Pappas's discussion, for example. He uses the term "part" in his formal statement of his necessary conditions to imply that if the object of perception is not the mind-independent object or a part of the object, then perception is not direct. This way of putting the point calls for drawing an important distinction on Reid's behalf. While relational properties are not mereological parts of objects, there seems to be a philosophically important sense of "part" at work here on which relational properties would meet the necessary condition. The importance of the term "part" lies in recognizing that if we perceive a property of the object directly, then we can be said to perceive the object directly. This non-mereological sense of "part" must be specified so as to recognize the philosophical importance of our seeing an objective, publicly observable, mind-independent property of objects.

by the rules of geometry and perspective, what must be its apparent magnitude and apparent figure, in each of those distances and positions. ... [O]pen your eyes and you shall see a table precisely of that apparent magnitude, and that apparent figure, which the real table must have in that distance and in that position. (EIP 2.14, 183/304b)

Hume seems to assume, wrongly, that the relationship between a seen figure and external object is subjective and mind-dependent. The systematic variation of the visible figure is evidence *for* the objectivity of its independence from one's mind. Reid continues in this same passage to argue that geometers from Euclid onward have assumed that there are mind-independent objects causing their visual experiences. Their geometrical demonstrations "about the various projections of the sphere, about the appearances of the planets in their progressions, stations, and retrogradations, and all the rules of perspective, are built on the supposition that the objects of sight are external" (EIP 2.14, 183/304a). This provides further evidence for the familiar allegation that it is difficult to ground the physical sciences on the systems of Berkeley and Hume.

4.10. Non-inferential Perceptual Knowledge

Reid in effect shows that (4.6) does not follow from (4.4) and (4.5), and that, were (4.6) true, (4.7) would not follow. So Hume cannot get to (4.8), that is, that we do not have non-inferential knowledge of mind-independent objects. At least, Hume must reach that conclusion through a means other than by appeal to perceptual relativity. And he might well attempt to do this by arguing that we have so attenuated Reid's theory that Reid cannot secure the epistemological benefits of a direct theory of visual perception. Let's call Hume's first and blocked pathway the "perceptual relativity" route and this new alternative the "epistemological" route.

One way to understand the epistemological route is as follows. Even if visible figure is external and publicly observable it does not follow that visible figure will necessarily represent the tangible figure accurately. It may seem, for example, that there is no logically necessary connection between my awareness of the seen figure of the crown tower and the present existence of the crown tower. Since there is no necessary connection it follows that by being aware of a seen figure of the crown tower I am not justified in believing in the existence of the tower. Since reaping epistemological dividends is arguably Reid's central purpose in adopting a direct theory of perception, the foregoing account of visible figure must be rejected, or at least recognized as dissonant with Reid's central philosophical motivations. So a Humean might argue.

Let me begin by saying a few things about non-inferential perceptual knowledge generally. The epistemological route requires assumptions about knowledge that we can make explicit. Hume may believe (i) that there must be necessary connections between a mind-independent object and the representational content of a belief in order to have non-inferential knowledge of that object. Reid also associates a type of internalism about knowledge with Hume. This might come in two crude forms: (ii) that each agent himself must show that there are such connections within his perceptions, or (iii) that someone or other must show that there are such connections.

Only card-carrying internalists about knowledge affirm theses like (ii). The majority of interpreters is correct to take Reid as endorsing—probably founding—a form of externalism about perceptual knowledge that denies requirements like (ii) (see De Bary 2002). According to most forms of externalism we can acquire non-inferential knowledge of our perceptual environment without fulfilling epistemic obligations and without having any meta-beliefs about our perceptual beliefs. What about the slightly weaker (iii)? If someone or other is to show that there are necessary connections between perceptual representations and objects, then they will face the insurmountable challenge of doing so while not presupposing any of their senses is reliable. Reid explicitly refuses to oblige Hume on this score by arguing that our faculties cannot be non-circularly proven reliable (IHM 5.7, 70–1/129–30 and IHM 6.20, 169/183b; see also Alston 1993).

Were he faced with (i), Reid would no doubt deny that the connection between object and belief state must be unfailing and necessary in order to have non-inferential knowledge of such an object. But Reid seems to claim that his account of vision meets such a condition anyway. For, on the basis of the success of Reid's geometry of visibles and the correlation between visible figure and tangible figure, geometrical figures model the real figures of physical objects necessarily. It is tempting to believe that seen figures inherit this trait from the geometrical figures from which they are built. Reid does say that the correspondence between visible figure and tangible figure "results *necessarily* from the nature of the two senses" (EIP 2.19, 225/326a, my emphasis). But whereas the demonstration of this necessity is perspicacious in the case of geometrical visible figure and (the facing sides of) tangible figure, instantiating the geometrical figure in the world scuttles the strict necessity claim. In the interests of charity we should take Reid as employing the notion of geometrical visible figure in the quotation immediately above, which bears a logically necessary relation to corresponding tangible figures. We could append Reid's proviso to the claim under discussion and suggest that seen visible figure necessarily corresponds to tangible figure "when the proper circumstances occur," but to use "necessity" in this way abuses that term. What we can say on Reid's behalf is that sight and touch reliably converge epistemically, contrary to the views of Reid's predecessors. We cannot go so far as to say that, for all seen figures y and for all corresponding tangible figures x, it is physically necessarily that y represents x. For example, the seen figure of a body on the other side of our sun will not necessarily represent the body because the light the body emits or reflects may be bent by our sun, which would distort our seen figure.

Reid does—at least to some small degree—characterize the non-inferential nature of perceptual knowledge positively. He argues that the mind typically becomes habituated to this correspondence. Since the information given us through our perception of seen figure about tangible figure is highly reliable and confirmed by daily experience, our mind instantiates an acquired suggestion relation (IHM 5.3, 59–61/121–2). This obviates the need to perform inferences in order to have knowledge of perceptual beliefs. This is true of all our sense modalities, including vision. Reid says:

[T]he visible appearance of things in my room varies almost every hour . . . . A book or a chair has a different appearance to the eye, in every different distance and position: yet we conceive it to be still the same; and, overlooking the appearance, we immediately conceive the real figure, distance, and position of the body, of which its visible or perspective appearance is a sign and indication. (IHM 6.2, 81/135a)

Reid's general reticence to prognosticate about knowledge will not obscure the fact that in passages like this he presumes that we are warranted in believing that the objects of which we are visually aware are as we think they are. Reid uses suggestion relations to explain how we acquire the contents we do, and he will go on to explain how our seen figure suggests beliefs about tangible figure in non-inferential ways. (In other words, visible figure conforms to our constraint (d), that seen figure regularly suggests our perceptions$_{C\&B}$ of bodies.) In short, the beliefs suggested to us by our sensations are warranted until proven guilty. Unique to vision, interderivability underwrites the reliability of immediately suggested, non-inferential beliefs about tangible figures. Contrary to (4.8), Reid is justified in concluding that we typically arrive at non-inferential knowledge of physical objects by being aware of visible figures.

Defending a robust account of non-inferential perceptual knowledge is not this easy. One might argue that if we are aware of seen figure, then knowledge of visual perceptual beliefs depends upon defending the intentional, *de re* acquaintance thesis I have earlier attributed to Reid. Second, though, is a host of more familiar objections, about which I can say a few things in partial defense of Reid. For example, we can see the visible figure of celestial bodies at great distances even if those bodies have vanished long ago. This time-lag argument causes prima facie trouble not only for his theory of non-inferential perceptual knowledge, but also for his interderivability thesis. In some cases light refracted from an object is altered before entering the eye, for example a paddle appears bent under water. Hallucination cases are used to show that the figures of items of which we take ourselves to be visually aware do not isomorphically represent the facing surfaces of tangible figures. These problems all seem to undercut Reid's thesis of non-inferential perceptual knowledge through vision, making it regrettable that Reid does not directly discuss them, especially hallucination arguments.

Several responses to these lines of criticism come to mind, though. First, the fact that dead stars sometimes misleadingly project visible figures of objects should not move Reid. Yes, Reid was unaware of several of the effects of light on visual perception, but we should not tailor a theory of visible figure to exceptional phenomena at the expense of adequately explaining typical phenomena. (This point serves to emphasize that the previous concession about the lack of necessity between seen and tangible figure is both correct and inconsequential.) The same may hold true of other problems for knowledge from vision. In each case Reid would invoke the environmental condition of his *ceteris paribus* clause. These cases are not cases in which my faculties are functioning properly in a truth-conducive environment, thus they fail to meet Reid's necessary condition for the "evidence of sense." Reid says he "shall take it for granted that the evidence of sense, *when the proper circumstances concur,* is good evidence, and a just ground of belief" (EIP 1.1, 229/328b, my emphasis). Second, about the perception of stellar objects (or rather, the light they have emitted or reflected), Reid might add that the visible figures projected from these bodies are mere points of light, lacking the rich geometrical figures possessed by other seen figures. Even if we could know that a certain distant star presently exists as we see its light, we could derive nothing from its seen figure as presented to bare eyes. We are quickly accustomed to cases in which objects are seen to have different properties from those they have—as the paddle under water. One Reidian response to such cases is to say that upon seeing seemingly bent paddles I form a rule so that such a seen figure suggests a straight paddle. This rule is a form of acquired perception for Reid.

This sketch of his response will meet with frustration from those who do not share Reid's epistemic intuitions. It is also unsatisfactory for those of us in Reid's corner. I will say more about Reid's account of perceptual knowledge in Chapter 8.

4.11. Metaphysical Problems with Visible Figure

When describing visible figure I expressed some reservations about Reid's use of the concept. His use of the term is not univocal, hence the need for the tripartite distinction we introduced. Once we distinguish amongst forms of visible figure his use of the concept appears less plausible. The explanation of his theory of visual perception given thus far does not remove some fundamental reservations about the nature of visible figure—about seen figure in particular. One objection to the account of seen figure stems from the intuition that this account is built on a theory of properties that is idiosyncratic, if not outright implausible.

James Van Cleve exploits the fact that Reid's geometry for visibles is non-Euclidean in an argument that implies that Reid's theory of visual perception is not direct. Reid facilitates his geometry of visibles by showing that, in Van Cleve's words, "objects have certain shape properties in themselves (that is, absolutely or nonperspectively) and other shape properties relative to various points of view" (2002, 404). These relational properties are undeniably real, which Van Cleve explains by saying, "The corner of the ceiling does not merely *look* obtuse from here—it *is* obtuse, from here. Compare: the mouth of a soccer goal does not merely *look* narrow from the sidelines; it *is* narrow from there, as shown by the greater difficulty of putting the ball in the net from there" (2002, 405). Thus far we are agreed on the relational status of visible figure. But Van Cleve believes this leads to an objection to the directness of Reid's theory of visual perception. He argues that either Reid advocates a genuinely non-Euclidean geometry for visible space, or he is capable of maintaining a direct theory of perception, but not both (2002, 399).

Reid understands that his geometry of visibles does not obey Euclid's theorems. In the history of geometry he says "not a single proposition do we find with regard to the figure and extension which are the immediate objects of sight" (IHM 102/147a), and adds that "those figures and that extension which are the immediate objects of sight, are not the figures and the extension about which common geometry is employed" (IHM 6.9, 105/148b). Most explicitly, his twelve propositions are each "not less true nor less evident [with regard to visible figures] than the propositions of Euclid, with regard to tangible figures" (IHM 6.9, 105/148a). The twelve propositions at *Inquiry* 6.9 are inconsistent with a number of Euclidean propositions. The parallel postulate is false in Reid's geometry of visibles, and the internal angles of visible triangles do not add up to $180°$. If those propositions are consistent, then, together with Reid's model, they seem sufficient for the establishment of a non-Euclidean geometry.

This proves to be a sticky point in Van Cleve's argument. Van Cleve eventually raises questions about what it is to construct a non-Euclidean geometry, and offers a sufficient condition: "If to propound a non-Euclidean geometry it suffices to point out that there are objects that have non-Euclidean properties from any point of view—even though these same objects are Euclidean in themselves—the answer would be yes" (2002, 406). In other words, if that is the sufficient condition of choice, then Reid succeeds in forming a non-Euclidean geometry. The key term in this condition is "objects," for Van Cleve proceeds to argue that the "objects" of Reid's geometry are either genuine sense-data or complex relational properties or something else. Reid will have developed a non-Euclidean geometry "only by introducing special visible objects for them to be facts about" from which it follows that "Reid can secure a non-Euclidean geometry only at the cost of abandoning a direct realism of vision" (2002, 406).

Two questions arise in relation to these considerations. First, what is an "object"? In the context it seems as though the term refers to a figure capable of bearing geometrical properties. Prima facie this does not preclude relational properties from being objects. Without an argument to this effect, it will not follow that Reid is committed to a theory of vision that posits ideas, sense-data, or perceived intermediaries. As argued, relational properties can themselves bear geometrical properties. Second, Van Cleve's observation neither implies that this condition is necessary for a non-Euclidean geometry, nor does Van Cleve claim it is necessary. Unless it is necessarily true that the "objects" of all non-Euclidean geometries cannot be relational objects, then Van Cleve's conclusion—no non-Euclidean geometry without sacrificing direct realism—seems unconvincing. Perhaps a set of necessary and jointly sufficient conditions can be constructed without reifying sense-data by relying instead upon Reid's denial of several of Euclid's propositions.

Van Cleve's questions take the form, "Does what philosopher X says imply theory A and, if so, does this imply he cannot adopt theory B?" In the present case the question is compelling for reasons of historical interest. Yet we mustn't lose sight of the fact that Reid neither debated the necessary and sufficient conditions of a geometry being non-Euclidean, nor employed highly sophisticated analyses of "direct realism" like those used by Van Cleve (2002, 375; and 2004b, 118). The foregoing argument does not succeed in showing that Reid, as a result of what he in fact says about the geometry of visibles, is committed to visible sense-data.

4.12. Summary

Given Reid's circuitous descriptions of visible figure codified through our constraints, and given the dialectical uses to which Reid puts visible figure, the preceding account marks a plausible way to interpret Reid and explain the texts at issue. Though Reid does not to his satisfaction determine its Aristotelian category of being (IHM 6.8, 98/144b), I have argued that we must discriminate between three types of visible figure: objects of geometrical analysis, objects of which we are visually aware, and objects of perception$_{C\&B}$. Seen figure—the immediate object of visual awareness—is the most important of the three. I showed that this distinction and my analysis of seen figure help to improve upon previous explanations. I then argued that, despite appearances, our account of visual perception is able to preserve the relevant philosophical difference between Reid's theory and the Way of Ideas. This is because being immediately aware of seen figure is not relevantly similar to being immediately aware of the Ideal Theory's ideas, since seen figures are mind-independent and objective. Reid can maintain his commitment to the psychological and epistemic immediacy of the objects of visual perception while avoiding pitfalls of the Way of Ideas.

5

The Purpose of Sensations

Philosophers, psychologists, and cognitive scientists widely recognize Reid as the first clearly to draw the distinction between sensation and perception.[1] Yet uncertainty prevails about what role sensations occupy in Reid's theory of perception. The purpose of this chapter is to improve our understanding of the relationship between Reidian sensation and perception. In what follows I will take for granted the analysis of the nature of sensations offered in Section 3.4. There I argued that sensations do not *have* or *take* mind-independent objects. Sensations are not states that are directed at the world; they do not have intentional content that is about bodies or their qualities. In the present context the issue is whether sensations are intentional objects of *other* mental states and, if so, what type of mental states takes them as objects.

The thrust of the chapter is to emphasize the thoroughgoing manner in which Reid marginalizes the role of sensation in perception. One way to analyze the role of sensations in perception is to offer some a priori definitions of "direct" and "indirect" perception, then tease out from Reid's corpus evidence that he accepts or does not accept those definitions. Reid does speak of directness and immediacy, but very rarely, and when he does, unsurprisingly, he appears to have different uses of those terms from the ones we have. On my preferred method, I will analyze what Reid says about sensations without imposing others' definitions of directness on the discussion. This leads to the conclusion that Reid holds that sensations have a very different purpose from the one they are typically thought to have by both philosophers of mind today and by Reid's commentators. Reid holds that sensations originally had very little to do with the perception of the external world. In his teleological account,

---

[1] A sampling includes Herrnstein and Boring (1965, 172); Pastore (1971, 114); Hatfield (1990, 281–2); Humphrey (1992, 46–50); and Hamlyn (1996, 5). Hatfield says that Malebranche makes something like what would become a sensation/perception distinction but in a form too inchoate to bear philosophical analysis. So Reid was first to make the distinction clear. Hamlyn implies that Reid is the first since Aristotle to make this distinction clear.

Reid suggests that their purpose was to enhance the survival of the human body. They do this, not by making us aware of mind-independent objects, but rather by causing our bodies to react to sensory stimulation. After explaining this account and its implications for the need of sensations for perception, I conclude with a remark about the origins of this "anti-sensationism" in Reid's reaction to Locke.

I have a procedural point to make before we go forward. Consistent with the methodology described in Chapter 1, Reid employs a first-person method of analysis by reflecting on the internal operations of his perceptual and sensory faculties. He sees no need to use anti-physicalist arguments to justify his belief that sensations exist and are not identical to or reducible to physical states, what he calls "material impressions." It is no surprise that those who argue that Reidian sensations are easily reducible to material or functional states do not show appreciation for or do not concur with Reid's method. One commentator says that Reid's "empirical case for such sensations is not decisive" (Chappell 1989, 56). But Reid holds that first-person experience of qualia is sufficient evidence on which to build a strong case for the independence of qualia from physical states.

Reid suggests that his readers concentrate upon their sensory experiences. He says, "The most simple operations of the mind, admit not of a logical definition: all we can do is to describe them, so as to lead those who are conscious of them in themselves, to attend to them, and reflect upon them; and it is often very difficult to describe them so as to answer this intention" (IHM 6.20, 166/182b; see EIP 1.1, 37/229b). For the investigations of a natural philosopher, these observations are of no less authority than the scientist's data that results from dissecting the eye. This methodological step is needed to prevent what has been called "consciousness neglect" (Siewert 1998). Elsewhere Reid argues that in order to have "a distinct notion of any of the operations of our own minds, it is not enough that we be conscious of them...: it is further necessary that we attend to them while they are exerted, and reflect upon them with care, while they are recent and fresh in our memory" (EIP 2.5, 96/258a). To participate with Reid in this exploration of our conscious mental life we must be willing provisionally to accept that this method is virtuous. Since this is a point of method closely echoed in contemporary work on consciousness, I do not expect it to be a stumbling block for most.[2]

---

[2] Siewert (1998) says he "will describe types of conscious experience, as well as cases in which certain kinds of conscious experience are or would be lacking.... I ask you to turn your attention to the first-person case. That is, I would like you to consider instances in your own life of the types of conscious experience I will describe" (4–5).

5.1. Sensations as Necessary for Perception

A number of philosophers hold both that Reid believes that sensations are not conceptually necessary for perception, and that he should believe they are. The forthright among this group infer that Reid was wrong, while the kindhearted attempt to repair Reid's theory, for better or worse. Interpreters claiming that Reid minimizes the role of sensation in perception have made this claim by citing different sources of textual evidence for this conclusion. Despite the widespread textual support for thinking that Reid intentionally marginalizes the role of sensation wherever he can, some commentators hold that Reid didn't intend to do this, or that doing so marks a slip on his part.

I want to invert this debate by repudiating a shared assumption of both groups. Reid intends to marginalize sensations in the perceptual process; this is no accident on his part. This leads me to diagnose attempts to show that Reid thinks sensations are conceptually necessary for perception as efforts motivated by a misguided sense of charity. Let's briefly look at what these scholars are suggesting.

Wolterstorff holds that if sensations were not intentional objects of awareness, there would be "an odd superfluity of information." The sensation, for Reid, "transmits information about the object to the perceiver" (Wolterstorff 2000, 12). But if we were directly perceptually acquainted with objects, then this information from our sensations would be overkill. "Given acquaintance with external entities, the sensory experience functioning as sign of the external entity is otiose; given the sensory experience functioning as sign of the external entity, acquaintance with the external entity is otiose" (2000, 13). Our direct perceptual acquaintance with external objects and our sensation experiences both yield the same thing. But "Double information is theoretically incoherent" (2001, 150). So sensations are useless if their job in the process of perception can be eliminated altogether, or just as easily performed by a material impression.

This, though, isn't exegesis of Reid; these passages voice Wolterstorff's own philosophical position. He notices Reid's anti-sensationism but believes that Reid cannot genuinely intend that sensations are useless in a theory of perception. But Reid doesn't unambiguously assert the necessity of sensation for perception. As others have noticed, Reid is "on the verge of plunging sensations into an insignificant role in our theories of mind and knowledge" (Daniels 1989, 73). Without finding sufficient texts for support, some commentators are driven on charitable grounds to construct an argument on Reid's behalf for the claim that sensation is not otiose for perception. (One straightforward way to insure their necessity in the perceptual process is to make them cognitive intermediaries, on which see Chapter 7.)

Vere Chappell (1989) thinks that Reid openly denies that sensations are necessary for perception. Chappell draws upon Reid's examination of the idiosyncrasies in visual perception in his statement of this objection. As we have seen, Reid holds that there are some visual perceptual experiences that do not proceed via sensations because we have no sensations of properties of visual space and figure. Chappell is savvy to the way Reid differentiates between vision and the other senses by claiming that seen figures are suggested directly by material impressions. This prompts Chappell rhetorically to ask: "[I]f such [material] impressions are capable of suggesting qualities directly, without the intervention of sensations, in some cases, why not in all?" (1989, 58).

Chappell and Wolterstorff differ about the nature of Reidian sensations but both their evaluations of Reid revolve around a mutual commitment to an intuition that sensation is in some way or other needed in an account of perception. But while Chappell uses this point to raze Reid's theory[3], Wolterstorff renovates.

Alston (1989) shares Chappell's analysis of the nature of Reidian sensation and his evaluation of Reid's theory. But whereas Chappell appeals to Reid's discussion of visual perception for evidence, Alston appeals to Reid's definition of perception for evidence that sensations play no role in perception. Alston emphasizes the formal elements of "perception$_{C\&B}$" from which it follows that Reid has left sensation out of his account altogether. He says, "perception

---

[3] Strictly speaking, Chappell attempts to show that sensations are "not all that different" from ideas (1989, 49). He says: "Reid attributes three special propositions to the idea theorist: [5.a] that all mental operations have ideas for their objects; [5.b] that ideas are the only things that are immediately thought and perceived; and [5.c] that ideas resemble their *representata*" (1989, 50). Chappell argues that we can replace "sensations" with "ideas" in (5.a)–(5.c) and Reid would accept the theses. If Chappell is correct, then Reid's account of sensations is confused. (If I am correct Reid denies each of (5.a)–(5.c) when recast about sensations.)

Chappell does not explicitly argue for the aforementioned replacement in each of (5.a)–(5.c). Indeed, he seems to argue for something else, namely: (5.d) "that sensations have representational properties" (1989, 52). I suppose his rationale is that (5.d) is more central to Reid's views on sensations than is (5.a) or (5.b), and also that (5.c) is dependent on (5.d). (5.d) would imply that Reidian sensations are not significantly different from his predecessors' ideas. Chappell says: "ideas are representative beings; they stand for or represent things distinct from themselves. The same again is the case with sensations. It is true that Reid rarely uses the language of representation in connection with sensations. What he says rather is that sensations suggest things to the mind in which they occur ... But representation too is a species of signification, as Reid acknowledges" (1989, 52). This charge fails to appreciate the differences in types of representation. On one definition of "representational,' even Aquinas' appeal to formal causes is representational. After all, the actual frog does not somehow enter my mind when I think about it, so I only think about the frog via something that is not itself the frog. Chappell presumes that sensations are intrinsically representational, whereas for Reid they are only conventionally representational.

is distinguished from thinking and believing precisely by incorporating an intuitive, sensory element. Perception *essentially* involves sensory awareness, awareness of sensory qualities.... So Reid has escaped a representational, ideational theory of perception only by talking about something else altogether" (1989, 38, my emphasis). It is true that Reid does not refer to sensations in his definitions of "perception" in either the *Inquiry* or *Intellectual Powers* (IHM 6.20, 168/183 and EIP 2.6, 96/258a). Since incorporating a sensation component in an account of perception is an a priori condition on an account for Alston, Reid's is doomed to failure.

In addition to the implications of his definitions of "perception," Reid's Sensory Deprivation argument also suggests that sensations are not physically necessary in perception. Keith DeRose says that the difference between a Berkeleyan theory of concept acquisition, which he calls a "sensationalist" theory, and Reid's is located in implications about the contingency of sensations. He says:

According to the sensationalist account, ... to have a concept of bodies just is to have a certain piece of such knowledge about sensations. According to Reid, on the other hand, it is possible for someone to know everything I know about sensations and their connections, and yet to lack a concept of bodies that I have. Likewise, it is possible for someone to have all the concepts of primary qualities of bodies that I have, and yet not to know anything at all about what sensations are like. (DeRose 1989, 342)

Reid's crucial test operates upon a radically anti-sensationist presupposition not shared by his interlocutors. This is a vital point, which we shouldn't miss on account of the introduction of epistemic terminology. DeRose might be claiming that, according to Reid, it is possible a human agent in our world can have concepts of all the primary qualities without ever having sensations. If so, then we might interpret Reid as claiming that it is physically possible that a human agent acquire these concepts without experiencing sensations. A retreat to metaphysical possibility would characterize a weaker claim. On this reading Reid asserts that it is possible that a human agent in some possible world or other acquires these concepts without experiencing any sensations.

We have several philosophers each developing a different pathway to the conclusion that Reid minimalizes the role of sensation in perception. Wolterstorff bases most of his argument for sensations as cognitive intermediaries upon an intuition that, counter to the textual evidence, Reid cannot intend that sensations are useless in the perceptual process. Chappell argues for the contingency of sensations in the perceptual process by appeal to Reid's claim that material impressions on the retina, not sensations, suggest to us perception of visible figures. Alston draws an inference to the same conclusion from

Reid's numerous definitions of "perception" that contain no mention of sensation. DeRose argues for the contingency of sensations from Reid's Sensory Deprivation argument.

These commentators unanimously believe that Reid errs by reducing the importance of sensation in perception in the ways he has. But I want to invert this debate by arguing that Reid intended to marginalize sensations in perception. Furthermore, far from this being obviously incorrect, there are good reasons for it.

Before defending these claims, we need more clarity about the logical relations involved than has yet been introduced. Here are some of the competing theses on this matter:

Conceptual Necessity of Sensation: it is necessary that, for all perceptual events over all possible worlds, sensation states are components.

Physical Necessity of Sensation: it is necessary that, for all perceptual events in the actual world, sensation states are components.

Contingency of Sensation: there exist perceptual events in the actual world in which sensation states are not components.

The Contingency of Sensation Thesis is inconsistent with the other two but is consistent with the claim that, normally, sensation is constantly conjoined with perception. These theses make no claim that, for all sensation events, there must be perception events. Such a biconditional cannot be attributed to Reid.

Reid does not affirm the Conceptual Necessity Thesis. Determining which of the other two Reid affirms is problematic. Reid's corpus offers no clear ruling, but his commitments are best captured by the contingency thesis. Sensations are a significant piece of Reid's philosophy of mind, but their importance is not captured by appeal to their role in forming perceptual beliefs. Instead Reid offers a proto-evolutionary explanation for their presence.

5.2. A Teleological Account

This dispute about the role of sensation is not a purely historical matter.[4] The Conceptual Necessity Thesis is affirmed and used today by those who

---

[4] I say that Reid offers a "teleological" account and not a "functional" account in order to distance my interpretation from those who have interpreted sensations in functionalist terms, as J. C. Smith has done. Smith says that sensations are not epistemic intermediaries of perception. This means that it is not a necessary condition upon our knowing facts about the external world through forming perceptual beliefs that we infer those beliefs from beliefs about sensations. "Perception counts as immediate knowledge even though it is mediated by sensation" because sensations do not have "objective

are constructing philosophical accounts of perception. But others, including the cognitive scientist Nicholas Humphrey, deny it. Moreover, Humphrey explicitly claims that Reid is the historical progenitor of the contingency thesis. It will help us understand Reid's theory if we describe the sharp contrast between Humphrey and advocates of the Conceptual Necessity Thesis.

For Brian O'Shaughnessy the notion of *perception* "must," he claims, "be classed as an *a priori* concept" (2000, 302). Those who do not include a qualitative experience, what he simply calls an "experience," in their analysis of perception are "throwing the baby out with the bath water" (413). He is targeting information-processing theories about visual perception. Such theories claim, in his words, "that *seeing is not necessarily an experience*" (419) and that "seeing has neither nominal nor real essence" (427). O'Shaughnessy objects not merely to information-processing accounts of perception, but also to the notion that sensation may not be a necessary component of perception. He exclaims that a theory denying the Conceptual Necessity of Sensation Thesis:

hardly seems to be a theory at all. Indeed, it is doubtful whether the recipe for seeing which it offers is equal to the task of designating *anything*! ... To my mind the danger facing such a theoretical position is, that in dispensing altogether with essences and demoting visual experience from its usual pre-eminence, they will have succeeded in dissolving seeing out of existence! They run the risk of denying it a nature of any kind! (427–8)

---

representational properties" (Smith 1990, 148, 145). Sensations "do not present objects to the mind by being conceptions of perceived objects," and "sensory operations are not ... representational" (Smith 1990, 177, 182).

Instead, they mediate in another way, according to Smith. Reidian sensations are akin to functional states. The qualitative experiences Reid calls "sensations" are reducible to the non-qualitative, non-conscious functional roles they play in the nexus of connections that constitute mental life. Smith generalizes from what he takes to be the role of sensation to all mental activity. "If one [cognitive faculty] is mediated, as perception clearly is by sensation, then they all must be mediated." Sensation is a "functional" intermediary in the perceptual process (Smith 1990, 150), which means it can be "decomposed" into "simpler subcapacities" (Smith 1986, 183, 180). His intriguing discussion leaves uncertain just what it means for sensations to "functionally" mediate perception. That is a substantial problem.

Here is another. Most of the texts that Smith cites are orthogonal to the task of determining whether Reid holds that sensations are functional intermediaries. The texts he typically cites (quoted and unquoted) are open-ended and edited. For example: "Under this account [i.e. an account of the "functional transduction" of a "descriptively specified" "sensory system"] the sensory operations occur in an arbitrarily systematic activity available as an underlying *uninterpreted* 'machine language' to any of the faculties, including the perceptual faculty" (Reid 1983, 14, 39). "This situation resembles the modern computational use of 'production systems,' which function independently whenever arbitrary formal relations of activity in the 'workspace' happen to meet pre-established conditions *internal* to those systems" (Smith 1986, 188–9). At the noted passages one finds no support for believing that Reid posits some type of language of thought in his account of cognition, let alone the other arcane aspects of the computational account of cognition to which Smith refers.

The perceptual experience, particularly seeing, "is endowed with an intrinsic essence" (435), echoing Alston's appeal to the "essential" inclusion of sensation in perception.

From Reid's point of view there is more bark than bite in this argument. First Reid does not believe that there is any "intrinsic essence" or conceptual "necessity" properly imposed upon accounts of perception. In fact, this is just the methodological feature of the Way of Ideas that Reid attacks. The Ideal Theorist begins, mistakenly, from a priori theorizing about the necessity of sense-data in perceptual experience, and from there is led to the coal pit of skepticism. Reid's empiricism constrains him from the heavy-handed use of a priori truths to signpost his theory of perception. Reid also preserves a robust metaphysical role for qualitative experience. As a substance dualist, arguably he is able to take the introspective aspects of qualitative experience more seriously and give them a more robust role in his philosophy of mind than is O'Shaughnessy. Third, Reid invokes notions of teleology and proper function in his account of perception. In this respect Reid's theory is arguably more contemporaneous than those offered by "essentialists." Claiming that by denying the Conceptual Necessity Thesis one's theory will not be capable of "designating *anything!*" and that such an explanation will be "denying [seeing] a nature of any kind!" is methodologically dubious.

In contrast, Humphrey lays stress upon the division of labor between our sensory and perceptual capacities. He says, "the two categories of experience—sensation and perception, autocentric and allocentric representations, subjective feelings and physical phenomena—are alternative and essentially non-overlapping ways of interpreting the meaning of an environmental stimulus arriving at the body" (1992, 47). Study of the evolution of sensation and experiments in the way sensory stimuli affect our perceptions draw him to this conclusion. Our ancestors evolved first merely with capacities for sensation, and only later with capacities of perception. The first living uni- and multi-cellular animals were able to react to their environments by receiving crude light and pressure stimuli. This ability to *react to* the environment was sensory, and it gave these organisms a survival advantage. The capacity to *represent* the external environment only later evolved when organisms found a survival advantage in possessing the ability to delay their responses to stimuli. Humphrey notes that Reid correctly asserts that "body surface stimuli," what Reid would call "material impressions," are responsible for both the qualitative state, and the cognitive, perceptual state. The sensation itself is thus not the cause of the perceptual event; it is only a natural sign.

While Humphrey believes that Reid is an early advocate of just this position, he calls Reid's view "interestingly ambiguous" (1992, 47 and 49). The best textual evidence for such an interpretation of Reid is this:

The external senses have a double province—to make us feel, and to make us perceive. They furnish us with a variety of sensations, some pleasant, others painful, and others indifferent; at the same time they give us a conception of and an invincible belief in the existence of external objects. This conception of external objects is the work of nature; so likewise is the sensation that accompanies it. This conception and belief which nature produces by means of the senses, we call *perception*. The feeling which goes along with perception, we call *sensation*. The perception and its corresponding sensation are produced at the same time. In our experience we never find them disjoined. Hence, we are led to consider them as one thing, to give them one name, and to confound their different attributes. (EIP 2.17, 210/318b)

Humphrey believes that in this comment Reid cuts to the core of the problem. The historical Reid only plays a cosmetic part in Humphrey's theory about the mind and its evolution, but, if correct, Reid is prescient on the point since empirical results show that the necessity of sensation theses are false. For example, only an affirmation of the Contingency of Sensation Thesis seems capable of reckoning with blindsight cases. These cases suggest that agents can perceive even if their experiences contain no sensuous content.[5]

Taking Humphrey's suggestion, I want to show why the balance of Reid's texts favors viewing sensations as an unnecessary part of the perceptual process. First I describe Reid's general opposition to imposing a priori constraints on an account of perception. Reid sets out a rule of thumb in this passage:

---

[5] Blindsight cases describe the severing of the relationship between visual sensation and visual perception. Victims do not acknowledge experiencing activity in portions of their visual field. This sensory deprivation is caused by damage to the visual cortex, but, from the first-person point of view, these subjects might as well lack receptors on their retinas. Despite the fact that blindsight subjects claim that they have no sensations of light and dark, of hue and brightness, or of visible figures, they remain capable of perceiving objects, much to their own surprise. Since patients deny they can "see" any such objects, experiments proceed by requesting that subjects take a guess about the nature of the objects in their visual fields—"guesses" which are remarkably accurate.

Though Reid is not aware of the blindsight phenomenon, he is aware of phantom pain cases in which one's sensations are not accompanied by the perceptual events that usually accompany them when one functions properly. In the case of phantom limb pain, if the subject "did not know that his leg was cut off, it would give him the same immediate conviction of some hurt or disorder in the toe" (EIP 2.18, 214/320b). This marks an aberration of the general rule that certain sensations are constantly conjoined to certain secondary qualities. In this case there is a sensation (of pain) and there is a secondary quality causing the sensation, but that cause it not the typical cause of the sensation of pain. "This perception, which Nature had conjoined with the sensation, was, in this instance, fallacious" (EIP 2.18, 214/320b). We can have sensations of pain without any accompanying perceptions, which supports this "double province" hypothesis. Blindsight cases support this hypothesis by being examples of the opposite phenomenon: cases in which perceptions are not accompanied by corresponding sensations.

Most operations of the mind, that have names, ... are complex in their nature, and made up of various ingredients, or more simple acts; which, though conjoined in our constitution, must be disjoined by abstraction, in order to our having a distinct and scientific notion of the complex operation. In such operations, sensation for the most part makes an ingredient. (EIP 1.1, 37/229b)

He applies this rule later to the issue at hand when he writes: "If we thus analyze the various operations of our minds, we shall find that many of them ... are compounded of more simple ingredients; and that sensation ... makes one ingredient, not only in the perception of external objects, but in most operations of the mind" (EIP 2.16, 197/311b). Reid's generalizations are unsatisfying. He says sensation is "for the most part" a component to operations of the mind, and it is an ingredient "in most operations" of the mind. He doesn't clarify or quantify. He is clear, though, that determining whether it is or is not a component part of perception is not a matter for armchair philosophy.

We must bear in mind that Reid puts sensations into the service of a different explanatory task from that of his interpreters. According to Reid sensations are intended by God for, and are physically necessary for, *our survival* (IHM 2.9, 40–43/112a–114b). Sensations are not directly fitted into an information-processing account of perception. Sensation and perception perform distinct functions in the life of the mind. In addition to the "double province" passage, Reid writes (in reply to Lord Kames):

You distinguish, I think very justly, two different Purposes of the external Senses; one to inform us of what passes about us, and one to give us Pleasure and Amusement. I distinguish two different Operations of the Senses, which almost always go together, and on that Account are confounded both by the Vulgar and by Philosophers; but which may be distinguished in thought. The first is *Perception*; by which I mean an Information of something about us by our Senses, and nothing more. The second is *Sensation*; by which I mean the feelings we have by our Senses whether pleasant painfull or indifferent. I can conceive a Being that has Sensations of various kinds without any Perception. (C 112)

Reid emphasizes the contingency of the relation between sensation and perception and in so doing openly denies the conceptual necessity of sensation. Reid gives us an explanation for why those two activities have been conflated in previous thinking about perception. We do not learn information about the world through sensations. Rather, sensations manifest our bodies' reactions to the world. In contrast, through perception we represent aspects of the mind-independent world—its objects and their properties. Sensations per se do not represent anything intrinsically. They suggest perceptual beliefs and signify qualities for most people most of the time. But its original and more important job is to regulate our behavior by furnishing us with pleasurable and painful qualitative experiences.

This leads Reid to adopt a teleological explanation of sensations. Reid says, speaking of our capacity for sensation, "The faculties which we have in common with brute-animals, are of earlier growth than reason" (EAP 3.1.2, 548b). In the *Intellectual Powers* Reid remarks on the wide variability amongst sensations. Some require effort to notice, while the presence of others demands our immediate attention. Some are caused from within our body, while others are caused by events external to our bodies. Most sensations assist us in prolonging our bodily existence. The state of being in need of nourishment, for example, produces sensations of hunger that in turn signals to the conscious mind a need for food (EIP 2.16, 196/311a).

Reid says, "the Author of Nature, in the distribution of agreeable and painful feelings, hath wisely and benevolently consulted the good of the human species, and hath even shewn us, by the same means, what tenor of conduct we ought to hold" (EIP 2.16, 198/312a). God has somehow brought it about that the sensations we experience condition us to develop patterns of response. Engaging in those patterns of behavior benefits us as organisms. Not only do sensations thus assist us in our attempt to survive, but they also are capable of rewarding us for behaviors beneficial to our bodies. The function of our possession of sensations is not to benefit us as epistemic agents but as embodied human beings. Far from benefiting us as knowers, the presence of sensations often befuddles us in our attempt to gain knowledge of the mind-independent world.

When the body's nervous systems lose their ability to function and to sense dangers to health, chaos erupts. Leprosy, for example, debilitates the cutaneous nervous systems. The lack of sensory cues renders victims of this malady unaware that they are doing grave harm to their bodies, which diminishes their ability to provide for their body's needs. Reid says, "The painful sensations of the animal kind are admonitions to avoid what would hurt us; and the agreeable sensations of this kind invite us to those actions that are necessary to the preservation of the individual or of the kind" (EIP 2.16, 198/312a). Reid extrapolates from this general principle by adding that one will have certain sensations of pleasure when exposed to beauty and sensations of disgust when exposed to "deformity." Furthermore, inactivity creates an idleness in our muscles that causes unpleasant sensations. We can see how this teleological analysis leads Reid to say:

Sensation, taken by itself, implies neither the conception nor belief of any external object. It supposes a sentient being, and a certain manner in which that being is affected;

but it supposes no more. Perception implies an immediate conviction and belief of something external—something different both from the mind that perceives, and the act of perception. (EIP 2.16, 199/312b)

Sensation "implies neither the conception nor belief of any external object" because that is not its divinely ordained purpose. God adapts each capacity for sensation in order to give us a reactive, sensory experience of the proper quality and intensity for each circumstance.

The upshot is that Reidian sensations are not fitted intrinsically to represent external bodies. Rather, the preponderance of texts implies that the purpose of sensations is to prompt our body to react to internal or external stimuli in ways that preserve its functionality.

5.3. Physically Necessary?

Reid says that God could have created us in such a way that we experience no sensations at all, or that our sensations would be matched with different physical causes from those with which they happen to be matched in the actual world. Reid also discusses several examples from the actual world in which perception can occur without a corresponding sensation. And yet he makes several other comments suggesting that sensations are physically necessary for perceptions. Let's look at evidence on both sides.

A respectable case can be made on behalf of the Physical Necessity Thesis. Reid says that tactual sensations "naturally *and necessarily* ... convey the notion and belief of hardness" (IHM 5.3, 60/122b, my emphasis). Given the clarity with which Reid denies any conceptual connection between sensations and perceptions, the modal claim in this quotation must be read as restricted to our actual world on charitable grounds. He also cannot mean that, necessarily, if one experiences a tactual sensation of pressure, then one forms the conception and belief of hardness. This is because we experience countless sensations of pressure throughout the day and most of us never form any discrete conception and belief of hardness. Yet the text stands on behalf of the physical necessity of sensations for tactile perception, to which this text is restricted. (One might distinguish between several forms of the Physical Necessity Thesis—one for touch, another for vision, and so on, in roughly the way we divided our analysis of forms of directness between vision and the other senses in Chapter 4. I refrain from doing this here.)

One point against the attribution of the thesis to Reid arises in his claims about conceivability. Above I quoted a passage about what is "perhaps actual." The full text reads: "I can conceive a Being that has Sensations of various kinds without any Perception. Perhaps this is actually the State of Children in the Womb and of Oysters & some other Animals. I can conceive also a Being that perceives all that we perceive without any Sensation connected with those Perceptions" (C 112). He is hinting, though not asserting, that fetuses have sensation without perception. Nonetheless, he can be interpreted as fostering some skepticism about the Physical Necessity Thesis since he clearly does not affirm it here when the opportunity arises.

It might seem from his discussion of the lack of visual sensations in visual perception that Reid does not believe sensations are physically necessary for perception. Reid says:

We might perhaps have been made of such a constitution, as to have our present perceptions connected with other sensations. We might perhaps have had the perception of external objects, without either impressions upon the organs of sense, or sensations. Or lastly, the perceptions we have, might have been immediately connected with the impressions upon our organs, without any intervention of sensations. This last seems really to be the case in one instance—to wit, in our perception of the visible figure of bodies. (IHM 6.21, 176/187b; see IHM 6.8, 100/146a)

He repeats this point elsewhere.[6] Our awareness of visible figure occurs without any special sensation and it is suggested immediately by a material impression. (For an objection and reply to this conclusion, see Section 4.2 and its notes).

But the entanglement surrounding visible figure prevents this from serving as much more than partial evidence against the Physical Necessity Thesis. Reid's claims that material impressions suggest our awareness of visible figure are nested in such a complex discussion (see Section 5.2; Yaffe 2003a and b; and Falkenstein and Grandi 2003) that I hesitate to rest the case for this "double province" interpretation upon them. Material impressions, not sensations, serve this role, but we know from our discussion of visible figure that Reid does not write clearly about the nature of our awareness of visible figure. Strictly speaking, when we visually perceive a red sedan, we do not merely perceive a visible figure. Rather, we perceive a red sedan, brimming with properties that visible figures—though robust in their own special way—lack. Sensations are not essential components in the perception or awareness of visible figure,

---

[6] "In answer therefore to the question proposed, there seems to be no sensation that is appropriated to visible figure, or whose office it is to suggest it. It seems to be suggested immediately by the material impression upon the organ, of which we are not conscious: and why may not a material impression upon the retina suggest visible figure, as well as the material impression made upon the hand, when we grasp a ball, suggests real figure? In the one case, one and the same material impression, suggests both colour and visible figure; and in the other case, one and the same material impression suggests hardness, heat, or cold, and real figure, all at the same time" (IHM 6.8, 101/146a).

but Reid believes that we are only rarely aware of or perceive visible figure. So actual exceptions to the physical necessity of sensations in our perceptual experience are infrequent.

Relatedly, consider Reid's claim that we have sensations of color. We cannot but sense color whenever we perceive visible figures. We have just witnessed him say, "there seems to be no sensation that is appropriated to visible figure, or whose office it is to suggest it." He also says that sensations do not "intervene" in our awareness of visible figure. But these comments are consistent with the fact that color sensations will be concurrent to the perception of visible figure. With the important exception of the sensations involved in seeing a white triangle on a black background, which Reid thinks is a colorless sensation, we have color sensations when seeing visible figure. Reid's point is not that we have no color sensations at all when seeing visible figures, but rather that there is no specific sensation corresponding to our visual perception of figure.

It is difficult to know what to do with this point in appraising the relation between sensation and perception in Reid. One might insist on these grounds that all visual perceptions have corresponding sensations of color. However, this appears misleading when we emphasize that sensations of color play no role in suggesting the perception of visible figures. We have been conditioned to experience sensations of color and perceptions of visible figures in tandem. From this training, sensations of color may artificially suggest figure. In a similar way, from birth I might have been conditioned to associate sensations of warmth with perceptions of visible figure. There is no substantive relation between the two. Put in Reid's terms, material impressions are the constitutional signs that suggest our visual perceptions. So the association between sensations of color and visual perceptions does not imply that it is physically necessary that sensations of color suggest visual perceptions.

The difficulties involved in identifying Reid's commitments about the Physical Necessity Thesis follow from a tendency in Reid's work. As it is stated, the thesis is a modal, broadly metaphysical claim. Reid is rarely comfortable issuing such declarations. He typically transmogrifies the metaphysical into the epistemic. In passages drawn from his unpublished abstract of the *Inquiry* and from the midst of the *Intellectual Powers*, he explicitly says that we cannot know that such statements are true:

For aught we know Nature might have given us Sensations of Mind such as we have without connecting them invariably with certain material Impressions made upon the bodily organs. In like manner for aught we know, Nature might have given us both the conception and the belief of external things, without connecting them invariably with certain Sensations. For no man can give a shadow of a reason why the latter should always precede the former. (Aberdeen MS 2131.6/I/2; see Norton 1976b, 129)

We know that, when certain impressions are made upon our organs, nerves, and brain, certain corresponding sensations are felt, and certain objects are both conceived and believed to exist. But in this train of operations nature works in the dark. We can neither discover the cause of any one of them, nor any necessary connection of one with another; and, whether they are connected by any necessary tie, or only conjoined in our constitution by the will of heaven, we know not. ...

Nor can we perceive any necessary connection between sensation and the conception and belief of an external object. For anything we can discover, we might have been so framed as to have all the sensations we now have by our senses, without any impressions upon our organs, and without any conception of any external object. For anything we know, we might have been so made as to perceive external objects, without any impressions on bodily organs, and without any of those sensations which invariably accompany perception in our present frame. (EIP 2.20, 227/327a)

Reid is claiming that three relations are contingent on the basis of a mild skepticism about modal knowledge. The relations are: that between a material impression and a sensation, that between a sensation and a perception, and that between a material impression and a perception. Reid makes the modal epistemic claim that *we cannot know that sensation is necessary for forming perceptual beliefs.* Far from contravening the "double province" interpretation, this complements it. But in the same breath Reid suggests that *we cannot know that sensation is unnecessary for forming perceptual beliefs* either.

Reid corroborates this epistemic pessimism when emphasizing his incapacity to fathom some aspects of sensation. In a discussion of "whether the Sensation and Perceptions takes place when I cannot in the least remember them next Moment," he says,

If therefore one Man says, that in this Case we had both the Sensation & Perception but were not conscious of them; another that we had both with Consciousness, but without any degree of Memory; a third that we had the sensation without the perception; & a fourth that we had neither; I think they all grop<e>in the dark, and I would not trust much to conclusions built upon any of these Hypotheses (C 214).

In effect, Reid refuses to affirm either the Physical Necessity Thesis or the contingency thesis on grounds that they are all underdetermined by empirical evidence. We might be psychologically compelled to think that there is a necessary connection, but this isn't a thesis that can be justified by philosophical argument. The "testimony of our external senses, which though on reflection, we can see no necessary connection between the feelings of the senses and external things, it is impossible for us to get over" (Edinburgh MS Reid

1763 Dk. 3.2, Lecture 40). Given his philosophical method (see Chapter 1) we should expect nothing less.

The points made in this section are neither individually nor collectively capable of showing that Reid does endorse what I have stated as the Physical Necessity Thesis. So far as I can see Reid is not inconsistent on this matter, even though Reid leaves us without the final answers about the relation between sensation and perception.

5.4. Locke's Mistake

At this juncture we're in danger of missing the forest for the trees. The point of overriding importance is that Reid marginalizes the perceptual role of sensations and qualitative experience to a degree unheard of in the history of realist theories of perception. Sensations, far from being necessarily perceived intermediaries, or the typical immediate objects of acts of perception, are not even contingent causal components in visual perception and are probably not even physically necessary corollaries to perception. We can best appreciate the meaning of the current observation, and glimpse its implications for a theory of perceptual knowledge, by examining a key difference between Reid and his predecessors.

Advocates of the Way of Ideas typically did not make any place for non-intentional, purely qualitative states in constructing their philosophies of mind. Locke started and Hume continued the debate by claiming that sensations and perceptions are both analyzable in terms of ideas. Representational theories of perception typically state that the immediate objects of awareness are private, mind-dependent ideas that represent features of the mind-independent world. Emphasis is placed upon the representational features of ideas at the expense of attention to the qualitative aspects of perceptual experience. Historically, these forms of representationalism about perception gave rise to information-processing theories of perception on which qualitative aspects of perception are typically ignored or passed to the phenomenologist to worry about. It is Locke who makes the implications of such a point of view upon an analysis of sensations most clear. Tacit assumptions in his commitment to the Way of Ideas lead Locke to propose his famous thought experiment about the visible spectrum. Locke says:

If by the different Structure of our Organs, it were so ordered, That *the same Object should produce in several Men's Minds different* Ideas at the same time; v.g. if the *Idea,* that a *Violet* produced in one Man's Mind by his Eyes, were the same that a *Marigold* produced in another Man's, and *vice versa*. He would be able as regularly to distinguish Things for his Use by those Appearances, and understand, and signify those distinctions, marked by the Names *Blue* and *Yellow*, as if the Appearances, or *Ideas* in his Mind, received from those two Flowers, were exactly the same, with the *Ideas* in other Men's Minds. (Locke 1975, 2.32.15/389)

The conclusion is distinctively epistemic: "this could never be known: because one man's mind could not pass into another man's body, to perceive, what appearances were produced by those organs."

Locke states his case without employing Reid's distinction between sensations and perceptions. Reid believes that distinction offers a key clarification over the Way of Ideas, which uses "idea" to refer to both representational and qualitative features of our internal mental states. To put the point in Reid's terms, Locke holds that if sensations are simply qualitative states, then they are superfluous. We can swap sensations as we wish and it wouldn't make a difference to our perception. This is the same assumption that guides the crew of Reid scholars to their unanimous verdict that Reid is guilty of making sensations otiose. They too affirm the conditional that, if sensations are merely qualitative states without any essential relationship to the perceptions they accompany, then they are superfluous. They add that Reid endorses the antecedent.

Though Locke presented this example with modest goals, cases of inverted spectra and inverted "worlds" have been put to uses Locke could have scarcely imagined. I raise this example only to show the way in which Reid would respond to Locke's own use of the case. Yes, the antecedent is true. But Reid would oppose Locke's conclusion that sensations are somehow useless by refuting his intermediate conclusion that we could not know that such a switch has taken place. Reid would deny this on the basis of the parallel operation of sensation and perception. Sensations began in the history of organic life as responses to stimuli, and not as a means of representing mind-independent reality. Thus there is no principled reason to think that, were our spectra inverted, a third party "could never know" that was the case. As a matter of fact, we can determine when this occurs for a range of sensations. Seeing a dazzling hue of red causes physiological changes, including increased heart rates, whereas blood pressure can be decreased by exposure to gentler colors.[7]

---

[7] Physiological data can be brought to bear on inverted spectrum cases and other sensation-switching thought experiments in order to block Locke's own epistemic conclusion. Studies on color preference and color avoidance have shown that certain (non-perceptual) behaviors and physiological changes are caused by some color sensations and not others. For example, when primates are placed in red environments their heart rates and body temperatures increase substantially in comparison with their rates and temperatures when in other chromatic environments (see Humphrey and Keeble 1977; and Humphrey 1975).

So Locke's claim that no one else could tell that my color sensations have been inverted is false. Locke errs in ignoring the qualitative features of sensations in favor of hypothesizing that they have representative properties, and that they resemble primary qualities.

Reid rightly insists that sensations matter—but for reasons of survival. But Reid also stands apart from those who lay claim to the conceptual or physical necessity of sensation. In the actual world sensations typically accompany perceptual events in most sense modalities, but they are physically and logically contingent components of such events.

5.5. Summary

The question of overriding importance in this chapter has been, "What is the relationship between perceptions and sensations?" Perception is the process by which we form perceptual beliefs about bodies in the mind-independent world through the use of our senses. Sensations are qualitative and not merely causal features of our interaction with the world. My answer to this question involved specifying just how perceptions depend upon sensations. Reid is best interpreted as claiming to know that sensations are at most contingently related to perceptions. He hedges bets about whether sensations are physically necessary for perception: he says they are for touch, but that we have difficulty knowing this to be true. I defend this interpretation with several texts and show that it coheres well with Reid's teleological approach to sensation: the purpose of our experience of sensations is to enhance our chances of survival, not to represent to us features of the mind-independent world.

This chapter leaves unanswered questions about the nature of our awareness of sensations, and whether that is in some way necessary for perception.

6

Qualities

I continue my analysis of the relation between sensation and perception by examining Reid's account of how we are perceptually aware of qualities. Reid says that the immediate objects of perception are qualities of bodies. Reid describes the process through which we perceive qualities of bodies in two different ways, depending upon whether the quality perceived is primary or secondary. In order to construct a plausible account of primary and secondary qualities, Reid must travel through an obstacle course. Locke's account of qualities favors a representationalist form of the Way of Ideas. Like Locke, Reid holds that there are mind-independent material bodies that we perceptually apprehend. But resemblance is an implausibly strong relation to posit between concept and primary quality. Reid must avoid appeal to resemblance, or any other similarly strong relation, while insuring that we are nonetheless aware of mind-independent material bodies. In other words, Reid must guard against Berkeley's dissolution of the distinction, and his conclusion that all qualities are mind-dependent. But Reid must keep an eye on Humean skepticism. Whatever ontology he gives to primary qualities, Reid must argue that we know them. The compass through the course is familiar: the doctrine of natural signs guides him.

Another motivation for his approach stems from his analysis of the ontology of visible figure. Reid's attempt to make clear the ontological status of the quality of visible figure was plagued by problems that led him to claim he didn't know what it was. As a result, Reid does not explicitly discuss where to place visible figure in his list of qualities, even though in hindsight it is a primary quality. A parallel agnosticism about traditional primary qualities—solidity, motion, extension—is unacceptable to Reid. Furthermore, Reid chooses to craft his distinction, not between types of qualities per se, but rather between types of awareness we experience in perceptual events. Reid approaches the problem of our qualities as someone constructing a theory of perception, not as a metaphysician.

I begin by describing how Reid structures the debate about qualities and our perception of them. I then turn to his inchoate analysis of primary and secondary qualities, devoting special attention to whether Reidian secondary qualities are dispositions. I develop this analysis by examining some potential problems with it. Some experts suggest Reid's distinction collapses; others claim that it implies a wrong-headed phenomenology of experience. My interpretation of Reid's analysis of qualities avoids those charges. However, Reid's primary/secondary quality distinction implies that we cannot directly perceive secondary qualities, a result which poses another threat to the coherence of his theory of perception.

The term "primary quality" deserves a brief remark. When Reid addresses the ontological make-up of qualities, he tacitly distinguishes between qualities themselves and their physical bases, following Locke. Locke often describes primary qualities but occasionally refers to an important subset of them—primary qualities of the "minute and insensible parts" of bodies. Locke says there is an "Ignorance of the primary Qualities of the insensible Parts of Bodies" but not of the primary qualities themselves (1975, 4.3.12/545). Reid describes primary qualities and only occasionally specifies what they supervene upon—that is, the primary qualities of the minute and insensible parts of bodies. Reid confesses that he is largely ignorant of what the physical basis of these insensible parts is like, but this does not prevent him from using the term "primary quality" ambiguously. Both quality and physical base are physical in character, though they occupy different levels of description. Reid says the quality of hardness is the firm cohesion of the parts of a body, but to specify its microphysical nature we must say something about the density of particles in the body.

6.1. Reid's Problems with Locke

Idealists, representative realists, and direct realists can in principle agree that apprehension of a secondary quality is a causal process. They differ with respect to the cause (an idea in God's mind, an idea of an object, or an object) and the effect (an idea, a sensation, or a concept)—and about whether there is any cognitive intermediary. Just as important is their disagreement concerning what, in this mix of causes and effects, is to be dubbed "the secondary quality." This is the inheritance of Locke for he is easily interpreted as using the term "secondary quality" to refer to the *cause* of the process,[1] its *effect*,[2] and, on the most common interpretation, *the process itself*, that is the relation between cause and effect.[3]

Locke's loose discussion of secondary qualities forms the backdrop for Reid's entrance into the debate. The source of Reid's difficulty in understanding Locke lies in Locke's appeal to ideas. Reid says Locke "thought it necessary to introduce the Theory of Ideas, to explain the distinction between primary and secondary qualities, and by that means, as I think, perplexed and darkened it" (EIP 2.17, 207/317a). Interpretations of Locke differ about how we apprehend qualities, and about the nature of secondary qualities themselves, which leaves two corresponding problems for Reid.

The first substantive problem concerns the distinction between sensation and perception. On the traditional interpretation secondary qualities are dispositions to cause ideas in us. But these ideas are underdescribed since secondary qualities frequently cause two mental states—a qualitative state and a propositional attitude. When smelling a rose, the perceiver possesses a mental state that has intentional and propositional content, which for Reid is a *perception*. Yet there is

---

[1] On one prominent interpretation, "colours, tastes, odours and sounds are not, for Locke, secondary qualities, but sensations; secondary qualities are colourless, tasteless, odourless and soundless textures of objects" (Alexander 1977, 212). Several texts favor this reading, and Locke's debt to Boyle also supports it. Locke's frequent appeal to "texture" favors his interpretation because texture for Boyle is an insensible physical property of corpuscles. Texture fails the inseparability test that Locke thinks that primary qualities pass (1977, 170 ff.). So secondary qualities are purely physical qualities.

[2] On another interpretation, secondary qualities are either conceptual or sensorial in nature, and neither physical bases of sensations nor dispositions causing those ideas. Locke says manna "has a power to produce the sensations of sickness, and sometimes of acute pains, or gripings in us. That these *ideas* of *sickness and pain are not in the* manna, but effects of its operations on us, and are no where when we feel them not: this also every one readily agrees to." The upshot of this passage is that "these *ideas*," presumably the ideas of sweetness and whiteness, and of sickness and pain, are "all effects of the operations of manna, on the several parts of our bodies" by the primary qualities (Locke 1975, 2.8.18/138). The ostensive reason Locke denies the vulgar view that the quality of pain is in the manna rests on the point that the idea of pain is not in the manna. "Locke is arguing that sweetness and whiteness are not really in manna, on the grounds that these qualities, *like other ideas* such as pain and sickness, are merely effects in a perceiver of the primary qualities of manna's atomic parts." If so, Locke "assumes that secondary-quality ideas are identical with secondary qualities themselves" (Dicker 1977, 465; see Bennett 1971, 115). These scholars identify textual reasons for such an interpretation, though they reject it out of charity.

[3] "[S]uch qualities, are nothing in the objects themselves, but powers to produce various sensations in us by their primary qualities.... These I call secondary qualities" (1975, 135). The description of secondary qualities as "powers" throughout this chapter of the *Essay* lends credence to a dispositional interpretation. Secondary qualities are alleged to be a special type of property describable as a state of affairs, namely: were an object O to produce sensation S in conditions C for person P, O would possess a secondary quality Q.

also a qualitative mental event the perceiver experiences, a *sensation*. The complex event of smelling the rose is caused by certain physical qualities of the rose:

> The object of my perception, in this case, is that quality in the rose which I discern by the sense of smell. Observing that the agreeable sensation is raised when the rose is near, and ceases when it is removed, I am led, by my nature, to conclude some quality to be in the rose, which is the cause of this sensation. This quality in the rose is the object perceived; and that act of my mind by which I have the conviction and belief of this quality, is what in this case I call perception. (EIP 2.16, 194/310a–b)

Our relation to the rose and its qualities is twofold: we can perceive the rose, and we can have a sensation of the rose. Reid distinguishes between the two effects of smelling a rose, which Locke does not, which leads to Reid's insistence on the independence of sensation from perception.

From Reid's point of view, the second deficiency with Locke's distinction concerns the nature of dispositional relations. A dispositional analysis of secondary qualities will identify them with our sensory (not perceptual) relation to qualities of objects. Reid is aware of some oblique motivations for this view. For example, he recognizes a syntactic relationship between sensation terms and secondary quality terms; they are "called by the same name" (EIP 2.16, 194/310b). Nonetheless, Reid believes there is a principled problem with Lockean appeals to dispositional "powers."

Though there is a systematic relation between certain properties of physical objects and certain properties of our mental lives, Reid does not believe this philosophically explains secondary qualities. Reid criticizes Hume's parallel appeal to associative relations on these grounds, saying:

> If a philosopher should undertake to account for the force of gunpowder in the discharge of a musket, and then tell us gravely that the cause of this phaenomenon is the drawing of the trigger, we should not be much wiser by this account. As little are we instructed in the cause of memory, by being told that it is caused by a certain impression on the brain. For, supposing that impression on the brain were as necessary to memory as the drawing of the trigger is to the discharge of the musket, we are still as ignorant as we were how memory is produced; so that, if the cause of memory, assigned by this theory, did really exist, it does not in any degree account for memory. (EIP 3.7, 281/354a)

Observing that specific qualities in objects regularly suggest or depend upon specific mental events is platitudinous, and neither illuminates the nature of those qualities nor explains how to bridge the chasm between the mental and physical worlds. Likewise, to stipulate that secondary qualities are relations between certain physical qualities and mental events is to avoid giving a philosophical explanation of secondary qualities. Reid knew that a dispositional account was one legitimate interpretation of Locke on secondary qualities, but he thinks this marks a return to medieval explanatory practices.[4]

In the context of criticizing Locke, Reid says: "The account I have given of this distinction is founded upon no hypothesis. Whether our notions of primary qualities are direct and distinct, those of the secondary relative and obscure, is a matter of fact, of which every man may have certain knowledge by attentive reflection upon them" (EIP 2.17, 202–3/314b). By "hypothesis," Reid is at least referring to Locke's adoption of the Way of Ideas, if not also to his corpuscularianism. So instead of focusing on what qualities are, as Locke had done, Reid attends to the means by which we become aware of qualities, which Reid describes as our notions of qualities.

6.2. Notions of Primary Qualities

Reid sees two philosophically important ways to distinguish between what he calls our "notions" of secondary and primary qualities. "Notion" is a somewhat technical term for Reid. When asked for clarification about whether mere notions can be true or false, he says in a letter of December 31, 1784, that they can be: "The notions we have of real existences, may with good reason be said to be right or wrong, true or false." He adds, "I am apt to think that true and false can only with propriety be applied to notions which include some belief" (C 172/EIP 64b). Elsewhere Reid says: "All men mean by it, the conception, the apprehension, or thought which we have of any object of thought. A notion, therefore, is an act of the mind conceiving or thinking of some object" (EIP 2.11, 155/289a). It is also equivalent to "having an idea of a thing" (EIP 4.1, 295/360a). In this sense "notions" can be and often are the intentional contents of perceptions. Since perception contains a belief component, the notions, as manifest in perceptual beliefs, are true or false depending upon whether they correspond with reality. Reid recognizes that merely entertaining a thought, such as "an abstract thought of a being with horns and cloven feet, without applying it to any individual" is something that is "neither true nor false" (C 172/EIP 64b). This is another way in which we can have a notion. The context for his discussion of qualities is his theory of perception. So I will be examining our notions of qualities insofar as they are the intentional and conceptual contents of perceptions, as

---

[4] This is not to say that Reid thinks there are no dispositional properties; rather, discovering that certain properties are dispositional does not illuminate our understanding of them. I am also not implying that Locke is unaware of the emptiness of appeals to dispositions (see Locke 1975, 4.3.13/545).

opposed to our notions of qualities insofar as they are objects of states of imagination.

The following passages contrast the formation of our notions of primary and secondary qualities. The first is from an early, undated manuscript, the second from Reid's 1763 correspondence with Henry Home, Lord Kames, and the last from the *Intellectual Powers*. In each of these texts Reid uses the term "direct" to describe our awareness of primary qualities:

The primary qualities of body we conceive, not relatively, but directly and clearly. They are not conjoyned in the imagination with the sensations which suggest them. (Aberdeen MS 2131/2/iii/03, no page)

You [Lord Kames] say that secondary Qualities have a Relation to a Percipient [see Home 2003 i, 170]. I would say rather that our Notion or Conception of them hath a relation to a percipient. The whiteness of this paper, is that Quality in it, which causes a certain sensation in me when I look upon it. Not knowing what this quality is in itself, I form a relative Notion of it viz That it is that, which causes such a Sensation in the percipient. It will appear evident to any one who considers the common use of the Word (whiteness) that we dont mean by it in common language, the Sensation, but that in the Body which causes the Sensation...

Of primary qualities Nature hath given us clear and direct perceptions. I know perfectly what figure and Extension are in themselves, as well as how they affect my sense. But of Secondary qualities we know onely how they affect the sense not what they are in themselves. (C 29)

I answer, That there appears to be a real foundation for the distinction; and it is this—that our senses give us a direct and a distinct notion of the primary qualities, and inform us what they are in themselves. But of the secondary qualities, our senses give us only a relative and obscure notion. They inform us only, that they are qualities that affect us in a certain manner—that is, produce in us a certain sensation; but as to what they are in themselves, our senses leave us in the dark. (EIP 2.17, 201/313b)

Building upon these passages, let's first examine how Reid believes our notions of qualities can be distinguished by their formation.

First, only in the case of primary qualities do sensations suggest qualities without themselves being objects of conscious apprehension; that is, they are not conceived and believed. We might infer that he uses "immediately" to this end in the following: "When a primary quality is perceived," says Reid, "the sensation immediately leads our thought to the quality signified by it, and is itself forgot" (EIP 2.17, 204/315b). Some may interpret "immediately" here as having a temporal implicature; his use of "direct" is less problematic. The point is that our sensations "directly" lead our minds onward to notions of primary qualities, which contrasts with the formation of our notions of secondary qualities. More formally, P's notion of quality Q is a notion of a primary quality only if P apprehends Q, and no intermediary is necessarily apprehended in the process.

This contrasts with the Way of Ideas on which our ideas of primary qualities can only be formed by way of experience of and, perhaps, attention to, our impressions. By saying that our notions of primary qualities are formed directly, Reid reaffirms his anti-sensationist commitments first discussed in Chapter 3.

Second, Reid says that we "have no way of coming at this conception and belief [about hardness], but by means of a certain sensation of touch" (IHM 5.3, 57/121a; see 61/122b). This type of passage was noted in the chapter on sensations as partial evidence for the claim that sensations are physically necessary for the conception of primary qualities like hardness, even though other primary qualities do not require the experience of a sensation. As others note, despite the connection between sensations and primary qualities, it remains true that "Primary qualities, in contrast, are those the concept of which makes no reference to sensation." In other words, it is not the case that "the concept of hardness is constitutively tied to sensation" (Hopkins 2005, 349–50).

The foregoing marks how notions of primary qualities are direct by Reid's lights. While directness concerns the *formation* of our concepts of qualities, Reid also argues that the *contents* of our conceptions of primary and secondary qualities differ in crucial respects. This marks the second means by which Reid draws his distinction. The contents of notions of primary qualities bear two traits that notions of secondary qualities lack: clarity and distinctness.

Notions of primary qualities are distinct, but Reid does not explain distinctness in the context of his discussion of qualities. Furthermore, studying Reid's discussion of simple apprehension, where distinctness also plays an important role, does not shed much light on this notion (EIP 4.1, 306–9/366–7). He may have a Cartesian notion of distinctness in mind according to which it refers to the way one apprehends a quality by distinguishing it from its surroundings and isolating it in one's mind.[5] In any case, Reid says that the distinctness of our notions of primary qualities "enables us to reason demonstratively about them to a great extent" (EIP 2.17, 203/315a).

---

[5] In the *Principles*, Descartes says: "I call a perception 'distinct' if, as well as being clear, it is so sharply separated from all other perceptions that it contains within itself only what is clear" (Descartes 1984–91 i, 207–8/AT VIIIA 22). The *cogito* conforms to this requirement but the statement "I have a pain in my foot" does not. Reid concurs with Descartes when Descartes says that the sensation of pain is clear and not distinct because "people commonly confuse this perception with an obscure judgement they make concerning the nature of something which they think exists in the painful spot and which they suppose to resemble the sensation of pain" (Descartes 1984–91 i, 208).

Clarity, not distinctness, is the more important means by which the contents of our notions of qualities differ. Reid explains that when a notion of some quality is clear, then "the thing itself we understand perfectly" (EIP 2.17, 201/314a). He continues: "It is evident, therefore, that of the primary qualities we have a clear and distinct notion; we know what they are, though we may be ignorant of their causes" (EIP 2.17, 201/314a). Reid doesn't amplify upon this remark at any length, which is unfortunate since the strength of this epistemic relation nearly implies that our apprehension of the physical nature of some primary qualities is incorrigible. The fact that we have clear notions of primary qualities indicates that the higher-level physical natures of those qualities are manifest and obvious to us through our senses. He says: "Every man capable of reflection may easily satisfy himself that he has a perfectly clear and distinct notion of extension, divisibility, figure, and motion" (EIP 2.17, 201/314a).[6] This indicates how Reid reigns in his claim about our incorrigibility about notions of primary qualities.

One way to develop this notion of clarity is by examining Reid's description of what he calls "manifest" qualities in the *Intellectual Powers*. At the highest order of classification Reid distinguishes qualities as being either *manifest* (apparent to the senses) or *occult* (occluded from the senses). Primary qualities are a species of manifest qualities, while secondary qualities are a species of occult qualities. A defining characteristic of this distinction is that the "nature of [primary qualities] is manifest even to sense" (EIP 2.18, 217/322a). According to Reid, hardness, a primary quality, is a high degree of cohesion of the parts of a body. While that describes the quality of hardness in physical terms, it leaves the nature of the deeper, microphysical bonds between parts of bodies open to discovery by science. He says: "the business of the philosopher with regard to [manifest qualities], is not to find out their nature, which is well known, but to discover the effects produced by their various combinations" (EIP 2.18, 217/322a). Further research on primary qualities lies in scientific analysis.

Occult qualities include secondary qualities, "disorders we feel in our own bodies," and those qualities we call "powers of bodies" (EIP 2.18, 217/322a). In contrast, we only know the existence of occult qualities through unaided sense perception; we do not know their natures through unaided sense perception.

---

[6] In the *Inquiry*, Reid enumerates extension, figure, motion, hardness and softness, and roughness and smoothness as primary qualities (IHM 5.4, 62/123a–b). In the *Intellectual Powers*, he describes Locke's primary qualities as including "extension, divisibility, figure, motion, solidity, hardness, softness and fluidity" (EIP 2.17, 201/313b). Locke would not endorse this list for it substitutes motion for mobility and divisibility for number, not to mention that it includes some qualities Locke does not (namely hardness, softness, and fluidity). Reid proceeds to discuss this latter list as though it marked his own distinction, but its differences with the *Inquiry* are obvious, if unimportant.

Reid gives an explanation of this division of labor by appeal to the "Author of nature," who found that it was not "necessary for the conduct of our animal life" that humans know the nature of occult qualities through sense perception (EIP 2.18, 217/322a). For example, color is an occult quality insofar as sense experience of color does not generate any knowledge about its physical or microphysical nature.

Thus we come to a second necessary condition on the conception of primary qualities: P's notion of Q at t is clear only if, of Q's physical nature E, P knows that E is the physical nature of Q.[7] Reid does not perfectly understand the physical nature of blue, for example, so his notion of blue is not clear. Thus, blue is not a primary quality for Reid.

A key implication of the criteria Reid describes in the foregoing passages is that geometrical and seen visible figures are primary qualities. He says that we do not conceive of visible figures by way of an awareness of sensations here: "In answer therefore to the question proposed, there seems to be no sensation that is appropriated to visible figure. ... It seems to be suggested immediately by the material impression upon the organ" (IHM 6.8, 101/146a). Our awareness of visible figures by seeing them appears to be "clear"—that is, manifest and not occult. However, this point can only be fully justified after a study of Reid's answer to the Molyneux question in Chapter 9, for there Reid explains how the properties of visible figure are open to transparent introspection.

6.3. Notions of Secondary Qualities

Reid says: "To call a thing occult, if we attend to the meaning of the word, is rather modestly to confess ignorance, than to cloak it" (EIP 2.18, 216/321b). Though this may not allow significant knowledge of secondary qualities per se, it is enough to permit an analysis of our notions of them. Since our notions of primary qualities are more direct and clear than our notions of secondary qualities, Reid defines secondary qualities in contrasting terms. I will first examine their formation then their content, but in this case the two are similar.

Sensations of secondary qualities are distracting and forceful in ways that sensations of primary qualities typically are not. When I smell a loaf of bread in the oven, I mentally attend to the olfactory sensation. This is not to deny that

---

[7] This entails neither that all clear notions are direct nor the converse, though it seems probable that clear notions will be direct. Direct notions will not be clear, since I may form a direct notion of some Q (without apprehending Q by means of its effects) and not understand the essential nature of Q "perfectly." This applies to my notion of things like imaginary numbers, automatic transmissions, and the ontological argument: they are direct but not clear.

the sensation signifies something. But the smell itself is an object of immediate attention in the way that the sensations that suggest primary qualities are not. So the formation of our notions of secondary qualities is mediated by awareness of sensations, i.e. such notions are not formed directly. Reid makes this crucial point when saying, "We may see why the sensations belonging to secondary qualities are an object of our attention, while those which belong to the primary are not" (EIP 2.17, 204/315a). Our notions of secondary qualities proceed by a suggestion relation that is not identical to the relation by which we form perceptual beliefs about primary qualities. Reid says: "We conceive [the secondary quality] only as that which occasions such a sensation, and therefore [we] cannot reflect upon it without thinking of the sensation which it occasions" (EIP 2.17, 204/315a). To be clear, both types of relation are members of the broad category responsible for suggestion of mental states wherein the connection between the sign and mental content is mysterious. They differ with respect to what is doing the suggesting—*sensation* in the case of primary qualities, and *awareness of* a sensation in the case of secondary qualities.

Due to the ties between sensations and secondary qualities, in normal circumstances the contents of our notions of secondary qualities are only of unknown causes of sensations. Echoing Berkeley, Reid gives voice to this stark contrast between our concepts of secondary and primary qualities. "The sensations of heat and cold are perfectly known; for they neither are, nor can be, anything else than what we feel them to be; but the qualities in bodies which we call *heat* and *cold*, are unknown. They are only conceived by us, as unknown causes or occasions of the sensations to which we give the same names" (IHM 5.2, 54/119b). We have no knowledge of the physical or microphysical nature of secondary qualities because we only conceive of them through sensations and "as unknown causes" of our sensation experience.[8]

Notions of secondary qualities are "relative." "A relative notion of a thing, is, strictly speaking, no notion of the thing at all, but only of some relation which it bears to something else" (EIP 2.17, 201/314a). Notions of secondary qualities are notions of the relation between the sensations that these qualities prompt in me. I placed emphasis on the relational character of visible figure earlier in an effort to emphasize that visible figure is not like an idea, but rather is mind-independent. Likewise it is important for Reid that secondary qualities

[8] That said, Reid is optimistic about acquiring knowledge of their microphysical natures: "No man can pretend to set limits to the discoveries that may be made by human genius and industry, of such connections between the latent and the sensible qualities of bodies. A wide field here opens to our view, whose boundaries no man can ascertain, of improvements that may hereafter be made in the information conveyed to us by our senses" (EIP 2.21, 241/334a).

are not ideas or sense-data. Our *notions* are relational, but the secondary qualities themselves are not. When attempting to identify the property of the rose that is the rose's smell, Reid says he is at a loss:

> I have a distinct notion of the sensation which it produces in my mind. ... The quality in the rose is something which occasions the sensation in me; but what that something is, I know not. My senses give me no information upon this point. The only notion, therefore, my senses give is this—that smell in the rose is an unknown quality or modification, which is the cause or occasion of a sensation which I know well. The relation which this unknown quality bears to the sensation with which nature hath connected it, is all I learn from the sense of smelling; but this is evidently a relative notion. The same reasoning will apply to every secondary quality. (EIP 2.17, 202/314b)

From my sense of smell I only learn *that* physical qualities in objects bear a causal relation to olfactory sensations, and nothing about the particular physical qualities involved.

   In addition to the traditional secondary qualities Reid inherits from Locke, he adduces a few new examples that aid in spelling out his view. Reid places gravity, the quality in bodies that attracts one to another, amongst the secondary qualities (EIP 2.17, 201–2/314a). We only directly observe gravity's effects on bodies so our notion of gravity depends upon notions produced by observing the attraction of bodies. Our notion of gravity, as opposed to the correlation between this unknown quality and certain effects, is not direct or clear.[9] Reid also discusses magnetism in this vein in the *Inquiry* to make largely the same points (see IHM 2.9, 40–3/113–14).

6.4 Dispositions or Physical Properties?

The texts we have adduced thus far do not point conclusively to any definition of "secondary quality." Specifically, they do not point to or away from an analysis of secondary qualities as dispositional states. These texts include comments that secondary qualities are conceived "as that which occasions such a sensation." Reid's use of the term "quality" is also neutral vis-à-vis this debate. Reid frequently says secondary qualities are "qualities in bodies." But this is not obviously evidence for interpreting secondary qualities as physical

---

   [9] While Locke does not classify gravity in his schema, he does say that our understanding of gravity is limited. God's alteration of the force of gravity is one of the more plausible explanations of the great flood. Locke then says: "I think it [gravity] impossible to be explained by any natural operation of matter, or any other law of motion, but the positive will of a superior being so ordering it" (Locke 1989, at §192).

base properties. In order to make headway, first consider this helpful schema for identifying what could be the secondary quality in the event of smelling a rose:

S is the fragrant sensation I am experiencing, the manifestation of the disposition
D is a property of the rose, a disposition to produce S in me
P is a physical property of the rose that causes S in me, the causal basis of D (McKitrick 2002, 487)

From the above discussion we can infer that secondary qualities are not sensations, since secondary qualities are those things that suggest sensations (given the fact that sensations do not suggest themselves). On the assumption that this schema is complete, ruling out sensations becomes helpful since it implies that evidence against identifying secondary qualities with dispositions is evidence for identifying them with physical base properties (and vice versa). In order to determine whether Reidian secondary qualities are dispositions or the physical bases of those dispositions we need to examine further texts.

Reid uses the term "disposition" only a couple of times and in those contexts he does not define what he means by that term. Given the multiple uses of that term in the context of discussions of secondary qualities, it is wise to be precise. Paradigmatically, solubility in water is a dispositional quality such that, were an object that possesses (this form of) solubility submerged in water, it would dissolve. Dispositional qualities are generally specified by counterfactual conditionals. A secondary quality Q is dispositional under standard circumstances for a properly functioning agent A if, were A to sense Q, A would experience sensation Q*. "Q*" refers to the sensation that we associate with Q in standard conditions. This use of terminology refers to the semantic connection between sensation experiences and secondary qualities. Using Reid's example, the smell of a rose is a dispositional quality for him if, were it smelled, he would experience a rose-infused olfactory sensation. The term "smell" can refer to the sensation produced by the rose in my mind, or it can refer to the mind-independent feature in the rose that causes that sensation.

This general idea is given precise form in the analysis of dispositionalism advocated by David Armstrong.[10] Suppose that it is a necessary condition for

---

[10] Armstrong 1973, 15; see McKitrick's comparison of Armstrong and Reid at 2002, 481. McKitrick tentatively suggests that "the secondary quality for Reid" is "the disposition *and* the causal basis, since they are one and the same property" (2002, 488). I disagree with that conclusion since Reid does not assert that there is an identity relation, i.e. does not assert that there is anything like Leibniz's law, that holds between dispositions and causal bases. Even positing identity *in a world* between a causal base and a disposition (if that is coherent) is too much for Reid given the rampant contingency in his metaphysics.

a dispositional interpretation of secondary qualities that the quality be *identified with* a set of counterfactual conditions having to do with how agents respond when in the presence of certain causal bases. Put otherwise, a secondary quality is *defined as* that property that fulfills this set of counterfactual conditions. Call this the "identity thesis." According to the identity thesis, dispositions are relational properties.

This type of analysis is often taken to make sense out of a unique feature of secondary qualities, which I will call the "semantic thesis." Secondary qualities are traditionally held to differ from primary qualities because we cannot form notions of secondary qualities in the absence of relevant experiences of corresponding sensations. In order to have the concept of red I require sensations of redness. This thesis in effect makes it a necessary condition for the possession of the concept "red" that the agent has experienced red*. It may be a further necessary condition that the sensations be experienced in appropriate ways.

Together these two necessary conditions can be considered as jointly sufficient for a robust dispositional analysis of secondary qualities. However, these two conditions are logically independent. The semantic thesis does not entail the identity thesis, and the identity thesis does not entail the semantic thesis. Denying that the identity thesis entails the semantic thesis may seem unusual since it is often assumed, to the contrary, that there is an entailment in that direction. But the semantic thesis deals only with the meanings of secondary quality terms, and is neutral about the ontology of what it is we decide to call "the secondary quality." Reid is much more concerned with the semantic thesis than the identity thesis.

Despite this comment, turning to textual evidence for dispositionalism, Reid does provide evidence for the identification of secondary qualities with dispositional properties. In fact this evidence has convinced some commentators that dispositionalism is his considered view. He says that color "is a certain power or virtue in bodies, that in fair daylight exhibits to the eye an appearance which is very familiar to us, although it hath no name" (IHM 6.5, 87/138a; see 2.9, 43/114a). By "appearance" Reid refers to a color sensation. So color is a relational property between a physical property of a body and a color sensation. He does not specify in what this relation consists, which is more problematic than may first appear. Despite that, this passage is much better explained on a dispositional interpretation of secondary qualities than on a physicalist interpretation. Specifically, if the "is" Reid uses is the "is" of identity, then this passage points to Reid's endorsement of the identity thesis.

Reid also says that sensations are semantically conjoined with our secondary quality terms. Sensations "bear a capital part in the notion we form of [the secondary quality]. We conceive it only as that which occasions such a sensation, and therefore [we] cannot reflect upon it without thinking of the sensation which it occasions" (EIP 2.17, 204/315a). This is a forceful comment in favor of the semantic thesis. Not only do sensations "bear a capital part" in our acquisition of concepts of secondary qualities, but those sensations are necessary for forming such concepts, as his use of "cannot" seems to imply. In addition, Reid uses the term "disposition" in this context when saying, "The disposition of bodies to reflect a particular kind of light, occasions the sensation of colour" (EIP 2.17, 204/315a). This indicates that he is aware of the important currency dispositions play in an analysis of secondary qualities. But this remark is unclear. Either "disposition" here refers to the physical base property (which would be an odd use of the term) or it refers to a relational property. Since he says a disposition "occasions" the sensation, this is tantamount to implying that the disposition has causal powers, and thus that it is not a relational property. The supporter of a dispositional interpretation of Reidian secondary qualities is wise not to rest a substantial portion of her case upon Reid's actual use of the term "disposition."

Other textual evidence points to an interpretation on which secondary qualities are mind-independent, physical or microphysical properties of objects. Reid's examples of secondary qualities favor this interpretation. He says, "We have no reason to think that any of the secondary qualities resemble any sensation.... It is too evident to need proof, that the vibrations of a sounding body do not resemble the sensation of sound, nor the effluvia of an odorous body the sensation of smell" (EIP 2.17, 203/314b). In this case the secondary quality causing sensations of smell is implicitly identified with effluvia, i.e. minute, airborne, physical particles. This type of example cannot be accommodated on a dispositional interpretation.

A considerable amount of textual evidence for a dispositional interpretation of secondary qualities involves Reid's discussions of color, but other things written about color undermine this appeal. First, consider the context of his comment that color "is a certain power or virtue in bodies" (at IHM 6.4, 87/138a). The title of this section is "That colour is a quality of bodies, not a sensation of the mind." The contrast the title invokes, is evidence against a dispositional interpretation of colors on its most straightforward reading. Less than a page later, in *Inquiry* 6.5, Reid says that what others regard as "one of the most remarkable paradoxes of modern philosophy," namely that color is not a quality of bodies, is "nothing else but an abuse of words.... We have shewn, that there is really a permanent quality of body, to which the common use of this word exactly agrees" (IHM 6.5, 87–8/138b–139a). He is said to reaffirm this point in some student notes.[11] This implies that colors are not sensations, and that colors are not likely to be dispositions, though this is less obvious. Dispositions are less fleeting and temporary than are sensations, but more unstable than physical qualities. A disposition of a lake to yield a visual sensation of cerulean blue for normal human beings may be "possessed" over time by the lake. But even if "possession" of this disposition is permanent, its exemplification may depend on qualities in the ambient light that occur once a year—or may never occur. The most plausible reading of this remark should be taken as evidence against thinking that colors are dispositions.

We needn't continue splitting hairs. In other passages about color Reid is more explicit. Reid's technical use of color terms is intended to refer only to the physical qualities of objects.[12] This judgment is based in part on passages like these:

That idea which we have called *the appearance of colour*, suggests the conception and belief of some unknown quality in the body, which occasions the idea; and it is to this quality, and not to the idea, that we give the name of *colour*. (IHM 6.4, 86/137b–138a)

The name of colour belongs indeed to the cause only, and not to the effect. But, as the cause is unknown, we can form no distinct conception of it but by its relation to the known effect…. Hence the appearance [of the color scarlet] is, in the imagination, so closely united with the quality called *a scarlet-colour*, that they are apt to be mistaken for one and the same thing, although they are in reality so different and so unlike, that one is an idea in the mind, the other is a quality of body. (IHM 6.4, 86–7/138a; see IHM 6.4, 85/137a and IHM 6.7, 95/142b)

When I would conceive those colours of bodies which we call scarlet and blue; if I conceive them only as unknown qualities, I could perceive no distinction between the one and the other. I must therefore, for the sake of the distinction, join to each of them, in my imagination, some effect or some relation that is peculiar. And the most

---

[11] Reid is recorded to have affirmed the semantic constancy of color-terms in the following way: "colour is a secondary quality, and is not necessary to the persistence of body. Yet though it be a secondary quality, it is not so ambiguous as the many other names of secondary qualities" (Edinburgh New College MS, Box 32.3, 9). Since color terms are not as ambiguous as some other secondary quality terms, this is a reason for thinking that they refer to mind-independent qualities.

[12] J. C. Smith does not think that there is a difference; he thinks that color terms are also ambiguous in Reid (1990, 141). Anthony Pitson agrees that they are "ambiguous" (2001, 18), but at pp. 20–1 Pitson says that, for Reid, "the term 'colour' *never* refers to the perceptual experience associated with our awareness of the quality itself." Hopkins assumes that when Reid says that "we never…give the name of *colour* to the sensation, but to the quality only" (IHM 6.4, 87/138a) he means that "colour terms only name the disposition" (2005, 348). In contrast to these thinkers, Falkenstein claims that Reidian color terms refer only to the physical causes of qualitative experiences (2000, 322; see 319). I concur with Falkenstein insofar as I believe that it is Reid's intention to use color terms to refer only to the physical causes of qualitative, color* experiences.

obvious distinction is, the appearance which one and the other makes to the eye. (I 6.4, 86–7/138a)

By the term "the appearance of colour" in the first inset passage Reid refers to our color sensations, for it is the sensation of color that suggests that there is a physical base property responsible for causing in us the color sensation. It is to these base properties that terms like "blue" and "red" refer. Reid goes so far as to say that "we never, as far as I can judge, give the name of *colour* to the sensation, but to the quality only" (IHM 6.4, 87/138a).[13] In the second passage Reid identifies colour terms as only referring to physical properties that cause sensations. These remarks point to Reid's denial of the identity thesis.

In addition to these textual problems for the identity thesis, a pair of philosophical reasons weighs against Reid's adoption of dispositionalism. I presented the first above (in 6.1) when I argued that Reid has a principled objection to dispositional analyses like Locke's. Reid implies that such analyses are philosophically unilluminating; thus he would not be likely to endorse the identity thesis since it is not useful for explanatory purposes. Second, Reid's description of our epistemic relation to secondary qualities contrasts with what we would expect on this dispositional view. According to Reid, our notions of things like green are not clear. On that basis Reid repudiates having knowledge of what the quality green is, other than repeating that it is the unknown cause of a known effect. Secondary qualities are conceived "only as the unknown causes or occasions of certain sensations" (EIP 2.17, 202/314b). If secondary qualities were nothing more than dispositions, and not the physical bases of these dispositions, Reid's frequent claims to the effect that he doesn't know what secondary qualities are would be nonsensical.[14]

---

[13] Falkenstein believes that this feature of Reid's theory necessitates a misleading semantics. This "sits uncomfortably with natural assumptions about the origin and use of words." "Reid is wrong," he says, "about what people mean when they use colour terms" (2000, 314 and 325). He is correct to think that something is amiss in Reid's semantics for color terms, but it can be accounted for by identifying one of Reid's motivations. We can understand Reid's penchant for wanting to put secondary qualities back into the world in light of the Way of Ideas, which was prone to locate qualities exclusively in the mind. Reid says: "Des Cartes, Malebranche, and Locke...made the secondary qualities mere sensations, and the primary ones resemblances of our sensations. They maintained, that colour, sound, and heat, are not any thing in bodies, but sensations of the mind: at the same time, they acknowledged some particular texture or modification of the body, to be the cause or occasion of those sensations; but to this modification they gave no name" (IHM 5.8, 73/131a). Ideal theorists were convinced that we only directly perceived ideas but, according to Reid, we directly perceive mind-independent objects and qualities. Hence, Reid has a principled reason to reject any heavy-handed demand to accommodate ordinary language in this particular dialectic.

[14] My argument here assumes that there is something about dispositional qualities that makes it likely that we *know* that a quality is dispositional when it is. Solubility, one might argue, provides a counterexample. I may work with salt for an indefinite amount of time and fail to apprehend that it possesses solubility. If this is correct, then describing our epistemic relation to secondary qualities

The preponderance of textual evidence suggests that Reid does not hold the identity thesis and thus denies the strong form of dispositionalism. Suppose it is a sufficient condition for an analysis of secondary qualities as physical base properties that the secondary quality is not itself a response-dependent property, but is mind-independent and physical or microphysical. On this construal the most charitable way to interpret relevant texts is as implying Reid's assent to this condition.

6.5. Sensations and Secondary Qualities

An intriguing aspect of Reid's theory is that he is best interpreted as endorsing a version of the semantic thesis, but denying the identity thesis.

A number of texts considered so far support this conclusion. In the second and third inset passages above, the relationship between base property and color experience is described as conceptually tight. An agent's ability to distinguish between those physical properties Reid describes as "colors" depends upon unique sensory experiences. Certain color sensations suggest the conception of certain color qualities. In the third passage Reid's language suggests that it is a necessary condition for an agent to possess the concept of a color that the agent should have experienced the sensation caused by the color. Reconsider Reid's claim that: "We conceive [the secondary quality] only as that which occasions such a sensation, and therefore [we] cannot reflect upon it without thinking of the sensation which it occasions" (EIP 2.17, 204/315a). These passages support the semantic thesis.

I say that the relation between the meanings of color* terms and our experience of those sensations that are caused by colors is "conceptually tight." By this I mean to avoid claiming that experiencing blue* is logically necessary

---

as transparent in the way I have just done is in error. Hence, Reidian secondary qualities might be dispositional qualities. (Thanks to George Pappas for this objection.)

However, due to a disanalogy between solubility and secondary qualities like green and heat, this criticism misses its mark. In the case of secondary qualities Reid is acquainted with a physical object and the effects that certain qualities of that object produce. Those effects are on our minds, not on a physical substance. Physical qualities of objects produce sensation experiences—qualitative mental states—in us. Reid is not a dispositionalist because he claims ignorance about the nature of secondary qualities *of whose sensory effects he is regularly and constantly aware*. Unlike solubility, the content needed to fill the counterfactual conditional is right at hand. If secondary qualities are dispositional, then green is identical with the following state of affairs: were a green surface brought into my visual field, I would experience a sensation of green. To know what green is does not require knowledge of what its physical base is since to be green is to be specified by a counterfactual conditional like this. If properly functioning (EIP 2.20, 229/328b), a perceiver's knowledge of what green is will be implied by a dispositional account of colors.

for acquiring the concept *blue* or using the term "blue." We already know that the relationship between secondary qualities and sensations is not one of logical necessity. God has conjoined certain sensations with certain physical qualities in objects for the benefit of our survival (EIP 2.16, 196–8/311b–312a). In contrast to the relationship between sensations and primary qualities, there are no physically necessary connections between any secondary quality and its corresponding sensation. The connection lapses in abnormal environments or when perceivers are malfunctioning, as in phantom limb pain (EIP 2.18, 214/320b).[15]

Why does he speak of acquiring concepts of colors and other secondary qualities as though this is virtually impossible to do without experiencing the sensations that they suggest in us? This is for two reasons. First, laws of nature for Reid are generalizations expressing relations between phenomena based upon empirical investigation; laws are neither exceptionless nor metaphysical truths about deep reality. Reid offers a theory of perception that purports to identify laws. Therefore his focus is always on explaining features of perception as manifest in standard environments for standard perceivers. Given that he specifies the initial conditions that govern the generalization he draws, this method suits him. In standard conditions we acquire concepts like "blue" by way of sensations of blue*. Second, Reid delivers his discussion in a context in which there was no science of color. He stresses this fact by continually referring to colors as "unknown qualitie." The physical or microphysical properties of colors at the time of his writing were unknown by scientists. Given Reid's attitude it would not be surprising if he thought scientists might never know them. Remarks about how color concepts, i.e. how concepts of the relevant physical properties, might be known in ways that did not require experience of color sensations would seem to be mere hypotheses to Reid.

Reid endorses the semantic thesis, but he only endorses a contingently true version of it. More clearly, the semantic thesis is an empirical generalization applicable to normal humans in normal environments. It is not intended by Reid to do anything profound, in the way that some philosophers think that metaphysical or modal conclusions can be drawn from the nature of language and meaning. So he endorses the semantic thesis while holding that secondary qualities are physical. Though uncommon in the history of philosophy, I see

---

[15] In the case of phantom limb pain, if the subject "did not know that his leg was cut off, it would give him the same immediate conviction of some hurt or disorder in the toe." In this case there is a sensation (pain) and there is a secondary quality causing the sensation, but that cause is not the typical cause of pains. "This perception, which Nature had conjoined with the sensation, was, in this instance, fallacious" (EIP 2.18, 214/320b).

no inconsistency in doing so, given a proviso about the semantic thesis being an empirical generalization, not a necessary truth.

These might be Van Cleve's motivations in a section of a paper in which he suggests that the following might be Reid's analysis of secondary qualities:

x is red in w=df x has in w some physical property P such that the following is a law of nature in @, the actual world: Things with P produce red* sensations in normal human observers. (2004a, 111)

Van Cleve says that the hybrid account is consistent with the following two claims: "(1) knowing what redness is requires knowing what red* sensations are like"; and "(2) redness supervenes on intrinsic physical properties, in the sense that anything just like a given red thing in all intrinsic physical respects would have to be red, regardless of its sensory effects on human observers" (2004a, 111). Van Cleve's ingenious proposal harmonizes threads in Reid's discussion, despite a few minor problems.

Van Cleve's analysis of secondary qualities is drawn in terms of the qualities themselves and not in terms of our notions of them. In contrast, Reid shows little interest in the metaphysics of qualities, and a great deal of interest in our differing forms of awareness of them. In addition, as this definition is stated, it appears to be true of primary qualities too. To show that this definition applies to primary qualities, replace "red" with "hard":

x is hard in w=df x has in w some physical property P such that the following is a law of nature in @, the actual world: Things with P produce hard* sensations in normal human perceivers.[16]

When I sit upon a wooden bench, I experience a sensation of hardness. That is, when my body experiences that physical stimulus, it produces in me a sensation of hardness. Likewise, when I see the brown bench, I experience a sensation of brownness. That is, when my visual system experiences that physical stimulus, it produces in me a brown sensation. If we assume that a definition of secondary qualities is supposed to be sufficient to distinguish secondary from primary qualities, then the above definition needs modification. (In the following section we will investigate this assumption.)

Scattered throughout Reid's manuscripts are further comments about the primary/secondary quality distinction, including his "aphorisms" (at Aberdeen

---

[16] I hesitate to call this sort of constant conjunction a "law of nature" on Reid's use of that term. For Reid, laws of nature are generalizations about empirical regularities derivative from inductive evidence. He is more comfortable speaking of "The *physical laws of nature*," which he says "are the rules according to which the deity commonly acts in his natural government of the world" (EAP 4.9, 628a–b). I expect Van Cleve's schema can be restated without any untoward implications about laws.

MS 2131/8/II/21, p. 6), but they bring no more clarity to his mature distinction. The futility of attempting to squeeze more precision from Reid's account brings us to a point of diminishing returns for an historical analysis such as this. Further understanding of the philosophical issues involved is best left to research more analytical in character. However, if I am correct, we have done enough to assuage the charge that Reid "doesn't speak consistently on the matter." Reid's texts cohere if he endorses a hybrid account of secondary qualities on which he upholds the sufficient conditions for weak dispositionalism and believes that secondary qualities are physical base properties.

6.6. The Relativity of Reidian Qualities

The two sets of qualities are distinguished in virtue of their differing epistemological effects on us. We form notions of primary qualities differently from the way in which we form notions of secondary qualities, and the contents of notions of primary qualities differ from the contents of notions of secondary qualities.

But in a sense Reid's distinction makes qualities relative to agents, since the two sets of qualities are identified as those things that cause certain conceptions in properly functioning agents. This relativity, coupled with the fact that the qualities are not distinguished on the basis of different physical constitutions, has led Reid experts to believe this feature sabotages his account. Lehrer says: "We may agree with Reid that we have a clear and distinct conception of primary qualities, but do we not also have a clear and distinct conception of some secondary qualities?" Clear and distinct notions of all qualities are caused in part by sensations. So Lehrer infers that "the distinction between primary and secondary qualities collapses because both are ultimately based on sensation" (Lehrer 1978, 186, 187). Ben Zeev echoes this point by criticizing Reid's epistemic/relational approach to this distinction on the grounds that "considerations which are valid in the case of those qualities admitted to possess a relational status are valid in the case of other qualities too. (This is Berkeley's criticism of the distinction between primary and secondary qualities.)" (1986, 113). This concern is understandable.

It seems to me that the reason the distinction is in danger of collapsing doesn't concern the fact that "ultimately" formation of both types of concepts "depends upon" sensations. For, first, we have witnessed the ways in which the two types of concept differ in their dependence upon sensations. More importantly, it is unclear why one is in principle unable to draw distinctions between two sets of concepts simply because members of each set depend upon sensations. We commonly draw distinctions between concepts upon many grounds.

But Lehrer's concern can be intuitively motivated in a different way. Reid takes the inebriating quality of wine to be a secondary quality (EIP 2.17, 204/315a). We now know the scientific nature of this quality—the molecular composition of alcohol—and how it destabilizes brain processes. Lehrer could argue that, on Reid's account, the inebriating quality of wine *is* a secondary quality, and is *not* a secondary quality since we know its scientific nature. Thus the very idea of a Reidian secondary quality is incoherent. Perhaps he has this in mind.

To this I say that the result that qualities might be relative to agents is part of Reid's theory, not a problem with it. We've seen above that Reid describes secondary qualities as "relative," but the relativity of qualities is not as radical as one might think. My notion of the microphysical nature of alcohol is not direct or clear since it is based on the testimony of chemists. So *for me* the quality in wine that causes inebriation is a secondary quality. Is the chemist's notion of the same quality a notion of a primary quality? The chemist's notion of the inebriating quality is neither direct nor, on Reid's use of the term, clear. So it too is a notion of a secondary quality. In this way Reid's analysis of secondary qualities shows that for chemist and connoisseur alike the notion of the inebriating quality of wine is a notion of a secondary quality. Reid's distinction does not make qualities relative to agents—at least not in the actual world.

On the basis of this point, though, we can build a more fanciful case that makes clear the way in which secondary qualities can in principle become primary qualities (and vice versa). Imagine a being that forms a direct and clear notion of the microphysical nature of the inebriating quality of wine (i.e. of the molecular composition of alcohol) merely on the basis of the sensation of tasting wine. Perhaps her taste buds process high degrees of information about the molecular make-up of substances she imbibes. This would resemble the manner in which our fingertips inform us of the physical nature of hardness (for Reid, the strong cohesion of the parts of a body) upon touching a wall. For this person the inebriating quality in wine is a primary quality because, on the basis of her sensory experiences alone, she forms notions of the physical *and microphysical* natures of alcohol. Reid's analysis allows that these states of affairs are possible.

To put this point generally, a body's having a certain primary or secondary quality is contingent and indexed to certain perceivers at certain times. Lehrer is correct to insinuate that the difference between a primary and secondary quality can "collapse" in some possible worlds. But rather than taking this as a criticism of the view, it is a compliment to it. It seems that this sense of the relativity of qualities to agents and worlds does not sap Reid's account from its explanatory power; further argument is needed for that conclusion. Moreover, a traditional distinction drawn on purely metaphysical lines would not be able to deal with such possibilities as smoothly. This versatility in Reid's distinction captures the radically different means by which we relate to these two types of qualities without assuming that all perceivers are properly functioning humans, that God had to design us as he has, or that the perceptual systems of human beings couldn't evolve or be redesigned.

6.7. Phenomenology of Reidian Secondary Qualities

We must again address the difficult status of color, this time from the point of view of the distinction between qualities. Lorne Falkenstein believes that Reidian secondary qualities—specifically, colors—fail to account for features of our experience. He says: "Once Reid's peculiar use of the term 'colour' is exposed, it is hard not to conclude that his position does not reflect what we think we see" (2000, 322). He continues:

the thesis that we do not experience our sensations of colour to be located on the visual field or compounded into extended and shaped aggregates is not even so much as uncertain or possible; it is false. Reid is wrong, both about what people mean when they use colour terms and about how they experience the sensations that coloured objects produce in their minds. (2000, 325)

Falkenstein indicates that we "see visible figures to be filled out with the sensations of colour that objects cause in the mind" (2000, 324). The problem is that "Colours, understood as the hidden qualities in objects that cause our sensations of colour are *hidden*—not actually seen, but only inferred." But colors are revealed to us through our sensations of them, urges Falkenstein. So Reid's account of color fails to accommodate the phenomenology of color vision (2000, 320).

Anthony Pitson has successfully addressed this objection as voiced against Reid (even though he does not address Falkenstein's presentation of it). I do not propose to better his analysis and refutation of this objection here, but I will bring to light the salient points of his argument. Pitson identifies what he calls the Revelation Thesis (to which Reid is opposed) as the claim that the "intrinsic nature of colours is revealed by ordinary visual experience." Pitson associates this thesis with Galen Strawson and Bertrand Russell. Since

Falkenstein objects to the hiddenness of Reidian colors, we can append his name to the list. This thesis is best understood as an epistemic claim. It comes in two forms. The strong form of the Revelation Thesis states that "the nature of colour as a quality is revealed in ordinary visual experience." The weak version states that "merely looking at something is sufficient for determining its colour" (2001, 25, 26). If I understand Falkenstein's discussion he seems to affirm both, and he surely affirms the weaker thesis.

Pitson argues that the strong version is false, and so Reid cannot be criticized on the grounds that his view is inconsistent with it. On the strong thesis colors are nothing more than qualitative mental events. But this doesn't account for the objectivity of our experience of color. Pitson argues that "we have to distinguish between the fixed colour of the object as a quality of the object itself, and the various colours it may appear to be under different circumstances" (2001, 27). This alone seems conclusive against the strong thesis.

He contends that the weaker thesis is false as well. More importantly, so does Reid. Reid thinks that terms like "scarlet" refer to physical causes of qualitative events, but let us grant the objector that "scarlet" always refers to the qualitative experience caused by some physical property. Even if this were the case, it will not follow that I can identify the color of the object of vision by looking at it. As Pitson notes, this is the point of Reid's example in which someone looks at a scarlet rose through green glasses, which makes the sensation of the *scarlet* rose like the sensation of a black rose. Reid says:

> The scarlet-rose which is before me, is still a scarlet-rose when I shut my eyes, and was so at midnight when no eye saw it. The colour remains when the appearance ceases; it remains the same when the appearance changes. For when I view this scarlet-rose through a pair of green spectacles, the appearance is changed; but I do not conceive the colour of the rose changed. To a person in the jaundice, it has still another appearance, but makes not the least change in the colour of the body. ... [W]e ought to distinguish between the colour of a body, which is conceived to be a fixed and permanent quality in the body, and the appearance of that colour to the eye, which may be varied a thousand ways. (IHM 6.4, 85–86/137b)

Reid also makes this point in correspondence with Lord Kames (from December 1778). He contrasts his view with Kames' and generalizes the result:

> As to what your Lordship calls *the Deception of placing Sound Colour and Smell upon the Objects that raise them*, I humbly think there is no deception. I think that Colour Sound and Smell are really and truly in the Objects that raise in us certain Sensations called by the same Name. ... Secondary Qualities therefore are really and truly Qualities of the Body to which Our Senses lead us to ascribe to them. (C 114–15)

I concur with Pitson's conclusion that Reid's idiosyncratic analysis of colors as physical qualities of bodies can be defended against an objection based upon the Revelation Thesis.

I want to make one addition to Pitson's case, which concerns a presupposition at work in appeals to the revealed knowledge of secondary qualities. Falkenstein says that people experience redness in the sense that, for example, a "triangle on their visual fields looks to be painted over its extension with … a mere sensation in the mind" (2000, 325). Locutions like "triangle on their visual fields" implicitly presume that the perceived triangle is not the actual triangle. Suppose I'm seeing a red, triangular road sign bearing the word "Yield." Falkenstein voices this criticism of Reid in a way that presupposes there is a perceived intermediary between my visual awareness and the yield sign—the visible figure of the triangle.

But, according to Reid's theory of visual perception, the red, visual triangle is not a reified, mind-dependent perceptual intermediary. As we have seen, it is instead a mind-independent relational property that Reid calls a "visible figure." A defense of the weak thesis, and a concomitant attack on Reid, will be much easier if we presuppose with the Way of Ideas that the object I see is a sense-datum of some sort. This intuition gives Revelation Theses their forceful, intuitive plausibility—and a dose of ambiguity. If I am right to think that the present objection to Reid's treatment of color is based upon the Way of Ideas' indirect realist account of perception, then to adjudicate the point properly one must take into account not only our analysis of Reid's theory of visible figure, but also his many arguments *against* just such a theory of perception. Once done, this militates against the Revelation Thesis and the objection that Reid's discussion of color qualities violates intuitions about the phenomenology of color vision.

6.8. Summary

Reid needed to construct his primary/secondary distinction so as to allow the idealist and representationalist forms of the Way of Ideas no foothold. Reid succeeds in crafting a distinction of his own. Contrary to Berkeley, a sensation of heat is not identical to heat, though it may be a sign of it (Jacquette 2003, 292). Contrary to Locke, pressure sensations do not resemble extension or hardness, though they may be signs of them. By forming states of intentional awareness of primary qualities, Reid insures we can conceptualize the world in ways that do not involve ideas. He has avoided their errors, and his discussion of qualities serves as a helpful supplement to his discussion of the workings of natural suggestion.

Understanding Reid's distinction between secondary and primary qualities necessitates understanding the nature of his departure from Locke's method. Reid chooses to ground his analysis in his concepts of qualities since he knows those well, as opposed to the scientific natures of qualities, which he does not. Concepts of primary qualities are clear, distinct, and direct, and bear fruit when placed in the service of science. Notions of secondary qualities lack all those features, chiefly because they are dependent on our mediating apprehension of the sensations they cause in us.

If this conceptual way of drawing the distinction is correct, then Reid should be seen as making a clear and radical break from Locke. Reid's distinction can be read as in sympathy with contemporary anti-realist interpretations of quantum phenomena on one key point, which illustrates his departure from the Way of Ideas. Secondary qualities occupy a place in Reid's ontology as do quantum unobservables for scientific anti-realists. This is because we in the actual world can only know secondary qualities by way of their effects upon our sensory systems. In contrast, we can form notions of primary qualities without reference to sensations. Indeed, in his discussion of Molyneux's question, Reid says a blind person can have notions of the primary quality of visible figure without having any visual sensations at all.

Reid's discussion of qualities exemplifies an intense devotion to empiricist standards in metaphysics and an abhorrence of what he would deride as "hypotheses." Given Locke's failure to clarify the distinction on speculative metaphysical grounds, Reid's empiricist turn should, despite the comparison just noted, retain the common-sense pedigree we associate with his work.

7

Our Awareness of Sensations

When philosophers advocate indirect theories of perception, they almost always hold that the immediate objects of awareness in acts of perception are mind-dependent mental states, whether they are described as sensations or ideas. I have argued that Reid minimizes the role of sensations in perception in those parts of his theory discussed thus far—in his account of concept acquisition, his theory of visual perception, and the function of sensation. In the previous chapter I argued that Reid's account of our notions of primary and secondary qualities contrasts with the Way of Ideas on the grounds that our notions of primary qualities arise directly, and not by an intermediating awareness of the sensations that signify primary qualities.

In this chapter I want to analyze what Reid says about the nature of our *awareness of* sensations in order to identify the degree of contact between our minds and the world. The purpose of doing this is not primarily to determine whether his theory is "direct" or not. My aim is to understand better Reid's theory on its own terms, and to facilitate our ability to assess the extent to which Reid's theory of perception departs from the Way of Ideas.

To put this issue in context, two broad trends have emerged in the interpretation of Reid's theory of perception as either "direct" or "indirect." In addition to leaning heavily on certain texts, broader, historical trends have emerged in the debate. Advocates of interpreting Reid's theory as a direct theory usually attend to what he says about suggestion as non-representational, and closely observe the contrast he builds between his theory and the Way of Ideas. Those who argue for an indirect interpretation typically intellectualize the process of perception by attributing to perceivers a robust sequence of mental states. They emphasize passages in which Reid attests to the fact that we are aware of our sensations, and they offer philosophical arguments to show that the most charitable reading says that it is in virtue of our awareness of sensations that we perceive objects. Both interpretations have merits.

This chapter begins with a summary of the reasons that have been discussed in passing in the preceding chapters for thinking that Reid's theory brings mind very close to world. I next discuss an interpretation according to which our awareness of the sensations that signify primary qualities renders our perception of primary qualities indirect. A handful of texts offer prima facie support for this view; in them Reid says we perform cognitive operations on those sensations by "interpreting," "conceiving," and "believing" them. I analyze these passages and their context to show that evidence on behalf of this interpretation fails fully to justify its attribution to Reid. I offer some reasons to think that determining the degree of directness of Reidian perception is intractable due to his coarse discussion of our awareness of sensations. But I conclude that we are justified in thinking that his theory of perception is more direct than indirect.

I restrict the discussion that follows to the nature of our awareness of primary qualities because Reid is up front that secondary qualities are not perceived directly. When perceiving secondary qualities the immediate object of mental awareness is a sensation and not its physical base, i.e. not the Reidian secondary quality. Reid emphasizes this contrast when saying that we do not mentally focus on sensations that accompany primary qualities: "the sensations belonging to secondary qualities are an object of our attention, while those which belong to the primary are not" (EIP 2.17, 204/315a). If the immediate object of awareness is a sensation, then it follows that the quality itself is not an immediate object of awareness. For example, when I am perceptually aware of the aroma of a rose by smelling it, I must be aware of an intermediary, namely the sensation accompanying my perception of the quality. This violates a minimal necessary condition on direct perception. Reid's suggestion relations provide us with concepts of primary qualities by taking sensations as their inputs (in the actual world for normal perceivers), but provide us with concepts of secondary qualities by taking *our awareness of* sensations as inputs.

This result complicates Reid's theory of perception, but not in unexpected ways. We have little to lose by conceding that secondary qualities are not perceptually, cognitively, or epistemically direct. Reid's theory of perception is already an unholy hybrid of direct and indirect features. Reid would have regarded it as an elementary mistake to construct a theory of perception in order to support the hypothesis that the process is direct. Reid constructs his theory in accordance with his observational method in order to account for the actual structure and operation of our senses. Furthermore, Reid is not claiming that we cannot be directly aware of our *sensations* since for Reid sensations are not secondary qualities. And from Reid's point of view the indirect features of our awareness of sensations aren't that surprising. After all, Reid speaks of secondary qualities as "unknown" (IHM 5.1, 54/119b) and "occult" (EIP 2.18, 216/321b).

7.1. The Cumulative Case for "Directness"

Concern about directness has overwhelmed discussion of Reid's theory of perception. Cases for and against are often prosecuted by close readings of thorny texts, in neglect of the ramifications of other features of Reid's theory of perception upon this interpretive problem. I want to observe how issues conceptually surrounding the topic of direct perception bear on what we attribute to Reid.

Points on behalf of a comparatively direct theory made thus far in the book include the following.

A. Reid's own inchoate views about directness typically do not cohere with the definitions of that term applied to Reid's theories in the literature on that topic (see Section 4.7–10). Though Reid does use the term "direct" to refer to our apprehension of primary qualities, often definitions of "directness" applied to Reid by his commentators have little to do with his meaning and are instead built out of the philosophical concerns of the commentator (see Copenhaver 2004 for a study of "directness" as it has been applied to Reid). I hope to leave the project of bagging and tagging definitions of directness, and evaluating their applicability to Reid, to others.

B. The claim that awareness of sensations mediates perceptions must be built upon an analysis of the types and "representative" characters of Reidian signs. Reid employs his theory of signs to preserve as much directness in our awareness of primary qualities as possible. We have explained the Berkeleyan considerations Reid cites in his Sensory Deprivation argument against Cartesian, intellectual attempts to use reflection and reasoning to "interpret" sensations and identify what they signify (Chapter 3). What makes the relation between sensation and the conception and belief stage in perception resistant to analysis is that sensation is not an informational or representational state. This seems to be his point in saying our awareness of primary qualities proceeds through a suggestion relation by "a natural kind of magic" (IHM 5.3, 60/122a). An interpretation upon which we need to decipher what sensations signify does not comport with Reid's discussion of our awareness of primary qualities.

C. We can conceive of and believe in visible figure, a primary quality, even though we needn't experience any sensation coupled with it (see Section 4.5). The material impressions on the retina, which Reid says suggest our perception of visible figure, are not immediate objects of awareness. So it appears that our awareness of the primary quality of visible figure is, in this sense, direct.

D. Some of the most forceful textual evidence for attributing a direct theory of perception to Reid arose in the previous chapter in our discussion of primary qualities. The means by which we acquire our concepts of primary qualities implies that our notions of them are formed without any interference by our awareness of sensations, in contrast to our awareness of secondary qualities (see Chapter 6). Reid says: "When a primary quality is perceived the sensation immediately leads our thought to the quality signified by it, and is itself forgot" (EIP 2.17, 204/315b), and, "our senses give us a direct and a distinct notion of the primary qualities" (EIP 2.17, 201/313b).

Related points on behalf of a comparatively direct interpretation of Reid's theory of perception yet to be discussed in these pages include E., Reid's analysis of the nature of inferential cognition in the formation of original and acquired perception. He insists that original perceptions about primary qualities require no reasoning at all, which suggests that his theory of perception is direct in an epistemic sense yet to be identified (see Chapter 8). In an allied discussion, F., Reid argues against there being any need to infer from our sensations to the existence of that which we (seem to) perceive. With Locke in his sights, Reid says that there is "no comparing of ideas, no perception of agreements or disagreements" in the process of perception (IHM 2.7, 38/111a), and no reasoning either (IHM 6.20, 172/185a).

Furthermore, G., Reid's unique response to Molyneux's question minimizes the role of sensations in the conception of the primary quality of shape (see Chapter 9). In the course of that discussion Reid contends that even a blind man can conceive of and form a belief about—thus, perceive$_{C\&B}$—a geometrical visible figure he had not even seen, so long as he is given data about the dimensions and distance of the object. This result appears to imply that it is possible for someone visually to apprehend one way the physical world is without his having any visual sensations.

H. The contrast to which I have alluded between Reid's theory and the Way of Ideas is stark. According to the Way of Ideas, ideas, latter-day sense-data, are the immediate objects of perceptual events. Ideas (for the Way of Ideas' realist subscribers) represent mind-independent objects and their qualities. In Locke's terms, "'Tis evident, the Mind knows not Things immediately, but only by the intervention of the *Ideas* it has of them. *Our Knowledge* therefore is *real*, only so far as there is a conformity between our *Ideas* and the reality of Things" (Locke 1975, 4.4.3/563). Locke asserts that we only ever immediately perceive ideas because they "intervene" between our minds and things. But he also makes an epistemic claim. Namely, our non-inferential knowledge is restricted to ideas.

In the *Inquiry's* dedication Reid explains his direct opposition to these theses. He says that the "sceptical system" (the Way of Ideas) that he plans to attack "leans with its whole weight upon a hypothesis … [t]hat nothing is perceived but what is in the mind which perceives it." The Way of Ideas says the mind is aware only of mental representations, but Reid implies that we do perceive what is not in the mind. Referring to ideas, he adds: "I cannot, from their existence, infer the existence of anything else: my impressions and ideas are the only existences of which I can have any knowledge or conception" (IHM 4/96a). If I am only ever aware of mental representations of things, then I will be unable to achieve knowledge of objects and qualities outside of my mind. If we are to take Reid at his word in his frequent repudiation of these aspects of the Way of Ideas, we have prima facie evidence to think that Reid did not endorse a theory of perception that conflicts with his case against the Way of Ideas.

I. Not least amongst these circumstantial points is Reid's theory of the purpose of sensations. Reid places sensations in the context of the human being as an animal, not as an information-processing engine. Their purpose is merely to alert us to the states of our bodies. From these origins they became useful for signifying primary qualities and suggesting our conception and belief of primary qualities. Unlike Humean impressions, sensations are not used as ingredients in the contents of perceptions per se. Distinguishing between a perception and a sensation is not merely a matter of determining which of the two is more forceful and vivacious, nor does Reid pretend that it is.

A.–I. constitute the main points in the cumulative case on behalf of the closeness of the connection between mind and world that Reid fosters.

7.2. "Directness" in Interpretations of Reid

Secondary qualities are not perceived as directly as are primary qualities. But disambiguating the senses of directness must come before developing the difference between our perceptions of the two types of qualities. I distinguish between three standard forms of directness to clarify our discussion of this point. (These forms resemble those applied to Reid in Pappas 1989 and Alston 1989.)

On the basis of Reid's comments that our concepts of primary qualities are "directly" formed, I construe Reid's own definition of that term in a cognitive manner. He says that my perceptual apprehension of a primary quality occurs without my being aware of an intermediating sensation. Reid's point seems to be that P's notion of primary quality Q at t is *cognitively direct* only if P apprehends Q, and no sensation is necessarily apprehended in the process. This implies that the direct intentional objects of cognition, as they occur within these acts of perception, are primary qualities and are not mental representations of primary qualities. He attests to a form of cognitive immediacy within perceptual events on several occasions (EIP 2.5, 96/258a; see EIP 2.19, 226/326b and IHM 6.20, 168/183a).

We can distinguish from this a thesis of perceptual directness on which P's notion of primary quality Q at t is *perceptually direct* only if P apprehends Q, and no intermediary is necessarily perceived in the process. Jackson (1977) and Pappas (1989) both offer definitions of "immediate perception" that have this structure. For example: "Typically we immediately perceive objects and their qualities, i.e., we perceive them without perceiving intermediaries" (Pappas 1989, 156). For a quality to be perceptually mediated it is necessary that P not only apprehends or conceives of the intermediary, but that P *perceives* the intermediary. In other words, P's awareness of the intermediary must be the same kind of mental operation as P's awareness of the quality. Only objects of perception are mind-independent qualities in virtue of the definition of the term "perception." He says: "Perception is applied only to external objects, not to those that are in the mind itself" (EIP 23/222a). So the thesis of perceptual directness will trivially hold of Reid's theory if we take Reid's definitions at face value (see Section 1.3).

Distinct from the cognitive and perceptual components is an epistemic form of directness. Often the principal motivation for endorsing a direct theory of perception is the thought that only such a theory enables one to affirm that perceptual beliefs are known immediately and non-inferentially. P's perceptual belief B at *t* is *epistemically direct* only if B is known by P, P has formed B in the appropriate way, and P has not needed to perform inferences in order to know B. If a theory of perception embraces epistemic directness, then no inferences from sensations or mental representations are needed in order to have perceptual knowledge of primary qualities. Reid's employment of the suggestion relation and his theory of signs foreshadow his commitment to epistemic directness. Though he rarely speaks about knowledge directly, he commits himself to this form of directness when saying that a perceptual belief "is immediate, that is, it is not [produced] by a train of reasoning and argumentation" (EIP 2.5, 99/259b).

Since cognitive directness is the most important form of directness for our study, let's look at how this notion is applied to Reid. (I set aside puzzles about the logical relationships between these theses.) Specifically, I want to state the case on behalf of the minority interpretation that Reid denies that perception of primary qualities is cognitively direct and affirms that his theory is cognitively *indirect*.

For Wolterstorff, Reidian sensations represent primary qualities. He begins his explanation by saying that sensations "are ... a sort of medium between the external object and our perception thereof" (2000, 11). To conceive of primary qualities one must first conceive of one's sensations: "Reid regularly speaks of tactile sensations as *signs* of external qualities; and he describes the conception and immediate belief of those external qualities, which these signs suggest, as interpretations of the signs. The conceptions and beliefs interpret the sensations." (2001, 148). He says, perception "involves reading the signs, interpreting the symbols" and "Reid regularly speaks of... conception and immediate belief... as *interpretations* of signs." Wolterstorff adds that we must use a "hermeneutic of signs" to understand the contents of our perceptual beliefs (Wolterstorff 2001, 119, 148, and 154). We conceive of, believe in, and interpret sensations in the course of having perceptions of primary qualities.

Interpreting a sensation is a cognitive matter involving the mind's movement from awareness of a sensation to awareness of what that sensation represents. Wolterstorff says: "It would not be wrong to describe our sensations as 'representing' external entities." Reid didn't describe them this forthrightly because "Reid has his eye throughout on one particular mode of mediation … : mediation by *imagistic* representations" (2001, 134). Sensations are the immediate objects of cognition but they are not pictorial representations. How do they represent? Wolterstorff comes closest to answering this question when saying: "The conceptions and beliefs interpret the sensations so as to extract the information about external qualities which the sensations carry by virtue of being signs of those qualities" (2001, 148). This makes it seem as though the internal structure of sensations contains information about primary qualities, which would be a form of intrinsic representation.

Wolterstorff's student J. Todd Buras updates and strengthens this interpretation by arguing that the "referent of perceptual belief is, for Reid, the object apprehended by the act of conception required for perceptual belief" (2002, 464), namely, the sensation (472). Sensations are the intentional objects of at least one type of perception$_{C\&B}$, but he suggests that bodies are also objects of an additional perception$_{C\&B}$—the two of which occur within the same perceptual event. This follows from Reid's claim that sensations are natural signs. "[I]f, say, we must apprehend bodily qualities by virtue of apprehending sensations—then perceptual beliefs are referentially mediated by sensations. They are about bodily qualities in virtue of being about sensations. In this case the mind would be thinking about bodily qualities by proxy, using sensations to represent them" (Buras 2002, 464). Buras doesn't soft-peddle Reid's cognitive commitments. "Reid is claiming that whenever there is a true material-object belief-statement of the form 'S believes of the *b* such that F*b* that *b* is G', there is not only a true statement to the effect that 'S feels sensation *e*'; but also a true sensational belief-statement 'S believes there is an *e* such that F*e*'" (Buras 2002, 469). Each perceptual event issues in, or incorporates, two distinct beliefs, including one that is about the sensation that suggests the other. Buras describes the cognitive chain-reaction hidden in each perception:

For we must have a thought about our sensations in order to have a sensation; and we must have a sensation in order to apprehend and hold beliefs about bodies; and we must apprehend and hold beliefs about bodies in order to perceive bodies. It is therefore by virtue of thinking about the sensations which signify bodily qualities that we have beliefs about bodily qualities in perception. (Buras 2002, 472)

So a sufficient condition for cognitive mediation of perception by sensation is that one "must apprehend bodily qualities by virtue of apprehending sensations."

Unlike Wolterstorff, Buras believes that sensations are reflexively conscious states as well. He emphasizes Reid's infrequent, but significant, comments that sensations are about themselves. For example, Reid says that sensation is distinguished from other mental states "by this, that it hath no objects distinct from the act itself" (EIP 1.1, 36/229a). The implication is that sensations are about themselves in a sense Reid leaves unexplained. Buras says that "sensations are purely reflexive modes of thought, thoughts which take only themselves as objects" (2005, 222; see 2002, 458).

For both Wolterstorff and Buras, sensations are *the objects of* intentional, cognitive states in the process of perceiving primary qualities. Buras uses the term "apprehension" synonymously with a mental state's "being about" something, which is inter-defined with "referential directness." Wolterstorff says "perception on the standard schema does not yield acquaintance with the world" (Wolterstorff 2001, 147) because perception "involves only the former sort of acquaintance," in other words, "acquaintance with sensations" (2001, 155). I understand this to be equivalent to attributing to Reid the belief that perception of primary qualities is necessarily mediated by our cognitive, intermediating awareness of sensations. Our awareness of primary qualities is cognitively indirect on this reading.

7.3. "Interpreting" Sensations

Several texts point to an interpretation on which Reid endorses the cognitively indirect theory of perception just described. These texts describe ways that our awareness of sensations is intentional. Perhaps due to the quality of evidence these texts offer this interpretation, advocates have needed to buttress the cognitively indirect interpretation with some philosophical arguments. These include an appeal to common sense,[1] an appeal to the similarities between

---

[1] Buras argues that common sense shows that an adverbial theory of sensation is false because adverbial states do not comport with what most people believe about our mental lives. Buras parses Reid's pledge of allegiance to common sense as a commitment that one should "think with the vulgar" (2005, 233). The vulgar have no conception of complex, adverbial states. Therefore, Reid does not endorse an adverbial theory of sensations. Therefore, Reid holds that sensations have intrinsic intentional content and are about something—themselves.

But the assumption that Reidian common sense is merely an appeal to majority opinion is inaccurate. This simplifies Reid's use of common sense in the way that his detractors, including Kant, thought

Reidian and Berkeleyan sensations,[2] and an argument to the effect that, if sensations and our awareness of them were not necessary for perception, then they would be useless in Reid's theory of perception.

These three arguments are sufficiently unconvincing that I won't consider them in the body of this chapter.[3] Instead, I will address whether Reid's texts

Reid did. Reid's use of common sense as a criterion in scientific explanation cannot be substituted into the argument so as to leave the reasoning intact. Besides, if this criterion were applied universally, Reid would not have been able to endorse any *theory* of perception.

[2] Buras next argues that Reid adopts Berkeley's theory of sensations. Reid notes several similarities between the two theories, including that sensations must be "in a sentient being" and that sensations cannot occur without being felt (Buras 2005, 226). He says that Berkeley thinks that sensations do have intentional content, then he says: "Reid does not explicitly attribute to Berkeley the claim that sensations are reflexive mental acts. But they are for Berkeley and Reid clearly recognizes this" (2005, 226). (By "reflexive mental act" Buras means that a given sensation takes itself as an intentional object.) Buras cites Cummins 1974 as offering the justification for the claims that Berkeleyan sensations have intentional content and that Reid attributes this thesis to Berkeley. This allows him to conclude that Reidian sensations also have intentional content.

This argument appears subject to a number of problems. First, I neither find justification for these theses in Cummins 1974, nor do I think that either thesis is intrinsically plausible. Second, the fact that Reid agrees with Berkeley that the phenomenal character of sensations is all there is to them seems to be evidence against attributing to Reid the "reflexive" interpretation. Also, if Reid "clearly recognizes" that Berkeley endorses a reflexive interpretation, then we can expect him overtly to say so because Reid explicitly states his three distinct points of agreement with Berkeley's theory of sensations. Fourth, Berkeley's theory of sensation presupposes features of the Way of Ideas to which Reid was unreservedly opposed. According to Berkeley, the immediate object of perception is a sensation and we cannot conceive of anything distinct from our sensations. Reid pointedly denies these conclusions, evidence that he finds much with which to disagree in what Berkeley says about sensations. There is the final point that the meaning of the claim at issue—that a given sensation takes itself as its intentional object—is unclear. Though Reid says this twice (at EIP 2.16, 194/310a and EIP 2.20, 36/229a), he leaves its meaning obscure. Hopefully, sensations on this interpretation are not bereft of their phenomenal content. Lastly, Buras's previous appeal to common sense on behalf of his case against the adverbial theory works against him here. The vulgar may understand higher-order states being about lower-order states, but would they understand how a state is about itself?

[3] Wolterstorff makes an argument like this (following Van Cleve 2004a): (6.a) We cannot acquire information about primary qualities both by being aware of sensations that represent primary qualities and by being directly, cognitively aware of primary qualities; (6.b) Sensations provide information about primary qualities via suggesting perceptual beliefs; (6.c) So direct cognition does not provide information about primary qualities; (6.d) If there were direct cognition of primary qualities, it would provide information about primary qualities; (6.e) So there is no direct cognition of primary qualities.

(6.a) is a philosophical claim justified independently of Reid's texts. (6.b) is supported textually, while (6.c) follows from those two premises. The conclusion means that we do not directly apprehend or conceive of primary qualities of mind-independent objects.

Van Cleve 2004a (408–10) offers two criticisms of this argument. First, if it were correct, then Wolterstorff's own account of visible figure would be erroneous. In the case of visual perception Reid says material impressions on the retina, not sensations, provide information about visible figures. But if material impressions do this without need of sensations, then we have a "superfluity" of information. Material impressions and sensations cannot both be a source of information about visible figures. Therefore, by parity of reasoning we have no direct cognition of visible figures. But Wolterstorff asserts that we do.

Second, consider the distinction between intrinsic and conventional representations. In Van Cleve's hands, X conventionally represents Y only if X represents Y and X only represents Y to or for a imply that in order to perceive objects, perceivers must form intentional mental states that take sensations as their objects.

In the first key passage Reid uses the term "interpretation" to refer to what we do to sensations:

The signs in original perception are sensations, of which Nature hath given us a great variety, suited to the variety of the things signified by them. Nature hath established a real connection between the signs and the things signified; and Nature hath also taught us the interpretation of the signs—so that, previous to experience, the sign suggests the thing signified, and creates the belief of it. (IHM 6.24, 190/195a)

Reid employs the term "interpretation" in reference to signs, which is a mark in favor of believing that our awareness of sensations is intentional. Wolterstorff uses this on behalf of saying that sensations are the objects with which we are directly acquainted in perception. It is necessary that we access the contents of sensation in consciousness, which makes perception cognitively indirect.

I have a few critical comments about this suggestive text, the first having to do with its context in the *Inquiry*. Were the cognitive, interpretive activity on our part an important aspect of our experience of sensations, it is reasonable to think that Reid would have described it (in some detail) in his most pointed treatment of the matter. He does not. Within the *Inquiry* advocates of cognitive indirectness travel quite far—a distance of tens of thousands of words—from Reid's formal treatment of sensations as natural signs to locate this passage. This is circumstantial evidence against the interpretation. The fact that key texts drawn on behalf of cognitive indirectness occur in Reid's discussions of other aspects of his philosophy of mind, and not within his formal analysis of sensation, indicates that, were he to endorse it, it is as ancillary to his aims as it is significant to his commentators'.

---

person P. A spoken description of Mt. Everest in English represents Mt Everest conventionally only because English has language users capable of hearing the description and understanding what the sound waves are used to mean. A spoken description does not represent Everest intrinsically. X intrinsically represents Y only if X represents Y and X does not represent Y conventionally. Wolterstorff says that sensations carry "information." Sensations might provide information by either being a conventional or an intrinsic fount of representation of the mind-independent world. If states provide information only if they intrinsically represent the objects of perception, then (6.b) is false. Sensations merely conventionally represent primary qualities. Yet, if states provide information either by convention or by their intrinsic content, then (6.a) is false, for both sensations and *de re* conceptions could therefore provide "information" (Van Cleve 2004a, 408–10).

Finally, the claim that sensations and acquaintance cannot both provide information about mind-independent bodies in (6.a) requires justification. The force of the modal claims needed to motivate the charge that Reid is "theoretically incoherent" is unclear. Merely because there are two sources of justification for a perceptual belief does not imply theoretical incoherence.

196 OUR AWARENESS OF SENSATIONS

Second, Reid gives no indication here that "interpretation" is a technical term with the cognitive connotations attributed to it by others. To the contrary, Reid suggests in this passage (and in the core material on the signifying capacities of sensations at IHM 5.3) that there is no higher-order cognitive activity needed in order for properly functioning human beings to experience sensations that signify primary qualities. Reid's use of the term seems inappropriate for Wolterstorff's ends because Reid says these are "interpretations" performed "previous to experience." Any genuinely cognitive process of interpretation would seem conceptually to require something from which something else is interpreted. Yet the source material for these "interpretations" cannot be previous experience.

Besides these observations, to the best of my knowledge Reid nowhere else uses this term to describe what we do to those sensations that signify primary qualities. If correct, this falsifies the claim that "Reid *regularly* speaks of ... conception and immediate belief ... as *interpretations* of signs" (Wolterstorff 2001, 148; first italics mine).

7.4. Signs as "Objects of Thought"

The second passage in favor of cognitive indirectness is more compelling and occurs in the context of Reid's discussion of Locke:

There is a sense in which a thing may be said to be perceived by a medium. Thus any kind of sign may be said to be the medium by which I perceive or understand the thing signified. The sign, by custom, or compact, or perhaps by nature, introduces the thought of the thing signified. But here the thing signified, when it is introduced to the thought, is an object of thought no less immediate than the sign was before. And there are here two objects of thought, one succeeding another, which we have shewn is not the case with respect to an idea, and the object it represents. (EIP 2.9, 134/278b; quoted in Buras 2002, 473–4)

Reid implies that we can perceive things like primary qualities "by a medium" like a sensation. The sign "introduces" the conception and belief of the primary quality. Then Reid implies that the sign "is an object of thought" by saying that the thing signified and the sign are both "immediate" objects of thought. The statement that "there are here two objects of thought" suggests that there are two instances of intentional awareness in perceptual events. This offers some evidence for Buras's theory that there are two distinct beliefs within every perception. Prima facie this passage offers substantial support for believing that Reid's theory of perception is cognitively indirect.

By appreciating the context in which this occurs, this support diminishes, but not entirely. Here Reid is appraising the "two-thought" theory of conception and perception endorsed by Locke. According to Reid's interpretation of Locke, Locke believes that when I conceive of Alexander the Great it is:

the image or idea of Alexander in my mind, which is the immediate object of this thought. The necessary consequence of this seems to be, that there are two objects of this thought—the idea, which is in the mind, and the person represented by that idea; the first, the immediate object of the thought, the last, the object of the same thought, but not the immediate object. (EIP 2.9, 133–4/278b)

Reid is laying stress upon the claim that my thought of Alexander is immediately about something other than Alexander, an idea, which is in turn about Alexander. The "immediate" object of my conception is "in the mind itself" and the final object is outside the mind.

The inset passage occurs at the end of the discussion, and can be interpreted as Reid attempting to be charitable to Locke by finding something in his theory to compliment. This is why Reid adopts the distant voice he does ("it may be said"). Reid's placid tone here should not mask the fact that he is unforgiving to the core tenets of Locke's theory.

First Reid says the theory is psychologically erroneous. Since "it makes every thought of things external to have a double object," Locke's theory does not correspond with our mental experience. "Every man is conscious of his thoughts, and yet, upon attentive reflection, he perceives no such duplicity in the object he thinks about. Sometimes men see objects double, but they always know when they do so: and I know of no philosopher who has expressly owned this duplicity in the object of thought" (EIP 2.9, 134/278b). This suggests that a mental state, whether an idea or something like it, such as a sensation, is not the intermediating object of intentional awareness in our perception. Furthermore, Reid claims that, with a little common sense, the man on the street can introspect on his perceptual experience and learn that sensation is not the object of attention in it.

Second, Reid insinuates that Locke's two-thought theory is incoherent. He professes that it is "very hard, or rather, impossible to understand what is meant by an object of thought that is not an immediate object of thought." He adds that "to think of any object by a medium, seems to be words without any meaning" (EIP 2.9, 134/278b). This passage occurs right before Reid throws Locke a bone by saying that "There is a sense in which a thing may be said to be perceived by a medium." Reid is silent about what that sense is.

As with the use of the previous passage, this text occurs far from Reid's central discussion of sensation. Not only does it not occur in the *Inquiry*, but it occurs in a section of the *Intellectual Powers* that is not focused upon developing his theory of perception. The language of sign and thing signified largely falls out in the *Intellectual Powers* anyway, so it is not surprising that we find Reid, after more than twenty years, making remarks about signs that are not strictly consistent with the *Inquiry*. In this respect we should modulate our interpretation of Reid on sensations in accordance with developmental considerations.[4]

However, I confess to lingering doubts about the extent of the contrast Reid intends to draw between his theory and Locke's. As it stands, he does not develop that contrast with any force. The implication of this discussion upon a determination about whether Reid endorses a cognitively direct theory of perception is uncertain. Specifically, if Reid had wanted to deny that perception contains two thoughts, he missed a fine opportunity to do so here. The leftover challenge is to explain the contrast between Reid and Locke as regards the relationship between our awareness of the sensation and the perception, as this contrast is manifest in this passage.

I take away from this passage Reid's insistence that the philosophically important point about the immediacy of perception is the *relationship between* its cognitive components—not how we divide up the process. There are two ways to parse the relationship between our awareness of the sensation and our perception.

First, the contrast between Reid and Locke could lie in a difference having to do with the *temporal succession* of the second thought from the first. Reid writes: "And there are here two objects of thought, one succeeding another, which we have shewn is not the case with respect to an idea, and the object it represents." Reid might be taken to mean that on his theory, chronologically, the sensation is the first object of thought and the external body is the second object of thought. He differs with Locke because, for Locke, this succession is absent since we have great difficulty in moving from an awareness of an idea to an immediately successive awareness of a mind-independent body. This both establishes the contrast between Reid and Locke, and serves to support the cognitively indirect reading.

But this reading of Reid's point is discordant with what he says elsewhere about the temporal relation between sensation and perception:

---

[4] This has been done before. Some argue that Reid changed his mind about the mediating role of sensations in perception between the two works (Immerwahr 1978). However, due to the contrasting interpretation of natural signs I offer, I believe that this inverts the pattern of Reid's shift. Immerwahr thought Reid believed that perception was mediated by sensation in the *Inquiry* but not in the *Intellectual Powers*. Assuming we are referring to cognitive, and not merely causal, forms of mediation, the shift probably goes the other direction given the texts from the *Intellectual Powers* we have considered.

When a man moves his hand rudely against a pointed hard body, he feels pain, and may easily be persuaded that this pain is a sensation, and that there is nothing resembling it in the hard body; at the same time, he perceives the body to be hard and pointed, and he knows that these qualities belong to the body only. (EIP 2.17, 205/315b)

The perception and its corresponding sensation are produced at the same time (EIP 2.17, 211/318a).

Reid says that the sensation and perception occur simultaneously in these passages. This offers us some reason to discount the passage as not reflecting what Reid says elsewhere. This is not to imply that the passage is no longer circumstantial evidence for the cognitively indirect interpretation. It is. Rather, my point is that this is tainted evidence by virtue of the fact that it runs counter to what Reid says elsewhere.

  Another option for explaining the contrast between Reid and Locke on the objects of awareness in perception involves pointing to a contrast in the *type of awareness* we have of sensations and of primary qualities. In a sense yet to be defined Reid implies that they are both objects of thought by saying, simply, that "there are here two objects of thought." Unfortunately, Reid does not describe what it is to be an object of thought here. Nothing in the passage implies that they are objects of the same kind of thought. If the two thoughts are both intentional thoughts, then the passage favors a cognitively indirect reading. If one thought is a state of phenomenal consciousness and another is intentional, then this favors a cognitively direct interpretation. In the next section I will attempt to identify the ways in which we are aware of sensations.

  This text offers partial support for attributing to Reid a cognitively indirect theory of perception, but this justification is insufficient to warrant attributing to Reid the view that, for each perception, the perceiver must have a mental state that takes a sensation as its intentional object of awareness.

7.5. "Conceiving" Sensations

We can begin clearing another trail to cognitive indirectness by noting Reid's widespread use of "conception":

Conception enters as an ingredient in every operation of the mind: Our senses cannot give us the belief of any object, without giving some conception of it at the same time … We cannot feel pain without conceiving it … In every operation of the mind therefore, in everything we call thought there must be conception. When we analyze the various operations either of the understanding or of the will, we shall always find this at the bottom, like the *caput mortum* of the Chemists, or the *material prima* of the Peripatetics. (EIP 4.1, 295–6/360b)

Reid insinuates that sensations, and all other mental states, are imbued with conceptual content of some kind. Since elsewhere Reid uses examples of pain to generalize about all sensations, we have reason to think that what is said here about pain applies across the board.

Reid makes similar comments prior to the publication of the *Inquiry*:

[E]ven though what philosophers mean by sensation is perchance sufficiently understood, namely, those operations of the mind that are brought into being with the external senses playing a middle role, the senses being sight, hearing, and the rest, nevertheless, I think that these operations are judgements rather than simple apprehensions. (Reid 1989, 56–7)[5]

In every sensation, therefore, the apprehension is not simple but joined with judgement and belief. (Reid 1989, 57)[6]

[T]he nature of sensation itself persuades us that it is not a form of simple apprehension. For in every sensation, the conception is not bare and simple, as in imagination, but joined to assent and belief. (Reid 1989, 75)[7]

Reid's statement that we conceive of each of our sensations can be parlayed into an argument for the indirectness of perception:

(7.1) All sensations are conceived or apprehended. (EIP 4.1, 295–6/360)

(7.2) Since all sensations are conceived or apprehended, all sensations are objects of intentional mental states. (definition)

(7.3) Since we only have perceptions by virtue of having a sensation, we only have perceptions by virtue of having sensations as the objects of intentional mental states. (from Reid's sign theory of sensations)

(7.4) P's notion of primary quality Q is cognitively direct only if P conceives or apprehends Q, and no sensation is necessarily conceived or apprehended in the process. (definition)

(7.5) So Reid's theory of perception is not a cognitively direct theory of perception.[8]

---

[5] "Quid per Sensationem volunt, satis forte intellegitur; eas nempe mentis operationes quæ mediantibus Sensibus externis exercentur, visu scilicet auditu & cæteris; tamen mihi videtur, has operationes, Judicia potius esse quam apprehensions simplices" (Reid 1937, 30–1).

[6] "In omni sensatione igitur est Apprehensio non simplex, sed cum Judicio & Fide conjuncta" (Reid 1937, 31).

[7] "Sensationem vero non esse simplicis Apprehensionis genus rei natura suadet. In omni enim Sensatione conceptio est non nuda et simplex, ut in imaginatione, sed cum assensu et fide conjuncta" (Reid 1937, 45).

[8] Buras uses the above passage, which he says is the "strongest" source of support for the cognitive indirectness (2005, 223), to argue as follows. "Acts of conception lie at the bottom of sensations. Where there are acts of conception, there are objects of thought. For acts of conception simply are

Since Reid says sensations are "conceived" and "apprehended," I use both terms in the premises of this argument.

Does Reid use the terms "conception" or "apprehension" in a way that is either identical to or implies that what is conceived must also be the object of intentional awareness? In other words, is (5.2) true? Theses about "cognitive" directness—also called "referential directness" (Buras 2005), "presentational directness" (Alston 1989), "perceptual direct realism" (Pappas 1989), etc.—are too coarse to be of much help resolving this issue. (We can make this concept artificially precise, but the thesis would then be inapplicable by virtue of its anachronism.) I propose a tripartite distinction between different forms of conscious awareness, though I do not do so in order to attribute it to Reid. Instead I want to show that, though Reid identifies phenomenal, intentional, and reflexive forms of apprehension, he does not adequately differentiate one from the other.

Sensations are states of phenomenal apprehension, or phenomenal consciousness, which can be described as states that seem or feel some way to a subject. When I smell a rose, my experiences seem a certain way to me—a way very different from the way the color of a passing coach looks to me. This what-it-is-like-ness picks out the way that we are standardly conscious of our sensations.

Other states are about something and, thus, intentional. Intentional apprehension refers to states of mind in which an object is represented to the mind. In Chapter 2 we discussed Reid's argument that the intentionality of mental states is a primitive and cannot be explained by appeal to other mental states, so this form of apprehension is familiar. A state of intentional apprehension can function as the content for a variable in an argument. My thought that "It will rain within the hour" is a state of intentional apprehension, which I can compile with other states. These states can be manifested in *de dicto* or *de re* form. I can form an intentional thought about a clock or an intentional thought that "The clock has struck 9." These states of awareness enable reasoning and the performance of directed actions, for example concluding that I'm late and ought to grab my umbrella before I depart.

Reflexive apprehension refers to states that are about other mental states— whether those states are phenomenal or intentional or are other states of reflexive apprehension. My intentional thoughts and my phenomenal states of consciousness need not be reflexive, but they can be. I may have the thought

acts of directing thought at objects... Conception is involved in every mode of thought, and thus object-directedness is an essential feature of mental operations" (Buras 2005, 223–4). Hence, perception is not "referentially direct." My argument attempts to capture the spirit and clarify the structure of this reasoning.

that I am now writing a book chapter or the thought about the way it feels to smell the aroma of the rose. For that matter, I could form a thought about my thought about writing a book chapter. In this sense, any instances of the three types of apprehension can serve as the objects of states of reflexive apprehension.

To rephrase the question posed in the previous section, is it necessary, physically or conceptually, that states of phenomenal apprehension are also states of intentional or reflexive apprehension? In other words, in order to experience a sensation, a way of feeling or sensing, must I form a thought about the sensation in order to perceive the primary quality that the sensation signifies? If so, then Reid's theory of the perception of primary qualities would be cognitively indirect. If not, then sensations are not the objects of intentional awareness, and perception is more direct.

When Reid says we conceive or apprehend or are conscious of sensations, he may not have meant that agents must have a higher-order state of awareness that takes a sensation as its intentional object. The underlying problem in the above argument is that key terms referring to forms of awareness and consciousness are not clearly defined. Perhaps when Reid says we are conscious of a sensation he means only that constitutive of experiencing a sensation of a rose is experiencing an episode of phenomenal consciousness—a what-it-is-like-ness. Since we can experience episodes of phenomenal consciousness without having an additional, higher-order thought about that episode, the sensation appears able to suggest the conception and belief of a primary quality even though the sensation itself is not the object of a state of intentional, conception-and-belief consciousness. Since that is what is required for a theory of perception to be cognitively indirect, Reid is not obviously committed to a cognitively indirect theory of perception.

Of course, the criticism I have just made does not by itself vindicate an interpretation that sensations are *not* typically objects of awareness in acts of perception. To do this, we need to look at further texts.

7.6. "Believing" Sensations

We can improve this discussion by studying Reid's direct remarks about conception. He distinguishes between forms of conception here:

"I conceive an Egyptian pyramid." This implies no judgment. "I conceive the Egyptian pyramids to be the most ancient monuments of human art." This implies judgment. When the words are used in the last sense, the thing conceived must be a proposition, because judgment cannot be expressed but by a proposition. When they are used in the first sense, the thing conceived may be no proposition, but a simple term only, as a pyramid, an obelisk. (EIP 1.1, 25/223b; see Section 2.1)

Reid loosely offers a distinction between *de re* and *de dicto* forms of conception, paralleling *de re* and *de dicto* forms of belief.

Reid says we conceive of sensations in both ways. Not only do we *conceive of* all our sensations, but Reid says that we form *beliefs about* them:

I can think of the smell of a rose when I do not smell it; and it is possible that when I think of it, there is neither rose nor smell any where existing. But when I smell it, I am necessarily determined to believe that the sensation really exists, that as they cannot exist but in being perceived, so they cannot be perceived but they must exist. I could as easily doubt of my own existence, as of the existence of my sensations. (IHM 2.3, 27/105b; see EIP 2.20, 228/327b, quoted in Section 1.4)

This thought is not merely restricted to the *Inquiry*. Moving to the *Intellectual Powers*, Reid remarks: "When I feel a pain, I am compelled to believe that the pain that I feel has a real existence" (EIP 4.1, 311/368a). This arguably offers more direct support for the claim that sensations are immediate intentional objects of thought than the passage about sensations being conceived. This is because Reid says "there can be no belief without conception" (EIP 2.20, 228/327b). Parallel to 7.1 and 7.2, we have:

(7.1′) All sensations are objects of belief. (IHM 2.3, 27/105b)
(7.2′) Since all sensations are objects of belief, the subject forms a belief attributing the sensation to herself.

This is arguably what Reid means when he says that, in sensations, "there is no object distinct from that act of the mind by which it is felt" (EIP 2.16, 194/310a; see EIP 1.1, 36/229a). Though sensations are forms of phenomenal consciousness, we cannot but form beliefs that take sensations as their intentional objects. One might bridge the gap between the nature of sensations and their reflexivity, and the relationship between sensation and perception this way. Surely, one might argue, if we formulate a belief about every sensation experience, sensations must be the objects of intentional awareness.

The problem of identifying what Reid means by saying that we form beliefs about all our sensations mirrors the problem of identifying what he means by saying that we form conceptions of all our sensations. One possibility is that he is literally suggesting that we discursively form propositional beliefs each time we experience a sensation. Buras opts for this reading, saying that "Reid is claiming that whenever there is a true material-object belief-statement of the form 'S believes of the *b* such that F*b* that *b* is G', there is not only a true statement to the effect that 'S feels sensation e'; but also a true sensational belief-statement" (2002, 469). This belief is reflexive in the sense that it is suggested by the sensation and is about the sensation. For example, if by sliding my hand over a table I experience a smooth tactile sensation, then Buras's Reid says that I form the propositional belief that "There is a smooth phenomenal experience that is occurring to me." Taking aboard the attributions about conception and belief, Buras interprets Reid as asserting that, for every sensation, the subject must conceive it as the intentional object of a thought, the subject must form a proposition attributing to the subject the experience of this sensation, and the subject must assent to this proposition. If we define "belief" and "conceive" in the formal ways Buras does, then Reid is committed to a cognitively indirect theory of perception.

But is Reid using "belief" in this way? A key text missing from the discussion thus far is Reid's claim that "belief admits of all degrees, from the slightest suspicion to the fullest assurance" (EIP 2.20, 228/327b). His many and varied uses of conception imply something similar is true of that mental operation. This gives us a reason to doubt that Reid has anything so structured in mind as Buras attributes to him. A distinction between narrow and wide uses of "conception" and "belief" may hold the key to steering around the inconsistencies and untoward implications that some earlier passages threaten to generate for Reid's theory of perception.

A wealth of circumstantial evidence suggests an interpretation on which Reid often uses "conception" and "conscious of" synonymously. When describing the architecture of the mind Reid attests to the ubiquity of consciousness:

As far as we can discover, every operation of our mind is attended with consciousness (EIP 2.15, 191/308b; see EIP 2.5, 96/258a)

[T]he whole train of thought passes in succession under the eye of consciousness (EIP 6.1, 420–1/420a)

All men are conscious of the operations of their own minds, at all times, while they are awake (EIP 1.5, 58/239b)

As far as we can discover, every operation of our mind is attended with consciousness, and particularly that which we call the perception of external objects; and to speak of a perception of which we are not conscious, is to speak without any meaning.

As consciousness is the only power by which we discern the operations of our own minds, or can form any notion of them, an operation of mind of which we are not conscious, is, we know not what; and to call such an operation by the name of perception, is an abuse of language. No man can perceive an object, without being conscious that he perceives it. No man can think, without being conscious that he thinks. What men are not conscious of, cannot, therefore, without impropriety, be called either perception or thought of any kind. (EIP 2.15, 189–91/308b)

From these passages it appears that the term "conscious" for Reid means something like the term "mental" does for us. He does not discuss non-conscious or subconscious mental states: if it is an operation of the mind, then it is conscious. When you place these texts alongside texts from the previous few sections, Reid appears to be saying that we are conscious of, we apprehend, we conceive of, and we form beliefs about our sensations. Taken at face value, this is endless, onerous mental work. Since we constantly experience multiple, changing sensations every waking moment, it is a wonder that we are able to occupy our minds with anything else.

But the cumulative effect of Reid's universal generalizations does not favor the cognitive indirect interpretation. Advocates of a cognitively indirect interpretation of Reid's theory of perception often interpret him as though he beat Brentano to Brentano's thesis through comments that echo and emphasize Reid's sweeping claims, e.g. "Conception is involved in every mode of thought" (Buras 2005, 223–4). But if we can identify any "mode of thought" that Reid believes is not characterized as an intentional, object-directed conception, we would have reason to pull apart Reid's use of "conscious of" and "conceive of" from our use of "intentional state about." This would in turn offer a reason to reject (7.2) and (7.2′).[9] This is because we will have found a mental state that is a form of awareness and yet does not possess representational or intentional content.

The nature of moods provides the source for a counterexample to this thesis. If "conceiving" is what we do when we are conscious of a state, then my melancholic mood, merely by being part of my mental life, is "conceived" even though I can experience this mood without forming an intentional mental state. I might not attend to the fact that I am feeling depressed and yet nonetheless, on this weak use of the term, I "conceive" of my depression.

To my knowledge, Reid does not discuss the nature of our awareness of moods. But he does offer another example that is equally instructive. Merely

[9] Buras parses the distinction between *reflecting on* and *being conscious of* in terms of a distinction between voluntary and involuntary mental states by saying: "The difference is rather between involuntary mental operations (which usually remain tacit) and voluntary mental operations (which are always explicit)" (Buras 2002, 473). Even if the categories invoked are extensionally equivalent, the voluntary/involuntary distinction does not illuminate the character of a conscious mental state. I submit that on standard uses of the term "conscious," if I entertain and assent to a belief attributing to myself the experience of a sensation, I would be conscious of the fact even if it is involuntary, as Reid says it is (EIP 1.5, 59/239a–240b). Being voluntarily or involuntarily formed has nothing to do with it. The reflex action of my knee is involuntary, but, when activated, I am consciously aware of it.

being conscious of something without attending to it "is like," he says, taking "a superficial view of an object which presents itself to the eye, while we are engaged about something else" (EIP 1.5, 59/239b). Extend your right arm and hold up your right index finger. Focus on an object, a candle, say, across the room. While you focus upon the candle, you will see your finger doubled. Reid explains:

[Y]ou may find a man that can say with a good conscience, that he never saw things double all his life; yet this very man, put ... with his finger between him and [a] candle, and desired to attend to the appearance of the object which he does not look at, will, upon the first trial, see the candle double, when he looks at his finger; and his finger double, when he looks at the candle. Does he now see otherwise than he saw before? No, surely; but he now attends to what he never attended to before. The same double appearance of an object hath been a thousand times presented to his eye before now; but he did not attend to it; and so it is as little an object of reflection and memory, as if it had never happened. (IHM 6.13, 134/164b)

Objects in the foreground or background of our visual field (relative to the object upon which we are visually focusing) are seen in double. Reid offers a physiological explanation for this; only when both eyes in binocular vision have symmetrical foci will we see one object (see *Inquiry* 6.13). In the present context I am instead interested in fact that Reid recognizes a form of non-attentive awareness ubiquitous in visual experience. Prior to shifting your visual attention from the candle to your finger, you were nonetheless conscious of it in an exceedingly weak sense. You did not form an intentional thought about it, but you did "conceive of" it in some elusive way that falls short of attention.

Here is a similar example. Suppose visually experiencing a figure/ground phenomenon is physically necessary for the visual perception of bodies. In order to see the visible figure of a table, it is physically necessary that I experience something else in my visual field in order to provide a contrast for my sighting of the table. Commonly, hues of color and shadings of light provide the contrasting ground needed to identify and individuate visible figures. In some sense it is true to say that I am aware of these cues when I see the table. That is to say, the figure/ground phenomena are not merely unconscious, purely physical features of my experience. In contrast, in no sense of the term am I "aware" of the electrical stimulation of my optic nerve. It is necessary that I perceive objects by virtue of being conscious of the figure/ground phenomenon as manifest in shadings of light and hues of color. Despite this, I do not form any higher-order intentional thought or any belief about figure/ground phenomena as I visually perceive the table. I also do not conceive of them in a discursive, intentional sense either. My awareness of them is so elusive and liminal that it resists description.

On some definitions of directness, including the one operative in the statement of cognitive indirectness, this elusive awareness of figure/ground phenomena in my perception of visible figures is sufficient to prevent my perception of visible figure from being direct. If this is a philosophically significant way to think about directness, then an unrecognized implication is that no theory of visual perception could be direct due to the need of an awareness of figure/ground phenomena for visual perception. This is in part why I do not believe that the form of directness that is sacrificed in this example is especially important to Reid, or especially important for philosophical concerns. Mere mediation is immaterial for ruling upon what is philosophically important about directness in the perceptual process.

We can return for a final example to our discussion of the Blind Book argument and Reid's analogy with syntax, words, and meanings. When reading the previous sentence, in one sense you interpreted the black markings that make up its words to know what the words mean and the sentence means. In another sense you did not. In a conventional sense, by virtue of seeing the black shapes you understood the meaning of each word. Furthermore, it is physically necessary and only by virtue of being in some sense aware of the black markings that you are able to understand the meanings of the written words.

However, remarkably, you came to know what the sentence meant without consciously forming any mental states about the black shapes as such—and without forming discursive propositions or beliefs about them. Those shapes suggest to your mind the meanings of the words that they represent by convention. To describe this process as "interpretation," or to say that you conceive of and form beliefs about black shapes by virtue of which you conceive of the meanings of the words they represent, doesn't comport with common uses of those terms. To think that we do form conscious beliefs of the form "S believes there is an e such that Fe" risks packing the mind with unobservable powers reminiscent of Helmholtzian "unconscious inferences." This cannot be done in Reid's name without observational evidence in accord with his Newtonian method to justify that conclusion. But this evidence is absent. This marked one of Reid's criticisms of Locke's theory: Locke proposed a "duplicity" of thoughts in the perceptual process that is not revealed to attentive introspection (EIP 2.9, 134/278b).

These examples, two of which derive from Reid, are evidence that there are modes of thought that are not object-oriented intentional states. Is it necessary, physically or conceptually, that states of phenomenal apprehension are also states of intentional or reflexive apprehension? If "Conception is involved in every mode of thought" (Buras 2005, 223−4) and if conception means what it is said to mean in (7.2), then the answer is yes. But the evidence we have presented in the examples just adduced indicate that it is false that we "conceive of" (as that term is defined in (7.2)) all our mental operations.

The second of our two questions carried over from the last section is unanswered: is our awareness of sensations like our awareness of moods, of the syntax of written language, and of the unattended aspects of visual awareness? Or is our awareness of sensations instead more like the formulation of discursive thoughts and beliefs, or like object-oriented perceptions of physical bodies?

Reid's description of our awareness of sensations that signify primary qualities indicates that it is intangible and uncertain. The "fugitive sensation" is "apt immediately to hide itself." In a comment revealing what he takes to be a key contribution to the history of philosophy, he says:

It is indeed strange that a sensation which we have every time we feel a body hard, and which, consequently, we can command as often and continue as long as we please, a sensation as distinct and determinate as any other, should yet be so much unknown as never to have been made an object of thought and reflection, nor to have been honoured with a name in any language; that philosophers, as well as the vulgar, should have entirely overlooked it, or confounded it with that quality of bodies which we call hardness, to which it hath not the least similitude. (IHM 5.2, 56/120b)

[The reason for this inattention is that] from their very nature, [sensations of primary qualities] lead the mind to give its attention to some other object. (EIP 1.6, 60/240b)

When a primary quality is perceived the sensation immediately leads our thought to the quality signified by it, and is itself forgot. (EIP 2.17, 204/315b)

He says: "our senses give us a direct and a distinct notion of the primary qualities" (EIP 2.17, 201/313b; see Section 6.2). This suggests that we needn't conceive of our sensations as intentional objects of thoughts in order to perceive a primary quality. It also suggests that, as Reid uses the term, our perception of primary qualities is cognitively direct.[10]

---

[10] One might suggest that it only *seems* to me that I'm not conceiving, formulating, and believing propositions that attribute sensation experiences to myself. Perhaps I am doing these things, but I am unaware that I am because these events occur at subliminal levels. Buras defends the attribution to Reid of a thesis asserting that we are aware of sensations on these grounds, tacitly invoking a kind of error theory about first-person states of consciousness. He says we should not think "inattentiveness amounts to unconsciousness. If it did, some might seek relief from our problem by burying the suggestive work of sensations beneath the level of conscious thought" (2002, 472). But if I am *conscious* of believing, each time I have a sensation, a belief of the form "S believes there is an *e* such that F*e*," then I'm uncertain why it doesn't seem like it to me.

In order to avoid interpretive myopia, I want to uncover a presupposition about mental awareness that I believe underlies arguments for cognitive indirectness in both Reid and others.

On some theories, to have a conscious mental state just means to be conscious of that mental state. Advocates of cognitive indirectness often make this assumption. However, as Rebecca Copenhaver puts it, "Reid can hold that consciousness is the awareness of one's own current mental states and refrain from holding that the awareness of one's own current mental states makes those states conscious" (Copenhaver 2005, 7). She defends an interpretation of Reid along these lines by distinguishing between types of consciousness similar to the ones used here. Copenhaver borrows the concepts "state consciousness" and "creature consciousness" to clarify the difference between using "conscious" as an adjective to describe a person and using it to describe a mental state. The key point is that what it is to be a conscious mental state does not imply that such a state must itself be the object of a further representational conscious state.

It is open to Reid to say that a state of phenomenal consciousness experienced when I smell a rose typically occurs without the occurrence of a further state of reflexive consciousness about that first-order consciousness. This nicely comports with what Reid says about our awareness of sensations that signify primary qualities. He repeatedly says that we are not typically aware of the sensations that signify primary qualities in the course of perceiving primary qualities (see Section 6.2). This insight also enhances my use of examples of moods, the awareness of figure/ground phenomenon, and the awareness of syntax. In these cases we have states of first-order awareness that need not (and typically are not) accompanied by a corresponding higher-order state of awareness.

The net effect is to show that the texts quoted and cited on behalf of the enumerated argument above do not offer unambiguous support for (7.2), which states that, merely because all sensations are apprehended, all sensations are the objects of intentional mental states. To justify (7.2) one must have an

Buras's answer invokes a distinction between "conscious of" and "attending to." Reid says that we are "conscious of many things to which we give little or no *attention*" (EIP 1.2, 42/231b; italics absent from Brookes's edition). Attention "is an act of reflection, an inward parallel of outward perception which takes mental operations as its objects" (Buras 2002, 473). Problems with this interpretation include the fact that the passage quoted to explain the difference addresses the contrast between consciousness and reflection, not attention. Second, Buras's discussion leaves the phenomenology of Reidian consciousness unclear. Reid's use of the term "conscious" as a matter of degree differs sharply from the way it is used today. Third, the error theory needed to account for the fact that we're all unaware of the huge numbers of beliefs we regularly but unwittingly form would be unbecoming to Reid due to his commitment to observation in the formation of philosophical explanations.

argument that shows that when a state is conceptual or is conscious, what makes it conceptual or conscious is the presence of a further conceptual or conscious state that takes the first state as its intentional object. We do not possess enough evidence from Reid to show that he endorses the position about the nature of awareness that the argument attributes to him. Moreover, we have sufficient evidence also to deny that he endorses the view. Instead, he endorses something much closer to the thesis of cognitive directness.

7.7. Summary

In this chapter I have attempted to identify and analyze key passages suggesting that we are aware of sensations, and to assess the implications of those passages for the relationship that our minds bear to the world in perceptual events. We are justified in attributing to Reid a fairly direct theory of perception, one that endorses the cognitive directness thesis on which a perceiver apprehends a primary quality without needing a higher-order intentional apprehension of the sensation that signifies that primary quality. I draw this conclusion on the basis of: (i) analysis of passages that appeared to support cognitive indirectness; (ii) the support of passages in which Reid attests to the directness of our awareness of primary qualities; and (iii) the cumulative case for cognitive directness. However, though we are justified in attributing to Reid a cognitively direct theory, I stop short of claiming that we have maximally justified that attribution.

This prompts a closing, cautionary point. Scholarship on Reid's theory of perception has been unduly focused upon identifying whether he offers a "direct" theory. But if I am correct, the support, though significantly in favor of one alternative, is not complete. I fear that the ongoing proliferation of varieties of Reidian "directness" in this niche in the history of Early Modern philosophy will be dismissed in a generation as a warmed-over scholasticism. I'm not a doxographical purist when doing the history of philosophy, but forcing an anachronistic clarity on to a corpus that cannot bear it risks offering a frictionless interpretation that has insufficient traction on the extant texts. I have attempted to maintain my goal as identifying what Reid means by what he says. As such, I hope that the partial agnosticism I am proposing about directness is as innocuous and sensible as it appears to be to me.

8

Perceptual Learning

We are now in a position to turn to Reid's discussion of perceptual knowledge. Reid offers a subtle analysis of stages of cognition in perception but we must be patient in sorting it out. Though he is known as an epistemologist he almost never discusses perceptual knowledge or knowledge *simpliciter*, and his discussion of the role of inference in the formation of perceptual beliefs is in some disarray.

The contrast he draws between original and acquired perceptions helps matters considerably, even if this distinction is itself rough. I regard the difference between the two as philosophically substantive, and as capable of informing us about the role of thinking in perception.[1] I will argue that Reid believes there is a philosophically significant difference between original and acquired perception. Reid uses the distinction to differentiate marginally cognitive events of seeing from events of visual perception, in which a perceiver applies conceptual categories to an object, i.e. perceives the chair *as* a chair.

Yet the implementation of this distinction does not resolve the following problem. Reid is often seen as holding that perceptual beliefs are non-inferentially known. In favor of this is his frank comment in the *Inquiry* that "There is no reasoning in perception" (IHM 6.20, 172/185a). But in the *Intellectual Powers* he makes numerous remarks that imply the contrary; for example he explains erroneous perceptual beliefs as arising from "conclusions

---

[1] Some have argued that the distinction merely picks out a temporal difference in the development of one's perceptual abilities. Ben Zeev says: "The distinction between original and acquired perception is not a distinction between two different types of perception (and cognition)—direct and indirect perception. The difference here is an empirical, historical difference concerning the time in one's history in which a certain perception has evolved. Original perceptions are present at birth, while acquired ones have evolved later" (1986, 108). He adds: "Reid is not always aware of the above implications of his stand, and sometimes treats acquired perception as having a different status (and not merely origin) than that of original perception" (1986, 109). The choice is between interpreting the original/acquired distinction as a substantive philosophical distinction between different types of perception (and cognition), or as a merely temporal distinction regarding the point at which a person's set of perceptions change. Alternatively the distinction could be temporal but refer to temporal properties of individual perceptions and not to a time in the historical development of one's perceptual faculty. Ben Zeev puts us on to the scent, but the dilemma he presents is a false one.

rashly drawn" from the senses (EIP 2.22, 244/335a). Since erroneous and veridical perceptual beliefs are formed in the same way with respect to our cognitive faculties, Reid implies that all such beliefs are in some sense the product of inferences or "conclusions" from the senses. This tension can stupefy those who attempt to interpret Reid on perceptual learning as offering a consistent theory over the course of the two major works.

Despite this tension, Reid holds that clarifying conflicts such as this are among the most important jobs philosophers have by saying that "Nothing is of more importance in the Culture of our Rational Powers, than to distinguish The Judgments of Nature which are the necessary result of our Constitution from opinions which we acquire from habit from Education (or) from Reasoning" (13 January 1765 at Reid 1990, 147). Interpreted properly, his theory of perceptual learning is subtle and plausible, though we must allow for its development through Reid's corpus. A central point emerging from his discussion in both the *Inquiry* and *Intellectual Powers* is that, for Reid, the epistemic justification of the majority of acquired perceptual beliefs depends upon the justification of other perceptual beliefs.

8.1. Immediate Perceptual Knowledge

In contrast to this aim, Reid offers his readers several reasons to attribute to him a non-inferential theory of perceptual knowledge. None of them is individually convincing, and each point has its difficulties. But taken together they constitute a convincing case on behalf of an interpretation in that vicinity.

The intuition that non-inferential perceptual knowledge would follow from (or, failing that, would plausibly accompany) direct perception has many sources of support. The first reason this intuition is positioned to find corroboration in Reid trades on a subtlety in his theory of perception. For Reid the process of perception culminates in a belief, the production of which is irresistible (see IHM 6.20, 168/182a–b; EIP 2.5, 96/258a; and EIP 2.16, 199/312b). Reid calls belief an "ingredient" of perception in his canonical definitions of the term "perception." Some may bristle at this terminology. "The belief of an Object that is perceived, I use to call an *ingredient* of the Act of Perception. But if any one dislikes this expression and chuses rather to call it a *concomitant*, which by the constitution of our Nature invariably attends Perception, I will not quarrel with him" (C 108). Whichever the term, Reid believes that perception contains a doxastic component. It seems quick work to argue that this immediately and irresistibly produced belief is justified. Commitment to non-inferential perceptual knowledge can be seen as an organic outgrowth of Reid's theory of the immediate perception of bodies.

Reasons for non-inferential perceptual knowledge also arise from philosophical commitments outside Reid's theory of perception. Reid contends that "original and natural judgments," for example believing there is a tree before me when it appears to be so, "are a part of that furniture which Nature hath given to the human understanding. They are the inspiration of the Almighty...They make up what is called *the common sense of mankind*" (IHM 7, 215/209b). Reid affirms that perceptual beliefs are God-given and are components of common sense. If a belief possesses these traits it seems we are prima facie warranted in believing that it is non-inferentially justified. For, since they are gifts of the Almighty, the implication is that we have not justified them of our own accord. So, second, we must seek to maintain the God-given, commonsensical account of perceptual knowledge. Any account failing to explain how children readily produce perceptual beliefs with positive epistemic status, for example, would violate this intuition.

We find the most far-reaching implication of the denial of non-inferential perceptual knowledge in Reid's relationship to skepticism. Those who struggle through the briar patch of objections to a direct theory of perception eagerly desire some philosophical recompense for their efforts. This takes the form of a dissolution of perceptual skepticism through an affirmation of non-inferential perceptual knowledge. Any alternative account must properly explain this relationship. Moreover, Reid lacks some of the resources that the proponents of the Way of Ideas possess for explaining how we might have inferential knowledge of the external world. Locke, for instance, makes an abductive case for the falsity of perceptual skepticism by appeal to a manifold of "conformity" between ideas (Locke 1975, 4.4.1/562-73). If what we perceive does not include ideas and mental images, and if we don't have non-inferential knowledge that the objects of certain perceptions are bodies and their qualities, then Reid must be careful to establish the justificatory status of perceptual beliefs without begging questions.

The previous points in favor of a non-inferential account of Reidian perceptual knowledge are circumstantial. In addition, compelling texts for this interpretation include this one, which comes from a letter to Dugald Stewart:

When a Man perceives the distance of an Object from the Eye, I apprehend the perception is as instantaneous as when he perceives the colour or visible figure of the Object. The first of these perceptions is acquired by Expirience, the last is original, but both are equally instantaneous. & I see no Evidence of any train of thought or reasoning interposed between the Appearance of the Object & the Judgment of its Distance. (C 214–15)

Reid emphasizes the temporal "instantaneousness" of the belief, switching seamlessly between temporal and epistemic senses of immediacy. "Temporal immediacy" refers to a short amount of time between one event and another, whereas "epistemic immediacy" refers to non-inferentially formed belief. He does not claim that we have epistemically immediate knowledge of our perceptual beliefs, and, besides, he is only talking about beliefs in terms of the distance of objects judged through vision—not perceptual beliefs *tout court*. Notwithstanding these points, he implies that he has no grounds to believe that one reasons from seeing the visible figure to forming a belief in terms of its distance. Such beliefs about distance are formed without reasoning.

The most frequently cited passage on behalf of an epistemically immediate interpretation of Reidian perceptual knowledge is this:

> If the word axiom be put to signify every truth which is known immediately, without being deduced from any antecedent truth, then the existence of the objects of sense may be called an axiom. For my senses give me as immediate conviction of what they testify, as my understanding gives me of what is commonly called an axiom. (EIP 2.20, 231/329a)

This too is not an endorsement of a non-inferential theory of perceptual knowledge, even though it moves us in that direction. Here Reid is arguing that we must take for granted that there exist mind-independent objects. He is not arguing for the conclusion that beliefs produced by my perceptual faculties are justified in virtue of the fact that the process is typically truth-conducive (Nichols 2002b, 566–9).

Some commentators hold that Reid identifies our psychological relation to perceptions with our epistemic relation to the same. Reid says: "we ask no argument for the existence of the object but that we perceive it; perception commands our belief upon its own authority, and disdains to rest its authority upon any reasoning whatsoever" (EIP 2.5, 99/259b, in Alston 1989, 37). Here Reid argues that we are powerless to use reason to override nature. By mixing psychological senses of immediacy with epistemic senses it becomes difficult to disambiguate his meaning in this passage. Reid seems to emphasize the psychological force our senses wield. He remarks in the preceding paragraph: "philosophy was never able to conquer that natural belief which men have in their senses" (ibid.). That the belief cannot be overridden by reason does not imply that it is known; it may be so near the center of the web of belief that it is psychologically impossible to give it up.

The most compelling textual evidence on behalf of a thesis of non-inferential perceptual knowledge comes in a letter in which Reid responds to the opinion of Henry Home, Lord Kames (Home 1785 i, 221–30), according to which perceptual belief is merely another means of conception and is not evidential. Reid sees this as giving too much ground to Hume and others who make different operations of the mind into "different Modes of the same Operation" (C 106). So Reid stresses the evidential nature of perceptual belief to sharpen this contrast. Though commentators have not yet alighted upon this text with a frequency proportional to its importance to the issue at hand, Reid might say more about perceptual knowledge in the following three paragraphs than in the rest of his published work combined:

By Perception I understand that immediate Knowledge which we have of external Objects by our Senses. This I take to be the proper meaning of the Word in the English Language. And I would wish Philosophers to keep by this meaning. The knowledge we have immediately by our five Senses is a particular kind; and deserves a particular Name, and I know no Name so proper as that of Perception. There is indeed a Figurative meaning of the Word which cannot easily be avoided. We use it to express any kind of Evidence which in its force & cogency resembles that of our Senses. As when we say that we *perceive* the force of a Demonstration meaning that we discern it as clearly as we do an Object placed before our Eyes.

By Knowledge, I think, we mean, Belief upon good Evidence. We know what is self evident, & we know what we can give good Evidence for. But we sometimes believe upon bad Authority or from Prejudice; & such Belief is not called Knowledge.

All knowledge therefore implies belief; but belief does not imply Knowledge. I know what I distinctly perceive by my Senses; I know what I distinctly remember; I know when I am pained; I know that two & three make five. In all these cases the knowledge is immediate. There is no *medium* of proof. But there is belief upon good Evidence. I know from undoubted Testimony that there is such an Island as Jamaica. I know from Demonstration a Mathematical Proposition. (C 107)

The terms in which Reid expresses his sentiments cannot be ignored. Reid appears to affirm two important points: that the concept of perception is evidential in nature, and that the knowledge delivered through perception is immediate and non-inferential.

Given the scarcity of texts about perceptual knowledge, the evidence now brought forth weighs significantly in favor of an interpretation on which it is gained non-inferentially. But even the last passage presents us with some reasons for pause. First Reid restricts his thesis in the third paragraph to say that which we "distinctly perceive" is "immediate" knowledge. On the basis of our study of qualities, we can venture a further clarification. Since Reid only describes our concepts of primary qualities as "distinct" and "clear," we can infer that our perceptual beliefs about primary qualities conform to a non-inferential theory of perceptual knowledge, and that, probably, our secondary qualities do not—a result that nicely conforms to the results from

Chapters 6 and 7. Second, and more perplexing, is the fact that these thoughts didn't make their way into the *Intellectual Powers* in the form in which Reid presents them to Kames. Had Reid wanted to, he could have easily included these passages in his later published work, for he often did adopt particular passages from letters for this purpose. In fact he uses the second half of this very letter in the *Intellectual Powers* at EIP 2.22, 244/335a–b. So he explicitly elected to omit the quoted passages from publication. I have no reason to think that he would not have placed these thoughts into his published work had they accurately represented his views. Perhaps his modesty about epistemic claims, along with the permanence of the printed word, conspired to forestall him from publishing.

In any event these sorts of circumstantial and textual considerations have motivated what I referred to as the canonical interpretation of Reid on this matter, which is that perceptual knowledge is non-inferential. Consider Pappas's definition of "epistemic direct realism" (or "EDR"), which he draws in reference to Reid:

EDR = (a) perceptual beliefs are (typically) justified solely in virtue of the perceptual process(es) that produces them; and (b) these beliefs are not justified in virtue of any conscious inference performed by the percipient from any other beliefs, whether about sensory states or about other perceptions.[2]

Reference to the "perceptual process" includes the application of concepts to the intentional objects of perception, but it does not incorporate inference. "Immediacy" in EDR means that there are no inferences between my sensory perception of an object and my knowledge of the object. This contrasts with the way "immediacy" is used in statements of direct theories of perception, in which cases it refers to the fact that there is no awareness of ideas, sense-data, or sensations intervening between my perception of an object and the physical object. Pappas explains epistemological direct realism as the view that perceptual knowledge of physical objects and their qualities is "typically direct or non-inferential, not being based upon immediately known, or immediately justified beliefs about sensations" (Pappas 1989, 159). On EDR perceptual

---

[2] See Copenhaver 2004 for an analysis and update on this schema. A systemic difficulty with this type of schema is the fact that it takes the concept of perception as primitive. In other words, Pappas and others are not interested in explaining what perception is, for Reid. They attempt to identify what is epistemically direct about perception. But in order to provide necessary and sufficient conditions for *epistemic direct perception* one must have an analysis of *perception* in hand. To assume that there is an uncontroversial analysis of Reidian perception and/or that Reid scholars agree on what that is, is dubious. This has not become a concern only because scholars have been typically interested in the matter of the directness of perception. But we have seen that all manner of complications arise for an analysis of Reidian perception in the form of necessary and sufficient conditions.

beliefs are normally known without inference, perhaps even thoughtlessly, as on contemporary forms of epistemological externalism. EDR is motivated by a desire to explain how the faculty of perception leads to knowledge that is non-inferentially formed. It can be understood as an attempt to nip skepticism in the bud.

It is no surprise that, though Pappas and Alston (1989)[3] are the only two explicitly to state such a thesis and interpret Reid as approving of it, many others make remarks that assume or imply a similar non-inferential account of Reidian perceptual knowledge. In this group belong Phillip Cummins, Tony Pitson, Aaron Ben Zeev, and Keith Lehrer, both on his own and with J. C. Smith.[4]

---

[3] Alston explains that perceptual knowledge for Reid possesses "epistemological directness," which a belief has when it is "justified, warranted, [and] rationally acceptable, apart from any reasons the subject has for it. It is 'intrinsically credible', 'prima facie justified', just by being a perceptual belief" (1989, 37). Alston does not believe Reid's view is lucid on this score because Reid's account of the "ground" of the belief is both psychologically descriptive and epistemologically evaluative (41–2). Nonetheless, after noting these reservations, Alston concludes: "there is no doubt but that Reid takes the perception of external objects to be immediate in [this epistemologically direct] way" (37). Despite obvious differences (e.g. that the first is a thesis about knowledge, while the second concerns justification), for the present I will not distinguish between Alston's "epistemological directness," Pappas's EDR, and my own statement of the view.

[4] Here is what they individually have to say on this point. Cummins states that: "Reid's position that perception is a first principle of contingent truth could be understood as the claim that basic perceptual beliefs provide the foundation for the total system of beliefs about material things which is common to all ordinary men. (By 'basic perceptual belief' I mean a belief—conception and assent—which is an element or ingredient in an act of perceiving.) It will be recalled that, according to Reid, basic perceptual beliefs have a very special status. They do not result from any process of reasoning and cannot be derived from any body of factual beliefs" (1974, 338). If such perceptual beliefs do not result from any reasoning, then they (a) non-inferentially, immediately acquire positive epistemic status, (b) do not have such status, or (c) have positive epistemic status in virtue of a process that cannot be resolved into a form of reason. That they would not be epistemically justified is anathema to Reid. How perceptual beliefs might be epistemically justified neither in virtue of facts about their irresistible production nor by a form of reasoning, yet in a way which coheres with the texts, is unclear at best. So, the most plausible extrapolation from what Cummins says is that he believes that since most perceptual beliefs are justified, they are justified non-inferentially in virtue of facts concerning their (reliable) production. This argument from elimination can be reapplied to the comments of other authors on this matter. Pitson says: "My own view is that when Reid says that perception arises from sensation, and that the operation involved is one of suggestion, he is referring to the fact that there is a causal—as opposed, for example, to an inferential—relation between the two" (1989, 82). Ben Zeev comments: "Reid says that a perceptual belief is not based upon internal processes such as reasoning or association from past experience" (1989b, 98). Lehrer says: "Reid holds that we have a natural and irresistible belief in the existence of external objects. This belief is, moreover, implied by our perception of external objects which involves a sensation giving rise to the conception and irresistible conviction of the qualities of the external object immediately, without reasoning, even reasoning concerning the sensation itself. ... Reid, in opposition to Hume, holds that the beliefs in question [i.e. perceptual beliefs] are not only natural but evident and justified as they appear irresistibly in us" (1987, 394).

Lehrer and Smith together present a subtle, meticulous account of the status of acquired perception. They hold that the operation of acquired perception "does not involve any reasoning of any sort. The

The view is headed in the right direction, but its proponents generally do not consider how some of Reid's discussions attenuate the attribution of EDR to Reid. I refer to what Reid says about perceptual skepticism, perceptual error, and the original/acquired distinction. The upshot is that EDR, though on the right track, is too sanguine for Reid. It better describes the epistemic views of James Beattie, the great popularizer of common-sense philosophy, since Beattie is considerably more confident of our knowledge of our perceptual beliefs than Reid.[5]

8.2. Skepticism and Error

What Reid says about perceptual skepticism and error blur the portrait of him painted by tradition. I want to develop these aspects of Reid's philosophical outlook as a counterpoint to the canonical interpretation.

First consider the following passage reminiscent of Hume:

For anything we can discover, we might have been so framed as to have all the sensations we now have by our senses, without any impressions upon our organs, and without any conception of any external object. For anything we know, we might have been so made as to perceive external objects, without any impressions on bodily organs, and without any of those sensations which invariably accompany perception in our present frame.

If our conception of external objects be unaccountable, the conviction and belief of their existence, which we get by our senses, is no less so. (EIP 2.20, 227/327a)

Given the philosophical pessimism present here, it is no wonder why Reid does not claim in print to possess perceptual knowledge of external objects, as opposed to "informations of the sense," as Roger Gallie has noticed (1989a, 47–8). Reid is reluctant to allow knowledge even that external objects produce our conceptions of what seem to us to be external objects. Passages like the following are striking: "We know that such is our constitution, that in certain circumstances we have certain conceptions; but how they are produced we know no more than how we ourselves were produced" (EIP 2.20, 226/326b). This evinces a mild form of second-order skepticism. Reid does not assert that we cannot know how our beliefs are produced in our minds. Yet saying

general principle yields a conception of the quality as the cause of the sensation without reflection or argumentation" (1985, 27–8).

[5] Compare Beattie (2000, 34–7) and Reid (EIP 6.5, 472–8/443–6) on their respective descriptions of the epistemic deliverances of perception. It is Beattie, not Reid, who uses terms like "knowledge" and "absolute certainty" to describe the deliverances of the senses.

that we do not know their origins is significant in light of some contemporary internalist definitions of knowledge on which justification for a second-order belief about the process causing the first-order belief is required for knowledge of the first-order belief. Reid's comments will be fodder for those interested in prosecuting his theory with BonJourian clairvoyance cases.

Though this wary, suspicious Reid contrasts with the established perspective, this Reid conforms well to the interpretation presented by Louise Marcil-Lacoste (1978). She argues that Reid is a mitigated skeptic about perceptual knowledge and says that though it "might be difficult to reconcile the seriousness of Reid's skeptical admissions with the tenor of many of his other statements," nonetheless, Reid's common-sense approach to philosophy will not allow him wholly to escape skepticism (1978, 321). Though beliefs about the existence of objects that are distinctly perceived have some type of justification, just what that amounts to Reid will not say.

Reid places surprising limitations upon perceptual knowledge in passages such as this, in which he follows Hume in distinguishing between the independent existence of an external object from its permanent existence. He says:

My senses do not testify that the Sun and Moon continue to exist when I do not perceive them. For any thing my Senses testify they might have been created the moment I perceived them and annihilated the moment after. If I have any where made their Existence when I perceive them not, to be the testimony of my Sense as distinguished from all my other Powers, I think it an Error. (Aberdeen MS 2131/3/II/3, 11; see Marcil-Lacoste 1978)

Our perceptual knowledge does not extend to knowledge of the permanence of objects we have perceived, but is instead coupled to those fleeting moments during which we perceive. I see something. I look away. The knowledge I have that it still exists is not a species of perceptual knowledge, but is of a species more difficult to obtain.

Reid's views about perceptual error also require special attention, for they create a conflict with the textual evidence in favor of interpreting Reid as advocating a non-inferential theory of perceptual knowledge. Reid's title of *Intellectual Powers* 2.22, "Of the Fallacy of the Senses," is misleading because in most cases in which we are apt to describe our senses as failing us, Reid would not. Despite this, Reid is secretly pleased that there are some errors of the senses. (To appreciate why, see Hume's *Treatise* 1.4.2.3−5/189.) His predecessors, in teaching "that the office of the senses is only to give us the ideas of external objects," brazenly assert that "there can be no fallacy in the senses" (EIP 2.22, 252/339b). Instead, he finds the common source of such errors in our cognitive manipulation of the outputs of our senses.

Reid packages his views on error in a fourfold division of the "appearances" of fallacies of the senses. Reid asks us to suppose that someone takes a guinea coin in payment for services rendered. Upon taking it she senses the coin with her eyes and hands. One may say her senses deceive her because she is not perceptually informed that the coin is a counterfeit. But in this situation her senses are not in error:

We are disposed to impute our errors rather to false information than to inconclusive reasoning, and to blame our senses for the wrong conclusions we draw from their testimony. Thus, when a man has taken a counterfeit guinea for a true one, he says his senses deceived him; but he lays the blame where it ought not to be laid: for we may ask him, Did your senses give a false testimony of the colour, or of the figure, or of the impression? No. But this is all that they testified, and this they testified truly. From these premises you concluded that it was a true guinea, but this conclusion does not follow; you erred, therefore, not by relying upon the testimony of sense, but by judging rashly from its testimony. (EIP 2.22, 244/335a–b; see C 114–15)

The error lies in "conclusions rashly drawn from the testimony of the senses" on the part of the subject (EIP 2.22, 244/335a), or as he puts it to Kames, "rash Judgments which are drawn or inferred illogically from the Testimony of Sense" (C 114). The reason his perceptual belief that the object before him is a guinea coin is not justified is due to the presence of illicit inferences taking him from seeing this object to seeing this object *as* a guinea.

Consider his next example. I take a piece of soft turf, "I cut it into the shape of an apple; with the essence of apples, I give it the smell of an apple; and with paint, I can give it the skin and colour of an apple. Here then is a body, which, if you judge by your eye, by your touch, or by your smell, is an apple ... This is a fallacy, not of the senses, but of inconclusive reasoning" (EIP 2.22, 245/335b). There is no sensory error present in my coming to believe that this object is an apple after sensory examination. This highly deceptive environment prompts the subject to conclude that the object is an apple. It was this sort of example Reid had in mind when stating the necessary condition on perceptual knowledge we observed above, namely, that he will "take it for granted that the evidence of sense, *when the proper circumstances concur*, is good evidence, and a just ground of belief" (EIP 2.20, 229/328b, my emphasis).

Reid explains the failure of justification for perceptual beliefs by explicit appeal to faulty inferences from what the senses convey to conclusions about what is actually the case. Though the type of reasoning Reid identifies as the source of error is not deductive, the error is not to be resolved into a breakdown in some automated and involuntary form of cognition. Reid would probably not contend that such conclusions are "rash" if he had in mind anything other than some type of inductive, inferential reasoning. Indeed, Reid uses the phrase "drawn or inferred illogically" in this correspondence. So we have a problem: Reid indicates that perceptual beliefs are immediately known but he also says that perceptual beliefs that are false are false because we make unjustified inferences. Reid voices these two commitments in the same letter no less (C 114).

I might form a visual perceptual belief about *that small, circular, thin object before me that appears to exhibit a silvery color*, or *that palm-sized, apple-like object that appears to exhibit a red hue*. Alternatively, I might form a perceptual belief in which the *de re* conception has as its content *that guinea coin before me*, or *that Macintosh Apple before me*. Roughly, the first sort of content is original, and the second acquired. Reid's use of the examples implies that acquired content is the product of some type of reasoning, and/or it contains more robust cognitive content than original perceptions do. If correct, this does not overturn an interpretation in the form of EDR since some perceptual beliefs remain non-inferentially formed. EDR and its cousins tend to oversimplify Reid's theories by omitting mention of the *scope or number* of perceptual beliefs to which they allegedly conform. Reid may hold that at least some perceptual beliefs are known non-inferentially, but that many, probably the majority, are known inferentially. Indeed, Reid says that acquired perceptions form the bulk of our perceptual beliefs. Put these two points together and it appears as though an EDR-style interpretation only services the minority of our perceptual beliefs.

One might object that we only draw inferences when perception goes wrong—otherwise it is non-inferential. But this solution is ad hoc and unpersuasive. One environment may be deceptive and another not, but they can appear qualitatively identical to me. In a pair of cases in which the objects of perception appear identical to me, my mind operates in precisely the same manner. So by parity of reasoning I not only "draw conclusions" when I err in acquired perception but in *all* acquired perceptions.[6]

This is the kind of claim with which Reid aficionados might take umbrage: how could Reid advocate a non-inferential theory of perceptual knowledge? I respond with two related observations. Philosophers of perception routinely overestimate the importance of propositional perceptual knowledge,

---

[6] There is a final constraint on Reid's account: error must not be attributed either to our faculties or to the world itself, as both are created by an all loving, omnipotent God. Reid needs to defend his supposition that the senses "are formed by the wise and beneficent Author of Nature" (EIP 2.22, 242/334a; see the Fourth Meditation at Descartes 1984–91 ii, 37/AT vii 53). Reid's account of error—and his theory of perceptual learning along with it—has been backed into a supernatural corner.

and routinely over-intellectualize the process. Defenders of theories like Reid's, and commentators on Reid's theories, emphasize the belief formation in Reidian perception. But consider the phenomenology involved in the perceptual process. The phone rings, I move to the adjacent room, find it, flip it open, and answer. I do not consciously form occurrent beliefs like *the phone is now ringing* or *the phone is in the next room* or *flip it open to answer*. (Neither do I form a perceptual belief with original content like *that there is a phone-like noise, seemingly originating from a nearby room*.) The majority of analyses of Reid's theory of perception, and of historical theories of perception generally, remain in the throes of a perspective on perception left over from A. J. Ayer and company. On this theory the (only) important questions are epistemic in character. But Reid does not intellectualize perception—perhaps he "under-intellectualizes" it. As argued in the previous chapter, when he speaks of "belief" he does not use the term in its conscious and propositional sense. He does not speak the language of "perceptual justification," "cognition," "inference," "information," or "knowledge." The penchant for such analyses of Reid's "direct realism" shows no signs of abeyance, but as this quest moves yet further from Reid's corpus it bears remembering that Reid was largely ambivalent to these issues.

My goal is to identify the type of reasoning Reid believes occurs in perception, while both refraining from imposing upon the texts ill-suited contemporary distinctions, and simultaneously bringing clarity to the issues. By closely charting the development of Reid's beliefs on the issue of perceptual learning and knowledge through published and unpublished texts, I hope to achieve this goal in the sections that follow.

8.3. Cognition and Inference in Original Perceptions

In the *Intellectual Powers* Reid abandons extensive talk of "natural signs" and "suggestion." He still believes that suggestion has work to do in his philosophy of mind because suggestion relations are needed to convert sensation experiences into perceptual contents. We observed that Reid uses suggestion relations in the *Inquiry* to explain conceptual phenomena at multiple levels in the perceptual process, saying for example: "When I hear a certain sound, I conclude immediately, without reasoning, that a coach passes by. There are no premises from which this conclusion is inferred by any rules of logic. It is the effect of a principle of our nature, common to us with the brutes" (IHM 38/117b). In this case the suggestion relation stands between an aural sensation and the perceptual belief that a coach is passing, a belief rich in content. We left our discussion of suggestion in Chapter 2 with Reid facing the problem of bridging this chasm between sensation and belief with robust content without appeal to any "natural kind of magic."

Reid sets his sights higher in the *Intellectual Powers*. He attempts to refine his analysis of suggestion by breaking down the process by which we form perceptual belief into its component parts. This results in his distinction between original and acquired perception. Reid's distinction between original and acquired perception, muddy though it is, enhances Reid's ability to explain how perceptual beliefs acquire their conceptual content. At the outset of the *Inquiry*, Reid's concern was to identify the miraculous mechanisms responsible for enabling us to form intentional thoughts about primary qualities at all. Reid uses his discussion in the *Intellectual Powers* to take a further step in analyzing this process by refining his goals. Here he wants to explain not merely how we are able to have perceptions of things *simpliciter*, but how we come to form the specific types of perceptual beliefs we do.

I construe this shift in emphasis as a progressive augmentation of material from the *Inquiry*. He does not replace his earlier views, but he enhances them. A key link between the major works is the claim that we directly perceive mind-independent objects and their primary qualities—as opposed to perceiving images, ideas, or other intermediaries. This point is overlooked at the peril of flummoxing Reid's response to the representational theory of perception put forth by his predecessors. Reid makes this point by saying:

As to independent Existence when the objects are perceived, that I take to be implied in the very nature of perception. What I perceive is not my self nor anything belonging to me; it is something external, that is, something of which my mind is not the Subject. and therefore independent of me ... I think the Faculty of Perception testifies that the object perceived is no quality of me nor any thing of which my mind is the Subject. or which depends upon my Existence. All this is no more than what is implied in its being external. (Aberdeen MS 2131/3/II/3, 11)

The nature of the objects of original perceptions is unambiguous; here I am concerned about the development of the broadly epistemic, or conceptual, content of those perceptions—about what I call "perceptual learning."

Reid's application of the original/acquired distinction anchors my interpretation of what he has to say about perceptual learning. In addition to this explicit distinction, he draws an implicit distinction between two types of acquired perceptions. The key task in assessing the role of inference in Reid's theory of perception lies in determining precisely how to understand the cognitive character of acquired perceptions.

Describing the original/acquired distinction in the *Inquiry*, Reid explains that:

When I perceive that this is the taste of cyder, that of brandy; that this is the smell of an apple, that of an orange; ... these perceptions, and others of the same kind, are not original—they are acquired. But the perception which I have by touch, of the hardness and softness of bodies, of their extension, figure and motion, is not acquired—it is original. (IHM 6.20, 171/184b)

The scope of simple, or original, perception is limited indeed. This distinction is not isomorphic to the primary/secondary quality distinction, but the pair shares some affinities. With sight, he adds that "we perceive originally the visible figure and colour of bodies only, and their visible place," and not the real figures of tables and chairs. The secondary quality of color is perceived originally—in the *Inquiry*. In a corollary passage in the *Intellectual Powers* Reid leaves color off the list. He says that by sight "we perceive visible objects to have extension in two dimensions, to have visible figure and magnitude, and a certain angular distance from one another. These, I conceive, are the original perceptions of sight" (EIP 2.16, 236/331b). In the analysis of the primary/secondary distinction, I contended that the distinction is conceptual in character. If primary quality perception were isomorphic to original perceptions (and secondary quality perception to acquired), this would indicate that there is a conceptual difference between original and acquired perceptions. Therefore, the similarities between the two sets of distinctions put us on to the right track without taking us far.

When forming an original perception I do not apply universals with which to differentiate the properties of the object from other properties. Reid describes the conceptual quality of original perceptions as follows:

To begin with the objects of sense. It is acknowledged, on all hands, that the first notions we have of sensible objects are got by the external senses only, and probably before judgment is brought forth; but these first notions are ... gross and indistinct, and, like the *chaos*, a *rudis indigestaque moles*. Before we can have any distinct notion of this mass, it must be analysed; the heterogeneous parts must be separated in our conception ...

In this way it is that we form distinct notions even of the objects of sense; but this process of analysis and composition, by habit, becomes so easy, and is performed so readily, that we are apt to overlook it, and to impute the distinct notion we have formed of the object to the senses alone. (EIP 6.1, 417/418a)

I'll address Reid's reference to habit shortly, but first let's try to understand the conceptual status of these "first notions," i.e. original perceptions.

From this and other comments it isn't easy to determine whether Reid believes original perceptions conform to his standard perceptual schema on which any perception incorporates conception and belief. He says original perceptions are merely products of the senses, but he also implies that in them are "notions." One might think that Reid has in mind something similar to some contemporary views about non-conceptual perceiving.[7] But I would opt with others for an alternative: original perceptions do conform to Reid's analysis and they do contain a conceptual component (see Van Woudenberg 2000, 74). Reid's definitions of perception and his examples of original perceptual belief support this view. But the conceptual quantity of original perceptions, to put it coarsely, is minimal.

The conceptual component in original perceptions is determinate and clear, but Reid describes it as "indistinct." We can think of original perceptions in terms of the conceptions that would be possessed by the subject of Reid's crucial test thought experiment. The subject obtains notions of extension and three-dimensionality through the coupling of sensation with his "natural constitution." But his notions will be rudimentary and lacking any substantive content. After discussing the differing ways a child and adult form perceptual notions about a cube of brass, Reid says: "There are, therefore, notions of the objects of sense which are gross and indistinct, and there are others that are distinct and scientific. The former may be got from the senses alone, but the latter cannot be obtained without some degree of judgment" (EIP 6.1, 419/419a). Reid has precious little to say about "distinctness" (see Section 6.2). Though this conceptual component can be determinant and clear, Reid is gesturing at the fact that it is nonetheless impoverished.

An example will be instructive. In vision we can form original perceptual beliefs about a clock (a) in regard to the quality of circularity and (b) that this circular object is present through my seen figure of the clock, as well as (c) that this circularity is a quality of a mind-independent (at least two-dimensional) object. However, while I can perceive the clock is circular, it seems that the original perceptual belief only contains demonstratives: this object seems thus-and-so. I cannot originally perceive (d) the clock as circular, since understanding the terms "circular" and "clock" is a matter of learning, and original perceptions *ex hypothesi* do not incorporate prior perceptual learning. To tip Reid's hand, option (d) seems to be the product of an acquired perception resulting from a confluence of original perceptions of sight and touch. If I can classify an object as a clock in a perceptual belief such a belief must be acquired, since my ability to apply (and my knowledge that

[7] For example, Alan Millar (1991) articulates and defends a "detachability thesis" that implies that "you could have had an experience of the very same type even if, for want of the appropriate concepts, the experience did not have the content in question. But it also implies that for any conceptual contents you care to mention, however tightly constrained, phenomenal character is detachable from those contents" (1991, 496; see Millar 1992 and, for a contrasting view, Hamlyn 1994).

I am correctly applying) this category depends upon cognitive abilities that transcend original perceptions. In fact, I for one cannot help *but* perceive the object before me as circular and as a clock, but someone with no experience of circularity or time-keeping devices would only perceive that object and its figure originally.

8.4. Cognition and Inference in Acquired Perceptions

Any reconstruction of Reid's epistemology of perception must give considerable attention to acquired perception. In both the *Inquiry* and *Intellectual Powers* Reid says: "In all our senses, the acquired perceptions are many more than the original, especially in sight" (IHM 2.20, 171/185a) and "the far greatest part [of the deliverances of perception] is acquired, and the fruit of experience" (EIP 2.21, 235/331a). When he makes the same point in his lectures on the cultivation of the mind he emphasizes the role of learning and habit explicitly. He says: "the far greater part of the perceptions we have by [the senses] are acquired and therefore must be learned by practice and Habit" (Reid 2004, 18). In fact, throughout these lectures Reid accentuates the role we as human beings have in improving our own faculties.

When we are initially presented with an apple, we don't originally see it *as* an apple, according to Reid. Rather we see a visible figure and a color pattern possessed by an external object that is typically associated with apples by those in the know. Somehow prior knowledge assists in the formation of acquired perceptions. Reid describes the dependence of acquired perceptions upon education in the first passage, and the broadly cognitive components of acquired perceptions in the second:

[D]ifferent acquired perceptions are produced by the same general principles of the human mind, which have a different operation in the same person according as they are variously applied, and in different persons, according to the diversity of their education and manner of life. (IHM 2.24, 192/195b)

[I]t requires some ripeness of understanding to distinguish the qualities of a body from the body ... if any one thinks that this distinction is not made by our senses, but by some other power of the mind, I will not dispute this point. I think, indeed, that some of the determinations we form concerning matter cannot be deduced solely from the testimony of sense, but must be referred to some other source. (EIP 2.20, 219/323a)

Had we never before seen an apple we could only form original perceptual beliefs of its qualities—observing its shape and color and relative position.

Without repeated perceptions of apples and the knowledge that the qualities we have perceived belong to them, we would be unable to formulate an acquired perception of the apple itself. However, when we have originally perceived several apples and observed their variations in color, size, and shape, we are in a position to formulate acquired perceptions of an apple in virtue of forming and applying the universal of, or what Reid calls a "general concept" of, *apple* (Castagnetto 1992).[8]

The first distinguishing mark of acquired perceptions is that acquired perceptual beliefs contain conceptual content absent in original perceptions. Reid's own example illustrates the point. When a globe is set before me I "perceive" that it has three dimensions and is a spherical figure, though I "see" a colored, circular, two-dimensional form.[9] A painter, in a rare exhibition of artistic aptitude, may deceive me into believing that what I see is a globe when it is not. The painter deceives me because she compels me to form a belief about a globe by seeing a two-dimensional figure (which is not the surface of a sphere). This contradicts the observed regularity found in the content of my acquired perceptions of globes (EIP 2.22, 247−8/337a). (This deception is successful only when the painting is in ideal conditions with respect to the eye (EIP 2.21, 237/332a), or when it is viewed through a keyhole from afar (IHM 6.22, 181−2/189b−190a).)

Globes reliably caused previous acquired perceptions of globe-like objects. In this deceptive case the visible figure seen by the eye is identical to what one would see while gazing at a globe of the same color and at the same distance and angle. Since the original perception of the imitation globe and the original perception of the genuine article are composed of a rudimentary *de re* content, it is possible the two original perceptions are identical. The difference between the two cases of perception lies in the content of the acquired perception and not in the nature of the object one visually apprehends. This distinction between original and acquired perception explains Reid's resolution

---

[8] In the *Lectures on the Culture of the Mind* Reid compares the difference in perceptual capacities of a human reared in society with those of a "wild man," a feral human being raised outside of human culture (see Reid 1990, 125−6).

[9] Here Reid follows Locke. At least, he seems to endorse Locke's comments about perceptual learning, but does not also endorse the presupposition that the object of perception is an idea. Just prior to introducing Molyneux's problem, Locke writes: "We are farther to consider concerning Perception, that the *Ideas we receive by sensation, are often* in grown People *alter'd by the Judgment*, without our taking notice of it. When we set before our Eyes a round Globe, of any uniform colour, *v.g.* Gold, Alabaster, or Jet, 'tis certain, that the *Idea* thereby imprinted in our Mind, is of a flat Circle variously shadow'd, with several degrees of Light and Brightness coming into our Eyes. But we having been accustomed to perceive, what kind of appearance convex Bodies are wont to make in us; what alterations are made in the reflections of Light, by the difference of sensible Figures of Bodies, the Judgment presently, by an habitual custom, alters the Appearances into their Causes" (Locke 1975, 2.9.8/145).

of his counterfeit guinea case. This difference between original and acquired perceptions regards their content.

The means by which they are formed—whether merely by the use of the senses or also by cognition or thinking—marks the second difference, but this is less clear in Reid than the previous point. Since acquired perceptions have more robust content than original perceptions, their formation is suitably more involved and requires more conceptual resources in the perceiver. That much is straightforward. Reid repeatedly denies that one must reason or draw inferences as one formulates an acquired perception. But what conceptual resources might be needed in their formation? A developmental discussion best captures Reid's way with this issue.

It seems that in the *Inquiry*, in drafts of sections of the *Intellectual Powers*, and in the *Intellectual Powers* itself, Reid provides discomfiting explanations of the formation of acquired perceptions. He implies that there both is and is not reasoning in their formation. Beginning with the *Inquiry*, Reid claims that reasoning is a necessary component in the formation of acquired perceptions. He says, for example, that the belief in the moon's three-dimensionality is a conclusion "not obtained by simple perception, but by reasoning" (IHM 6.2, 172/185b). Yet immediately before this he says:

Perception ought not only to be distinguished from sensation, but likewise from that knowledge of the objects of sense which is got by reasoning. There is no reasoning in perception, as hath been observed. The belief which is implied in it, is the effect of instinct. But there are many things, with regard to sensible objects, which we can infer from what we perceive; and such conclusions of reason ought to be distinguished from what is merely perceived. (IHM 6.2, 172/185a)[10]

This implies that I cannot have visual perceptual beliefs that any of the heavenly bodies are three-dimensional. Since such beliefs are produced "by reasoning," and since perception contains "no reasoning," they are not perceptual beliefs.

Heavenly bodies serve as intriguing examples. We do not visually perceive the dark side of the moon, and thus do not know anything about that side through visual perception, let alone through tactual perception. This leads to the speculation that Reid may believe that the moon's three-dimensionality cannot be in the perceptual content of a visual perceptual belief. But one might think that my acquired visual perception of the moon could include in its content the moon's three-dimensionality once I make a habit out of perceiving it as a sphere. In this passage Reid insists that this does not follow—though this does not imply that no acquired visual perception can

---

[10] A similar passage occurs at EIP 2.6, 101/260b, though Gallie correctly observes that the epistemic optimism in this latter text is an aberration (1989a, 44).

include three-dimensionality in its content. However, what he says in this passage is consistent with what he says about guinea coins and apples, and implies that many beliefs that we intuitively construe as perceptual beliefs are actually not perceptual beliefs. Strictly speaking, Reid implies one does not perceive guinea coins and apples—and moons. Rather, in these passages he uses the term "perceives" to refer to one's original perceptions of these things.

It seems he holds that only original perceptions are worthy of being called "perceptions." However, when amplifying this point he says: "Perception, whether original or acquired, implies no exercise of reason; and is common to men, children, idiots, and brutes" (IHM 6.2, 173/185b), applying "perception" to both. But he insists that acquired perceptions arise without the help of "reason." Apparently, so long as acquired perceptions do not require "reasoning," Reid will allow them to be, with original perceptions, claimants to genuine perception.

The difficulty becomes clearer upon reading drafts of the "Of the Fallacy of the Senses" chapter of the *Intellectual Powers*. Here Reid desires to carve out a conceptual space for acquired perceptions between original perceptions and "conclusions drawn by reasoning." In this manuscript he writes:

The habit of judging of small distances by the eye is got so early and so much confirmed by daily experience that it resembles original perception very much, it is called perception in common language and can be distinguished from original perception only by philosophers. As this distinction is important I have taken the liberty to call it acquired perception to distinguish it on the one hand from original perception and on the other conclusions drawn by reasoning from what we perceive. (Aberdeen MS 2132 7/V/26, 2)

In this vital unpublished passage Reid struggles to establish that acquired perceptions are more cognitive in character than original perceptions, while also holding that they do not require the subject actively to draw an inference in order to formulate each acquired perception. Not two but three categories are at work.

In a 1768 manuscript Reid says that we "learn" to form at least some acquired perceptions: "[W]e learn to perceive the distance of an object by our eyesight ... by means of intervening or contiguous objects whose distance is otherwise known" (Aberdeen MS 2131/4/II/16, 1 Dec. 1768, 30). We do not learn that particular acquired perceptions (of distance) are true. We learn to correlate the perceived sizes of intervening objects with the distances of those behind them, implying that we reason in at least some stages of habit formation. The use of the active voice and the term "learn" here represents a shift in tone, albeit a subtle one. Reid is aware that the categories in his architecture of the mind are inadequate. In a forthright passage on the "Principle of Induction" he explicitly states the source of the interpretive problem with which we have been grappling. "Not onely our acquired perceptions but all inductive reasoning and consequently the greatest part of that knowledge we get by experience and all that we know in natural philosophy is founded upon [the Principle of Induction]. Simple perception, common understanding & philosophy run into each other so that it is difficult to fix their limits accurately" (Aberdeen MS 2131/4/II/16, 1 Dec 1768, 30). He recognizes the limits of analysis of the mind's cognitive activity in "perception."

Several years later in 1778—also between the two works—we read a similarly ambiguous characterization of the difference between original and acquired perception that occurs in a letter to Kames. Reid explains why he gives the matter renewed reflection. He writes:

> In some cases the Perception is connected with the Sensation by our Constitution, previous to all Experience. This I call original Perception. Sometimes the Sensation is connected with the Perception by Experience & Custom. This I call acquired Perception. Thus I hear a Drum; Originally, I should onely have a certain Sensation of Sound, but by Custom I perceive it to be a Drum. A forreign Writer has censured me for calling this Perception, he thinks it ought to be called Judgment. I dispute not about the Name. I think it is called Perception in common Language. And it is so like to Original Perception in Nature, tho not in its Origin, that I think the Name of Perception may be applied to it without Impropriety. (C 113; about the "forreign Writer," see C 294)

At this point in the development of Reid's distinction he thinks original perceptions are generated by sensation alone, whereas for acquired perceptions one needs the sensation and the assistance of custom or habit. This introduces a type of cognition into the process of forming acquired perceptions, which is why his critic believes they are better denominated as judgments. These categories are rough around the edges at this point.

As late as the *Intellectual Powers* he echoes the anti-reasoning line found in the *Inquiry*. "This power which we acquire of perceiving things by our senses, which originally we should not have perceived, is not the effect of any reasoning on our part: It is the result of our constitution, and of the situations in which we happen to be placed" (EIP 2.21, 238/332b). But toward the end of the *Intellectual Powers* he seems to change his mind sharply, saying: "Acquired perception is not properly the testimony of those senses which God hath given us, but a conclusion drawn from what the senses testify" (EIP 2.22, 247/336b). These contrasting texts prevent any smooth resolution to the tension regarding whether acquired perceptions require reasoning. That said, even at this late point in his career, having reflected on these issues for a few decades, Reid remains unsure what to make of this category. He wonders "whether this acquired perception is to be resolved into some process of reasoning" or perhaps "from some part of our constitution distinct from reason, as I rather believe" (EIP 2.22, 247/336b). He is marking the divide between inductive inference, and mere association.

Perhaps it is on the basis of textual considerations like these that Lehrer and J. C. Smith hold that forming acquired perceptual beliefs is a process that uses inductive reasoning. These authors distinguish various principles, some of which generate acquired and others original perceptions. They claim that Reid's "inductive principle accounts for our conception of secondary qualities," conceptions which are included within acquired perceptions. They remark, "The operation of such a principle in yielding the conception of secondary qualities does not involve reasoning of any sort" (Lehrer and Smith 1985, 27). But a page prior they describe the deliverances of acquired perception as being produced by "inductive reasoning" (1985, 26).

The major problem with Lehrer and Smith's interpretation arises as a result of an equivocation on "reasoning" and the tacit assumptions they make about induction. They inadvertently track Reid too closely. While acquired perceptions result from inductions, it is difficult to determine whether Lehrer and Smith believe that one reasons (and if so, how one reasons) in performing an induction. They are quite right to apply this term to Reid because, when he describes the process of experiential learning, he says: "Upon this principle of our constitution, not only acquired perception, but all inductive reasoning, and all our reasoning from analogy, is grounded: and therefore, for want of another name, we shall beg leave to call it *the inductive principle*" (IHM 6.24, 198/199a). Even so, their use of the term "reasoning" is ambiguous, and they do not discuss whether, on Reid's use of that term, acquired perceptions can aptly be described as "products of reasoning." In contrast to Reid's circumspect application of the term "knowledge," his use of the term "reasoning" is quite broad. Furthermore, finely tuned distinctions between Reid's uses of "reasoning" would only be of value in this context if it can be shown that such distinctions apply to the very uses of that term describing acquired perceptions. Drawing a distinction between types of acquired perceptions, which I propose to do now, will produce precision in Reid.

8.5. Inferential and Habituated Perceptions

The principal problem before us is twofold. Charity requires that we attempt to make Reid's discussion of acquired perception consistent by determining just what it does and does not involve, and attempt to account for the relation between the categories of original and acquired perception in the most coherent way possible. Several options for interpretation are available.

We might argue that acquired perception does require reasoning and is not a form of perception$_{C\&B}$. This would allow us to contend that "perception" is univocally non-inferential in Reid and only refers to original perception. On this interpretation, original and acquired "perception" differ in kind.

Three points favor this interpretation. First, some cited texts support the claim that acquired perception is only an analogical form of perception. Second, this reading mops up the problems quickly by distinguishing these forms of belief formation. Also, "acquired perception" can be used in a loose sense to refer to perceptual beliefs about objects that are not present to the perceiver at the time the belief is formed. For example, I may form a belief about David Beckham when my son misses a penalty kick in an important match. Some Reid experts interpret that sort of perceptual belief as an acquired perception, and infer that acquired perceptions do not conform to Reid's stated theory of perception$_{C\&B}$. Even though a visual perception of my son's kick moving wide right suggests to me a belief about David Beckham, since Beckham is nowhere near the pitch I cannot be said to form a perceptual belief about Beckham (see Van Cleve 2004b, 127–8).

These advantages do not persuade me to opt for this interpretive solution. I doubt Reid would call the belief about Beckham an "acquired perception." There are scant texts to support that type of reading. Besides, his many examples of acquired perception are much less controversial and problematic, for example one's perception of a guinea coin. When I use the term "acquired perception," it conforms to Reid's formal definition of perception, which includes the conception and belief components. Consistent with our description of perception$_{C\&B}$, acquired perception includes both an intentional aspect and a doxastic aspect. Consistent with our discussion of sensation, acquired perception will also incorporate a sensation component so long as Reid's *ceteris paribus* requirements are met. We can restrict our attention without any difficulty to the (subset of) acquired perceptions in which the content of the intentional state picks out something in the vicinity that has physical presence.

The first two benefits of this interpretation are not without corollary problems. It is true that some texts favor this reading, but those are rare. Furthermore, an abundance of texts describe acquired beliefs as beliefs formed through perception, to which his frequent use of the term "acquired perception" attests. To overlook the great similarities between these two forms of belief formation is too high a cost for this interpretation.

Given the developmental evidence we have researched, Reid is stretching the category of "acquired perception" beyond its conceptual limits. The conceptual content of acquired perceptions is richer than in original perception. Reid stresses two features of non-original perceptual beliefs: sometimes they require some reasoning, for example beliefs about the moon's three-dimensionality, and other times they are formed through habit, as are our judgments of distance from the eye. These two features are sufficiently different that, to anchor my interpretation of acquired perception, I propose making a distinction within that category between *inferential* and *habitual* perceptions. The first requires conscious reasoning and the second does not.

This type of distinction captures Reid's description of some examples. Reid is clear that when I first perceive a globe-like object, I do not know non-inferentially that the object I perceive is a globe. Were I to form an acquired perceptual belief that it is a globe, then, if that belief is justified, it must be inferred—on the basis of a tactile experience of the object, for example. Once I have repeated this inference several times I habituate my original perception of the globe-like object, which enables me to form an acquired perceptual belief about the presence of a globe. Once habituated, I need not consciously reason in the formation of my acquired perceptual belief. Instead, the original perception will suggest the non-inferential, acquired perception of a globe.

I'm drawing the term "habit" and its cognates directly from Reid. In the *Inquiry* he says: "The word *gold* has no similitude to the substance signified by it ... yet, by habit and custom, it suggests this and no other. In like manner, a sensation of touch suggests hardness" even though it has no logical connection to the quality of hardness per se. "The difference," he continues, "betwixt these two signs lies only in this—that, in the first, the suggestion is the effect of habit and custom; in the second it is not the effect of habit, but of the original constitution of our minds" (IHM 5.3, 58–9/121b). In passages like this we see evidence that there is a category of perceptual belief, members of which are formed neither originally nor through cognition, but through habituation.

These categories of inferential and habituated perception are mine and not Reid's. I propose them not as what Reid held, but as what I take to be the most promising way of understanding what he held. Since they are my creation I will provide necessary (but not sufficient) conditions for them:

X is an *inferential perception* only if (a) there is an object or property originally perceived (i.e. heard, seen, etc.); (b) the original perceptual event causes an intentional conception of the object or property; (c) from this conception one performs conscious explanatory reasoning to hypothesize that the object or property originally perceived is P, is a P, is caused by P, or has property P; (d) the explanatory reasoning culminates in the belief that the object originally perceived is P, is a P, is caused by P, or has property P.

By "conscious explanatory reasoning" I mean to avoid implying that only deduction can move us from an original conception to an acquired perceptual belief. More frequently the process of conscious reasoning proceeds by the process of elimination or induction. This analysis does not state the conditions for knowledge of inferential acquired perceptual beliefs.

The need to formulate inferential perceptions in order to generate justified perceptual beliefs is not restricted to situations in which I have never before formed a perceptual belief about the type of object under consideration. Reid's examples of error illustrate this. In certain contexts it will be an open question whether or not one's acquired perceptual beliefs (of either type) will be justified. If I live among a cabal of counterfeiters, from Reid's description of error, then I must draw inferences in order to be justified in assenting to certain acquired perceptual beliefs about legal tender. Reid simply does not provide us requisite detail with which to reconstruct what he holds about the knowledge or justification of perceptual beliefs.

As an example of inferential acquired perception, consider the following case, adapted from Reid (IHM 2.7, 38/111a and IHM 4.2, 50/117a–b). I sit in my living room, windows open, and I hear a sound. I form the conception and belief that the sound is a mule drawing a cart because that is the best explanation for the particular clip-clop noise and the fainter grating sound of what seem to be wheels against a hard road surface. This is the first time I have heard such a sound and, for me, hearing the sound does not suggest a mule and a cart. To be explicit, none of my suggestion relations operate in such a scenario. Reid says that "suggestion is not natural and original; it is the result of experience and habit" (IHM 2.7, 38/111b).

Suppose that when I look out the window after forming this belief I see a slow-moving horse and carriage, not a mule and cart. Since the belief is false, it is not known; since it was my first hearing of such a sound, I was not justified forming the belief in the first place. The next time I hear a similar sound I tentatively infer that it is caused by a horse and carriage, and this time I am correct. My inferential acquired perception is known and justified, but that justification depends crucially on a process of conscious, abductive reasoning. Building on this we can say the following:

X is a *habituated perception* only if (a) in the past the subject has formed a number of inferential perceptions of an object or property of an object under relevantly similar circumstances; (b) by doing so, the subject has instantiated a suggestion relation that conjoins the original perception of X with the inferential acquired perceptual belief that the object is P, is a P, is caused by P, or has property P in the mind of the subject.

To continue with our previous example, if the same sound were repeated nightly, a type of suggestion relation—one cued by my awareness of the sensation—would soon be created. This is because, with enough experience associating the sound and belief, I would be disposed to move *without inference* from hearing the clip-clop sound to forming the perceptual belief that there is a horse and carriage passing on the road. Rarely, however, is the suggestion relation created without any error. Suppose for a week a horse and carriage pass on the road nightly, but then a mule and cart pass, making a similar sound. The embryonic suggestion relation in this case generates a false belief. Such relations will be subject to correction and standardization in different environments prior to causing justified, habituated perceptual beliefs.

One advantage of this interpretation is that it is phenomenologically realistic. It describes the way in which we develop perceptual habits, which Reid attempted to, but did not, capture. This is a process that requires some attention and direction. Through the use of this distinction we need not force on Reid the unwelcome consequence that each time I formulate beliefs about roses I engage in a form of conscious inductive inference in going from sensations to beliefs. This resonates with the spirit, though not the letter, of EDR, because habituated perceptual beliefs are not formed through any process of conscious reasoning.

Reid refers to the example we have been using in a manuscript in which he describes the form of perception achieved through habitual association of a sign with what it signifies:

The thing signified by the sign is something which has been found by experience connected with that sign in the course of nature. Such is our constitution that having observed this connection frequently in our experience we believe the same connection will always subsist and we acquire a habit of passing from the sign to the belief of the thing signified, and that without any reasoning. Instances. 1 Sound of a coach. 2 The visible figure and appearance of a man a sign of his distance. (Aberdeen MS 2131/4/II/15, 5 Dec. 1766)

Reid might mean that no reasoning is used in forming the perceptual belief through the connection between it and the sensation that suggests it, or that no reasoning is used in the formation of the habit of believing the perceptual belief through that connection. At minimum Reid insists that there is no reasoning in the formation of perceptual beliefs formed through the use of a habit. In other words, there is no conscious reasoning employed by the agent in the formation of the token occurrent belief that *a horse and carriage are passing by*. Reid is correct provided the habit is well established. This interpretation of Reid's comment that acquired perceptual beliefs are formed "without any reasoning" correctly describes what Reid holds.

Indeed, this claim is so obvious from a first-person point of view that it is a wonder that its dispute in the context of interpreting Reid has created so much controversy. From the phenomenological perspective that Reid often favors in his analysis of perception, an ounce of introspection reveals that one almost never performs any conscious reasoning as one forms a perceptual belief of items one has perceived before.

This does not imply that the inset passage could not also mean that we do not consciously reason in the formation of the habit itself. In other words, Reid might intend that no conscious reasoning occur in either the formation of token perceptual beliefs or in the building up of a habit through experience of the suggestion and thing signified. However, it is obvious that Reid intends at least to deny there is immediate reasoning in the formation of most perceptual beliefs.

The use of reasoning in perception will often be intermittent and occur when glitches enter the stream of belief formation, which is indicated by his discussion of perceptual error. Furthermore, some of Reid's examples of perceptual belief-forming habits more obviously require conscious reasoning for development than others. (Note that habituated perceptions as I intend them are only a species of acquired perception, rich in conceptual content. We may form habits as we perceive originally, but those habits are subject to very different requirements.) Nonetheless, once the habit is developed, one's perceptual beliefs are formed seamlessly, immediately, and without any reasoning.[11]

---

[11] Reid addresses his ongoing struggle to account for the role of cognition in acquired perception in this unpublished manuscript: "[Our reasoning powers develop] by degrees; and before we come to the use of reason we learn much and many usefull habits by some part of our constitution which cannot be called reason but is common to us with brute animals" (Aberdeen MS 2131/7/V/26, 2). This can be read as a problem text for my interpretation insofar as it implies that some habits are developed by human beings before they possess a reasoning faculty, and, therefore, without reasoning at all. Clearly some habits conform to this description. Therefore, what he calls "learning" would seem to be an intellective process requiring fewer cognitive resources than does reasoning. But these non-rational habits are not habits to form acquired perceptual beliefs rich in conceptual content. In other words, many of the habits needed to form acquired perceptions necessitate sophisticated abilities of perceptual discrimination, and those habits, and the perceptual beliefs to which they give rise, are not common with animals. In addition, the use of this passage in interpreting Reid must be tempered with the realization that it is unpublished and marked for deletion.

8.6. Reasoning and Justification in Habituated Perceptual Beliefs

Let's take stock. I have introduced the distinction between inferential and habitual perception, given analysis of those terms, and applied these categories to a few of Reid's examples in an attempt to give the distinction some phenomenological appeal. One philosophically important implication of this distinction now merits extended discussion.

A key issue is whether the justification of acquired perceptual beliefs is independent of the justification of other perceptual beliefs. The great ambiguity of "immediacy" and its cognates has thwarted greater progress on this point. We commentators have not distinguished this issue from the more coarse discussion about stages of reasoning in perception. But neither did Reid. A belief may depend upon other beliefs for its justification, but not itself be formed through a process of conscious reasoning. Only inferential perceptions are *formed by* conscious reasoning. But habituated perceptual beliefs are not formed by conscious reasoning, even though they *depend upon* prior reasoning for their justification. In other words, they depend for their justification upon other perceptual beliefs upstream in the belief-forming and habit-forming processes. In this sense, habituated perceptual beliefs could not serve as basic beliefs in a foundationalist theory of the structure of empirical knowledge.

This implies that a measure of the positive epistemic status possessed by my habituated perceptual belief derives from the justification of the inferential perceptual belief through which the suggestion relation has been developed. I may form a habituated perceptual belief about the proximity of a horse and carriage on the basis of an (original) aural perception. Yet we may imagine that in my repeated exercises of explanatory reasoning I negligently misidentify the sound as being caused by a mule and cart when it was actually the product of a horse and carriage. The error I have committed explains why the beliefs I form about horses and carriages based merely on aural perceptions lack sufficient justification for knowledge.

We form original perceptual beliefs about physical objects and their qualities non-inferentially. Upon repeatedly forming such thinly conceptual original perceptual beliefs, our minds quickly generalize from associated qualities in order to classify the objects with natural kind terms in inferential acquired perceptions. Children engage in just this sort of inductive reasoning when they are learning to classify the objects of their perceptions as belonging to a single species or genus, for example, when differentiating between wolves, coyotes, and common dogs. Reid briefly states his own examples of the phenomena to which I refer:

Not only men, but children, idiots and brutes, acquire by habit many perceptions which they had not originally ... The farmer perceives by his eye, very nearly, the quantity of hay in a rick, or of corn in a heap. The sailor sees the burthen, the built, and the distance of a ship at sea, while she is a great way off. (IHM 2.20, 171–2/185a)

Consider the first stage of the sailor's perceptual belief formation. The sailor originally, visually perceives a visible figure of minute proportions on the edge of the blue horizon. At the next stage he perceives this and similar figures as seafaring vessels. At more advanced stages he learns to perceive such an object as having a keel of 80 feet, as built at the Whitehaven yard, or as at a distance of 17 nautical miles. Later still he can perceive this ship as the *Monarch*. Consider the perceptual belief *that schooner has a tonnage of 100 and is fully laden*. It is as misguided and of as little use to insist that there is no cognition involved in his forming this perception$_{C\&B}$ as there is to say that this belief is obviously formed through inference. The first option fails to recognize the extensive learning required by the sailor enabling him to extract such sophisticated data from a fleeting visual experience. The second option omits recognition that, when learned well, his learning can be applied with effortless ease. To explain the complexity in perceptual belief formation in examples like these we need the inchoate distinction Reid was beginning to draw between inferential and habitual perceptions.

Reid seems to recognize that how we describe the case can create undue controversy if definitions of terms are not used with care. At the second stage of perceptual belief formation, explanatory inferences are required in order consistently to form perceptual beliefs that correctly distinguish one object (or quality) from another. Once relations between certain original perceptions and certain inferential acquired perceptions have been developed, a suggestion relation is instantiated during future perceptions of the objects. This allows the mind to move from an inferential perception to a habituated perception. When I have developed appropriate suggestion relations between original perceptions of ships and inferential perceptual beliefs in which I classify the object of sight as a deepwater schooner and not a tea clipper, my perception of that object has become habituated.[12]

---

[12] Another potential advantage is that the distinction offered here can be used to avoid imputing to Reid implausible claims about the epistemology of perceptual belief. Consider Van Cleve's helpful interpretation of Reid's first principle of perception (EIP 6.5, 476/445b). Either it is a principle of truth alone as in (8.1), or it is a principle of evidence as in (8.2). Where "p" refers to a perceptual belief, and

One objection to this understanding of habituated perceptions is that it is inconsistent with Reid's earlier comments about the immediacy of knowledge. The above distinction separates those beliefs that are formed by conscious reasoning, from those that are dependent for their justification upon the justification of other beliefs. Reid's use of "immediate" to describe perceptual beliefs could pick out either form of epistemic immediacy. This term may refer to the fact that some set of perceptual beliefs is not formed through a process of conscious reasoning, or it may refer to the fact that the justification of the belief does not depend upon the justification of other beliefs.

In response, first, in many contexts Reid refers to "perception" generally, and does not apply his distinction between original or acquired perception. In these cases it can be especially difficult to identify which type of meaning he has in mind with the term. More to the point, if "immediate" is used in the first sense—referring to perceptual beliefs that are not formed through conscious reasoning—then habituated perceptual beliefs are immediate, or immediately known. As is the case with most of Reid's uses of "immediate knowledge," in the following passage it seems Reid is using the term in this way. Recall he says: "By Perception I understand that immediate Knowledge which we have of external Objects by our Senses. This I take to be the proper meaning of the Word in the English Language" (C 107).

This solves the problem just voiced, but arguably lands us in another one. Inferential perceptions do require conscious reasoning, and thus they are not strictly speaking "perceptions$_{C\&B}$" for Reid. This is an implication of my use of the distinction, but it is not a problem. Reid has no recipe for identifying those beliefs that are perceptual beliefs from those that are not. One would like to say that perceptual beliefs are those formed by the faculty of perception, and no other faculty. But Reid allows that multiple powers and faculties are frequently used in concert in the formation of a single belief, in just the way

---

"Pp" means "I perceive that p," the principles are: (8.1) "It is a first principle that (p) (Pp — > p)": (8.2) "(p)(Pp — > it is a first principle that p)." (1999, 6).

Van Cleve finds textual evidence favoring one over the other to be inconclusive, but he presents a cumulative case for preferring (8.2) over (8.1). According to (8.2) our perceptual beliefs are justified merely by being formed in the appropriate way. So Reid endorses an externalist (even if not reliabilist) theory of justification (1999, 16–20). Reading Reid as sanctioning (8.2) has advantages over competing interpretations, but critics will believe it appears far too permissive and allows as justified a large quantity of unjustified perceptual beliefs. The present interpretation of Reid as tacitly drawing a distinction between forms of acquired perception can be used to constrain the scope of this principle by specifying boundaries on the content of those perceptual beliefs that are justified merely by being formed appropriately. This maneuver will require restricting the scope of the universal quantifier, but the distinction gives us a principled means of discriminating between those perceptions that are justified merely by being formed and those that require some reasoning on our part. This point can be used to meet the critic's demands in a way that arises naturally from Reid's corpus and is not ad hoc.

that sub-faculties within the faculty of perception conspire jointly to form a belief. The distinct experiences of smelling and tasting may jointly suggest a perception$_{C\&B}$ of a cinnamon roll. Likewise, suppose I am told that I will probably see Jack and Amy at the park, and that once there I find myself forming a belief that the figures in the distance that I see are Jack and Amy. In this case the formation and justification of that belief are the joint product of my testimonial knowledge that they are probably there and my awareness that the figures I see are probably figures of them.

In the case of inferential perceptions, the faculties of reasoning and perception are both at work—perhaps more reasoning than perception. If we interpret Reid strictly in the above remark, we can denominate inferential perceptions as primarily products of reasoning, not perception. If we interpret him loosely, then inferential perceptions can still lay claim to being perceptions$_{C\&B}$ in the privileged sense. Nothing much hinges on this point, though. The aforementioned comment that various powers "run into each other so that it is difficult to fix their limits accurately" (Aberdeen MS 2131/4/II/16, 30, 1 Dec. 1768) makes this clear.

The confluence of perception with other faculties in the formation of beliefs—"coordinated perception"—is worthy of further comment, especially since Reid emphasizes this point in both the *Inquiry* and *Intellectual Powers*. It is important for Reid that the process of perceptual belief formation be accompanied by what we can describe as social dimensions of knowing. Reid is keen to describe the importance of our interactions with others in gaining knowledge. We are created as social beings, to which end God has provided us with "social intellectual powers," as Reid puts it. Many faculties only operate in a social context and many faculties can only arise within an individual who is part of a society. Into this second group Reid places reasoning, language-use, conception of abstract ideas, and moral perception (Reid 2004, 40–2).

The usefulness of testimony in gaining knowledge confers upon it special importance to Reid. "Testimony is a social act, and it is essential to it to be expressed by words or signs" (EIP 6.1, 407/413a–b). Testimonial knowledge, including that through which we learn to identify objects of perception, represents a confluence of the work of our individual intellectual powers, including faculties of perception, testimony, and judgment. Giving and receiving testimony requires more than the solitary exercise of intellectual powers. "They may be called intellectual, because they can only be in intellectual beings: But they are neither simple apprehension, nor judgment, nor reasoning, nor are they any combination of these operations" (EIP 1.8, 68/244b). Reid correctly observes that asking an expert a simple question, and receiving the answer, is a complex process employing a number of different abilities.

Our inferential perceptions often come by way of the subtle transmission of knowledge through testimony. The adult sailor's broad perceptual beliefs about the make, tonnage, length, speed, and distance of ships qualifies as a social form of knowledge if only because the belief-forming habits he employs have been developed under the tutelage of more experienced sailors.

This might raise worries that it therefore is incumbent upon Reid to provide a rationale for the transmission of justification or knowledge from testimony to perceptual beliefs. In response he will appeal to his twin principles of veracity and credulity. The principle of veracity is a "propensity to speak truth, and to use the signs of language so as to convey our real sentiments" (IHM 6.24, 193/196a). The principle of credulity disposes us to "confide in the veracity of others, and to believe what they tell us" (IHM 6.24, 193/196a). These two principles are psychologically descriptive and epistemically efficacious. Reid holds that belief based upon testimony is reliable. Indeed, Reid explicitly conjoins the processes of forming acquired perceptions and believing on the basis of testimony (IHM 6.24, 192/195b). But the problem of justifying testimonial beliefs is largely orthogonal to the thrust of this chapter, and, in any event, it has received capable analysis in the hands of others. Wolterstorff's remarks about the nature of cognition in the absorption of testimonial knowledge are particularly helpful, and he recognizes the difficulty of categorizing the type of reasoning at work in this process (2001, 179–82).

8.7. Textual Consistency and Historical Continuity

This interpretation is able to explain the apparent discrepancies in Reid's descriptions of acquired perceptions and the continuity of Reid's thought better than alternative proposals. John Immerwahr offers one of only a handful of developmental analyses of Reid's views on perception. He believes with some justification that, due to the nature of the suggestion relation, Reid holds that perceptual knowledge is inferential in the *Inquiry*. He remarks that Reid "believes that external objects are only known indirectly by means of sensations which act as natural signs of the external world" (1978, 250). Immerwahr develops a sharp contrast between the major works in this regard when saying: "In the *Inquiry* Reid does not really eliminate this barrier between the mind and the external world. He merely shows us a novel way to get through the barrier. He sees sensations as an innate language that suggests knowledge of the external world ... In the *Intellectual Powers* the barrier is eliminated altogether" (1978, 250–1). Because sensations are (or at least can be) objects of direct awareness in the *Inquiry*, Immerwahr concludes that the external world "is known only indirectly" (1978, 248). Though I believe this is an interpretive mistake, given Reid's confounding use of "suggestion" and the fact that it drops out in the *Intellectual Powers*, it is a very understandable one. One problem with Immerwahr's interpretation is philosophical: the fact that sensations are causally relevant in the production of perceptual beliefs has no bearing on whether or not perceptual beliefs are known directly. Ambient light is causally relevant to the production of visual perceptual beliefs, but simply because my eyes require light to perceive certain objects visually is itself no reason for holding that such beliefs are produced inferentially. More importantly, the distinctions now available show that interpretations asserting that perceptual knowledge is or is not wholly inferential (even when restricted to only one of Reid's works) are erroneous. The evidence for the distinction between original and acquired perception is present in both works, and that between inferential and habitual perception latent in both. With these distinctions in hand, Reid can contend that some justified perceptual beliefs are non-inferential (original), others inferential, and yet others habituated.

We can appreciate the continuity between the two works on this score, and the reason Reid did not overtly draw the distinction between habituated and inferential acquired perceptions, by attention to two passages:

When I look at the moon, I perceive her to be sometimes circular, sometimes horned, and sometimes gibbous. This is simple perception, and is the same in the philosopher and the clown: but from these various appearances of her enlightened part, I infer that she is really of a spherical figure. This conclusion is not obtained by simple perception, but by reasoning. (IHM 2.20, 172/185a–b)

[W]hen a globe is set before me, I perceive by my eyes that it has three dimensions and a spherical figure. To say that this is not perception, would be to reject the authority of custom in the use of words ... but that it is not the testimony of my sense of seeing, every philosopher knows. I see only a circular form, having the light and colour distributed in a certain way over it. (EIP 6.22, 247/337a)

These passages, respectively drawn from the *Inquiry* and *Intellectual Powers*, show that Reid consistently holds that original perceptions are non-inferential. What has confused us is his tendency to use "perception" ubiquitously in his later work. The second passage is helpful on this score. He reveals that his uses of "perception," which encompass beliefs about the three-dimensionality of an object, are not technical uses but rather uses which conform to "custom." In his unpublished writings he also humbly complies with common usage. He writes that:

We are liable to many errors in acquired perception which are commonly called fallacies of the senses, but improperly. Acquired perception is not properly a testimony of the senses which God hath given us, but a ~~conviction arising from a certain improvement which they receive~~ conclusion drawn from past experience ... When such conclusions come by habit to be immediately made from what the senses really testify, they come to be confounded with the testimony of sense and get the name of perception in common language ... And this conclusion which was originally grounded on experience becomes so ready and habitual that it resembles immediate perception and gets the name of perception in all languages. (Aberdeen MS 2131/7/V/26, 3; see EIP 2.22, 247–8/336b)

"Conviction" does not appear strong enough to describe the nature of some acquired perceptions, so Reid replaces it with "conclusion." Also, he insinuates that when suggestion relations are properly instantiated, perceptual beliefs will become "habitual" (see EIP 6.1, 417/418a, above, and EIP 2.21, 237–8/332a–b). In both the *Inquiry* and the *Intellectual Powers* Reid shows too much deference to customary usage in the development of his theory of perception. These considerations go some way toward explaining why he chose not to make overt the further distinction between inferential and habituated acquired perceptions and clutter his theory.

As ever, visual perception would require some special treatment in the context of describing the content in stages of original, inferential, and habitual perception. The previous example about stages of perceiving a clock illustrates the fact that original visual perceptions would have visible figures, not real figures, as their intentional contents. Reid begins to address the confluence between the unique status of visual perception and the original/acquired distinction here:

The objects which we see naturally and originally ... have length and breadth, but no thickness nor distance from the eye. Custom, by a kind of legerdemain, withdraws gradually these original and proper objects of sight, and substitutes in their place objects of touch, which have length, breadth, and thickness, and a determinate distance from the eye. (IHM 6.19, 167/182a)

Reid's odd description of the active role of custom here draws our attention to the fact that he is not settled on how best to account for the process. But he is clear that a key development in one's history and development as a perceiver involves gaining the custom or habit of associating the awareness of certain visible figures with the perception and belief of real figures of tables and chairs. Reid's makes a case on behalf of the need for perceivers to perform reasoning about original perceptions in order that they move from the perception of visible figure to the perception$_{C\&B}$ of real figure. This takes dramatic form in the following chapter about the skills required of the subject of Molyneux's problem.

In addition to the fact that a division between habituated and inferential perceptions best explains several perplexing texts, Descartes, a likely influence on Reid on these matters, serves as a historical precedent for that distinction. In Descartes' Sixth Replies he argues that the process of perception is best resolved into three grades: a level of sensation, a level of mentality, and a judgmental level. Descartes, like Reid, indicates that the reasoning present in habituated perceptions has allowed us to use intentional predicates to speak of the senses "learning" to perform an operation (Descartes 1985, 295). Reid echoes this hybrid position: inferences are present in the formation of our initial perceptual beliefs about three-dimensional objects, but their formation becomes unconscious and merely dependent upon prior inferences once they are performed at "great speed because of habit," or in Reid's terms, once they become "ready and habitual."[13]

Where does this leave us with regard to a theory of Reidian perceptual *knowledge*? Since Reid seldom uses normative epistemic terminology to describe perceptual beliefs, prognosticating about "knowledge" will not easily improve our understanding of the historical Reid. For example, Reid comments that though a man "can give no reason for believing his senses, his belief remains as firm as if it were grounded on demonstration." He adds that "the evidence of sense [is] no less reasonable than that of demonstration" (EIP 2.20, 230/328b). Explaining what epistemic work the term "evidence" is doing here and elsewhere is fraught with difficulty in part because Reid "give[s] the name evidence to whatever is a ground of belief" (EIP 2.20, 230/328b). As a result, Reid's views on perceptual knowledge will appear more similar to Hume's views than to the received interpretation of Reid, until his treatment of stages of cognition in the process of perception is studied further.

8.8. Summary

Original perceptual beliefs are justified independently of the justification of other perceptual beliefs, and are formed without conscious reasoning. In accordance with our discussion of the suggestion of (original) perceptions in Chapter 3, these perceptual beliefs contain rudimentary conceptual content.

---

[13] Foremost among objections to be voiced against this interpretation is the charge that Reid's theory of perceptual learning is inconsistent with his rejection of the Way of Ideas. For, if we need to perform inferences of any kind, then our knowledge of the world must leap the very same gap that Reid says ideas cannot bridge. The Way of Ideas leads to skepticism by creating the need for inferences in the first place. Either perceptual knowledge is non-inferential, or we are damned to the coal pit. But this interpretation of Reid on the Way of Ideas is naive to a fault. I've discussed and dismissed this charge elsewhere (Nichols 2002b, 587–90), and won't revisit it here.

There are two forms of what Reid describes as "acquired perception." Inferential perceptual beliefs, the first, are formed through conscious reasoning. Habituated perceptual beliefs, the second, are not formed through conscious reasoning. Inferential perceptual beliefs represent a comparatively small portion, and habituated perceptual beliefs a majority, of the total number of perceptual beliefs. The content of inferential and habituated perceptual beliefs is considerably richer than that of original perceptions. The distinction between these two types of perceptions is warranted on the basis of a systematic ambiguity in Reid's notion of "acquired perception," and its utility in explaining a number of Reid's examples of perceptual belief formation.

9

Answering Molyneux

In general form William Molyneux's famous question to Locke asks whether a blind subject (call her "S") whose sight is newly restored will be able to distinguish between and identify a sphere and a cube presented to her at a distance outside of her grasp. Much has been written about this question, but the question's ambiguity is greater even than its publicity.

I propose to identify Reid's answers to Molyneux's questions and draw out implications of his response for his theory of perception. If Gareth Evans is right, Reid's answer is unique in the history of philosophy (Evans 1985, 393–4). In his "Molyneux's Question," Evans begat interest in Reid's response by claiming that Reid stands out as the philosopher who thought most highly of our cross-modal perceptual abilities, and who gives the strongest "yes" answer (i.e. "yes, the formerly blind subject can discriminate between spheres and cubes in her visual field"). Though Evans quotes Reid, his interests are not historical in nature and he does not take steps to develop Reid's actual analysis of this problem. This is the task before us.

The major difficulty facing any interpretation of Reid on Molyneux's question is that he addresses the Molyneux problem on three distinct occasions and he gives opposite answers at different places in the same book (first a "no", then two "yes" answers). This disregard for his readers has led some to argue, understandably, that his account is inconsistent (Davis 1960, 403–4). Yet a careful reading of his texts, coupled with an understanding of the different forms of Molyneux's question circulating in Reid's milieu, will aid in resolving the confusion.

Reid requires great specificity in the question prior to offering any definitive answer—specificity absent in the historical treatment of the question. Depending on how it is qualified, Reid may answer "yes," "no," or "maybe." The apparent vacillation in Reid's analysis of the problem can be explained by the cautiousness called for by his Newtonian method. In the following discussion I'll attempt to show that Reid's aim is to continue to build his case against the Ideal Theory, which he does by eliminating the necessity of sensations for the perception of visible figure and shape.

9.1. Historical Ambiguity

The ways in which Early Modern philosophers rephrase Molyneux's question tells us as much about their philosophy of perception and views about concept acquisition as do the ways they answer the question they rephrase. (To be clear, "Molyneux's" question is asked by one philosopher to another, whereas "cube/sphere" questions are asked of newly sighted subjects.) It is beyond the scope of this chapter to detail the ways the question was formed in Reid's milieu, though Table 2 contains a condensed version of the intriguing differences in historical forms of the question. Here I will identify Molyneux's original statements of the question and then advance to Reid.

Molyneux wrote to Locke twice about the problems encountered by a congenitally blind man in arriving at spatial concepts. The first letter was written on July 7, 1688, the second on March 2, 1693. Consider the relevant passage of the first:

A Man, being born blind, and having a Globe and a Cube, nigh of the same bignes, Committed into his Hands, and being taught or Told, which is Called the Globe, and which the Cube, so as easily to distinguish them by his Touch or Feeling; Then both being taken from Him, and Laid on a Table, Let us suppose his Sight Restored to Him; Whether he Could, by his sight, and before he touch them, know which is the Globe and which the Cube? Or Whether he could know by his sight, before he strechd out his Hand, whether he Could not Reach them, tho they were Removed 20 or 1000 feet from him? (Locke 1976–89 iii, 482–3; no. 1064)

Molyneux poses two questions here. In the first he imposes one constraint: that the subject be made to answer which object is the globe and which the cube "before he touch them." The subject presumably may perform other actions—pass his hand before his eyes, say—before answering. This question is typically known as *the* Molyneux question and can be stated as:

(9.1) Could the subject know, by sight and prior to touching the objects, which is the cube and which the globe?

The second of his two 1688 questions is about distance perception:

(9.2) Could the subject know, by sight, prior to touching the objects, and prior even to passing his hand through his visual field, whether the cube and globe are within his grasp?

Molyneux does not inquire whether the subject knows how distant the objects are. Rather, assuming the objects are placed "20 or 1000 feet" away from the subject, he could know that they are placed at some distance or other from his eye, as presumably opposed to the thought that the objects might be "seen" as impinging upon the very surface of the eye. (9.2) can be made interesting in its own right, but in Molyneux's letter the question is not especially well-formed. Few people have examined the issue of distance perception qua Molyneux's question because most believed that the answer was clearly "no."[1] In part this is because it is difficult to determine the full angular range of one's arms, and even more difficult to use that information in conjunction with visible figures to answer to (9.2). Reid is perhaps an exception for he does discuss (9.2), though he too is more concerned with (9.1).

The distinct philosophical interest of (9.1) over (9.2) is why Locke chose to publish a quotation from Molyneux's 1693 letter, which restates (9.1) and avoids mention of (9.2). Molyneux's 1693 question asks:

Suppose a Man born blind, and now adult, and taught by his Touch to Distinguish between a Cube and a Sphere (Suppose) of Ivory, nighly of the same Bignes, so as to tel, when he felt One and tother, Which is the Cube which the Sphære. Suppose then, the Cube and Sphære placed on a Table, and the Blind man to be made to see. Quære whether by his sight, before he touchd them, he could now Distinguish and tel which is the Globe which the Cube. I answer, Not; for tho he has obtaind the Experience of How a Globe, how a Cube affects his Touch. Yet he has not yet attaind the Experience, that what affects my Touch so or so, must affect my Sight so or so. (Locke 1976–89 iv, 651: no. 1609, March 2, 1693)

Locke reproduces this in his essay with only cosmetic differences (1975, 2.9.8/146). This question can be stated as:

(9.3) Could the subject distinguish, by sight and prior to touching the objects, which is the cube and which the globe?

The differences in the 1693 letter are, first, that Molyneux asks whether the subject "could now" distinguish the globe from the cube. Strictly speaking, even the odd "yes" response is qualified by saying that the subject must be given a few moments to orient his visual perceptions. But this requirement can also be seen as a way to preclude the subject's use of reasoning once he is given sight, for using reason might require that the subject pause and reflect on the

---

[1] Molyneux's own "no" answer to (9.2) was to have a profound effect on Berkeley and others. In his *Dioptrica Nova* Molyneux says: "In Plain Vision the Estimate we make of the *Distance* of Objects (especially when so far removed, that the Interval between our two Eyes, bears no sensible Proportion thereto; or when look'd upon with one Eye only) is rather the Act of our *Judgment*, than of Sense; and acquired by *Exercise* and a Faculty of *comparing*, rather than *Natural*. ... For *Distance* of it self, is not to be perceived; for 'tis a Line (or a Length) presented to our Eye with its End towards us, which must therefore be only a *Point*, and that is *Invisible*" (Molyneux 1692, 113).

answer. I refer to this form of reasoning as "abstract" rather than "a priori" because it requires the use of data given in experience, even though the relevant data is not given to the subject in his experience. Second, in the 1688 letter, Molyneux asks epistemic questions, using "know" in his statements of what I have paraphrased as (9.1) and (9.2). These qualifications make it both more difficult and easier for the subject to answer the cube/sphere question: more difficult, because the response must directly follow the operation without time to adjust, but more easy because merely distinguishing between the cube and sphere is a less burdensome cognitive demand than is knowing which is the cube and which the sphere. Notice I am not claiming that Molyneux *intended* to ask different questions in 1688 and 1693, but rather that he did ask different questions.

Locke restates (9.3) and provides his answer as follows: "the Blind Man, at first sight, would not be able with certainty to say, which was the Globe, which the Cube, whilst he only saw them" (Locke 1975, 2.9.8/146). From this answer we can see he is asking a slightly different question than (9.3). He seems to have answered something like (9.4):

> (9.4) Supposing that there is nothing else in his visual field, could the subject know with certainty and immediately, by sight and prior to touching the objects, which is the cube and which the globe?

(9.4) captures several of the constraints that Locke imputes into the question: the subject must answer immediately ("at first sight") and "with certainty," and, seemingly, there must be nothing else in his visual field (insofar as that proves possible).

The question is typically taken to be philosophical rather than empirical. In other words, the phrase "could the subject tell" typically refers to what it is conceptually possible for the subject to know. However, experimental results were taken to confirm the negative answer. William Cheselden removed cataracts from a fourteen-year-old boy in 1728, which offered an opportunity to supplement answers to the philosophical forms of the question with answers to empirical forms of the question. Cheselden reports in *Philosophical Transactions* in 1728 (reprinted in Degenaar 1996) that his patient failed visually to recognize his cat upon being given sight. This "young Gentleman ... when he first saw ... was so far from making any Judgement about Distances, that he thought all Objects whatever touch'd his Eyes" (Degenaar 1996, 55). Most philosophers addressing the question in the century after Cheselden's surgery address this experiment in some way.

Berkeley makes heavy use of this result, but to uncertain effect. In *Theory of Vision Vindicated* Berkeley summarizes the Cheselden case incompletely and inaccurately, then concludes: "Thus, by fact and experiment, those points of the theory which seem the most remote from common apprehension were not a little confirmed, many years after I had been led into the discovery of them by reasoning" (TVV §71/WGB i, 276). On the contrary, despite the amusing story about the boy's cat with which Cheselden flavors his lab report, this case throws little light on the Molyneux question. The boy was not congenitally blind. He had lost his sight as a young child, though at just what age we do not know. Cheselden only repaired one eye at a time. There were months between the two operations. This would be relevant since binocular vision may figure prominently in answering Molyneux from purely physiological data. At least, were the boy to answer a cube/sphere question negatively with one functioning eye, such a response would not provide an adequate ruling upon the philosophical question. If he were to answer after both eyes are functioning, this would also be inadequate since this gives the boy time to associate in experience his monocular experiences of visible figures with his tactile sensations. Furthermore, Cheselden did not ask his patient any of Molyneux's questions. It is unlikely Cheselden even knew of Molyneux's question(s) at the time. Natural philosophers, including Cheselden, were keenly interested in the visual acuity of the patients after the operation but, without an adequate experimental environment, even the empirical form of Molyneux's question could not be ruled upon. Besides, were such a patient to answer "no" under the most favorable of circumstances, even this would not show that it is not conceptually possible for some human being or other to distinguish the cube from the sphere.

Unfortunately, questions about the logical status and modal scope of the questions were rarely if ever addressed. Condillac is the exception. He must have Berkeley in mind in the *Treatise* when he says, of philosophers addressing Molyneux's problem: "We set forth the question poorly, we do not even know how to set it forth, and yet we claim to have resolved it" (Condillac 1982, 3.3/277; see his detailed recommendations on what went wrong in Cheselden's case and on how to create ideal conditions for observation for a patient after the removal of cataracts in Condillac 1982, 3.5–3.6/290–5).

Together, Molyneux and Locke came to set the standard conditions upon which the question can be posed and answered in such a way as to yield important philosophical results. Cheselden's conditions were taken by Berkeley to be such conditions, but they were not. What I will call the "standard conditions" under which a Molyneux question is posed are these. The subject has been blind since birth and has his sight restored in both eyes simultaneously. The subject answers the question only by seeing, and not touching, the objects. Objects are set at a distance far enough from the eyes to allow the subject to focus on both at once, but near enough that people with normal sight would answer "yes." The objects must be of a similar size. The question asks the subject to determine which object is the cube (or square) and which is the sphere (or circle). An unstated *ceteris paribus* clause filters aberrant and unforeseen features of the subject, the perceptual environment, and the question.

This is not to say that there were not other conditions that individual philosophers placed upon the question. Reid's treatment of the problem was shaped by the twists put upon the question by his predecessors (see Table 2).

All the major players differ in their statement of the problem itself, their understanding of the implications of the problem, and/or in their answers to Molyneux's original question(s). Even when there is apparent unanimity on a "no" answer, as with Locke and Berkeley, the arguments they each give on its behalf are not only different but, in that case, mutually incompatible (Park 1969).

I must clarify some assumptions about the questions. One assumption present in the standard conditions is that the subject is capable of taking seen visible figures as intentional objects of perceptual belief. Berkeley does not assume that the subject has discrete visual figures or color patches as the intentional objects of those first perceptual states. For Berkeley, the subject's visual perception resembles the visual experience of infants who, in an evocative phrase from William James, experience "a blooming, buzzing confusion." Infants, he says, "must go through a long education of the eye and ear before they can perceive the realities which adults perceive" (James 1981, 724). For Berkeley, the subject will not misidentify the cube as the sphere; rather, there are no determinate figures in his field of vision that could stand as the intentional objects of perceptual beliefs. Rich perceptual experience is needed even to have intentionally directed visual perception of two-dimensional visible figures.

This assumption drives only Berkeley's radical perspective on the question. In effect, determining the nature of the subject's visual experience is an empirical matter. If research on the visual capacities of neonates is any guide,

Table 2. Responses to Molyneux's Questions

	Molyneux 1688a	Molyneux 1688b	Molyneux 1693	Locke	Berkeley[2]	Leibniz[3]	Condillac[4]	Diderot[5]	Reid a	Reid b	Evans
PERCEPTION											
Standard Conditions	A	A	A	A	D?	A	A	D	A	A	A
S's perception has intentional content	A	A	A	A	D	A	A	A	A	A	A
S perceives objects as 3-D	A	A	A	A	D	A	D	D	D	?	?
AGENT											
S is totally passive		A					A[6]				
S employs reasoning						A		D[7]	D	A[8]	
JUDGMENT											
S must visually perceive depth				A	A		A		A	D	D
S asked to measure distance	A			A				D		D	
S asked whether S "knows"	A			A[9]		A		?			A[9]
S asked to answer immediately			A	A		D	D				
OBJECTS											
Q posed about cube and sphere	A	A	A	A	A	A	A	D	A	A?	A
Q posed about square and circle								A		A	A
S sees no other objects				A		A[10]					
ANSWER	No	No	No	No	No	Yes	No	Yes	No	Yes	Yes

Key: "A"=agrees; "D"=disagrees; "?"=response uncertain in text; "□"=conceptually necessary. Blank cells indicate that the author did not address the point. "Reid a" refers to his discussion of the capacities of Cheselden's cataracts patient. "Reid b" refers to his discussion of the capacities of Nicholas Saunderson.

² Berkeley's preferred version of the question is this: "a man born blind would not at first reception of his sight think the things he saw were of the same nature with the objects of touch, or had anything in common with them" (NTV §128/WGB I, 223). With his "no" answer Berkeley allies himself with the thesis that there is no inter-modal sharing of information. The subject would believe the question is "downright bantering and unintelligible" (NTV §135/WGB I, 226). Berkeley employs his "no" answer elsewhere in order to vindicate his empiricist account of distance perception (NTV §41/WGB I, 186) and his discussion of magnitude (NTV §79/WGB I, 203).

³ Leibniz says, "by applying rational principles to the sensory knowledge which he has already acquired by touch," the agent will be able to distinguish them. The subject can determine which figure is of the cube and which is of the sphere because "in the case of the sphere there are no distinguished points on the surface of the sphere taken in itself, since everything there is uniform and without angles, whereas in the case of the cube there are eight points which are distinguished from all the others" (Leibniz 1981, 136–7, 2.9.8).

⁴ Condillac's discussion of Molyneux-like problems is so rewarding it cannot be adequately summarized in a note. Also, the column for Condillac is misleading insofar as he does not address himself to Molyneux's questions. He describes what his statue would experience, given its wealth of reflection upon its other senses, once sight is added to touch. Then he separately analyzes cases of the removal of cataracts.

First, befitting his focus upon the succession of sensations from a first-person point of view, Condillac urges caution in the evaluation of "no" answers based upon allegedly scientific cases. Patients having undergone surgery for the removal of cataracts would require time to adjust to the experience of light and color, develop acuity in their visual perceptions, and formulate a judgment about entirely novel experiences. At *Treatise* 3.6.3 he advocates some unusual controls on the experiment, including placing S in a glass chamber, and setting objects of various sizes, shapes, and colors on the outside of the chamber (Condillac 1982, 294–5). Second, there he suggests that S "could not have seen colors outside of his eyes if touch had not taught him to see them," thus the outness of colors depends upon the sense of touch, even if only putting one's hands before one's eyes. Third, in his most explicit discussion of cubes and spheres Condillac explains the dependence of shape concepts upon tactile experience and argues that S's initial visual impressions (that is, those occurring prior to S seeing himself touching objects) will only contain 2-D content. When initially seeing a sphere, the statue's impression "represents only a flat circle mixed with shade and light. Thus it does not yet see a sphere, . . ." (3.3.11/278).

⁵ Diderot was the first to recognize that to require of the subject that he see a 3-D cube and 3-D sphere unnecessarily burdens a "yes" answer by making it depend upon a form of depth perception. Someone with newly restored sight might be capable of distinguishing a 2-D, four-sided figure from a 2-D, circular figure, and yet be incapable of doing the same for cubes and spheres. No one made this point until Diderot partly because Molyneux's first question about cubes and spheres, and, worse, his second one is about distance. If one wishes to ascertain cross-modal perceptual abilities, then posing the question about squares and circles is a more efficient way of achieving that end.

⁶ Condillac requires that S is passive in the sense that he not move his hands through his visual field, but he requires that S is active in the sense that S must be allowed to learn to "look" as opposed to "see." "In a word, our eyes must analyze" (*Treatise* 3.3.6; Condillac 1982, 276).

⁷ Diderot poses the question to several different people, a "dullard," a "metaphysician", and a "geometer." The metaphysician and geometer both give "confident" affirmative answers to square/circle questions. The geometer does not use a priori reasoning, but does use abstract reasoning through which tactile experience is compared with visual experience (Diderot 1972, 134–6).

⁸ The second form in which Reid poses the question requires that S employ not merely abstract reasoning, but advanced geometrical and spatial reasoning.

⁹ Locke and Evans both place the epistemic bar high. Locke asks whether S knows "with certainty" which is which.

¹⁰ Leibniz requires that there are no objects in S's visual field, and that S *knows* that there are no other objects in S's visual field.

then Berkeley is incorrect.[10] But even if this research prima facie indicates that Berkeley's analysis of visual experience is wrong, there are at least some cases in which it is correct. When restricted to those with damage to or a deterioration of their visual cortex, Berkeley's claim is probably correct. But I will be assuming, with Reid, that the subjects of whom we speak have a functional visual cortex, optic nerve, and eyes. This is my second assumption.

This qualification raises an important point about quantifying over the set of subjects involved. These questions are posed to a theoretical subject, who is intended to represent everyone in such circumstances, but some people will have cerebral damage or impaired conceptual abilities from which would follow aberrant answers. Someone might think, of subjects to whom Molyneux's questions are posed, that (a) all of them are incapable of distinguishing a cube from a globe (or a square from a circle); that (b) some of them are capable, and some incapable, of distinguishing a cube from a globe; or that (c) all of them are capable of distinguishing a cube from a globe. Evans's appeal to quasi-transcendental considerations indicates that he might endorse a universally generalized answer like (c). Of their respective formulations of the question, Locke, Molyneux, and Berkeley answer with (a); indeed, one might argue that Berkeley takes (a) to be a necessary truth. A stance on this scope issue may imply an analysis of the implicit modal operator in several forms of the question. Most respondents offer universally generalized answers intended to range over all properly functioning perceivers, but this is a methodological assumption Reid does not share.

9.2. Cheselden's Boy: "No"

Reid first discusses blindness and distance perception at *Inquiry* 6.3. The discussion is primarily about the distance issue in (9.2), and it occurs in the context of his analysis of visible figure and the visible appearance of objects. The reason that this discussion intermingles with a discussion of visible figure is that the immediate object of visual experience for the subject, when the blindfolds are removed, is a seen visible figure (see Section 4.4). However, in the midst of this discussion, Reid also addresses object-identification issues. At this point he fails to distinguish clearly between the two points.

---

[10] Sight in neonates has received attention by psychologists interested in determining spatial perception skills, the onset of cross-modal perception, and other features of early perceptual learning. They have concluded that newborns exhibit abilities that can be best explained by hypothesizing that their various sense modalities are capable of sharing perceptual information in a matter of hours from birth. Thus very young infants "register the same information about the shape of the object even if it is picked up through two different modalities, touch and vision" (Meltzoff and Moore 1993, 224).

Reid makes the general point that we err in believing that we can ascertain distance via sight alone. As we know from our study of visible figure, "it is certain that visible appearance hath no more than two [dimensions], and can be exactly represented upon a canvass which hath only length and breadth." Reid adds: "it appears certain, that distance from the eye is no immediate object of sight" (IHM 6.3, 84/136b). In the *Intellectual Powers* Reid says: "The objects which we see naturally and originally ... have length and breadth, but no thickness, nor distance from the eye" (IHM 6.20, 167/182a). So long as the objects between which the subject must discriminate are three-dimensional, the subject must possess the concept of depth in order to answer affirmatively. To acquire the concept of depth, one must have tactile sensations. This is the result of what we have learned both about Reid's explanation of the origins of primary qualities and about his qualified claim that tactile sensations are physically necessary for the perception of some primary qualities. An alternative way of putting this point is to emphasize an observation made in the previous chapter—namely that distance is an object of acquired perception and is not original to vision (see also Hopkins 2005, 343).

Reid emphasizes the implications of the two-dimensionality of visible figure with his thought experiment about the "Idomenians"—creatures "endued with sight only, without any other external sense." An Idomenian would be incapable of arriving at a concept of distance. "We must not conceive him disposed by his constitution, as we are, to consider the visible appearance as a sign of something else" (IHM 6.9, 106/149a). Reid adds: "He might perceive visible objects to have length and breadth, but could have no notion of a third dimension, any more than we can have of a fourth. ...It would not be possible for him to conceive one object to be behind another, or one to be nearer, another more distant" (IHM 6.9, 106–7/149a). This treatment of question (9.2) is idealized and the product of a thought experiment, but Reid explicitly addresses (9.2) in the following passage:

[D]oes not every man, by sight, perceive the distance of the book from his eye?... [I]t appears certain, that distance from the eye is no immediate object of sight. There are certain things in the visible appearance, which are signs of distance from the eye, and from which, as we shall afterwards shew, we learn by experience to judge of that distance within certain limits; but it seems beyond doubt, that a man born blind, and suddenly made to see, could form no judgment at first of the distance of the objects which he saw. The young man couched by Cheselden thought, at first, that everything he saw touched his eye, and learned only by experience to judge of the distance of visible objects. ... To a man newly made to see, the visible appearance of objects would be the same as to us; but he would see nothing at all of their real dimensions, as we do. He could form no conjecture, by means of his sight only, how many inches or feet they were in length, breadth, or thickness. He could perceive little or nothing of their real figure; nor could he discern that this was a cube, that a sphere; that this was a cone, and that a cylinder. His eye could not inform him that this object was near, and that more remote (IHM 6.3, 84–5/136b–37a).

In the first part of this passage Reid wants to know the means by which one is able to perceive the approximate metric distance of an object like a book from oneself. But in the second part he addresses the thickness of objects and discusses the perception of different three-dimensional objects. Reid thereby seems to conflate two distinct issues in the visual perception of all three dimensions. For his part, when saying that we cannot visually perceive depth, he means that we cannot perceive the distance an object is from an eye and that we cannot perceive objects as inhabiting a dimension extending at angles out from the eye.

Reid is not alone in overlooking this ambiguity. On one hand are the visual perception of metric distance of an object from the eye and visual perception of relative distance between two objects (distinct issues we will conjoin for now). On the other is the visual perception of the depth or metric depth of objects themselves. To describe the two types of visual perception in this second group, the subject may see the book as possessing three, and not merely two, dimensions, and the subject may see the book as being about $5'' \times 8'' \times 2''$. In the present context these distinct issues can be conflated without serious concern provided we are explicit that in both kinds of case the subject must possess and apply the subject's concept of the third dimension, of "outness," as Berkeley called it. To see the book as being about 20 feet in front of me, and to see it as being thicker than my forearm, both require an application of a depth concept.

In order to interpret this passage appropriately, we need to identify which question it is that Reid is addressing. He evinces an interest in the cube/sphere question. Depth cues would only be useful in a response to it, not to the circle/square question. Reid holds that the boy of Cheselden's experiment could not know whether the cube and globe are within his grasp. Why?

First, it seems that we do perceive distances (of both sorts) through vision. The application of depth concepts to our visual perceptions becomes a habituated perception for properly functioning agents, but Reid is tacitly speaking of original perceptions here. These habitual perceptions depend upon cross-modal coordination with touch. I observed Reid to say in a manuscript that "The habit of judging of small distances by the eye is got so early and so much confirmed by daily experience that it resembles original perception very much, it is called perception in common language and can be distinguished from original perception only by philosophers." But he adds that he calls it "acquired perception to distinguish it on the one hand from original perception and on the other [from] conclusions drawn by reasoning from what we perceive" (Aberdeen MS 2132 7/V/26, 2). To employ concepts of distance in acquired perceptual beliefs, one must make use of information derivative of sight *and* touch. This results in Reid's "no" to (9.2) (see Daniels 1989 and Ganson 1999 on distance perception in Reid).

In the last two sentences of the passage Reid gives us his definitive answer. Though the subject's awareness of visible appearances and visible figures is identical to ours, the subject cannot see them as mind-independent, three-dimensional objects because he lacks concepts of depth. This can be expressed using Reid's terminology by saying that a visible figure of a book suggests to me the presence of a book, but such suggestion relations are absent from the subject's experience. Merely through exposure to the visible figures of cubes and spheres, the subject is unable to distinguish which is the cube and which the sphere. Strictly speaking, the subject does not perceive cubes and spheres at all, even though Reid says that his perceptual experience does contain intentional content. Note that in this discussion Reid does not remark upon the subject's abilities to perceive two-dimensional figures.

For the sake of completeness, we can formulate Reid's version of the question as discussed in this context as:

(9.5) Could a subject who does not employ abstract reasoning before or immediately after having his vision restored, prior to touching the objects, perceive and distinguish between a three-dimensional cube and a globe?

I use the term "perceive" in the question in order to indicate that Reid seems to assume in this context that the subject needs to be able to perceive the objects in his visual field as being a cube and a sphere in order to answer affirmatively. (This reflects the importance of the first line in the "judgment" category on the table regarding whether visual perception of depth is required for a "yes" answer.) I also explicitly describe the cube and sphere as being "three-dimensional" to capture the fact that in *Inquiry* 6.3 Reid explicitly considers the relevance of their "thickness" to an answer to Molyneux's question. Once he rejects these assumptions and adopts a more lax reading of the question, the answer changes.

9.3. Saunderson and the Cube/Sphere Question: "Yes"

Upon having his vision restored, Cheselden's patient is unable to perceive depth and is unable to determine which is the cube and which the globe. But not only does Reid refrain from generalizing this result as applying to all human beings in such circumstances, he discusses another case in which a subject answers affirmatively to one of Molyneux's questions. This is possible when the person of whom the question is asked is changed from an inexperienced boy to Cambridge University's Lucasian Professor of Mathematics. Reid imagines it is the blind mathematician Nicholas Saunderson, whom Reid met on his travels to England as a young man, whose sight is restored. Rather, Reid imagines an idealized agent who possesses all of Saunderson's skills and more, and who is blind from birth; I will use "Saunderson" to refer to Reid's idealization of Saunderson. In this section I want to examine the stage of the process by which Reid says Saunderson can give a "Yes" answer.

Reid brings Saunderson into the discussion of the Molyneux problem in two different contexts. In the first and more oblique, the subject of this section, Saunderson's facility in deriving geometrical visible figures of objects is used to draw a conclusion about his capacity to answer Molyneux's question as posed about cubes and spheres. In the second and more pointed context (assessed in the next section), Reid discusses Saunderson's response to a question about squares and circles.

The switch of subject from a boy to Saunderson carries particular importance as a result of the discussion of visible figure in Chapter 5. Reid attests that visible figure and real figure are interderivable. By knowing the real dimensions of a figure and the distance of it from a given set of coordinates, an expert geometer, though congenitally blind, could exactly calculate what the appearance of that object would be as modeled from those coordinates. The figure that a blind mathematician would come to know would not, of course, be what we have called *seen* visible figure, the apprehension of which requires a functioning visual system. But the blind mathematician would be able to calculate the dimensions of the geometrical visible figure and model how the object would appear to the eye when set at a particular distance.

Of course, before a blind person can come to such rich concepts, he must have more rudimentary geometrical concepts. Reid believes that Saunderson has a number of geometrical concepts, including concepts needed to build Euclidean figures—foremost among them "point" and "line". The justification for this belief is based upon Reid's observation of Saunderson's extensive mathematical and geometrical knowledge. First, if presented with ropes fashioned into squares, circles, rhombuses, etc., Saunderson will correctly identify those shapes by touching and tracing each length of rope with his hands. Second, many concepts in geometry—the most important—are defined in terms of points, which are non-spatial. On this front, the abilities of the sighted and of the blind are on a par.

Reid prepares the way for this intermediate conclusion with his earlier remarks about the Idomenians. That discussion occurs in the context of his development of his geometry of visibles. In a version of that discussion Reid presented to the Aberdeen Philosophical Society, he explicitly describes the geometrical concepts he believes the Idomenians, unfeeling seers, can acquire. Imagine that the Idomenians are presented with white circles of different sizes and distances from them, and that some circles are divided by lines. Reid says that "by comparing the objects of sight & reasoning upon them, he might by degrees acquire the idea of points, angles, right obtuse & acute, of lines streight & curved, & of spaces bounded by lines; he might discover the relations of these & form Geometrical conclusions built upon self evident principles" (Reid 1997, 273; see IHM 108/150a). A sense of touch is not necessary to acquire these geometrical concepts. The last one—space bounded by lines—is especially important for answering Molyneux's questions.

Once Reid allows Saunderson these concepts, the second stage of the process by which Saunderson can conceive of visible figures involves the conception of Euclidean planar figures. Since Saunderson knows the geometrical definition of a triangle, he can make a mental model of its shape. A triangle is simply a figure composed of three straight lines enclosing a space. Reid is silent on whether this requires use of knowledge Saunderson has gained from touch—perhaps Reid would go so far as to say that an unseeing and unfeeling agent can conceive of a mental model of a triangle (see below). But in Saunderson's case, he has the help of his hands and can trace out a triangle in space.

At the third stage, Reid describes Saunderson's use of Reid's model for his geometry of visibles:

The visible figure, magnitude, and position, may, by mathematical reasoning, be deduced from the real.... [W]e may venture to affirm, that a man born blind, if he were instructed in mathematics, would be able to determine the visible figure of a body, when its real figure, distance, and position, are given. Dr Saunderson understood the projection of the sphere, and perspective. Now, I require no more knowledge in a blind man, in order to his being able to determine the visible figure of bodies, than that he can project the outline of a given body, upon the surface of a hollow sphere, whose centre is in the eye ...

A blind man can conceive lines drawn from every point of the object to the centre of the eye, making angles. He can conceive that the length of the object will appear greater or less, in proportion to the angle which it subtends at the eye; and that, in like manner, the breadth, and in general the distance, of any one point will appear greater or less, in proportion to the angles which those distances subtend. He can easily be made to conceive, that the visible appearance has no thickness .... He may be informed, that the eye, until it is aided by experience, does not represent one object as nearer or more remote than another. Indeed, he would probably conjecture this of himself. (IHM 6.7, 95–6/142b–143a)

Imagine an idealized blind mathematician possessing these reasoning skills to be given sight. Reid's guiding thought is that such a subject will be able through abstract reasoning to compare the geometrical properties of visible figures of cubes that he has in his mind's eye with the two two-dimensional visible figures that now appear in his field of vision. The geometry of visibles ranges over two- and three-dimensional objects; in other words, blind Saunderson can calculate the geometrical visible figures of plane circles and three-dimensional spheres on a couple of conditions. He must be provided with their dimensions, their distance from the eye, and their angle of orientation to the eye (IHM 6.7, 96/143a).[11] (This data is not necessary in order for Saunderson to answer affirmatively.[12]) Also, the objects must be sufficiently different so that they cannot project identical visible figures to the same set of coordinates.[13]

So Saunderson can "project the outline of a given body, upon the surface of a hollow sphere." At the third stage, Saunderson's abilities imply that he can form a notion of visible figure. To show this Reid must define the concepts "real figure" and "visible figure." He says: "as the real figure of a body consists in the position of its several parts with regard to one another, so its visible figure consists in the position of its several parts with regard to the eye." He adds:

---

[11] Despite other similarities with Condillac about the nature of the Molyneux question, Condillac holds in the *Treatise*, contrary to Reid, that "if we were to give our statue a perfect knowledge of optics, it would be no further advanced" (Condillac 1982, 3.3/274).

[12] The two-dimensional figure of a cube will be significantly more complex than the figure of a sphere since for each degree of rotation on the X-, Y- and Z-axes, a new two-dimensional seen figure of the cube will be manifest. This makes it easier on Saunderson—so easy, in fact, that he needn't antecedently know their angles of orientation to his eye, their respective sizes, or their distances. If he knows he is working with a cube and a sphere, that is enough. Likewise, knowledge that he is working with a square and circle will also be sufficient.

[13] At least, Saunderson will be able to identify and differentiate any real figures in virtue of the geometrical figures they produce, so long as the three- or two-dimensional objects under investigation are incapable of producing coincident geometrical figures. That is, depending upon the subject's orientation and distance, the subject may not be able to determine that object X is a cube and object Y a rectangle. This would occur if he unluckily occupies coordinates from which X and Y produce identical geometrical visible figures. Imagine X is a cube, Y a rectangle, and Z a square. Suppose the dimensions of the side of X and the side of Y that face the subject are identical. Suppose also that the surface of square Z faces the subject head-on (as opposed to edge-on), and that the dimensions of the surface of Z are also equal to the sides of X and Y seen by the subject. Then the subject might be incapable of distinguishing between any of them. He will see a $5'' \times 8''$ expanse, say, and be unable to identify the object—X, Y, or Z—to which it belongs.

In Molyneux's question the two visible figures at issue, those of a cube and a sphere, have no coincident visible figures (see Section 5.4). Even in the square/circle question this holds true. This is critical because, had they possessed coincident visible figures, our subject's reasoning would not lend his answer certainty.

As he that hath a distinct conception of the situation of the parts of the body with regard to one another, must have a distinct conception of its real figure; so he that conceives distinctly the position of its several parts with regard to the eye, must have a distinct conception of its visible figure. Now, there is nothing, surely, to hinder a blind man from conceiving the position of the several parts of a body with regard to the eye, any more than from conceiving their situation with regard to one another; and, therefore, I conclude, that a blind man may attain a distinct conception of the visible figure of bodies. (IHM 6.7, 96/143b)

Because the idealized geometer's conceptions of visible figure are distinct, Reid infers that the subject can uniquely separate and distinguish the visible figures of the sphere and the cube (and square and circle). In effect, to say the blind man may "attain a distinct conception of the visible figure of bodies" is equivalent to saying that a blind man may conceive of the way that an object looks, in contradistinction from the surrounding visible figures. He says: "[A]s to the visible appearance of the figure, and motion, and extension of bodies, I conceive that a man born blind may have a distinct notion, if not of the very things, at least of something extremely like to them" (IHM 6.2, 79/133b). At this point it is essential to recall our distinction between types of visible figure. Reid is invoking a type of visible figure that does not require the subject to have seen anything at all. The subject acquires the concept of a visible figure as it would appear to the subject, *ceteris paribus*. At minimum, the subject acquires the concept of the object's geometrical visible figure.

Someone will object that Saunderson cannot have acquired a concept of visible figure given the data available to him. Reid is aware of this objection and addresses it obliquely. He says that the blind man's conceptions of the visible figures of an object are highly abstract and mathematical, but this is no reason to think that he could not successfully apply this knowledge to figures he sees, were he given sight. Many sighted people conceive of a variety of geometrical forms purely abstractly and without having seen or touched them. For example, we sighted people can take the definition of a dodecahedron and form a mental model of how the object would look were one to enter our field of vision. "The blind man forms his notion of visible figure in the same manner," via abstract geometrical analysis, as someone who has formed "his notion of a parabola or a cycloid, which he never saw" (IHM 6.8, 97/144a). The means by which the subject forms his notion of visible figures is clearly different from the way that sighted people do so. "The blind man forms the notion of visible figure to himself, by thought, and by mathematical reasoning from principles; whereas the man that sees, has it presented to his eye at once, without any labour, without any reasoning, by a kind of inspiration" (IHM 6.8, 97/144a).

Commentators concur that a blind subject's concept of a visible figure of a square that he has not seen, and a sighted subject's concept of a visible figure of a square he has seen, are identical. To reach this conclusion, these commentators lean upon operational analyses of concept possession (see Daniels 1989, 72; and Hopkins 2005, 356). With this way of looking at it, the second Molyneux question vindicates Reid's analysis by allowing the blind subject to confirm Reid's theory about concept acquisition and concept application behaviorally. Gareth Evans pioneered this way of interpreting the process of concept acquisition in Reid in this context.[14]

Though he hedges his response with a number of qualifications, Reid answers this version of Molyneux's question affirmatively. The most important ways in which Reid molds the question to suit his answer are these. First, he implicitly poses the question of subjects with certain abilities. Reid's subject uses a geometry for visible space through which he can calculate the shape of the objects as they will appear to the eye. (I presuppose the results in Yaffe 2002.) Such an individual will be able mentally to model the position of three- (and two-) dimensional objects in this geometry, as if the facing sides of these objects were represented on the inner surface of a hollow sphere. This is why Reid says that the breadth of objects in this model will appear to the subject in direct proportion to the size of the angle the object presents to the center-point of the sphere. Since this blind subject can deduce the visible figures of spheres and cubes (and circles and squares), he will be able to differentiate one from another when he sees their visible figures. The blind subject performs these inferences "by information and reflection" and not by using any sensations.

In a sense this broad requirement that subjects possess certain abilities is present in others' answers too, for example the newly sighted people must not

---

[14] Evans implies that to know one is presented with a square visual array is to be disposed to reach in certain ways. He says: "no explanation can be given of what it is to have a perceptual representation of space—to be given perceptually the information that objects of such-and-such a character are arranged in such-and-such a way in one's vicinity—except in terms of the behavioural propensities and dispositions to which such information gives rise" (Evans 1985, 371). From this he mounts what seems to me to be a transcendental argument about the necessary structure of experience in our spatial behavioral framework, to the effect that it must be profoundly unitary. Evans concludes, with Kant, that "it is not possible to have a conception of an objective world—a world whose states and constituents are independent of one's perception of them—without conceiving of that world as spatial, with oneself as located within it and tracing a continuous path through it" (Evans 1985, 369; see Cassam 1997, chapters 2 and 3).

There is some conceptual distance between Evans's response and Reid's, though I do not think the distance invalidates Evans's approach to Reid. While Evans and Reid both return strong "yes" answers, Evans's response appeals to the status of the subject's "behavioral framework." Evans's answer marks a stronger "yes" than either Leibniz's or Reid's because Evans's appeal to the structure of the manifold of human experience lends itself to an interpretation on which it is necessarily the case that the subject will know a cube from a sphere under Molyneux's conditions. Neither Reid nor Leibniz would be comfortable with that way of putting the point.

have too much degradation in their visual cortex, must have fully functioning tactile faculties, and so on (Denis Diderot and Adam Smith appreciated this point better than did Reid.[15]) Has Reid's use of Saunderson left the bounds of the questions' implicit *ceteris paribus* clauses? Molyneux does not explicitly prohibit the use of abstract reasoning after sight is restored in (9.1) and (9.2), though in (9.3) and (9.4) Molyneux and Locke invoke temporal constraints upon answers (the subject's judgment must be given "immediately" and "at first sight"). In neither case, though, is there a prohibition on abstract reasoning *prior* to posing the question to the subject.

When discussing Saunderson, Reid's second alteration to Molyneux's question involves a subtle interpretation of its relative clause. This point assists in understanding what Reid holds to be the role of depth perception in addressing Molyneux's questions (see Evans 1985). Molyneux wants to know the answer to question (9.1): "Could the subject know, by sight and prior to touching the objects, which is the cube and which the globe?" This question is ambiguous in a crucial way. Molyneux might be inquiring about (9.1.i) which *three-dimensional object is* the cube and which *is* the globe. But he might be inquiring about (9.1.ii) which *two-dimensional visible figure represents* the cube and which *represents* the globe.

In the foregoing discussion of Saunderson's affirmative answer to the cube/sphere question, Reid interprets the question as asking which two-dimensional visible figures represent the cube and sphere. This is because

---

[15] This point must not be overlooked if one wants an empirically adequate answer to any of Molyneux's questions. This also cautions any hasty comparison between the visual abilities of the blind and of neonates. Reid mentions that inactivity creates an idleness in our muscles that causes unpleasant sensations (EIP 2.16, 197–9/312a–b). But he does not bring the effects of idleness to bear upon the Molyneux problem, and so overlooks the role of developmental physiology on the problem. Adam Smith does not make this mistake, instead showing an acute awareness of the fact that our faculties deteriorate without use. He emphasizes the importance of the observation that Cheselden's boy was not totally blind (1980, 158). Smith says: "though it may have been altogether by the slow paces of observation and experience that this young gentleman acquired the knowledge of the connection between visible and tangible objects; we cannot from thence with certainty infer, that young children have not some instinctive perception of the same kind. In [the subject] this instinctive power, not having been exerted at the proper season, may, from disuse, have gone gradually to decay, and at last have been completely obliterated. Or, perhaps, (what seems likewise very possible,) some feeble and unobserved remains of it may have somewhat facilitated his acquisition of what he might otherwise have found it much more difficult to acquire" (1980, 161).

He adds that children "appear at so very early a period to know the distance, the shape, and magnitude of the different tangible objects which are [visually] presented to them, that I am disposed to believe that even they may have some instinctive perception of this kind; though possibly in a much weaker degree than the greater part of other animals. A child that is scarcely a month old, stretches out its hands to feel any little play-thing that is presented to it" (1980, 163). Lacking any opportunity to develop and sustain our visual system puts a congenitally blind Molyneux subject's visual system in worse shape than any infant's system, as has been shown through studies of the development and growth at the neuronal level in the visual cortex.

the subject could use abstract reasoning to understand the nature of the isomorphic representational relationships between his two-dimensional visible figures (which technically exist in three-space; see Ch. 4, fn. 4) and the three-dimensional objects responsible for them.

Were Reid to interpret the question in accord with (9.1.i), then he will answer "no" because of his denial that Molyneux's subject will have any concepts of distance or depth. Such concepts are required to entertain that question. In order to know which three-dimensional object is which, the subject must be capable of applying spatial concepts like depth to the figures in his field of vision, and Reid denies that any subject could do that. In the previous section I explained Reid's "no" answer, which he justifies in part on the grounds that Cheselden's says that his patient "thought, at first, that everything he saw touched his eye" (IHM 6.3, 85/137a). This, and its context, reveal Reid's stress upon the inability of the subject to see objects as having depth. This marks a reason to infer that in his discussion of Cheselden's boy, Reid was answering (9.1.i).

One final point in this connection is about Molyneux's work. By introducing Saunderson into the question, Reid sharply amends Molyneux's principal aims in posing the question. Molyneux was known by Reid primarily to be concerned with distance perception. This constitutes the major theme in Molyneux's forgotten *Dioptrica Nova: A Treatise of Dioptricks*, the highlight of which is a proof that distance cannot be perceived (1692, 113 ff.). This background provides another reason to think that Reid assumed that Molyneux's question about the recognition of cubes and globes was actually intended to test whether concepts of depth could be acquired through a virginal, untrained use of vision. In contrast, it is improbable that Reid would have believed that Molyneux was merely interested in a question about object individuation and identification.

So Reid's "no" is consistent with his "yes," since he is in effect answering (9.1.i) with a "no" and (9.1.ii) with a "yes."

9.4. Saunderson and the Square/Circle Question: "Yes"

Cheselden's young patient was asked a question about cubes and globes, which tacitly required him to possess and apply concepts of depth to his new visual perception in order to distinguish between them. This is so on Reid's assumption that visual perception of depth is required to answer that question affirmatively. It is in that context that Reid insists that distance is not an object of sight, and that the subject could form no judgment about the distance of objects from him. He repeats Cheselden's claim that the boy thought that all the objects abutted his eye. He can't perceptually distinguish cubes from spheres in his visual field if he thinks that all seen shapes are touching his eye, because it is a necessary condition for individuating a cube in his visual field that he understands that at least some angled lines on the edges of the cube retreat from the eye's surface.

Here is another way of expressing the point behind this necessary condition. If the boy cannot determine the difference between a *square* and a *cube*, then he cannot make a bona fide claim to be able to distinguish a *globe* from a *cube*. This is because, for all the boy knows, he could be distinguishing what in his experience is a square from the globe (or, for all he knows, from the circle) even though he thinks he is distinguishing a cube from a globe. In Cheselden's report of the case, the boy's claim about the objects all abutting the surface of his eye implies, on Reid's interpretation, that the boy was not able to distinguish between a square and a cube. With these attempts to specify the conditions upon an answer we glimpse the depth of, and philosophical trouble generated by, Diderot's alteration of the question.

Reid's discussion of Saunderson's abilities perceptually to discriminate objects upon having his sight restored occurs in *Inquiry* 6.7, which we have just examined. Reid continues the debate in *Inquiry* 6.11 but to a different purpose. In 6.11 Reid hypothetically poses of Saunderson not a cube/sphere question, but a square/circle question. This passage is more explicitly directed at the Molyneux problem than is 6.7.

Why two distinct discussions both mentioning Molyneux-like problems? It seems open to Reid to reason as follows to eliminate the need for a second discussion:

Suppose I am correct in arguing that Saunderson would reply affirmatively to the cube/sphere question. Saunderson would give the same answer to a square/circle question. This is because a square/circle question is considerably easier to answer insofar as it removes from the question all the muddy, inchoate issues about depth and depth perception. So my argument for Saunderson's "yes" answer to the cube/sphere question entails a "yes" to the square/circle question. QED.

However, Reid did not approach the square/circle question in this way. He chooses to treat it more or less independently of his previous discussion. It is worthwhile to learn what motivates Reid to pose the question in yet another form here.

He begins this discussion by saying:

[L]et us suppose such a blind man as Dr Saunderson, having all the knowledge and abilities which a blind man may have, suddenly made to see perfectly. Let us suppose him kept from all opportunities of associating his ideas of sight with those of touch, until the former become a little familiar; and the first surprise, occasioned by objects so new, being abated, he has time to canvass them, and to compare them, in his mind, with the notions which he formerly had by touch; and, in particular, to compare, in his mind, that visible extension which his eyes present, with the extension in length and breadth with which he was before acquainted. (IHM 6.11, 117/155a)

Reid says Saunderson has "all the knowledge and abilities which a blind man may have." We might call Reid's Saunderson "tactilely omniscient," for he has every concept that can be suggested to him by his tactile sensations. This marks a great contrast with the actual subject Cheselden examined.

Someone such as Saunderson will be able to identify through vision "the figures of the first book of Euclid." The first book includes descriptions of squares, triangles, rhombuses, parallelograms, and other multilateral figures. Reid also discusses other plane figures, like circles, earlier in this context (IHM 6.11, 118/155a). This context is clearly about the subject's ability to distinguish between two-dimensional objects under Molyneux's conditions. Saunderson can answer such a question affirmatively.

Diderot reformulates Molyneux's question to be about two-dimensional figures in part because he believes that cube/sphere questions constitute an ambiguous amalgamation of distance questions with perceptual discrimination questions.[16] In cube/sphere questions the emphasis may be placed upon the newly sighted subject's ability to see three-dimensional objects like a cube and a sphere at all. Alternatively, the question may *presuppose* that the subject can see that an object exists in three dimensions, and instead focus upon the subject's ability perceptually to discriminate between and identify the two distinct three-dimensional objects. (This is the shift we identified in Molyneux's earliest questions in the 1688 letter.)

Due to this presupposition, Diderot's question is thought to offer a purer means to assess the extent of our cross-modal perceptual capacities. It is a mistake to think that the only means by which I can see what I can touch is by seeing three-dimensional objects. If I trace a square on a flat surface with my

---

[16] "I have substituted a circle for a sphere and a square for a cube, because there is reason to think that we only judge of distances by experience; and of course he who uses his eyes for the first time sees only surfaces without knowing anything of projection, since a projection consists in certain points appearing nearer to us than others" (Diderot 1972, 137).

finger, I tactilely experience a two-dimensional figure. Even if upon having my vision restored I cannot visually apprehend that a figure has depth, I would not for that reason alone be unable visually to apprehend that a figure is a square and not a circle. Diderot's question poses a test for the cross-modality of perception without assuming that, if perception is cross-modal, depth must be visually perceived.

The fact that Reid addresses a Diderot-style question indicates that he is savvy to this nuance of the debate. But for Reid the square/circle question does not take on the importance that it does for someone like Diderot himself. Diderot holds that the square/circle question can be answered affirmatively but that the cube/sphere question cannot. Since Reid tacitly offers an affirmative answer under the stringent conditions of the cube/sphere question by way of appeal to abstract reasoning, the square/circle question becomes less interesting. This is because Reid rejects Diderot's assumption that in order to answer a cube/sphere question affirmatively, the Molyneux subject must visually perceive the depth of cubes and spheres. Reid holds that Saunderson can distinguish the cube from the sphere *even though he cannot visually apprehend the depth properties of either the cube or sphere.*

9.5. The Role of Tactile Sensations in Affirmative Answers

Is it a necessary condition on an affirmative answer that the subject compare the representational features of his visible figures with his previous tactile experiences?

The answer to this question demarcates the boundary between what we might call "strongly affirmative" and "weakly affirmative" answers to Molyneux's questions. Leibniz brings some important qualifications to his affirmative response that render it only a weak "yes." Having felt cubes to have edges and points, and having felt spheres to have neither, the newly sighted person can correctly identify the sphere and cube as presented in his visual field. For Leibniz a "yes" will be forthcoming if the agent is informed that the two objects he is looking at are a cube and a globe, if the agent needn't answer immediately, and the agent compare his new visual ideas with his former tactile ideas of cubes and spheres.[17]

[17] "It may be that Mr Molyneux and the author of the *Essay* are not as far from my opinion as at first appears... If you will consider my reply, sir, you will see that I have included in it a condition

In the *New Essays* 2.9 §8, Leibniz says, "by applying rational principles to the sensory knowledge which he has already acquired by touch," the agent will be able to distinguish them. The newly sighted man can determine which figure is of the cube and which is of the sphere because "in the case of the sphere there are no distinguished points on the surface of the sphere taken in itself, since everything there is uniform and without angles, whereas in the case of the cube there are eight points which are distinguished from all the others" (Leibniz 1981, 136–7). The subject can compare what it was like to handle a cube and handle a sphere with what it is like to see the figure of a cube and see the figure of a sphere. Leibniz alleges that this comparison is of sufficient phenomenological richness that the subject can answer affirmatively.

On these grounds Leibniz agrees with Berkeley and Locke on a crucial presupposition about the meaning of Molyneux's problem: it can be resolved by determining the extent to which there is resemblance between our perceptual experiences across the sensory modalities of touch and sight. Locke and Berkeley happen to think that there is no resemblance of the relevant sort. Leibniz thinks that there is enough resemblance to allow the subject to map his tactile sensations of edges on to the straight lines in the visible figure of the cube. Leibniz's version of the question can be put as follows:

> (9.6) By the combination of (i) abstract reasoning, (ii) antecedent knowledge that the only objects in his visual field are a cube and a sphere, and (iii) successful comparison of aspects of tactile sensations that suggest cubes and spheres with seen visible figures that represent cubes and spheres, and prior to touching the objects in his visual field, could the subject distinguish the cube from the globe?

On the basis of (9.6.iii) Evans comments that Leibniz seems to be an advocate of Berkeley's general position about the acquisition and application of spatial concepts as requiring multi-modal experience (Evans 1985, 379–80). Both hold that the role of tactile sensations in an agent's behavioral framework is "the most fundamental issue" raised by Molyneux (Evans 1985, 372). We must compare tactile sensations or ideas with visual sensations or ideas. Leibniz thus offers a weak "yes" because it is beholden to this presupposition.

It appears that at least one of Reid's affirmative answers is committed to the same requirement. In *Inquiry* 6.11 Reid explicitly says that Saunderson would "compare ['ideas of sight'], in his mind, with the notions which he formerly

---

which can be taken to be implicit in the question: namely that it is merely a problem of telling which is which, and that the blind man knows that the two shaped bodies which he has to discern are before him and thus that each of the appearances which he sees is either that of a cube or that of a sphere" (Leibniz 1981, 2.9.8/136).

had by touch; and, in particular, to compare, in his mind, that visible extension which his eyes present, with the extension in length and breadth with which he was before acquainted" (IHM 6.11, 118/155a). Reid adds:

[W]hen this visible extension and figure are presented to his eye, will he be able to compare them with tangible extension and figure, and to perceive that the one has length and breadth as well as the other; that the one may be bounded by lines, either straight or curve, as well as the other. And, therefore, he will perceive that there may be visible as well as tangible circles, triangles, quadrilateral and multilateral figures. (IHM 6.11, 118/155a)

Reid envisions someone in Saunderson's situation employing all the resources at hand in an effort to answer Molyneux's question, including by comparing sensations. Reid does not say that the subject must do a comparison, but he suggests that through such a comparison the subject can answer "yes." So Leibniz and Reid, in *Inquiry* 6.11, offer a similar, weak answer.

Evans himself offers a strong "yes" because no comparison on the agent's part is required due to his quasi-transcendental considerations about concept identity. Evans hints that Reid offers a strong "yes" because Reid offers his affirmative answers *without* requiring that the subject engage in a cross-modal comparison of sensations. This runs against the passage just quoted from Reid, but Evans is correct about this. This is because Reid's answer in *Inquiry* 6.7 does not invoke any requirement that the subject compare sensations.

Strictly speaking, we need to distinguish between its being necessary for a "yes" answer *that a subject has tactile sensations at all* and its being necessary *that the subject compare his new visual experience with his former tactile sensations*. It is possible that tactile sensations are needed in order for the agent to understand the question, but that no comparison between tactile sensations is needed: that is, tactile sensations are needed in order to acquire the concepts "cube" and "sphere."

Yet the answer Reid offers in *Inquiry* 6.7, as posed of the visual representations of a cube and sphere, is constructed so that a "yes" is forthcoming even though Saunderson does not actively compare his experiences of touch with his new visual experiences. This feature of Reid's answer in *Inquiry* 6.7 makes it a strongly affirmative response, in contrast to Leibniz's weakly affirmative response. That is, Reid denies (9.7.iii) is a necessary condition on a "yes" answer. (This is not to say that Reid does not also offer a weakly affirmative response. He does, and we have studied it in *Inquiry* 6.11.)

To justify this claim, let's first summarize a few conclusions. First, Reid says that the Idomenians can possess concepts of a figure with four sides of equal lengths, for example. This generalizes to humans under the conditions of

Molyneux's questions. Suppose that, in addition to being congenitally blind, Saunderson had never experienced any tactile sensations. In adulthood his sight is restored, though he is still unfeeling. Reid would suggest that merely by reasoning through the definitions of the terms "square" and "circle," Saunderson could distinguish between them and offer up a "yes" answer. Thus, for the square/circle question, I suggest that Reid does not believe that any tactile sensations are necessary.

Next, could the Idomenians acquire concepts of the geometrical figures of cubes and spheres? In my discussion of geometrical visible figure above in §4.3, I described this form of visible figure as being the geometrical representation of the facing surfaces of a three-dimensional object as that object is modeled on the surface of a sphere in accordance with Reid's geometry. Reid explicitly says that Idomenians can have no notion of a third dimension (IHM 6.9, 106–7/149a). Nothing prevents them from seeing the visible figure of a cube and contrasting that with a visible figure of a sphere. But they are unable to have a concept of those figures as representing anything in three dimensions. This result generalizes to any unfeeling human subject. The implication is that tactile sensations of a cube are necessary to acquire the concept "cube" and understand the meaning of saying that the two-dimensional visible figure isomorphically represents a three-dimensional figure. This implies that in order to understand a question posed about the geometrical figures of a cube and sphere, the subject must have had some experience of a third dimension. (Reid gives no indication that the needed tactile experiences must be of cubes and spheres. Presumably a "yes" answer to Molyneux's question will be forthcoming so long as the agent can extrapolate from his tactile experience of cylinders and pyramids.)

As we turn from *Inquiry* 6.11 to *Inquiry* 6.7, Reid eschews talk of comparing information from touch and sight. Reid makes different remarks about the relation between tactile sensations and "yes" answers. Recall from our discussion of visible figure that visual sensations are unnecessary for the formation of Saunderson's concepts of geometrical visible figures. Blind Saunderson does not need visual sensations in order mentally to model the geometrical visible figures of specific objects. This is what leads Reid to say: "it is worthy of our observation, that there is very little of the knowledge acquired by sight, that may not be communicated to a man born blind" (IHM 6.2, 78–9/133b). However, to come to such understanding Saunderson must be provided with information derivative from tactile sensations. Distance concepts must enter his abstract reasoning about the way geometrical visible figure will appear to his eye in two ways. He must be given the size of the objects in three dimensions and their distance from his eye. So he must employ depth and distance concepts he acquires from touch in order to respond to Molyneux's questions affirmatively. This represents a distinct way in which tactile experience bears on "yes" answers.

At *Inquiry* 6.7 Reid says that he "require[s] no more knowledge in a blind man, in order to his being able to determine the visible figure of bodies, than that he can project the outline of a given body, upon the surface of a hollow sphere, whose centre is in the eye" (IHM 6.7, 95/142b). Here Reid tacitly implies that the blind person does not need to do any comparing of visual and tactile sensations in order to identify and distinguish between visible figures of different lengths and breadths. This is a feature that differentiates Reid's *Inquiry* 6.7 "yes" answer from Leibniz's "yes" answer. Reid does not require that the agent compare the degree of resemblance between a tactile sensation and a visual sensation.

We can see in Leibniz's writing on this matter the presence of what Reid took to be a hallmark of the Way of Ideas. Leibniz requires the comparison of tactile sensations with newly present visual sensations. This appeal to the agent's comparison resonates with the Way of Ideas' presupposition that sensations are needed to arrive at primary quality concepts. (This remains true even though Leibniz denies such a requirement in other contexts.) Reid says the Way of Ideas affirms that "no material thing, nor any quality of material things, can be conceived by us, or made an object of thought, until its image is conveyed to the mind by means of the senses." This implies that "to every quality and attribute of body we know or can conceive, there should be a sensation corresponding, which is the image and resemblance of that quality" (IHM 6.6, 91/140b). It was the burden of Chapter 3 to show how, through his Sensory Deprivation argument, Reid denies this condition for concept formation. His "yes" answer further confirms the conclusion of that argument.

9.6. "Yes" Answers and the Perception of Mind-independent Objects

Reid's discussion invites us to rethink what the Molyneux problem means for a theory of perception. I said at the outset of the chapter that through an analysis of Reid on Molyneux's problem we would draw together several of the themes discussed earlier in the book. In order to fulfill this promise I need to step back from the minutiae of Reid's arguments and discuss what he believes is the philosophical significance of the questions.

Most philosophers have taken the central consequence of the debate as illuminating the nature of cross-modal perception by asking such questions as: can information between our sensory systems be shared even without cross-modal experiences of similar objects? If so, then what is the extent of this sharing? If not, then has Locke accurately described the mind as a *tabula rasa*? Locke's negative answer to Molyneux's question shows that having cross-modal sensory experience is necessary for the formation of visible figure concepts. Berkeley's "no" confirms that the "objects" of which we speak are not mind-independent objects different in kind from our sensations. In broad terms Reid's affirmative answer shows that we can attain empirical knowledge about a mind-independent reality with a bare minimum of sensation experience.

To understand the way this fits into Reid's quiver of objections against the Way of Ideas, compare his approach to Molyneux's problem and his Sensory Deprivation argument. Through this argument and its accompanying thought experiment, Reid concludes that tactile sensations are *insufficient* for our formation of primary quality concepts (IHM 5.3, 61/122b). In addition to the fact that tactile sensations are insufficient for acquisition of primary quality concepts, comparing tactile sensations with new visual experiences is not necessary for affirmative answers to Molyneux's object-identification in the style of (9.2).[18] His "yes" answers to Molyneux's questions finish what his crucial test started.

The major thrust of Reid's response to Molyneux's questions is to reduce the dependence of concepts and knowledge upon sensations, and thereby oppose a core tenet of the Way of Ideas. We have seen this at work throughout this book, and especially in Chapter 5. Reid stands between these views and says that *some* sensations are needed for the formation of concepts of visible figure. This implies that Reid is not claiming that we have innate ideas of primary qualities. He argues that we needn't have any *visual* sensations in order to form concepts of visible figure. Hopkins emphasizes this point:

> Reid is pursuing a core ambition, that of showing, *contra* the Ideal system, that some of our most important concepts are not constitutively tied to sensation. He focuses on the concept *visible figure*, not just because it is in general his most extensive illustration of that point, but because, in the context of Molyneux's question, it allows him to argue the point in a distinctive way. If a blind subject can grasp that concept, it cannot be tied to sensation, since the blind lack *any* of the candidate sensations. (Hopkins 2005, 352)

Concepts that can be formed through the use of visual sensations need not be formed through the use of visual sensations. Framing Reid's response in

---

[18] This emphasis elucidates why our earlier discussion of the role of sensation in perception was attenuated. The most we could squeeze out of Reid's remarks on sensation was that tactile sensations are probably physically necessary for the acquisition of concepts involving depth and three-dimensional extension. The physical necessity of sensation thesis could not be given broader scope because Reid holds that we need not have visual sensations to form concepts of visible figures.

this manner reveals the extensive continuity between Reid's discussion of Molyneux's questions, his Sensory Deprivation argument, and his analysis of the mind-independence of visible figure.

The matchlessness of this plan and Reid's fascinating execution of it is so novel for the Early Modern period that it may be difficult to appreciate. But reconsidering core commitments of Hume and Berkeley can help us. One of Hume's claims about impressions and ideas—one of the "articles of inquisition"—is that each idea must be traceable back to a corresponding impression. This is why, for example, Hume worries about the missing shade of blue. To appreciate the anti-sensationism in Reid's answers to Molyneux we can see Reid's "yes" answer as offering another counterexample to Hume's thesis. According to the Way of Ideas, impressions determine the semantics of the idea and they provide the subject with the ability to acquire the idea in the first place (Hopkins 2005, 353). But Reid has shown that subjects are capable of forming rich visible figure concepts without any visual sensations, and with a minimal set of tactile sensations.

Hume misunderstood this theme in Reid's work, which is apparent from his comments upon Reid's Inquiry (which are reprinted in Wood 1986). The way Reid discharges sensations from the purposes they served in the systems of his predecessors led Hume to the inference that Reid endorses a theory of innate ideas. But the advanced copy of the Inquiry that Hume was able to read did not include the final, longest, and all-important chapter of the Inquiry about sight (Wood 1986, 413). Had he been, he would have more clearly understood why Reid does not rely upon innate ideas. Reid shows through Saunderson's case that, when human beings do their utmost with what they are provided through their senses, they can gain knowledge.

As Reid diminishes the role of sensations, he reclaims the role of the mind-independent world in determining the intentional objects of perceptions. Reid holds that the speculative principles about ideas, too frequently conflated with a commitment to empiricist accounts of perception, lead Berkeley and Locke astray on the Molyneux problem. Reid's response displays his Newtonian methodology, and contrasts with theirs.

Berkeley says nothing is like an idea but another idea. He repudiates representative realist versions of the Way of Ideas in favor of his idealism on these grounds. We cannot perceive mind-independent primary qualities because in order to do so there must be a resemblance between my sensory idea and my quality idea. Berkeley's argument led him to claim that there was also no resemblance between what we see and what we touch, and thus there are no "common sensibles"—no qualities perceived by more than one sense faculty. Reid believes that his study of Molyneux's questions rebuts this claim. He says:

Hence it appears that small visible figures (and such only can be seen distinctly at one view) have not only a resemblance to the plain tangible figures which have the same name, but *are to all sense the same*: so that, if Dr Saunderson had been made to see, and had attentively viewed the figures of the first book of Euclid, he might, by thought and consideration, without touching them, have found out that they were the very figures he was before so well acquainted with by thought. (IHM 6.11, 118/155a–b, my emphasis)

Reid infers that "Bishop Berkeley therefore proceeds upon a capital mistake, in supposing that there is no resemblance betwixt the extension, figure, and position which we see, and that which we perceive by touch" (IHM 6.11, 119/155b).

One might object that Reid is willing to proceed on this point without having accurate experimental data at hand. I accused Berkeley of doing just that; perhaps a defender of Berkeley would reply with the same charge. True, the Cheselden case aside, Reid is willing to give an answer to the hypothetical question. But he cautiously answers this hypothetical question, and does not universally generalize in the way others had. Some blind people, upon being given sight, can distinguish the visible figures of cubes from the figures of spheres. Others cannot. Besides, through his research into the nature and phenomena of vision—work on upside-down retinal images, parallel motion of the eyes, images on both retinas, and research on the phenomenon of squinting—Reid reasons from an extensive body of empirical evidence. This informs his inferences about the physical abilities of the blind to create mental models for visible figures.

Good evidence of his Newtonian approach to Molyneux lies in the chief implication of his affirmative answer. Berkeley claims that objects of sight and of touch are incommensurable. If one is concerned to preserve our causal relations to the mind-independent world in our perceptual experience, then Berkeley's response to Molyneux is a notable disappointment. According to Reid, the objects of sight and touch are unified in mind-independent space and "are to all sense the same." With his defense of the homogeneity of the objects of perception across the senses Reid argues that tangible and visible experience is integrated. Reid believes this result to be of paramount importance for natural science:

The rules [geometers] have demonstrated about the various projections of the sphere, about the appearances of the planets in their progressions, stations, and retrogradations, and all the rules of perspective, are built on the supposition that the objects of sight are external. They can each of them be tried in thousands of instances. ... Add to this, that, upon the contrary hypothesis, to wit, that the objects of sight are internal, no account can be given of any one of those appearances, nor any physical cause assigned why a visible object should, in any one case, have one apparent figure and magnitude rather than another (EIP 2.14, 183/305a).

The foundation for the triumph of a unified perceptual space lies in Reid's theory of vision. The Molyneux problem composes an intriguing and rigorous test case for the application of Reid's theory of vision to a perceptual problem.

Due to the conceptually tight relation between the objects of vision and of touch, Reid grounds a realist science of vision—a feat made difficult for his predecessors. For Berkeley such a relation, and a science, is in principle impossible, or so it is argued (Falkenstein 2004, 165). Reid instead argues that visual space is fundamentally objective across perceivers, and is not relative but real. This answer proceeds from his earlier work on the geometry of visibles and the perceptual and ontological status of visible figure. Reid's insistence on the objectivity and unity of space spans across one's sense of vision and of touch, as well as across perceivers themselves. In his discussion of Molyneux Reid adopts a position with respect to the nature of our awareness of space. But this is of a piece with his understanding of the objectivity and unity of space itself. Reid's sentiments about the vituperative controversy early in the eighteenth century surrounding the status of space as absolute (Newton and Clarke) or relative (Berkeley and Leibniz) are clearly with Newton. At the highest remove, the implications of Reid's response to Molyneux's questions resonate with Reid's claims on behalf of Newton, Clarke, and Colin Maclaurin that space is absolute and objective, and that there is an absolute frame of reference. I leave the explorations of this connection, and of Reid's views on the nature of space, for another time.

9.7. Summary

Reid's reflections on the unity of the senses and on our multifaceted perceptual relationships to the mind-independent world arise through his discussion of Molyneux's questions. A standard form of Molyneux's question is: "Can someone who has been blind from birth and who has newly been given sight, determine through vision alone which object in her field of vision is a globe and which is a cube?" In order to identify and appreciate Reid's responses to these questions, we first determined the forms that different versions of the questions have taken. Reid provides different answers to different historical forms of the question. As posed to young, inexperienced, and uneducated people, Reid claims that the answer is "no," while when the question is posed of people adept at geometry and spatial reasoning the answer is "yes."

We considered what occurs when Diderot's alteration in the content of the question—a shift between three-dimensional objects to two-dimensional objects—is made. Here Reid also answers affirmatively. His geometry for visibles serves his "yes" answers.

Reflection upon these monosyllabic answers offers considerable insight into Reid's theory of perception, and its differences with competing theories. Reid is committed to commonsensical claims about our relation to the mind-independent world. We routinely perceive things in it. We routinely perceive the same mind-independent objects over time and with different sense faculties. We perceive the same objects. We routinely have knowledge of our perceptual beliefs. "No" answers to Molyneux questions threaten commitments such as these by dividing our perceptual apparatus into incommensurable functional units, by implying that ideas mediate our perceptions, and by inhibiting scientific inquiry about the mind-independent world.

I drew together aspects of Reid's theory of perception by explaining the correlation between Reid's Sensory Deprivation argument, his theory of sensation, and his answer to Molyneux. Reid claims that Saunderson can attain knowledge of geometrical figures, which Saunderson could apply to the seen figures of globes and cubes, were he given sight. This resonates with Reid's discussion of the relation between sensation and perception because he believes that sensations are not necessary for perception and perceptual knowledge. In this way his response to Molyneux's problem finished what his Sensory Deprivation argument started: sensations need not and in fact do not obstruct our perceptual capacities.

10

Empiricism and the Way of Ideas

The purpose of this book has been to interpret and critically evaluate Reid's theory of perception. I have referred to Reid's predecessors and his relation to them in the course of achieving this goal, but it has not been a priority to discuss to whom he responds with which features of his theory of perception. Too often Reid's theories are presented as mere responses to the Way of Ideas, as though his own philosophical system does not merit detailed research. Due to this systemic tendency in the presentation of Reid's views, and to Reid's status as a peripheral figure in the Early Modern canon, I conclude this book by comparing and contrasting Reid's method with what has come to be known as "empiricism."

In some sense we should all be "Newtonians." Likewise, we should all be empiricists in the vapid sense that we should modulate our beliefs to experience. In the eighteenth century, this meant something important. In the twenty-first, in the context of analytic philosophy or the natural sciences, it does not retain vim and vigor. One question that emerges as a way to clarify the problem is this: what are the proper aims of the empiricist?

For Reid, the aims are to ground knowledge of self and world. Reid emphasizes the role of broadly epistemic concerns throughout his discussion of perception because, and not in spite of, his enduring aim to demarcate the limits of knowledge. Whereas Hume attempts to reduce philosophical questions to psychological questions by searching for naturalistic mechanisms to explain our ideas, Reid turns what had been thought to be metaphysical questions into epistemic ones.

Reid distinguishes between types of perceptual content—original, inferential, and acquired—in virtue of their varying epistemic character. His interest in the preservation of privileged access leads him to take uncommon steps to preserve it, resulting in his construction of an unusual account of fictional objects perhaps unique in the history of philosophy. His distinction between primary and secondary qualities is drawn in virtue of the immediacy of our concepts of the respective types of qualities. He sees Molyneux's problem from a striking new angle and argues that the use of all our epistemic faculties, including our ability to reason a priori, yields an affirmative answer to the question.

Does this render Reid an empiricist? I want to clarify in what senses Reid's system bears the hallmarks of empiricism and in what senses it does not. Unfortunately, the history of the term "empiricism" and its cognates has been influenced more by polemical concerns than by philosophical argument. The briefest historical tour through the use of the term shows the intractability of applying it with much propriety.

Bacon, the first to put cognates of the term to philosophical use, describes empiricists as those who "like ants, simply accumulate and use; Rationalists, like spiders, spin webs from themselves; the way of the bee is in between" (Bacon 2000, 1.95/79). For Bacon, empiricists are those who make observations, and extrapolate their results only in order to infer judgments about specific future events; empiricists do not formulate general laws. But Reid believes that observing the world, making inductions on the basis of those observations, and finally formulating laws is precisely the task of natural philosophy. So Reid is not an "empiricist" in Bacon's sense; he is able to find a home in Bacon's third category. In fact, Reid admires bees, and their seemingly mathematical instincts in the creation of their hexagonal cells, which are designed "in order to make the greatest possible saving, or the least expense, of material and labour" (EAP 2.1.2, 546b). The fact that it is the bee who crafts this idealized construction would not have been lost on someone who kept Bacon and his vision for science close to heart.

Leibniz follows Bacon on this use of the term in some ways, but he makes the distinction between empiricists and rationalists clearly epistemic. Rationalists claim to have some a priori knowledge of substantive or synthetic truths, while empiricists deny having such knowledge (Leibniz 1981, 50). As for Reid, he claims that some synthetic truths can be known a priori. Reid has a lengthy list of "first principles of necessary truth" that includes theses in ethics, for example "that no man ought to be blamed for what it was not in his power to hinder" (EIP 6.6, 494/453b), and in metaphysics, for example "that whatever begins to exist, must have a cause which produced it" (EIP 6.6, 497/455a). Reid is not an empiricist on Leibniz's definition of the term, nor does it seem that Reid is an empiricist in the sense in which Locke, Berkeley, and Hume are called the "British Empiricists," for Reid posits original principles that these philosophers do not—and denies their original principles. Reid's empiricism "is not, as in Berkeley and Hume, a matter of limiting what we can know to the immediate contents of experience but of interpreting the natural signs in sensation, much as we must interpret artificial signs in conventional languages" (Jacquette 2003, 295).

Reid's empiricism is not what Kant in the *Critique of Pure Reason* famously identifies with the antitheses of his four antinomies. According to Kant, the empiricist believes: (i) that the world has no beginning in time and no limits in space; (ii) that there is nothing in the world that is simple; (iii) that there is no freedom, or in other words, that everything in the world is the product of laws of nature; and (iv) that there is no necessarily existent being (A426–61/B494–504). Reid's faith commitments and views about agent causation preclude him from being Kant's sort of empiricist.

According to these and other *historical* definitions of empiricism, Reid is thus not an empiricist. Reid's failure to fit the inherited paradigm for empiricism is no coincidence, given that Reid is arguably the only Early Modern philosopher who both understood Newton and employed Newton's method. According to Larry Laudan:

Although histories of philosophy often bracket Newton with the classical British empiricists, Locke, Berkeley, and Hume, such a conjunction is more misleading than illuminating, at least so far as the history of the philosophy of science is concerned. Indeed, those three empiricists are surprisingly un-Newtonian when it comes to questions of scientific method. Locke, for instance, died before most of Newton's *pronunciamentos* on methodology were published, so we look in vain for signs of Newtonian influence there. Berkeley, on the other hand, though undoubtedly aware of Newton's inductive empiricism, developed a theory of scientific method and concept formation which is almost as alien to Newton's views as any could be.... The situation is not vastly different with Hume, who seems to have taken little or no cognizance of Newton's numerous methodological *obiter dicta*. In fact, when Hume did come to grips with methodological issues (e.g., induction and causality), his conclusions were diametrically opposed to the then usual interpretation of Newton's doctrines... [M]ost of the available evidence seems to indicate that Reid was the first major British philosopher to take Newton's opinions on induction, causality, and hypotheses seriously. (Laudan 1970, 105–6; see Ellos 1981, 24)

Reid's devotion to Newton forms the methodological basis of his repudiations of hypotheses about ideas and the foundation of his realist theory of perception.

The subtitle of Hume's *Treatise* pays homage to Newton and Newton's method. Hume insists upon and sanctions the antagonism of Newtonian natural philosophy to human knowledge. Newton merits the highest praise from Hume as being "the greatest and rarest genius that ever arose for the ornament and instruction of the species." He says: "While Newton seemed to draw off the veil from some of the mysteries of nature, he shewed at the same time the imperfections of the mechanical philosophy; and thereby restored her ultimate secrets to that obscurity in which they ever did and ever will remain" (Hume 1770, viii, 350–1). Through Hume's lens, Newton aspires to very little knowledge of the world. Through Reid's lens, it is Hume, not Newton, who is the skeptic. Reid believes Newton is principally a scientist who seeks knowledge of the world consistent with an appropriately modest estimation of the human capacity for doing so. Given this confluence of interpretations, Hume's claim to extend Newton's work strikes Reid as mistaken.

Reid's opposition to the Way of Ideas is broad in scope, encompassing refutations of the "British Empiricists" and "Continental Rationalists," and their first principles and final conclusions. Reid's diagnostic history of philosophy focuses upon errors at the outset of the philosophical systems spawned by the Way of Ideas. He offers his reproach both for the epistemically skeptical conclusions of the "British Empiricists" and for the metaphysically fanciful conclusions of the "Continental Rationalists." In his theory of perception, he is more concerned about warding off skepticism than he is in refuting continental theories of perception. However, it is important for Reid to set limits upon his empiricist method in order to blaze a path between skepticism and hypotheses, like Leibniz's, that appear fantastic from the point of view of empirical science.

Here Newton's comments in the General Scholium on hypotheses (inserted into the second edition of the *Principia*, twenty-six years after the first) make their way into Reid's method. Newton says:

I have not as yet been able to deduce from phenomena the reason for these properties of gravity, and I do not feign hypotheses. For whatever is not deduced from the phenomena must be called a hypothesis; and hypotheses, whether metaphysical or physical, or based on occult qualities, or mechanical, have no place in experimental philosophy. In this experimental philosophy, propositions are deduced from the phenomena and are made general by induction. (Newton 1726/1999, 943)

Reid's devotion to Newton's implicit commitment to parsimony can be debated (see Dea 2005) and is clearly not beyond criticism (see Nichols 2007, and Tapper 2003). Nonetheless, when taken as a middle way between two traditions, Reid approximates Newton's instructions about hypotheses better than other philosophers, even if his replies to Hartley and Priestley about method are unconvincing.

Reid says that in practice, the "Newtonian philosopher inquires what proof can be offered" for a phenomenon, such as "the existence of magnetic effluvia, and can find none. He therefore holds it as a fiction, a hypothesis; and he has learned that hypotheses ought to have no place in the philosophy of nature." Instead, "his business, as a philosopher, is only to find from experiment the laws by which it is regulated in all cases" (EAP 1.7, 526b). Finding laws is the principle aim of the experimental method. Laws mustn't be confused with hypotheses or with efficient causes. The "grandest discovery ever made in natural philosophy," the law of gravitation, did not delude the discoverer into thinking he had found a "real cause." Reid says that when natural philosophers "pretend to show the cause of any phenomenon of nature, they mean by the cause, a law of nature of which that phenomenon is a necessary consequence" (EAP 1.7, 527a).

While certain broad emphases can be used to demarcate the British Empiricists from philosophers of the Continent in the century and a half before Reid begins writing, Reid finds an unsettling commitment to theses that are not the product of experience in fellow British philosophers. By this I refer to Reid's devotion to Newton's first rule of philosophy, which has two components: the truth condition and the sufficiency condition: "No more causes of natural things should be admitted than are both true and sufficient to explain their phenomena" (Newton 1999, 794; see Section 1.1). If Reid were forced to choose one maxim as most influential to his philosophical method and his empiricism, this would be it.

This rule provides a needed corrective for the errors Reid finds promulgated in the history of philosophy. Those errors have to do with the multiplication of hypotheses. "Hypothesis" is best defined for Reid in terms of Newton's first rule. Hypotheses are proposed explanations of natural phenomena that meet only the sufficiency condition of the first rule (Callergård 2006, chapter 3). This is why Reid was incensed at Priestley's reformulation of the first rule, which omitted the truth condition. "The first of these rules as laid down by Sir Isaac Newton, he [Priestley] says, is that we are to *admit no more causes of things than are sufficient to explain their appearances.*" But, Reid asks:

Did the interpreter imagine that these two phrases, *such as are true* and *such as are sufficient to explain their appearances* meant one and the same thing, and that Sir Isaac in expressing a rule had been guilty of an useless tautology which needed his correction? If the words themselves and the character of the Author had admitted this construction, it is precluded by the disjunctive particle *both*, which must imply two things and can never be applied to one. (AC 186)

Reid continues his denunciation of Priestley by taking aim at features of his materialism that Reid believes fail to abide by the full version of the first rule. An explanation fails to meet the test of the first rule if it has no source in observation.

Following on the first rule is Newton's second, which is also dear to Reid. Newton joins the first and the second by "Therefore" implying that the two are logically related. Of the second rule, he writes: "Therefore, the causes assigned to natural effects of the same kind must be, so far as possible, the same" (Newton 1999, 795). Reid comments: "The proper caution therefore with regard to this Rule is, not that we assign effects to the same cause *as far as is possible*, but that we be sure the effects be of the same kind before we assign them to the same cause" (AC 189). Reid endeavors to interpret Newton as using the second rule to caution natural philosophers enamored of simplicity. Robert Callergård explains that Reid departs significantly from Newton's own purpose in introducing the second rule; Reid sides with Bacon instead (Callergård 2006, chapter 3).

But insisting on the misleading capacity of simplicity resonates with Reid's diagnosis of the errors of the Way of Ideas. In perception, the Way of Ideas holds that our experience can be accounted for by a commitment to the existence and immediate awareness of mental intermediaries. But this alluring hypothesis is too simple to account for the complexity of our perceptual experience, and arguments on behalf of the Way of Ideas, for example the perceptual relativity argument, make assumptions that oversimplify the data.

Reid says that his philosophical doctrines are built from the ruins of those he criticizes. And his criticisms of earlier theories generally hinge either upon showing that they oversimplify data and fall afoul of the second rule, or upon showing that they fail truly to account for the phenomena they seek to explain and fall afoul of the first. Sometimes theories are guilty of both errors.

Hume's foundational division between impressions and ideas is one such hypothesis. It is not itself the product of the use of the experimental method. Reid believes it is facile and derives neither from our observations of the workings of our minds nor from our observations of the natural world:

Hume would argue that if it be neither an idea nor an impression, it cannot be. But it will equally follow from these premises that these divisions are imperfect. Upon this account, till they are able to demonstrate the perfection of them, we ought never to look upon them as conclusive, nor exclude any one thing from being because our notions of it don't tally with the beds made for them. (Edinburgh MS Reid 1763 Dk. 3.2, Lecture 15)

We are not to begin with a conceptual division between types of notions and apply it to the world. Hume's "articles of inquisition" violate Newton's first and second rules. If adherence to Newton's first and second rules for natural philosophy is necessary in order for a philosopher to qualify as an empiricist, Hume is not an empiricist. Instead, Hume has engaged in hypotheses on the grounds that they are the simplest explanations available.

Reid is preoccupied with avoiding hypotheses—to a fault. He goes so far as to restrict laws to phenomena. Laws do not describe efficient causes. He declares that: "supposing natural philosophy brought to its utmost perfection, it does not discover the efficient cause of any one phenomenon in nature" (EAP 1.7, 527a; see Dea 2005 and Tuggy 2000). This methodological limitation on natural philosophy appears to commit Reid to something akin to contemporary "constructive empiricism" about scientific explanation. Reid should be credited for pouring those foundations even if he did not always build directly, or wisely, upon them.

Bas van Fraassen (to whom the foregoing discussion in this chapter is indebted) claims that the rejection of metaphysical theorizing is central to modern-day empiricism. Van Fraassen and Reid differ sharply about central issues in the philosophy of science, including whether the designedness of the world should be a feature of scientific explanations and whether every event has a cause. Despite these disparities, van Fraassen makes comments about contemporary analytic metaphysics that profoundly resonate with Reid's critique of his predecessors. Consider these two remarks:

I see metaphysical concoctions not as underpinnings but as the canopies of baroque four-poster beds ... Metaphysical theories purport to interpret what we already understand to be the case. But to interpret is *to interpret into* something, something granted as already understood. Paradoxically, metaphysicians interpret what we initially understand into something hardly anyone understands, then insist that we cannot do without that. (2002, 3)

What exactly are the targets of the empiricist critique? As I see it, the targets of traditional empiricism are forms of metaphysics which (a) give absolute primacy to demands for explanation, and (b) are satisfied with explanations-by-postulate, that is, explanations that postulate the reality of certain entities or aspects of the world not already evident in experience. (2002, 37)

Van Fraassen argues that the empiricist is one who is willing to reject "demands for explanation at certain crucial points." Reid refuses to capitulate to demands for explanation, satisfied to note the darkness surrounding our best efforts. As for (b), there can be no more infamous explanation-by-postulate in Early Modern philosophy than the multifarious appeal to "ideas"—as Locke defines it, "whatever is the object of understanding when a man thinks"—which Reid battled throughout his work. Van Fraassen and Reid share an interest in criticizing metaphysicians who demand explanations in cases that seem to be theoretically underdetermined.

Some of van Fraassen's comments could be interchanged with remarks from Reid without much notice. To proponents of what he dubs the "metaphysical enterprise," van Fraassen pleads: "But most of all, please admit that this putative pursuit of truth runs on a fuel of probabilities and values extraneous to its enterprise. For what is there inside this project besides the delight in puzzle-solving?" (2002, 17). Reid remarks, of proponents of the Way of Ideas, that: "When a man has laid out all his ingenuity in fabricating a system, he views it with the eye of a parent; he strains phenomena to make them tally with it, and makes it look like the work of nature" (EIP 6.8, 535/472b). This statement is as true and biting in 1785 as it is in 2002 (see Nichols 2006). Reid holds that this is, lamentably, the inheritance of the history of philosophy:

The dark cave and shadows of Plato, the species of Aristotle, the films of Epicurus, and the ideas and impressions of modern Philosophers, are the productions of human fancy, successively invented to satisfy the eager desire of knowing how we perceive external objects; but they are all deficient in the two essential characters of a true and philosophical account of the phaenomenon: For we neither have any evidence of their existence, nor, if they did exist, can it be shewn how they would produce perception. (EIP 2.20, 226/326b)

Reid and van Fraassen both attempt to renew philosophy by refocusing attention to worthwhile epistemological questions, and embrace a contented quietude about questions that cannot be answered. In so doing, they acclaim distinctively Newtonian natural science as the paradigm of rational inquiry.

Reid's metaphors for the Way of Ideas differ with van Fraassen's for what he dubs "the metaphysical enterprise." Van Fraassen says he sees "a dead man walking." Its hypotheses are like "the canopies of a baroque four-poster bed." Reid describes the Way of Ideas' tendency to exorcise sound philosophy as being like "the Trojan horse" that "carries in its belly death and destruction to all science and common sense" (IHM 6.1, 75/132b). The Way of Ideas, he says, "is a rope of sand" (IHM 5.7, 70/128b). But most evocative of Reid's metaphors and similes, and most instructive about Reid's response to it, is another. The Way of Ideas, he says, is "like Nebuchadnezzar's image, whose feet were partly of iron and partly of clay" (EIP 6.4, 457/436b). Reid refers to the dream recorded in the Book of Daniel. Daniel responds to the king's request for a statement and interpretation of the king's dream with this:

Thou, O king, sawest, and behold a great image. This great image, whose brightness was excellent, stood before thee; and the form thereof was terrible. This image's head was of fine gold, his breast and his arms of silver, his belly and his thighs of brass, his legs of iron, his feet part of iron and part of clay. Thou sawest till that a stone was cut out without hands, which smote the image upon his feet that were of iron and clay, and brake them to pieces. Then was the iron, the clay, the brass, the silver, and the gold, broken to pieces together, and became like the chaff of the summer threshing floors;

and the wind carried them away, that no place was found for them: and the stone that smote the image became a great mountain, and filled the whole earth. (Daniel 2: 31–5)

The Way of Ideas was a beautiful conceptual artifice, but it was constructed atop foundations that failed to bear its weight. Reid supplants it with the theory of the mind that I have attempted to present through an analysis of the intellectual power of perception. By building his account of perception upon sound meta-philosophical foundations Reid has placed knowledge of self and world on firmer footing.

Bibliography

Alexander, Peter (1977). "The Names of Secondary Qualities," *Proceedings of the Aristotelian Society* 77: 203–20.

——(1985). *Ideas, Qualities and Corpuscles: Locke and Boyle on the External World*. New York: Cambridge University Press.

Allen, Richard (2002). *David Hartley on Human Nature*. Albany, NY: SUNY.

Alston, William (1985). "Thomas Reid on Epistemic Principles," *History of Philosophy Quarterly* 2: 435–52.

——(1989). "Reid on Perception and Conception," in Dalgarno and Matthews, eds., 1989, pp. 35–47.

——(1993). *The Reliability of Sense Perception*. Ithaca, NY: Cornell University Press.

Angell, R. B. (1974). "The Geometry of Visibles," *Noûs* 8: 87–117.

Atherton, Margaret (1984). " 'Suppose I am Pricked with a Pin': Locke, Reid and the Implications of Representationalism," *Pacific Philosophical Quarterly* 65: 149–65.

——(1990). *Berkeley's Revolution in Vision*. Ithaca, NY: Cornell University Press.

Aquinas, Thomas (1981). *The Summa Theologica of St. Thomas Aquinas*, ed. and trans. Fathers of the English Dominican Province, 2nd and revised edn., 5 vols. Allen, Tex.: Thomas More.

Armstrong, David M. (1973). *Belief, Truth, and Knowledge*. Cambridge: Cambridge University Press.

Bacon, Francis (1831). *The Works of Francis Bacon*, ed. Basil Montagu, 14 vols. London: William Pickering.

——(2000). *The New Organon*, L. Jardine, ed. M. Silverthorne, trans. Cambridge: Cambridge University Press.

Barker, Stephen F., and Beauchamp, Tom L., eds. (1976). *Thomas Reid: Critical Interpretation*. Philadelphia: Philosophical Monographs 3.

Barron, William (1806). *Lectures on Belles Lettres and Logic*. 2 vols. London: Longman, Hurst, Rees & Orme.

Beanblossom, Ronald E, (1975). "In Defense of Thomas Reid's Use of 'Suggestion'," *Grazer Philosophische Studien* 1: 19–24.

Beattie, James (2000). *An Essay on the Nature and Immutability of Truth*, ed. J. Fieser, *Opposition to Sophistry and Scepticism*. Bristol: Thoemmes Press.

Benbaji, Hagit (2000). "Reid's View of Aesthetic and Secondary Qualities," *Reid Studies* 3: 31–46.

Bennett, Jonathan (1971). *Locke, Berkeley, Hume: Central Themes*. New York: Oxford University Press.

——(2001). *Learning from Six Philosophers*, 2 vols. New York: Oxford University Press.

Ben Zeev, Aaron (1986). "Reid's Direct approach to Perception," *Studies in the History and Philosophy of Science* 17: 99–114.

___ (1989a). "Reexamining Berkeley's Notion of Suggestion," *Conceptus* 23: 21–30.

___ (1989b). "Reid's Opposition to the Theory of Ideas," in Dalgarno and Matthews, eds., 1989, pp. 91–101.

___ (1990). "Reid and the Cartesian Framework," *Journal of the History of the Behavioral Sciences* 26: 38–47.

Berkeley, George (1948). *The Works of George Berkeley*, 9 vols, eds. A. Luce and T. Jessop. London: Nelson and Sons.

Block, Ned (1995). "A Confusion About a Function of Consciousness," *Behavioral and Brain Sciences* 18: 227–47.

Boghossian, Paul (1989). "Content and Self-Knowledge," *Philosophical Topics* 17: 5–26.

BonJour, Laurence (1991). "Is Thought a Symbolic Process?", *Synthese* 89: 331–52.

Brentano, Franz (1973). *Psychology from an Empirical Standpoint*, ed. O. Kraus and trans. A. C. Rancurello, D. B. Terrell, and L. L. McAlister. London: Routledge & Kegan Paul.

Brett, George Sidney (1921). *A History of Psychology*. London: G. Allen & Company, Ltd.

Brooks, G. P. (1976). "The Faculty Psychology of Thomas Reid," *Journal of the History of the Behavioral Sciences* 12: 65–77.

Brown, Thomas (1828). *Lectures on the Philosophy of the Human Mind*, 2 vols. Hallowell, Me.: Glazier & Co.

Browne, Peter (1728). *The Procedure, Extent, and Limits of Human Understanding*. London: W. Innys.

Buras, J. Todd (2002). "The Problem with Reid's Direct Realism," *Philosophical Quarterly* 52: 457–77.

___ (2005). "The Nature of Sensations in Reid," *History of Philosophy Quarterly* 22: 221–38.

Butts, Robert, and Davis, John, eds. (1970). *The Methodological Heritage of Newton*. Toronto: Toronto University Press.

Callergård, Rabert (1999). "The Hypothesis of Ether and Reid's Interpretation of Newton's First Rule of Philosophizing," *Synthese* 120: 19–26.

___ (2006). "An Essay on Thomas Reid's Philosophy of Science," PhD dissertation, Stockholm University.

Cantor, G. N. (1971). "Henry Brougham and the Scottish Methodological Tradition," *Studies in the History of Philosophy of Science*, Part A, 2: 69–89.

Cartwright, R. (1960). "Negative Existentials," *Journal of Philosophy* 57: 629–39.

Cassam, Quassim (1997). *Self and World*. Oxford: Oxford University Press.

Castagnetto, Susan V. (1992). "Reid's Answer to Abstract Ideas," *Journal of Philosophical Research* 17: 39–60.

Chappell, Vere (1989). "The Theory of Sensations," in Dalgarno and Matthews, eds., 1989, pp. 49–63.

___ (1991). "Locke's Theory of Ideas," in *The Cambridge Companion to Locke*, ed. V. Chappell. Cambridge: Cambridge University Press, pp. 26–55.

Cheselden, William (1728). "An Account of some Observations made by a young Gentleman, who was born blind, or lost his Sight so early, that he had no Remembrance of ever having seen, and was couch'd between 13 and 14 Years of Age," *Philosophical Transactions of the Royal Society* pp. 54–6; reprinted in M. Degaaner 1996, pp. 447–50.

Chisholm, Roderick (1957). *Perceiving: A Philosophical Study.* Ithaca, NY: Cornell University Press.

Cohen, I. Bernard (1962). "The First English Version of Newton's *Hypotheses non fingo*," *Isis* 53: 379–88.

Condillac, Abbé de, Etienne Bonnot (1982). *Treatise on Sensations*, trans. F. Philip. *Philosophical Writings of Etienne Bonnot, Abbé de Condillac*, 2 vols. Hillsdale, NJ: Lawrence Erlbaum.

Copenhaver, Rebecca (2004). "A Realism for Reid: Mediated but Direct," *British Journal for the History of Philosophy* 12: 61–74.

——— (2005). "Reid on Consciousness." Unpublished.

——— (2006). "Is Reid a Mysterian?", *Journal for the History of Philosophy* 44: 449–66.

Cummins, Phillip (1974). "Reid's Realism," *Journal of the History of Philosophy* 12: 317–40.

——— (1975). "Berkeley's 'Ideas of Sense'," *Noûs* 9: 55–72.

——— (1987). "On the Status of the Visuals in Berkeley's *New Theory of Vision*," ed. E. Sosa, *Essays on the Philosophy of George Berkeley.* Dordrecht: D. Reidel, pp. 165–94.

——— (1990). "Pappas on the Role of Sensations in Reid's Theory of Perception," *Philosophy and Phenomenological Research* 50: 755–62.

Cuneo, Terence (2003). "Reidian Moral Perception," *Canadian Journal of Philosophy* 33: 229–58.

——— (2004). "Reid's Moral Philosophy," in Cuneo and Van Woudenberg, eds., 2004, pp. 243–66.

——— and Van Woudenberg, René, eds. (2004). *The Cambridge Companion to Thomas Reid.* New York: Cambridge University Press.

Dalgarno, Melvin, and Matthews, Eric, eds. (1989). *The Philosophy of Thomas Reid.* Dordrecht: Kluwer.

Daniels, Norman (1976). "On Having Concepts 'By Our Constitution'," in Barker and Beauchamp, eds., 1976, pp. 35–43.

——— (1989). *Thomas Reid's Inquiry: The Geometry of Visibles and The Case for Realism.* Stanford: Stanford University Press.

Davenport, Alan (1987). "Reid's Indebtedness to Bacon," *Monist* 70: 496–507.

Davis, John (1960). "The Molyneux Problem," *Journal for the History of Ideas* 21: 392–408.

Dea, Shannon (2005). "Thomas Reid's Rigourised Anti-hypotheticalism," *Journal of Scottish Philosophy* 3: 123–38.

de Bary, Phillip (2002). *Thomas Reid and Scepticism: His Reliabilist Response.* London: Routledge.

De Beer, E., ed. (1978). *The Correspondence of John Locke*. New York: Oxford University Press.

Degenaar, Marjolein (1996). *Molyneux's Problem*. Dordrecht: Kluwer.

DeRose, Keith (1989). "Reid's Anti-Sensationalism and His Realism," *Philosophical Review* 98: 313–48.

Descartes, René (1984–91). *The Philosophical Writings of Descartes*, 3 vols, ed. and trans. J. Cottingham, R. Stoothoof, and D. Murdoch. Cambridge: Cambridge University Press.

Ellos, William (1981). *Thomas Reid's Newtonian Realism*. Washington, DC: University Press of America.

Dicker, George (1977). "Primary and Secondary Qualities: A Proposed Modification of the Lockean Account," *Southern Journal of Philosophy* 15: 457–71.

——— (1998). *Hume's Epistemology and Metaphysics*. London: Routledge.

Diderot, Denis (1972). *Diderot's Early Philosophical Works*, ed. and trans. M. Jourdain. New York: Burt Franklin.

——— (1983). "Thomas Reid's Analysis of Sensation," *New Scholasticism* 57: 104–14.

Emerson, Roger (1989). "Science and Moral Philosophy in the Scottish Enlightenment," in Stewart 1990, pp. 11–36.

Evans, Gareth (1985). *Gareth Evans: Collected Papers*, ed. A. Phillips. Oxford: Clarendon Press.

——— (1996). "Molyneux's Question", in *Gareth Evans: Collected Papers*. Oxford: Oxford University Press, pp. 364–99.

Everson, Stephen (1988). "The Difference between Thinking and Feeling," *Mind* 97: 401–13.

Falkenstein, Lorne (2000). "Reid's Account of Localization," *Philosophy and Phenomenological Research* 61: 305–28.

——— (2002). "Hume and Reid on the Perception of Hardness," *Hume Studies* 28: 27–48.

——— (2004). "Reid and Smith on Vision," *Journal of Scottish Philosophy* 2: 103–18.

——— (2005). "Condillac's Paradox," *Journal for the History of Philosophy* 43: 403–35.

Falkenstein, Lorne, and Grandi, Giovanni (2003). "The Role of Material Impressions in Reid's Theory of Vision: a Critique of Gideon Yaffe's 'Reid on the Perception of the Visible Figure'," *Journal of Scottish Philosophy* 2: 117–33.

Feibleman, James (1944). "Reid and the Origins of Modern Realism," *Journal of the History of Ideas* 5: 113–20.

Flage, Daniel (1991). *David Hume's Theory of Mind*. New York: Routledge.

Fodor, Jerry (1980). *Language of Thought*. Cambridge, Mass.: Harvard University Press.

Gallie, Roger (1989a). *Thomas Reid and 'The Way of Ideas'*. Dordrecht: Kluwer.

——— (1989b). "Hume, Reid and Innate Ideas: A Response to John P. Wright," *Methodology and Science* 22: 218–29.

——— (1993). "Lehrer on Reid on General Conceptions," *British Journal for the History of Philosophy* 1: 126–38.

Gallie, Roger (1997). "Reid: Conception, Representation, Innate Ideas," *Hume Studies* 23: 315–35.

Ganson, Todd (1999). "Berkeley, Reid and Thomas Brown on the Origins of our Spatial Concepts," *Reid Studies* 3: 49–62.

—— (2002). "Reid on Colour," *British Journal for the History of Philosophy* 10: 231–42.

Gracyk, Theodore (1987). "The Failure of Thomas Reid's Aesthetics," *Monist* 70: 465–82.

Graham, Jody (1997). "Common Sense and Berkeley's Perception by Suggestion," *International Journal of Philosophical Studies* 5: 397–423.

Grandi, Giovanni (2003). "Thomas Reid's Theory of Vision," PhD dissertation, University of Western Ontario.

Greco, John (1995). "Reid's Critique of Berkeley and Hume: What's the Big Idea?", *Philosophy and Phenomenological Research* 55: 279–96.

Greenberg, A. (1976). "Sir William Hamilton and the Interpretation of Reid's Realism," *Modern Schoolman* 54: 15–32.

Gregory, James (1765). *A Comparative View of the State and Faculties of Man with those of the Animal World.* London: J. Dodsley in Pall Mall.

Grene, Marjorie (1994). "The Objects of Hume's *Treatise*," *Hume Studies* 20: 163–77.

Hagar, Amit (2002). "Thomas Reid and Non-Euclidean Geometry," *Reid Studies* 5: 54–64.

Haldane, John (1989). "Reid, Scholasticism and Contemporary Philosophy of Mind," in Dalgarno 1989, pp. 285–304.

—— (1993). "Whose Theory? Which Representations?", *Pacific Philosophical Quarterly* 74: 247–57.

—— (1997). "The Forms of Thought," in L. Hahn, ed., *The Philosophy of Roderick M. Chisholm: Library of Living Philosophers.* Chicago: Open Court, pp. 149–70.

—— (2000). "Reid on the History of Ideas," *American Catholic Philosophical Quarterly* 74: 447–69.

Hamlyn, D. W. (1994). "Perception, Sensation and Non-Conceptual Content," *Philosophical Quarterly* 44: 139–53.

—— (1996). *Understanding Perception: The Concept and its Conditions.* Aldershot: Avebury.

Hanink, J. G. (1986). "Thomas Reid and Common-Sense Foundationalism," *New Scholasticism* 60: 91–115.

Hartley, David (1971). *Observations on Man, his Frame, his Duty, and his Expectations.* Gainesville: Scholars' Facsimiles & Reprints.

Hatfield, Gary (1990). *The Natural and the Normative: Theories of Spatial Perception from Kant to Helmholtz.* Cambridge, Mass.: MIT Press.

Herrnstein, Richard J., and Boring, Edwin G., eds. (1965). *A Source Book in the History of Psychology.* Cambridge, Mass.: Harvard University Press.

—— (1785). *Elements of Criticism*, 2 vols. Bristol: Thoemmes Press.

Hopkins, Robert (2005). "Thomas Reid on Molyneux's Question," *Pacific Philosophical Quarterly* 86: 340–64.

Hume, David (1770). *A History of Great Britain from the Accession of James I to the Revolution in 1688*, 8 vols. London: T. Cadell.

—— (1975). *Enquiries Concerning the Human Understanding and Concerning the Principles of Morals*, 3rd edn., L. A. Selby-Bigge, ed. P. H. Nidditch, rev. edn. Oxford: Clarendon.

—— (1978). *A Treatise of Human Nature*, L. A. Selby-Bigge, ed. P. H. Nidditch, rev. edn. Oxford: Clarendon.

—— (1993). *Dialogues Concerning Natural Religion*, ed. J. Gaskin. Oxford: Oxford University Press.

—— (2000a). *An Enquiry concerning Human Understanding*, ed. T. Beauchamp. New York: Oxford University Press.

—— (2000b). *A Treatise of Human Nature*, ed. D. F. Norton and M. Norton. New York: Oxford University Press.

Humphrey, Nicholas (1975). "Interactive Effects of Unpleasant Light and Unpleasant Sound," *Nature* 253: 343–48.

—— (1992). *A History of the Mind*. New York: HarperCollins.

—— (2000). "The Privatization of Sensation", in L. Huber and C. Heyes, eds., *The Evolution of Cognition*. Cambridge, Mass.: MIT Press, pp. 241–52.

—— and Keeble, Graham (1977). "Do Monkeys' Subjective Clocks Run Faster in Red Light than in Blue?", *Perception* 6: 7–14.

Hutcheson, Francis. (1756). *Logicae Compendium*. Glasgow: R. & A. Foulis.

Immerwahr, John (1978). "The Development of Reid's Realism," *Monist* 61: 245–56.

Jackson, Frank (1977). *Perception*. New York: Cambridge University Press.

Jacquette, Dale (2003). "Thomas Reid on Natural Signs, Natural Principles, and the Existence of the External World," *Review of Metaphysics* 57: 279–300.

James, William (1981). *The Principles of Psychology*, 2 vols. Cambridge, Mass.: Harvard University Press.

Kames, Lord, Henry Home (1754). "Of the Laws of Motion," *Essays and Observations, Physical and Literary* 1: 1–69.

Kant, Immanuel (1999). *Critique of Pure Reason*, ed. and trans. P. Guyer and A. Wood. Cambridge: Cambridge University Press.

Kantor, Jacob Robert (1969). *The Scientific Evolution of Psychology*. Chicago: Principia Press.

Kemp, Catherine (2000). "The Innateness Charge: Conception and Belief for Reid and Hume," *Reid Studies* 3: 43–54.

Kivy, Peter (1970). "Lectures on the Fine Arts: An Unpublished Manuscript of Thomas Reid's," *Journal of the History of Ideas* 31: 17–32.

Koyre, Alexander (1968). "Newton's 'regulae philosophandi'," in A. Koyre, ed. *Newtonian Studies*. Chicago: Chicago University Press, pp. 261–72.

Laird, J. (1943). "Impressions and Ideas: A Note on Hume," *Mind*, 52: 171–7.

—— (1967). *Hume's Philosophy of Human Nature*. New York: Anchor Books.

Laudan, Larry (1970). "Thomas Reid and the Newtonian Turn of British Methodological Thought," in R. Butts and J. Davis, eds., *The Methodological Heritage of Newton*. Toronto: Toronto, 103–31.

Lehrer, K. (1978). "Reid on Primary and Secondary Qualities," *Monist* 61: 184–91.

—— (1986–7). "Reid on Consciousness," *Reid Studies* 1: 1–9.

—— (1987). "Beyond Impressions and Ideas: Hume vs. Reid," *Monist* 70: 383–97.

—— (1989). *Thomas Reid*. New York: Routledge.

—— (1998). "Reid, Hume and Common Sense," *Reid Studies* 2: 15–26.

—— and Smith, J. C. (1985). "Reid on Testimony and Perception," *Canadian Journal of Philosophy*, Supplemental vol. 11: 21–38.

—— and Warner, Bradley (2000). "Reid, God and Epistemology," *American Catholic Philosophical Quarterly* 74: 357–72.

Leibniz, Gottfried (1981). *New Essays on Human Understanding*, ed. and trans. P. Remnant and J. Bennett. Cambridge: Cambridge University Press.

Lennon, Thomas (1979). "Hume's Ontological Ambivalences and the Missing Shade of Blue," *Southern Journal of Philosophy* 17: 77–84.

Livingstone, Donald (1984). *Hume's Philosophy of Common Life*. Chicago: Chicago University Press.

Locke, John (1975). *An Essay concerning Human Understanding*, ed. P. Nidditch. New York: Oxford University Press.

—— (1976–89). *The Correspondence of John Locke*, 8 vols., ed. E. DeBeer. New York: Oxford University Press.

—— (1989). *Some Thoughts Concerning Education*, ed. J. and J. Yolton. New York: Oxford University Press.

McCosh, James (1875). *The Scottish Philosophy*. London: Macmillan.

McDowell, John (1994). *Mind and World*. Cambridge, Mass.: Harvard University Press.

McGinn, Colin (2000). *The Mysterious Flame*. New York: Basic Books.

McKitrick, Jennifer (2002). "Reid's Foundation for the Primary/Secondary Quality Distinction," *Philosophical Quarterly* 52: 476–94.

McRae, Robert (1969). "Hume on Meaning," *Dialogue* 8: 486–91.

Madden, E. H. (1986). "Was Reid a Natural Realist?", *Philosophy and Phenomenological Research* 47: 255–76.

Marcil–Lacoste, Louise (1978). "The Seriousness of Reid's Skeptical Admissions," *Monist* 61: 311–25.

—— (1982). *Claude Buffier and Thomas Reid: Two Common-Sense Philosophers*. Kingston and Montreal: McGill-Queen's.

Maund, Constance (1937). *Hume's Theory of Knowledge: A Critical Examination*. New York: Lea Press.

Meltzoff, A. N. and Moore, K. (1993). "Why Faces are Special to Infants—on Connecting the Attraction of Faces and Infants' Ability for Imitation and Cross-Modal Processing," in B. de Boysson-Bardies, ed., *Developmental Neurocognition: Speech and Face Processing in the First Year of Life*. Dordrecht: Kluwer, pp. 211–225.

Michael, Emily (1999). "Reid's Critique of the Scottish Logic of Ideas," *Reid Studies* 2: 3–18.

—— and Michael, Fred (1987). "Reid's Hume: Remarks on Hume in Some Early Logic Lectures of Reid," *Monist* 70: 508–26.

Michael, Fred (2001). "Reid and Occam's Razor," *Reid Studies* 5: 3–16.

Millar, Alan (1991). "Concepts, Experience and Inference," *Mind* 100: 495–505.

——— (1992). "The Nonconceptual Content of Experience", in T. Crane, ed., *The Contents of Experience: Essays on Perception.* New York: Cambridge University Press, pp. 105–35.

Mishori, Daniel (2003). "The Dilemmas of the Dual Channel: Reid on Consciousness and Reflection," *Journal of Scottish Philosophy* 1: 141–55.

Molyneux, William (1692). *Dioptrica Nova: A Treatise on Dioptricks.* London: Benjamin Tooke.

Nagel, Thomas (1965). "Physicalism," *Philosophical Review* 74: 339–56.

Nauckhoff, Josefine C. (1994). "Objectivity and Expression in Thomas Reid's Aesthetics," *Journal of Aesthetics and Art Criticism* 52: 183–91.

Newton, Isaac (1959–1977). *The Correspondence of Isaac Newton,* 7 vols., eds. H. Turnbull and A. Hall. Cambridge: Cambridge University Press.

——— (1999). *Mathematical Principles of Natural Philosophy,* ed. and trans. I. Cohen and A. Whitman. Berkeley: University of California Press.

Nichols, Ryan (2002a). "Reid on Fictional Objects and the Way of Ideas," *Philosophical Quarterly* 52: 582–601.

——— (2002b). "Learning and Conceptual Content in Reid's Theory of Perception," *British Journal for the History of Philosophy* 10: 561–90.

——— (2002c). "Visible Figure and Reid's Theory of Visual Perception," *Hume Studies* 28: 49–82.

——— (2003). "Reid's Inheritance from Locke, and How He Overcomes it," *Journal for the History of Philosophy* 41: 471–92.

——— (2006). "Why is the History of Philosophy Worth our Study?", *Metaphilosophy* 37: 34–52.

——— (2007). "Natural Philosophy and Its Limits in the Scottish Enlightenment," forthcoming in *Monist* 90.

——— (unpublished). "Reid on Science, Dualism and the Limits of a Philosophy of the Mind."

Norton, David Fate (1976a). "Hume and His Scottish Critics," in D. Norton, N. Capaldi, and W. Robinson, eds., *McGill Hume Studies.* San Diego: Austin Hill Press, pp. 309–40.

——— (1976b). "Reid's Abstract of the Inquiry into the Human Mind," in Barker and Beauchamp, eds., 1976, pp. 125–32.

Ockham, William (1967–89). *Scriptum in librum primum Sententiarum ordinatio* in *Opera Theologica,* 4 vols. St. Bonaventure: Franciscan Institute Press.

O'Shaughnessy, Brian (1989). "The Sense of Touch," *Australasian Journal of Philosophy* 67: 37–58.

——— (2000). *Consciousness and the World.* New York: Oxford University Press.

Pappas, George (1986). "Common Sense in Berkeley and Reid," *Revue internationale de Philosophie* 40: 292–303.

——— (1989). "Sensation and Perception in Reid," *Noûs* 23: 155–67.

Pappas, George (1990). "Causation and Perception in Reid," *Philosophy and Phenomenological Research* 50: 763–66.

——— (2000). *Berkeley's Thought.* Ithaca, NY: Cornell University Press.

Park, Désirée (1969). "Locke and Berkeley on the Molyneux Problem," *Journal of the History of Ideas* 30: 253–60.

Pasnau, Robert (1997). *Theories of Cognition in the Later Middle Ages.* New York: Cambridge University Press.

Passmore, John (1980). *Hume's Intentions.* London: Duckworth.

Pastore, Nicholas (1971). *Selective History of Theories of Visual Perception 1650–1950.* Oxford: Oxford University Press.

Pitcher, George (1977). *Berkeley.* London: Routledge.

Pitson, Tony (1989). "Sensation, Perception, and Reid's Realism," in Dalgarno and Matthews, eds., 1989, pp. 79–90.

——— (2001). "Reid on Primary and Secondary Qualities," *Reid Studies* 2: 17–34.

Porterfield, William (1759). *Treatise on the Eye: the Manner and Phenomena of Vision,* 2 vols. Edinburgh: Hamilton and Balfour.

Price, H. H. (1940). "The Permanent Significance of Hume's Philosophy," *Philosophy* 15: 10–36.

Priestley, Joseph (1774). *An Examination of Dr. Reid's Inquiry in to the Human Mind, on the Principles of Common Sense; Dr. Beattie's Essay on the Nature and Immutability of Truth; and Dr. Oswald's Appeal to Common Sense in behalf of Religion.* London: J. Johnson.

——— (1775). *Hartley's Theory of the Human Mind on the Principle of the Association of Ideas, with Essays relating to the subject of it.* London: J. Johnson.

——— and Price, Richard (2003). *A Free Discussion of the Doctrines of Materialism, and Philosophical Necessity, in a Correspondence between Dr. Price, and Dr. Priestley.* Whitefish, Mont.: Kessinger.

Putnam, Hilary (1981). *Reason, Truth and History.* Cambridge, Mass.: Harvard University Press.

Quine, W. V. O. (1956). "Quantifiers and Propositional Attitudes," *Journal of Philosophy* 53: 177–87.

Ramsay, John, of Ochertyre (1888). *Scotland and Scotsmen in the Eighteenth Century,* ed. A. Allardyce, 2 vols. Edinburgh and London: William Blackwood and Sons.

Raynor, David (1990). "Hume and Berkeley's *Three Dialogues,*" in M. A. Stewart 1990, pp. 231–50.

Reid, Thomas (1763). *A System of Logic Taught at Aberdeen, 1763, by Dr. T. Reid.* [Lectures to students at Aberdeen in 1763. John Campbell, transcriber, 1774.] University of Edinburgh Library. Shelf Mark Dk.3.2.

——— (1768–9). *Student notes of Dr. Reid's Lectures, Professor at Glasgow.* University of Edinburgh, New College, Divinity Library. Shelf Mark Box 32.3.

——— (1775). Review of "Hartley's Theory of the Human Mind, on the Principle of the Association of Ideas; with Essays relating to the Subjects of it," by Joseph Priestley. *Monthly Review* 53: 380–90 and 54: 41–7.

_____ (1937). *Philosophical Orations of Thomas Reid* (Latin), ed. W. R. Humphries. Aberdeen: Aberdeen University Press.

_____ (1981). *Thomas Reid's Lectures on Natural Theology*, ed. E. Duncan. Washington, DC: University Press of America.

_____ (1982). "*Cura prima*: Of Common Sense," ed. D. F. Norton in Marcil-Lacoste 1982, pp. 179–208.

_____ (1983). *Inquiry and Essays*, eds. K. Lehrer and R. Beanblossom. Indianapolis: Hackett.

_____ (1989). *The Philosophical Orations of Thomas Reid*, ed. D. D. Todd, trans. S. D. Sullivan. Carbondale: Southern Illinois University Press.

_____ (1990). "<Georgica Animi>: A Compendium of Thomas Reid's Lectures on the Culture of the Mind," ed. Charles Stewart-Robinson, *Rivista di storia della filosofia* 1: 113–56.

_____ (1994a). *An Inquiry into the Human Mind on the Principles of Common Sense*, in *The Works of Thomas Reid*, vol. 1, W. Hamilton, ed. Bristol: Thoemmes Press.

_____ (1994b). *Essays on the Intellectual Powers of Man*, in *The Works of Thomas Reid*, vol. 1, W. Hamilton, ed. Bristol: Thoemmes Press.

_____ (1994c). *Essays on the Active Powers of Man*, in *The Works of Thomas Reid*, vol. 11, W. Hamilton, ed. Bristol: Thoemmes Press.

_____ (1994d). *A Brief Account of Aristotle's Logic, With Remarks*, in *The Works of Thomas Reid*, vol. 11, W. Hamilton, ed. Bristol: Thoemmes Press.

_____ (1995). *Thomas Reid on the Animate Creation*, ed. P. Wood. University Park: Pennsylvania State University Press.

_____ (1997). *An Inquiry into the Human Mind on the Principles of Common Sense*, ed. D. Brookes. University Park: Pennsylvania State University Press.

_____ (2001). "Of Power," ed. J. Haldane, *Philosophical Quarterly* 51: 3–12.

_____ (2002a). *Essays on the Intellectual Powers of Man*, ed. D. Brookes. University Park: Pennsylvania State University Press.

_____ (2002b). *The Correspondence of Thomas Reid*, ed. P. Wood. University Park: Pennsylvania State University Press.

_____ (2004). *Thomas Reid on Logic, Rhetoric, and the Fine Arts*, ed. A. Broadie. University Park: Pennsylvania State University Press.

Robinson, Daniel (1976). "Thomas Reid's *Gestalt* Psychology," in Barker 1976, pp. 44–54.

_____ (1989). "Thomas Reid and the Aberdeen Years: Common Sense at the Wise Club," *Journal of the History of the Behavioral Sciences* 25: 154–62.

Rollin, Bernard E. (1978). "Thomas Reid and the Semiotics of Perception," *Monist* 61: 257–70.

Ross, Don (1991). "Hume, Resemblance and the Foundations of Psychology," *History of Philosophy Quarterly* 8: 343–56.

Sacks, Oliver (1995). *An Anthropologist on Mars*. New York: Vintage Books.

Schuhmann, K. and Smith, B. (1990). "Elements of Speech Act Theory in the Work of Thomas Reid," *History of Philosophy Quarterly* 7: 47–66.

Searle, John (1980). "Minds, Brains, and Programs," *Behavioral and Brain Sciences* 3: 417–24.

—— (1983). *Intentionality: An Essay in the Philosophy of Mind*. New York: Cambridge University Press.

—— (1993). *The Rediscovery of the Mind*. New York: Cambridge University Press.

Sell, Alan (1979). "Priestley's Polemic Against Reid," *Price-Priestley Newsletter* 3: 41–52.

Siewert, Charles (1998). *The Significance of Consciousness*. Princeton: Princeton University Press.

Silver, Bruce (1974). "A Note on Berkeley's New Theory of Vision and Thomas Reid's Distinction between Primary and Secondary Qualities," *Southern Journal of Philosophy* 12: 253–63.

Sinclair, Alistair (1995). "The Failure of Thomas Reid's Attack of David Hume," *British Journal for the History of Philosophy* 3: 389–98.

Sleigh, Robert (1987). "Reid and the Ideal Theory on Conception and Perception." in Barker 1976, pp. 77–85.

—— (1990). *Leibniz & Arnauld: A Commentary on Their Correspondence*. New Haven, Conn.: Yale University Press.

Smith, Adam (1980). *Essays on Philosophical Subjects*, eds. W. Wightman and J. Bryc. Oxford: Clarendon Press.

Smith, J. C. (1986). "Reid's Functional Explanation of Sensation," *History of Philosophy Quarterly* 3: 175–93.

—— (1990). "Reid and the Contemporary View of Consciousness", in J. C. Smith, ed., *Historical Foundations of Cognitive Science*. Dordrecht: Kluwer, pp. 139–59.

—— (2002). "Reidian Intentionality," *Reid Studies* 5: 53–64.

Smith, Norman Kemp (1941). *The Philosophy of David Hume: A Critical Study of its Origins and Central Doctrines*. London: Macmillan.

Smith, Robert (1738). *A Compleat System of Opticks*, 2 vols. Cambridge: Cornelius Crownfield.

Somerville, James (1995). *The Enigmatic Parting Shot*. London: Avebury.

—— (1998). "Whose Failure, Reid's or Hume's?", *British Journal for the History of Philosophy* 6: 247–60.

Sosa, Ernest and Van Cleve, James (2001). "Thomas Reid," in Stephen Emmanuel, ed., *Blackwell Guide to the Modern Philosophers*. Oxford: Blackwell, pp. 179–200.

Stanistreet, Paul (2001). "Hume's True Philosophy and Reid's Common Sense," *Reid Studies* 4: 55–70.

Stecker, Robert (1992). "Does Reid Reject/Refute the Representational Theory of Mind?", *Pacific Philosophical Quarterly* 73: 174–84.

Stewart, Dugald (1803). *Account of the Life and Writings of Thomas Reid*. Edinburgh: William Creech.

—— (1854). *The Collected Works of Dugald Stewart*, ed. Sir William Hamilton, 13 vols. Edinburgh: Thomas Constable & Co.

Stewart, M. A., ed. (1990). *Studies in the Philosophy of the Scottish Enlightenment*. Oxford: Clarendon Press.

Strawson, Galen (1989). *The Secret Connexion*. Oxford: Oxford University Press.

_____ (1990). Review of *Thomas Reid* by K. Lehrer, *London Review of Books* 22 February.

Stroud, Barry (1977). *Hume*. London: Routledge.

Tapper, Alan (2003). "Reid and Priestley on Method and the Mind," in J. Haldane and S. Read, eds., *The Philosophy of Thomas Reid: A Collection of Essays*. Oxford: Blackwell, pp. 98–112.

Tuggy, Dale (2000). "Thomas Reid on Causation," *Reid Studies* 3: 3–28.

Turnbull, George (2005). *The Principles of Moral and Christian Philosophy*, 2 vols, ed. A. Broadie. Indianapolis: Liberty Fund.

Van Cleve, James (1999). *Problems from Kant*. New York: Oxford University Press.

_____ (2002). "Thomas Reid's Geometry of Visibles," *Philosophical Review* 111: 373–416.

_____ (2004a). Review of *Thomas Reid and the Story of Epistemology*, by Nicholas Wolterstorff, *Mind*, 113: 405–16.

_____ (2004b). "Reid's Theory of Perception," in Cuneo and Van Woudenberg 2004, pp. 101–33.

van Fraassen, Bas (2002). *The Empirical Stance*. New Haven, Conn.: Yale University Press.

Van Woudenberg, René (2000). "Perceptual Relativism, Scepticism, and Thomas Reid," *Reid Studies* 3: 65–85.

Waxman, Wayne (1994). *Hume's Theory of Consciousness*. New York: Cambridge, University Press.

Weldon, Susan (1982). "Direct Realism and Visual Distortion: A Development of Arguments from Thomas Reid," *Journal for the History of Philosophy* 20: 355–68.

Winch, Peter (1953). "The Notion of 'Suggestion' in Thomas Reid's Theory of Perception," *Philosophical Quarterly* 3: 327–41.

Winkler, Kenneth (1991). "The New Hume," *Philosophical Review* 100: 541–79.

Wittgenstein, Ludwig (1953). *Philosophical Investigations*, ed. G. E. M. Anscombe and R. Rhees, trans. G. E. M. Anscombe. Oxford: Blackwell.

Wolterstorff, Nicholas (2000). "Thomas Reid's Account of the Objectivated Character of Perception," *Reid Studies* 4: 3–15.

_____ (2001). *Thomas Reid and the Story of Epistemology*. New York: Cambridge University Press.

Wood, Paul (1976). "Reid on Hypotheses and the Ether; a Reassessment", in Barker and Beauchamp, eds., 1976, pp. 433–46.

_____ (1985a). "Thomas Reid and the Scottish Enlightenment: an exhibition to celebrate the 200th anniversary of the publication of Thomas Reid's Essays on the intellectual powers of man 1785," prepared for the Thomas Fisher Rare Book Library, University of Toronto.

_____ (1985b). "Thomas Reid's Critique of Joseph Priestley: Context and Chronology," *Man and Nature/L'homme et la Nature* 4: 30–41.

_____ (1986). "David Hume on Thomas Reid's 'An Inquiry into the Human Mind, On the Principles of Common Sense'; A New Letter to Hugh Blair from July 1862," *Mind* 95: 411–16.

Wood, Paul (1994). "Hume, Reid and the Science of the Mind," in P. Wood and M. Stewart, eds., *Hume and Hume's Connexions*. Edinburgh: Edinburgh University Press, pp. 119–39.

Wright, John (1983). *The Sceptical Realism of David Hume*. Minneapolis: University of Minnesota Press.

—— (1987). "Hume versus Reid on Ideas: the New Hume Letter," *Mind* 96: 392–8.

—— (1991). "Hume's Rejection of the Theory of Ideas," *History of Philosophy Quarterly* 8: 149–62.

Yaffe, Gideon (2002). "Reconsidering Reid's Geometry of Visibles," *Philosophical Quarterly* 52: 602–20.

—— (2003a). "Reid on the Perception of Visible Figure," *Journal of Scottish Philosophy* 2: 103–15.

—— (2003b). "The Office of an Introspectible Sensation: A Reply to Falkenstein and Grandi," *Journal of Scottish Philosophy* 2: 135–40.

Yolton, John (1984). *Perceptual Acquaintance from Descartes to Reid*. Minneapolis: University of Minnesota Press.

Zabeeh, Farhang (1960). *Hume: Precursor of Modern Empiricism*, 1st edn. The Hague: M. Nijhoff.

Index